Book has card

Healing and Christianity

HARPER & ROW, PUBLISHERS
New York, Evanston, San Francisco, London

1817

MORTON T. KELSEY

Healing
and Christianity

*In Ancient Thought
and Modern Times*

234,131

Ke H

248.7

HEALING AND CHRISTIANITY. Copyright © 1973 by Morton T. Kelsey.

FIRST EDITION

STANDARD BOOK NUMBER: 06-064380-3

LIBRARY OF CONGRESS CATALOG CARD NUMBER: 72-78065

Designed by C. Linda Dingler

Contents

To my children—Myra, Chip and John

Preface

Some years ago when I became interested in the healing ministry of the church and looked around for a comprehensive study of the subject, the only work I found that even came close was Evelyn Frost's *Christian Healing*. This, of course, is an excellent and fairly recent study, but it covers only a small part of the church's history and does not attempt to deal with the findings of either depth psychology or psychosomatic medicine. Since then book after book has come out on religious healing, still leaving these areas relatively untouched.

It became clear that I would need the material—I was lecturing on healing in various parts of the country—and so I started collecting it myself. It turned out to be a large order. This was nearly fifteen years ago, and I have gone on learning about healing while three other books took shape and were completed.

What was needed was not a documenting of case histories. There are dozens of good books (several will be found in the bibliography) which carefully detail occurrences of sacramental healing in the present day. What was needed, and what I try to present, is an *understanding* of the ups and downs of healing in the Western Christian tradition, in actual history from Old Testament times on. If Christian healing was indeed as vital a reality for people now as it appeared to be, then it was necessary to offer a rationale for practicing healing in the church today. This I have tried to do, at the same time considering why modern theology on the whole has avoided the subject. The attitude of modern medicine also had to be examined, with the resulting discovery of some fascinating things about a growing comprehension in medicine of the effect of emotions on the body; there are even medical men, I found, who suggest that real healing depends as much upon the operation of a transpersonal power as upon physical factors.

In short, this is not a book on the method or practice of religious healing. Instead it is an attempt to provide a theological foundation, based on historical and scientific understanding, for a serious ministry of healing today.

My introduction to the healing ministry, almost twenty-five years ago, came in a roundabout way through Agnes Sanford's first book, *The Healing Light*. My wife, to pass the time while she was getting over the flu, started to read it one day. When I came home that evening she handed it to me, saying, "Here, you'd better read this. Either this woman is completely off base or she's saying something pretty important." I soon found that I had to agree, and then a chance came to try out the suggestions in the book. To my utter amazement I found they worked. I began to realize that healing did still occur sacramentally. Later I met Mrs. Sanford and we became fast friends.

A few years later I first met the group of psychologists in Los Angeles who are followers of Dr. C. G. Jung. These men demonstrated a very sophisticated belief in psychological and religious healing operating quite apart from the organized church. Dr. Max Zeller, Dr. and Mrs. James Kirsch, and others introduced me to the thinking of Dr. Jung and the firm foundation he laid for both psychological and religious healing. It is impossible for me to express adequately my appreciation of their personal interest as well as the wise understanding they have shared freely over so many years.

Because of this I began to search the New Testament to see what the Christian tradition actually held. This led me to the church fathers, and then into the Old Testament. A study of modern theology showed clearly why the healing ministry was so completely neglected by most mainline churches. I was soon asked to lecture for the Schools of Pastoral Care founded by Edgar and Agnes Sanford. The substance of many of these pages was prepared for those lectures in one part of the country or another.

It has been my privilege to know many of the leaders of the healing movement in this country, for instance John and Ethel Banks, Starr Daily, and Robert Bell, as well as some leaders in England, such as Thomas Roy Parsons. I also came to know many in the Pentecostal movement, all of them interested in healing. Through Francis Whiting I was introduced to Tommy Tyson, and others involved in healing in the Baptist church. Since then I have talked with ecumenical groups interested in healing from California to Massachusetts and from Florida to the state of Washington. Whatever I can say to thank these groups will only begin to express my gratitude for what I have received from each of them, often from their questioning.

Thus it will be seen that the editorial "we" often used in this volume is more than a mere convention. It includes in feeling all those who have made the book possible, though I must take full responsibility for the opinions voiced.

For twenty years I was rector of St. Luke's Church in Monrovia, California. Soon after I came there we instituted healing services, and the sacrament of healing has been an important part of the life of that growing and vital parish through all these years. I had a great deal of help in this program from my associate, Stuart Fitch, whose healing ministry has been a significant part of the church's life. Through forums and personal discussions we struggled with questions about healing, forging some of the answers presented here. The people of St. Luke's and their support and interest in the subject have been the stuff of which this book is made. Even though they are hardly mentioned, these people were the proving ground for the answers we offer.

Throughout the years Mrs. Sanford has been a close friend as well as a wise consultant on all matters relating to sacramental healing. In recent years she has also made her home in Monrovia and been a member of St. Luke's Church. At present my students at the University of Notre Dame—students in the Department of Graduate Studies in Education—are continuing to question, and have helped me formulate many of the conclusions found in this book. Both the vestry of St. Luke's Church and Dr. James Michael Lee, former chairman of the department at Notre Dame, have encouraged me to take the time to lecture on this subject and to put the material into book form.

Two friends have been of special help in formulating many of the ideas presented. With John A. Sanford I have spent hundreds of hours discussing the problems, the questions, and their answers. His books, *The Kingdom Within* and *Dreams: God's Forgotten Language*, have also been of great help in showing the relation of Jungian thought to various aspects of modern Christian living. Dr. Leo Froke has been of inestimable value both as a friend and as a mine of information on literature, psychiatry, psychology, medicine, and psychosomatic medicine in particular. He has also read and checked the medical sections of the manuscript.

In addition, I have been fortunate to have as personal physician and friend Dr. Leland Hawkins, who understands the importance of dealing with psychological as well as physical factors in medicine, and has done much to keep me both healthy and informed.

In the writing itself, Paisley Roach has done yeoman service. Twice she has edited this manuscript, and much of the research for chapters seven and eight was done by her. The book in its present form is to a large degree the result of her hand. I have appreciated her years of interest and her skill in both phrasing and accurate documentation.

My family has suffered through hundreds of hours of "father at the typewriter." My children, who have grown up and two of them married since the "healing book" was first conceived, have given me real encouragement. My wife has corrected and criticized the drafts, checked references, and helped with a multitude of tasks so that I could be free to write, and I am truly grateful to each of them.

My appreciation also goes to Carmela Rulli and the most efficient secretarial staff at Notre Dame for their cooperation and services in putting the final draft into legible form.

One last and very important note: it is somewhat frightening to write on the subject of sacramental healing. It is almost like testing the fates. I am certainly not a paragon of physical health, nor am I unusually gifted as a healer. But I have experienced the effects of healing in my own life, ministered by another, and I have also seen the quickening power of new health come to some of those to whom I have ministered. I have seen the things of which I write.

MORTON T. KELSEY

University of Notre Dame
Notre Dame, Indiana

Healing and Christianity

1

Is the Question Settled?

Not many things in this world interest modern man quite as much as his health. He not only talks about it—in public as well as in private—but he spends a great deal of energy on it one way or another. In the United States alone billions of dollars are spent to preserve health and prolong life. Every socialistic state, as part of its total program for the individual, provides all-inclusive medical care from birth to disintegration and death. In these times, when belief in a significant spiritual world is almost at a vanishing point, men seem to become as absorbed in staying alive and healthy as they once were in preparing for life after death. Even when the zest for living is gone, taking care of life in the here and now seems almost an obsession. It does not occur to most people that religion itself might have some influence on this matter of mental and physical health.

Yet in the history of man for a very long time that was the generally accepted view. It was understood that his religion, by affecting his relationship with spiritual powers, both good and evil, could have a powerful influence for health or illness. It was believed that certain individuals could have a profound effect upon the diseased condition of others because these persons were either official mediators of such spiritual powers or were given special faculties by them. This point of view is found very clearly

3

in the teachings of Jesus of Nazareth and in the practice of the early church.

Although this idea was generally abandoned by the western Protestant church after the Reformation, the question was never directly put: What is the place of the Christian idea of healing in the world that men are shaping? Instead, the sacramental and devotional practices directed toward healing were simply discouraged or discontinued, while theology turned its attention elsewhere. Today there is an almost total lack of theological support for such ideas or practice. Yet at the same time there are several indications that the question is not exactly settled. In fact, when it is asked directly we find, not that healing has finally died out in the Christian world, but rather that we have poked into a whole hornet's nest of divergent practices and ideas about it.

There is first of all the movement that started in the 1800s, spearheaded by New Thought and Christian Science. These groups have continued to grow. Then there are the Pentecostal churches, now the fastest-growing bodies of Christendom. At first their revival of the healing ministry was only incidental to their emphasis on tongue speaking and other gifts of the Spirit. The early leaders were surprised to find healing occurring when converts were baptized and spoke in tongues. As a result, healing practices became a part of the Pentecostal way of life. Meanwhile services for healing had begun to appear in a few of the more orthodox Protestant churches, while among Catholics the occurrences at Lourdes and other shrines brought renewed interest in healings taking place in this way.

In addition, our century has seen the growth of an essentially new interest in psychological healing, arising out of the relatively new professions of the psychiatrist and psychologist. These men have found that it is quite possible to heal a patient's neurosis by doing nothing other than talking with him. Not only is the mind of a patient affected by such psychic causation, but his physical condition often changes as well. Sometimes, it has been discovered, a whole host of physiological problems, of hysterical or other origin, will disappear as a man's emotional integration improves.

Finally, in the past thirty years or so men in other areas of medicine have come to realize that many physical illnesses can have a psychic factor, and have published some of their findings. With growing realization that man cannot be treated piecemeal, physicians have begun to discuss the need to treat him as a whole functioning organism, including his social and religious life. It has even been suggested recently that medical schools offer courses on man's religious beliefs to give the doctor the understanding he needs in order to help his patients.[1] In 1954 the Academy of Religion and Mental Health was founded for much the same purpose, and this group, now with its own journal, continues the effort to establish a bridge between the healing and the religious professions.

But the average orthodox clergyman is not much interested in practices that would convey healing. The "orthodox" Christian, whether liberal or conservative, has little exposure to such sacramental acts and little or no interest in physical or mental healing through religious means. This fact has been brought home to me graphically on several occasions. One was the experience just a few years ago of a friend who is state commissioner of health for one of the large eastern states. At his instance a group of doctors and clergy were called together to discuss the whole subject of spiritual healing. While the physicians on the whole were deeply involved in the discussion, the clergy who attended hardly treated the subject as a serious one.

1. Milton O. Kepler, M.D., "The Importance of Religion in Medical Education," *Journal of Religion and Health* (October 1968), pp. 358 ff.; see also Lester J. Evans, *The Crisis in Medical Education*, pp. 36 ff. Note that full publishing data for references cited, if available in the Bibliography, will be omitted from the footnotes.

At about the same time a similar meeting was called by a large western hospital which has a department of religion and health. A selected group of clergy and medical men were invited to meet together and discuss the problems. All but one of the physicians responded and 80 percent of them came, while barely 50 percent of the clergy even answered the letter and less than 30 percent of them attended the meeting.

What, then, *is* the place of healing in the Christianity of the modern world? What I have mentioned above suggests that there is quite a difference of opinion among Christians today on this subject. But there is far more than that. In reality, this difference over the value of sacramental or religious healing in the church is only one symptom of a fundamental division among Christians about how God acts in human life. The points of view are so diametrically opposed and so deeply divided that they are often unspoken, each side simply accepting the validity of its own view without question.

Thus, in the Christian churches today we find two conflicting attitudes toward the ministry of healing of Jesus of Nazareth and the apostles—a ministry that was practically unbroken for the first thousand years of the church's life. On one hand, among certain religious groups today we find an increasing interest in this spiritual ministry of healing. On the other, we come face to face with the fact that in most Protestant churches today there is actual hostility to the practice of religious healing—hostility even to the idea of it. How has the church become so divided? Which point of view is nearer the heart of a vital Christianity? Which attitude fits better the knowledge we have of man and his world?

In order to find answers to these questions, we must sort out some complex and rather difficult material. We shall consider first of all the case against spiritual healing in the church—the outlook of probably by far the largest segment of modern Christianity. A short but revealing study of ancient ideas about healing follows, particularly as shown in the Old Testament. I shall then go on to outline the healing ministry of Jesus of Nazareth in relation to this cultural and religious background, showing how unusual his ministry was as against the contemporary scene and what a radical innovation it was religiously. This will take us to a careful consideration of the actual preaching and practice of Jesus in regard to healing. We shall next examine the attitudes and practices of the early church, and then follow the status of healing through its later history.

We shall then turn to the medical profession to see what it has to tell us about the relation of the emotions, mind, and body, and whether the teaching and practice of Jesus and the early church make any sense in terms of modern medical practice. This will take us on to the relation of religion to man's mental attitude and a consideration of modern psychological thought. In conclusion, we shall turn to philosophy and theology to see whether there is any place for the healing ministry or action of the church in contemporary sophisticated thinking.

It is strange—even ironic—to realize that this interest in the effect of spirit on man's material body may make it necessary to reconsider the whole question of the place of spirit in man's life and religion. Since the source of such interest lies somewhat beyond the ordinary field of religion today, let us begin by looking carefully at the church's own arguments for the negative.

2

The Case against Christian Healing

Most modern Christian churches believe that they have nothing to do officially with healing the sick. They do not feel that the church's actions—its religious acts—have any direct effect on human health. It is true that religious groups do build hospitals and medical centers, but this does not differ from any other act of charity or compassion. Until recently many such hospitals did not even have chaplains to serve their patients. In fact, it has come to be widely believed that there is no particular relation between the practice of Christianity and sound health of mind and body.

Oddly enough, this constitutes an about-face in Christian belief. In the Roman communion it can be traced to about the tenth century, when the service of unction for healing was gradually transformed into extreme unction. Thus the one sacrament for healing the bodies of men became a rite of passage for dying, a service to "save" the individual for the next life and speed him quickly and easily into it. Still, it must be emphasized, healing interest was not dropped entirely from this major division of Christendom. But it shifted from the official sacramental action of the church as such to the efficacy of shrines and relics. We shall see more about this later.

Among Protestants, who dismissed these later popular practices as so much popery and superstition, there was left no action of the church, official or popular, dedicated to religious healing. What took over instead was quite different—so different that it finally became a positive hostility to the idea that healing might or ought to take place within the church. Indeed, a set of attitudes arose to show *why* healing does not and should not take place as a function of Christianity.

In order to see just what reactions are involved here, we shall consider four different but overlapping views of healing within the modern Protestant church: First, the materialistic conviction that man's body can be cared for by medical and physical means alone and that religious help is superfluous. Next, the idea of sickness as God's direct and disciplinary gift to men, as expressed in the English Office of Visitation to the Sick. Then the conviction known as dispensationalism: the belief that God originally gave such ministries as healing only for the time being, in order to get the church established. And last, the theology of Bultmann: the understanding that there is no supernatural agency which can break through natural law. Since Bultmann and those who go along with him are in theological ascendancy at present, this all adds up to a very strong case against spiritual healing.

The "Orthodox" Medical Point of View

Well before the turn of the century it was apparent that the materialistic approach to human life would take over the healing professions lock, stock, and barrel. What was happening in the clinics of Berlin and Vienna as they became the medical centers of the world was not just a victory for physical medicine, but a rout of all uncertainty. Human illness could be dealt with like any other problem involving matter—a complex one, it is true, but quite susceptible to careful medical regulation. As the new century began, it even seemed that illness might be banished entirely, given only enough knowledge about the body and its chemistry and a free hand for the scientist.

So successful was this approach that by 1956 the average American might expect to live twenty years longer than he could have hoped for in 1900; the death rate had dropped by an amount equal to one percent a year. In its 1960 study of the statistics, the National Health Foundation concluded:

> Between 1900 and the present . . . the communicable diseases—gastritis, tuberculosis, and influenza and pneumonia—decreased sharply as causes of death and lost their places in the front ranks of major killers. They were replaced by heart disease, cancer, vascular lesions of the central nervous system, and accidents.
>
> Although they were considerable in the first quarter of this century, the declines in mortality actually accelerated in the latter part of the second quarter. The improvement in infant and maternal mortality, and the decline of the communicable diseases . . . coincided generally with an acceleration in the pace of new medical advances, introduction of the sulfa drugs and the antibiotics and improvements in the standard of living. However, within the most recent period, the mortality rates generally have reached a plateau, and it may be that further declines will be slow, even though health progress steadily continues.[1]

Behind this amazing change in the health patterns of Americans, and also most western Europeans, is a point of view that can be put rather simply. The task of medicine is to heal the body, and since this physical mechanism (or an isolated part of it) responds to treatment, this is all that is important. The patient is essentially a set of assorted organs and physical processes which can be regulated by physical means: by surgery, drugs, hormones, rest, diet, and the like. Only his body is real and significant; his mind and emotions are merely mechanical functions of the brain and nerve cells. In fact, as techniques are more and more pinpointed, the causes of even mental and emotional

1. Odin W. Anderson and Monroe Lerner, *Measuring Health Levels in the United States, 1900–1958* (1960), p. 37.

illness will be isolated—in the brain or somewhere else—and the specific physical cure will be found even for them.

Most of us, clergy included, have accepted this view of medical healing. Any criticism has generally come from doctors themselves, usually like the bit of satire written a few years ago by Dr. F. G. Crookshank, a British physician. Discussing physical reactions to stress, he remarked,

> I often wonder that some hardboiled and orthodox clinician does not describe emotional weeping as a "new disease," calling it paroxysmal lachrymation, and suggesting treatment by belladonna, astringent local applications, avoidance of sexual excess, tea, tobacco and alcohol, and a salt-free diet with restriction of fluid intake, proceeding in the event of failure to early removal of the tear-glands.[2]

In the last thirty years the medical view has been changing. With the advance of psychiatry and the increasing importance of chronic illness, medicine is taking a new look at the factors that cause disease.[3] Many physicians are giving very serious attention to the possibility that the mind and emotions of man have a significant effect upon his physical well being. But since this is a complex matter, often requiring medical background and judgment, most people feel that it is foolish, if not downright dangerous, for lay persons like the clergy to meddle in healing. There appear to be two quite separate categories of disease; where the causes are purely physical, religious healing can have no effect except by encouraging or interfering with treatment. In the case of emotional or psychosomatic illness, the outlook is a little different, but even here the need is mostly for technical knowledge and analysis rather than for any change of attitude or belief.

The church has reasons of its own for being in general agree-

2. Quoted from the *British Journal of Medical Psychology* by Flanders Dunbar in her *Emotions and Bodily Changes* (1954), pp. 83 f.

3. In reality this is not a very *new* look. It is the understanding of psychosomatic medicine, which can be traced as far back as Hippocrates.

ment with this conclusion. Ever since the Middle Ages in the Christian outlook a split has been growing between man's soul and his being and life here and now. Gradually the church has come to accept the idea that reality in the immediate world is all derived from the physical—from matter, which acts according to rational functions. With such materialism almost axiomatic, how can the soul, the nonmaterial, possibly affect the body? The answer seems obvious, and so the church must keep its efforts strictly divided.

There is a nonmaterial world in which man's soul has eternal significance, and although it is somewhat difficult to pin down, the task of religion is certainly to save the soul for eternal life. But these efforts do not carry over to the immediate world where man's problems are being created and solved. Here the job of the church is to impart ethical and moral values by teaching and example or by social action. There is no way to bring in healing, nor any need for it. It is accepted by faith that there is some untraceable effect upon the soul's life later on if men simply learn to behave in accordance with the Christian gospel—that is, with parts of it.

The elements of the Christian message that do not fit one category or the other are ignored or rationalized—the healings done by Jesus and his followers (which alone account for one-third of the narrative portions of the Gospels), the outpouring of the Holy Spirit along with other strange phenomena at Pentecost and in apostolic times, the dreams and visions, the references to angelic and evil spirits in the New Testament, indeed the whole emphasis on interrelation of body, soul, and spirit. One begins to wonder how it is possible to take the ethical and moral teachings of Jesus seriously when nearly half the verses of the New Testament must be avoided because these other things—chiefly healing—intrude into them.

Modern Christians, however, have found several quite acceptable ways of avoiding the unmodern elements in these stories. One way is to hold that the New Testament writers were simply mistaken about the facts they were trying to describe; another is to suggest that the stories themselves were a later addition to the text by the more credulous early church.

In a world where recognition of healing was still part of the norm for the church, and demons too, there were of course innumerable stories at second hand and pure leaps of the imagination or hearsay as well. Like fraud and delusion in medicine or love, this bulky evidence of man's credulity in no way disproves the real thing, whether in modern times or ancient. It is simply the inevitable increment of human folly and lively emotion or imagination upon the real experience of life. In the record and at a distance it is often hard to know one thing from another. We must accept this; we cannot always tell. Wordings that sound strange or impossible may refer to quite real things, and vice versa. But part of our wisdom must be the ability to perceive that both exist—the false and the true—as they do in most basic things, whether now or long ago. We must be able to refrain from regarding the whole matter of healing as a tight categorical question of either/or (wholly true or wholly false), and accept rather an untidy but truer both/and. We do not throw away the values of love or wisdom in this life because of the follies or pretenses that belie them. Nor should we discard this. When one's world view has little place for religious healing most instances tend to be discarded.

A number of reasonable explanations are also given for the healings. My own mother, who was deeply religious, accepted many of these ideas. I remember asking as a child why we didn't see these things happen any more, and being told that we know more about such things now. The blind who were healed were merely hysterically blind; the lepers were just suffering from an allergy. Since then I have heard many such explanations: the lame were psychologically bound; the dead were only in a coma or a catatonic state. For many persons with some scientific knowledge this provides quite a satisfactory way of looking at the "irrational" elements in these stories.

Today, however, the principal approach to such matters is simply to show how irrelevant they are, either by ignoring them entirely or by concentrating only on an allegorical meaning. For instance, the seventh volume of the *Interpreter's Bible* offers an excellent introduction to the New Testament, discussing everything from the life and teaching of Jesus to the cultural background and beliefs of the early church. This is probably as fine and comprehensive a survey of the Bible as anyone has made. Yet its two-hundred-and-fifty-page introduction to Christianity devotes less than two pages to the healing ministry of Jesus and his followers. It finds almost nothing to say about events which take up more than one-fifth of the entire text of the Gospels and Acts.

In the commentaries many of these stories are also treated allegorically. It is suggested, for example, that in healing the blind Jesus was really trying to show that blindness of the spirit could be healed; or that his raising of the dead was actually a demonstration of the fact that one who is dead in spirit may find life again. In this way, by concentrating on a symbolic level of meaning, it is possible to avoid looking at Jesus' healings as factual in relation to our present point of view.

Indeed, in one way or another a great many modern Christians seem to have reconciled some sort of belief in the New Testament with the fact that the healings, which constitute a larger part of the New Testament narrative than any other single element, make no sense at all to them. This kind of healing is apparently unknown today; there no longer seems to be any need for it. With its technical knowledge, modern medicine should be quite able to look directly at a sick body or mind and its various environments, diagnose the trouble, and correct it. There is no reason to worry about healing through the soul or spirit of man. Indeed—spirit? Soul? Where, in what organ, would it be found?

But the reality of healing by spiritual means persists, and Christians have found other ways of looking at the problem. One of these is an older idea which is apt to creep into people's thinking today even though it seems passé. This is a notion clearly expressed in the service for the sick still found in the *Book of Common Prayer* of the Church of England.

A Service for the Sick

In the English Office of the Visitation of the Sick we find sixteenth-century Christian thinking about illness crystallized in an implicit attitude still influencing most Protestants today. In fact, this service expresses the outlook of popular modern Protestantism perhaps better than any other document. It is *still* the official service of *The Book of Common Prayer* of the Church of England!*

The Office is introduced by a rubric (a direction originally printed in red) which specifies: "When any person is sick, notice shall be given thereof to the Minister of the Parish; who coming into the sick person's house, shall say. . . ." The minister—when ministers used the Office—then began by invoking God's mercy upon the miserable sufferer, and after the Lord's Prayer and a few versicles and responses, he went on:

Hear us, Almighty and most merciful God and Saviour; extend thy accustomed goodness to this thy servant who is grieved with sickness. . . . Sanctify, we beseech thee, *this thy fatherly correction to him; that the sense of his weakness may add strength to his faith, and seriousness to his repentance:* That, if it shall be thy good pleasure to restore him to his former health,

*It is difficult to believe that this service is still found in all copies of the English *Book of Common Prayer* and that the sixteenth-century views have not been officially changed, but such is the case.

he may lead the residue of his life in thy fear, and to thy glory: *or else,*
give him grace so to take thy visitation, that, after this painful life is ended, he
may dwell with thee in life everlasting; through Jesus Christ our Lord.[4]

One or both of the following exhortations was then read—
perhaps to a person dying of cancer or a man watching his sick
child suffer. If the person was too sick to comprehend more, only
the first was used.

Dearly beloved, know this, that Almighty God is the Lord of life and
death, and of all things to them pertaining, as youth, strength, health,
age, weakness, and sickness. Wherefore, *whatsoever your sickness is, know*
you certainly that it is God's visitation. And for what cause soever this
sickness is sent unto you; *whether it be to try your patience for the example*
of others, and that your faith may be found in the day of the Lord laudable,
glorious, and honourable, to the increase of glory and endless felicity; *or else*
it be sent unto you to correct and amend in you whatsoever doth offend the eyes
of your heavenly Father; know you certainly, that if you truly repent you
of your sins, and bear your sickness patiently, trusting in God's mercy,
for his dear Son Jesus Christ's sake, and *render unto him humble thanks for*
his fatherly visitation, submitting yourself wholly unto his will, it shall
turn to your profit, and help you forward in the right way that leadeth
unto everlasting life.

If one had a chance of getting well, however, and might be
redeemed by his illness, the following advice was also read to
him:

Take therefore in good part the chastisement of the Lord: For (as Saint Paul
saith in the twelfth Chapter to the Hebrews) whom the Lord loveth he
chasteneth, and scourgeth every son whom he receiveth. If ye endure
chastening, God dealeth with you as with sons; for what son is he whom
the father chasteneth not? *But if ye be without chastisement, whereof all are*
partakers, then are ye bastards, and not sons. Furthermore, we have had
fathers of our flesh, which corrected us, and we gave them reverence;

4. The italics throughout these quotations are mine.

shall we not much rather be in subjection unto the Father of spirits, and live? For they verily for a few days chastened us after their own pleasure; *but he for our profit, that we might be partakers of his holiness.* These words, good brother, are written in holy Scripture *for our comfort and instruction; that we should patiently, and with thanksgiving, bear our heavenly Father's correction, whensoever by any manner of adversity it shall please his gracious goodness to visit us.* And there should be no greater comfort to Christian persons, than to be made like unto Christ, *by suffering patiently adversities, troubles, and sicknesses.* For he himself went not up to joy, but first he suffered pain; he entered not into his glory before he was crucified. So truly our way to eternal joy is to suffer here with Christ; and our door to enter into eternal life is gladly to die with Christ; that we may rise again from death, and dwell with Him in everlasting life. *Now therefore, taking your sickness, which is thus profitable for you, patiently,* I exhort you, in the Name of God, to remember the profession which you made unto God in your Baptism. And forasmuch as after this life there is an account to be given unto the righteous Judge, by whom all must be judged, without respect of persons, I require you to examine yourself and your estate, both towards God and man; so that, accusing and condemning yourself for your own faults, you may find mercy at our heavenly Father's hand for Christ's sake, and not be accused and condemned in that *fearful judgment.* Therefore I shall rehearse to you the Articles of our Faith, that you may know whether you do believe as a Christian man should, or no.

The rubrics then required the priest to stop and examine the sick person to be certain that he really believed every part of the Apostle's Creed, and was truly repentant and ready to make restitution for anything he had done wrong. At this point the Office was reinforced in the 1800s by a special prayer book for the sick, with complete forms of examination and instruction. One most enlightening story is found in the advice it offered ministers. A man who had had a heart attack confessed to the priest who was called that he had trouble believing in the incarnation; it took the priest several hours of prayer and instruction about the faith of learned men before he could go on with the Office, and very soon after he left, the man died. This supplementary prayer book—which was used until nearly 1900—remarked that the case, of course, is "painful and unsatisfactory . . . but is here recorded to show the difficulties sometimes experienced in examinations of faith, and the means that may be taken in dealing with those difficulties."[5]

When the minister was satisfied of the sick man's faith, freedom from worldly cares and charity for all men, he was to remind him to make a will, remembering the church, and pay all his debts. Then the Office concluded with a Psalm and brief prayers for mercy and such relief as seemed expedient to God.

This service is still the only official form of prayer for visiting the sick in the Church of England, and until 1928 the same thing was also true in the Episcopal Church in America. The present Office of Visitation in the American Prayer Book has added a great deal of more comforting material. Some of the emphasis has been shifted, placing it directly upon the discretion of the indi-

5. *Visitatio Infirmorum* (1854), pp. lix f. This volume of over eight hundred pages contains services, penitential Psalms and suggestions for almost every difficulty and affliction—all cast in the same intellectual rigidity about faith and morals.

Among the long forms of examination, one by John Kettlewell, called "the Trial and Judgment of the Soul," pp. 499–513, begins: "Are you persuaded that your present sickness is sent unto you by Almighty GOD? . . . And that all which you now suffer is far less than you have deserved to suffer? . . . Are you fully sensible and convinced now, how little there is in (all your possessions), and how soon you may be, or are like to be taken from them?" Another form, based on baptismal vows, pp. 514–42, suggests an incredible number of specific questions, such as: "Have you not secretly rejoiced at the losses, crosses, disgraces, or death of any?" "Have you flattered with your lips, professing more love and respect to any than has been truly in your heart towards them?" After making the most of "lusts" and "wanton imaginings" it concludes: "Have you brought forth fruits meet for repentance, that is . . . more frequent and hearty devotions for your sins of ungodliness; almsgivings for your sins of unrighteousness; fasting for your sins of intemperance? If the tree of repentance bring not forth such fruits, it is neither lively, nor likely to be accepted." These forms were actually used for examining sick people in any condition short of dying. They seem to have been seriously proposed in a sincere belief that this was the best way to help a sick person.

vidual priest today, but without suggesting to him any fundamental need for changing his way of thinking. The two long exhortations I have quoted are deleted, but their essential meaning is shifted to a rubric. The idea of sickness as a time to catch a person and get his conscience and his ideas of faith straightened out intellectually is still to be found. Another attitude is added to it, but no reconciliation is made between them. This is still the official statement of this church on its ministry to sick people.[6] There is little idea in it that the service should bring healing, but rather comfort and strength.

Of course, the words of the service are seldom read any more, either in England or America; indeed the Office is ignored for the most part. But used or unused, it still stands as a major statement of the Christian attitude. Anyone who has done much pastoral work knows how thoroughly this outlook permeates the less conscious ways in which people look at and accept themselves

6. In the new services for trial use in the Episcopal Church, nothing remains of the pointed references to sickness and punishment for sin, but it is clear from the choice of New Testament passages, the place given to confession, and the care not to push spiritual healing, that this attitude is still at work. Aside from the brief optional prayer for laying on of hands, one is to pray mostly for the doctors and medical means of treatment, or else for strength and release from sin, and then for health. In the Church of Canada, where the Visitation Office was replaced in 1959 with an excellent set of services for "The Ministry to the Sick," the discussions occasioned by these services show that much the same thing is true there.

A casual reading of the Visitation of the Sick in the American *Prayer Book* would seem to indicate a belief in spiritual healing. This impression is derived largely from the addition of the Unction of the Sick in the 1928 revision of the *Book of Common Prayer* in the American Episcopal Church. However, this addition is neither historically nor organically related to the Visitation office. Following the work of Percy Dearmer and others, the Anglican Bishops at Lambeth approved the idea of healing. Thus the service of Unction was added, but in no way integrated into the stripped down version of the English Prayer Book which is the basis of the American office. Two quite different ideas about healing are here superimposed upon each other, but not molded into one service. Many of the clergy of the Episcopal service find the Visitation office ideas more congenial than those of the service of Unction of the Sick. Only a small portion of Episcopal churches would use the Unction service, or the Visitation office, but the basic attitude of most clergy follows that of the Visitation office.

when sickness strikes. Whether a man expresses it religiously or medically or sociologically, the question is foremost: "Why did *I* get myself into this? How did *I* make a mistake that was so displeasing to God? so sinful—or stupid—or clumsy?" When a child is involved, the parents' reasoning becomes even more clear.

This moralistic relationship of man to God, which the sixteenth-century church made so explicit in the Office of Visitation, is still at work, because it has not yet been replaced by a different point of view. The church has not yet come to a rethinking of the basic reality represented by this service.

Not long ago the English Visitation Office was read as part of a paper on healing to a group of the chief rectors of one of the large Episcopal dioceses in this country. The reactions of these men were quite typical of modern clergy. None of them had ever used this service. None of them had read it through in many years. Yet a majority still supported its basic theology and were very hesitant about any need to change it.

If this is typical of what the church and its clergy feel about the relation of God and his church to the sick, and if it represents the unspoken view of the average Protestant, then certain conclusions are inevitable. In general they are five.

1. God is responsible for sickness. There is no indication that evil or what might be expressed as the devil or demons may be the cause of any of it. Since there is apparently no other place for it to come from, sickness, along with other adversity and calamity, even though produced by material cause and effect, must be "given" or allowed by God for a reason.

2. The reason must be that God as Father shows his love to men as human fathers are assumed to do—by giving their children needed correction and chastisement. According to this psychology, which we shall discuss later, the only way to change an individual is by education and punishment. Sickness, then, is

seen as a natural punishment administered by God, and we become more dear to God the more he punishes us. In the words of the Visitation Office, those who receive no chastisement—the punishment of illness included—are bastards and not sons of God.

3. God's purpose in sending sickness is twofold. First, it is given to show men that they have sinned so that they may repent. Second, it is given to try their patience, because it enables the sufferer to grow in faith and become more saintly. In other words, sickness is a good, given either to correct men in their evil ways or so that their faith may be equal to Job's. Once this has been seen in certain instances, it becomes easier to suggest that sickness in general makes better people. It must also be man's fault that God sends destructive diseases like cancer and mental illness.*

4. It is the minister's task to save a person's spiritual health and his soul no matter what this does to his mental or physical condition. There is really no better time for it than when the person is seriously ill—when he can be guided into repenting and set on the right track. If these ideas sound more like the arguments of the friends of Job than the spirit of the New Testament, this is not too important, since almost no one in the church articulates them any more. The trouble is . . . they have left a hollow echo.

5. The Christian minister is left with no healing function. Christianity has no particular mission toward men's bodies, toward their physical and mental health. With sickness considered a cross sent by God to make people more aware of their defects and help them to become more mature, the church will obviously not undertake to remove it. The individual may go to a doctor, and churches may provide hospitals and even medical missionaries. But the church itself, by its own religious and sacramental

*These three points can only be seen by implication in the current American Prayer Book. We shall speak later of how the healing service was added to the Visitation Office.

actions, does little with an actual sacramental healing ministry. The church offers support and consolation which may have a healing effect, but in a secondary manner.

None of these approaches, however, has appealed very much to the more literal and fundamentalist churches, and so they have taken another tack. In doing so they have arrived at quite a different theory.

Healing and Dispensationalism

The theory that goes by this name has appeared among the more conservative churches that cherish the historical value of the New Testament and wish to maintain it, but find that certain elements in it, such as the healing ministry, are no longer present in the church today. This can be explained, as they see it, by God's having given a special dispensation for these mighty works only for a particular period and purpose.

The same problem was faced when the Protestant churches first began, and Luther came to admit that no one raised the dead any more and that what passed for healing miracles seemed to him to be the Devil's artifices and not miracles at all. The day of miracles is past, he concluded, and the real gift of the Holy Spirit is to enlighten Scripture, for "now that the apostles have preached the Word and have given their writings, and nothing more than what they have written remains to be revealed, no new and special revelation or miracle is necessary."[7] Or in Calvin's words,

7. *Sermons on the Gospel of St. John*, chaps. 14–16, *Luther's Works*, 24:367. Although in the end Luther added another view of the experience of healing (see pp. 233 and 221 f.), this did not happen until late in his life. In these earlier sermons the sixteenth-century attitude toward healing and miracles is expressed with a vehemence and color which few other writers displayed. In fact, the same spirit is sometimes found in them as in the contemporary English Office of Visitation to the Sick. Luther expressed two attitudes towards healing. He never reconciled them and the church followed the one more congenial to the world view of the 17th to 19th centuries.

The gift of healing disappeared with the other miraculous powers which the Lord was pleased to give for a time, that it might render the new preaching of the gospel for ever wonderful. Therefore, even were we to grant that anointing was a sacrament of those powers which were then administered by the hands of the apostles, it pertains not to us, to whom no such powers have been committed.[8]

The influence of these two men can hardly be stressed too much. Practically all Protestant theology begins from one or the other of them. Whatever reason they had for rejecting miracles —whether they were reacting to an emphasis in the medieval church, or perhaps responding to the first whispers of sophisticated humanism, or to the developing implications of Aristotelian thought—makes little difference. Calvin and Luther alike left the precedent that healing was a dispensation for a former time, and the matter was settled for later "orthodox" Protestants. The fact that the church fathers up to Aquinas, as well as the Orthodox churches, had a different point of view does not seem to have been much considered.

The thinking of these Reformation giants has been continued in a refined way by that modern giant of theology, Karl Barth. More careful than either Luther or Calvin, he has neither denied or affirmed the healing ministry for today. Instead, in the third volume of *Church Dogmatics, The Doctrine of Creation*, Barth even presented the great German healer J. C. Blumhardt in a very positive light, particularly by comparison with Mrs. Eddy. But when he came to consider how the Holy Spirit and the gifts of the Spirit act in man, he could see no real function for the Spirit except to open men's minds to understand and accept the original biblical revelation.[9] Healing was simply dismissed

8. John Calvin, *Institutes of the Christian Religion* IV.18 (1953), 2:636.
9. Barth's understanding of the work of the Holy Spirit is clearly shown in his discussions in *Church Dogmatics* (1936–1969), in various volumes, as follows: 1, *The Doctrine of the Word of God*, pt. 1, sec. 12.1, 526 ff.; 2, *The Doctrine of God*, pt. 2, secs. 33.1 and 34.3, 105 f., 118, and 249 f.; 3, *The Doctrine of Creation*, pt. 4, secs. 54.3 and 55.1, 320 ff. and 369 ff. (including the discussion of Blumhardt); 4, *The Doctrine of*

by neglect rather than by being denied.

For a long time this conclusion remained more or less implicit among Protestants. Most people simply accepted that there were two parts to God's history; that miraculous events like healing had happened in one of them, but would not happen again. It was assumed that no intelligent Christian of our age would encourage an interest in such things. But in time some serious questions were raised, and it became necessary to examine just what the church did mean by its rejection of miracles in current experience.

One of these early formulations is found in a little volume from England, *The Silence of God,* written about the end of the last century by Sir Robert Anderson. In it he stated:

The dispensation of Law and covenant and promise—the distinctive privileges of the favoured people—was marked by the public display of Divine power upon earth. But the reign of grace has its correlative in the life of faith. Ours is the higher privilege, the greater blessedness of those "who have not seen and yet have believed." And walking by faith is the antithesis of walking by sight. If "signs and wonders" were vouchsafed to us, as in Pentecostal days, faith would sink to a lower level, and the whole standard and character of the discipline of Christian life would be changed. The sufferings of Paul denote a higher faith than "the mighty deeds" of his earlier ministry. Not until miracles had ceased, and he had entered on the path of faith as we now tread it, was it revealed to him that his life was to be "a pattern to them that should afterwards believe."[10]

In the end, when some quite intelligent Christians did become interested and actually involved in a healing ministry, taking the meaning of the New Testament stories seriously, the theory of

Reconciliation, pt. 1, 64.1 and 2, 648 f. and 666 ff.; pt. 2, 64.4 and 68.4, 320 ff., 648 f., and 825 ff. In his discussion of Romans 15:18–19 in *The Epistle to the Romans* (1963), p. 532, Barth completely ignores the significance of Paul's words about "signs and wonders" and "the power of the Holy Spirit."

10. Sir Robert Anderson, *The Silence of God* (1952), pp. 153 f.

dispensationalism was ready for use in specific rejection of miracles of healing.[11]

Probably the most specific explanation of dispensationalism in relation to healing was set down by Dr. Wade Boggs in 1956. His work, *Faith Healing and the Christian Faith*, is an excellent study of the difficulties raised for the practice of a healing ministry within the framework of orthodox Christianity. By sticking logically and consistently to the point of view that faith healing has no place in the modern Christian church, Dr. Boggs opens up a great many of the problems that must be faced.

His thesis is basically this: There is no doubt that Jesus spent a large portion of his ministry healing the sick, and it is also clear that the apostles healed the sick in both body and mind. But this was only a dispensation for the period of the New Testament. God permitted these healings to take place in order to establish the Christian church; once the reality of the new faith had been demonstrated, the dispensation was withdrawn. Thus the healing ministry, being given only for a special period, has no application to our time. And since the healing ministry of Jesus was given mainly to establish his message and to prepare the church to evangelize it, healing was not meant to relate to our situation. Even the apostles, Boggs remarks, made use of oil—the best medicinal agent available to them, which was partly responsible for their effectiveness.

Dr. Boggs points up the fact that in recent years most of the emphasis on religious healing has come from fringe groups about which there is reason to be skeptical. Christian Science (and Mrs.

11. Although the idea of divine dispensations is an old one theologically, the term "dispensationalism" has come into use quite recently and is not always employed in this sense. The theory of a Christian dispensation of grace is used by Pentecostal writers to signify that, from the founding of the church on, tongues, healing, and other gifts of the Holy Spirit have been available to all Christian believers. One of the basic differences between Pentecostal and fundamentalist thinking is the interpretation given to the word "dispensation."

Eddy is certainly a controversial figure) is one example. New Thought with its dubious ancestry in the theory and practice of animal magnetism is another. The Pentecostal churches with their orgiastic practices and disregard for the laws of hygiene form yet another class, and he discusses such figures as Oral Roberts, Little David, Aimee Semple McPherson, and others. The implication is that, because the ministry of healing has sometimes been associated with ridiculous practices and foolish persons, therefore that ministry is itself ridiculous.

On the very practical side, Boggs calls attention to the tragic consequences that sometimes occur when faith healing is allowed to take the place of accepted medical practices. He deals specifically with the fact that people have died as a result of their refusal to have a doctor because this was against the belief of their sect. In addition, the connections seen in the Old Testament between sickness and sin and between sickness and God's displeasure are discussed at length, as well as Paul's mention of a thorn in his side, which is the only New Testament passage given much emphasis. All in all, this very consistency of approach in the book allows it to state some very difficult problems clearly and well.

These are much the same problems as were faced by the United Lutheran Church in 1962, with the result that its two and a half million members were warned to steer clear of religious healing. A committee of doctors, ministers, and theologians appointed by the church looked very carefully at the "religious quackery" practiced by certain faith healers. Their report made three specific charges: faith healers often have desire enough for money and personal power to exploit human desperation; they ignore the God-given gift of proven scientific methods; and they generally blame their own failures on the sick person's lack of faith and so endanger the spiritual life of many. For these and certain theological reasons the committee concluded that, while God does sometimes perform miraculous cures, these should not be sought, since "it cannot be assumed that, because of Christ's victory in their lives, Christians can expect healing effects not available to other people."[12]

Unquestionably dispensationalism has faced a difficult problem. It has taken the New Testament seriously and still faced the fact that most orthodox Protestant churches do not practice any ministry of religious healing to the sick in mind or body. The truth is, spiritual healing, whether within the church or by individuals outside it, is simply not a familiar event in modern life, nor does the average person feel at all capable of it.

Existential Theology and Healing

From the same starting point, current religious philosophers have taken quite a different path to arrive at an even more conclusive interpretation of the whole problem.

Philosophically the church has found itself in an equally tight spot. Liberal theology in the nineteenth century was bedded down, seemingly complacent, between the idealism of Hegel and the scientific naturalism of Darwin. But this was a crowded bed. It did not leave much room for man's individuality or spiritual worth, and it was soon under severe attack from Kierkegaard on one side and Nietzsche on the other. Unfortunately neither of these thinkers was quite equipped for a Boccaccian role; but they provided thought at the right time, and it is to Kierkegaard and Nietzsche that many religious philosophers have turned in the effort to find some reasonable base for Christian faith in the sophisticated modern world. As a result, the two schools of thinking which have come to the fore—Christian existentialism and the "God is dead" movement—both make a complete case against

12. *Anointing and Healing: Statement*, adopted by the adjourned meeting of the 1960 convention of the United Lutheran Church in America, June 25–27, 1962, Detroit, Mich., p. 23.

such experience as Christian healing. They find no more place
for healing than did naturalism or Hegelian idealism.

In Christian existentialism the philosophy of Husserl[13] has
been joined with the ideas of Kierkegaard and the method of
Hegel. For the followers of Husserl—Heidegger, Jaspers, Sartre,
Marcel, Merleau-Ponty—nothing is real but the present moment
of existence. Subject and object are dismissed as undiscoverable
entities. Any idea of supernatural nonphysical reality existing
apart from personal psychic material is discarded. The value of
history is questioned, and a scientific understanding of the world
as a closed system of reality is accepted as axiomatic. The course
of nature cannot be broken into or interrupted by any powers
beyond "existence"; instead meaning comes to men as they au-
thentically live in this immediate, conscious situation. They then
discover the ground of their being.

Kierkegaard also made it quite clear that the supernatural is
beyond the historian's province and thus irrelevant in Christian
thought. Only Christ who is paradoxically known is of value, not
Christ the healer.[14] Kierkegaard saw little of value to be found in
the history of Jesus of Nazareth. Husserl followed much the same
view in his discussion of mythical-religious ideas as opposed to
scientific and theoretical ones. Husserl's statement—ex cathedra
and without evidence—was that there is no value to the religious
belief that higher powers can influence human life in this space-
time existence.[15]

One large segment of Continental theology has accepted this
point of view and tried to interpret the Christian message in
these terms. Bonhoeffer, Tillich, and Bultmann have been the

13. Or phenomenology, which stresses the careful description of phenomena
in all domains of experience without regard to traditional epistemological questions.
14. Søren Kierkegaard, *Training in Christianity* (1944), pp. 9–39.
15. Edmund Husserl, *Phenomenology and the Crisis of Philosophy* (1965), pp. 169–
172.

leaders in this thinking, while Bishop Robinson and the early Bishop Pike have popularized it in England and the United States. And so this has become the most widely accepted way of thinking in Christian academic circles today.

This theology is quite satisfied that there is no basis for Christian healing in the known world. It would be a typical example of intervention into the natural order by supernatural powers, a break-through that changes the foregone conclusion. Bultmann, who is the clearest and most consistent representative of this school, views the Gospel account of healing as "mythology." These events, he holds, did not take place in actual fact, but were created by the faith of the early Christian community. Even the resurrection experience was a result of that faith rather than a fact in the strictest sense.

As Bultmann expresses it,

The whole conception of the world which is presupposed in the preaching of Jesus as in the New Testament generally is mythological; i.e., the conception of the world as being structured in three stories, heaven, earth and hell; the conception of the intervention of supernatural powers in the course of events; and the conception of miracles, especially the conception of the intervention of supernatural powers in the inner life of the soul, the conception that men can be tempted and corrupted by the devil and possessed by evil spirits. This conception of the world we call mythological because it is different from the conception of the world which has been formed and developed by science since its inception in ancient Greece and which has been accepted by all modern men.[16]

In order for modern man to accept the Christian message, the kerygma, Bultmann finds it necessary to demythologize the early Christian documents. Only then can we appreciate Jesus Christ and experience the power of the early Christian community.

From this point of view all angels and demons, all extrasensory

16. *Jesus Christ and Mythology* (1958), p. 15.

knowledge, the experiences of prophecy and tongues, the value of dreams and visions, as well as every account of healing the demon-possessed and the physically ill, must simply be rejected. They did not happen as such. Obviously, since they did not happen then, there is no reason to believe that they happen now. If one believes that they do, or that they should, it is because he is still under the domination of a "mythological" point of view which is untenable in the modern world. Christian healing, therefore has no place in today's Christianity, which is dealing with men where they are. It need not be considered, and any modern accounts of it are probably distortions of fact.

This point of view has been carried to its logical conclusion in the radical theology of the "God is dead" movement. Hamilton, Altizer, and Van Buren have done much of the talking for this school, which leans heavily on Nietzsche. Obviously, with God no longer active in the world the basis for any spiritual reality of healing no longer exists. It does not make much difference whether divine healing ever did exist, since there are no longer any terms in which this could be discussed. Religion—aside from direct activism, no longer directed by God—is a matter of waiting for the silent God to repeat himself once more.[17]

A Clean Sweep

Certainly most Christian thinking, both Catholic and Protestant,[18] has been swept clean of any idea of Christian healing. On one hand the successes of medicine have made it unnecessary, and on the other, modern theology has made any belief in it untenable. There has been, first, the acceptance by the church of

17. The historical development and present-day significance of these schools of thought are discussed in detail in my book, *Encounter with God* (1972).
18. Thomist theology, still the basis for the official Roman Catholic position, is discussed in chap. 9. See pp. 213ff.

the need to deal with the natural world rationally and on its own natural, material terms. Then there has been an acceptance of sickness as a part of that world, put there by God. Dispensationalism has found a way to divide this world so that healing, once seen as one of the greatest divine gifts, no longer seems needed or even wholesome. Finally, existential theology has made clear in ample reasoning why it did not happen at all.

Meanwhile the churches have gone on finding ways to adjust to a religion without the expectation of healing or other experiences of that nature. For a long time just talking about the nonmaterial soul and its salvation for a nonmaterial heaven was sufficient. To support this emphasis material things were produced. Churches went on constructing buildings and conducting campaigns for money using modern business techniques. They went into public relations and advertising, emphasizing numbers and attendance, and even made use of billboards like the one picturing a beautiful little white church, and parents and children well enough dressed to be attending a fashion show, with a caption two feet high: IT IS SMART TO GO TO CHURCH.

But today the awareness of huge dilemmas in our world has developed almost concurrently with a theology which has room only for a direct, existential way of solving difficulties. To find some more effective approach to people's problems, and something really to show for its morality, the church has turned to social action. The emphasis then is on the picket line or political activity, on meeting people and problems "just as they are." Religious healing does not fit in with either of these atmospheres. It is neither smart nor social-action-oriented—nor, in fact, generally considered *possible*—and so is ignored by practically the whole modern official Christian community.

In spite of this, let us take a fresh and honest look at the cultures that lie behind our own—Hebrew and Greek as well as

Christian—to discover what they have to say as to the value and reality of religious healing. Let us then see what sense the Gospel narrative makes on its own, and what evidence there is in later and modern experience to bear it out.

3

Religious Healing in the Ancient World

If we are to look intelligently at the healing described in the New Testament, so as to assess it critically together with the practices that followed, the description of these events must be seen in relation to the world in which they occurred. For one thing—perhaps strangely—we are so accustomed to the modern idea that it is good to heal that we forget how peculiarly Christian this is. It is surprising to find how much Jesus of Nazareth differed with the thinking of both his Judaic heritage and the Hellenistic world of which he was a part. His religious concern for the physical and mental welfare of men represented a departure. Although primitive peoples have always had their magic for relieving illness and pain, although other great faiths, such as Hinduism and Buddhism, have in certain areas developed elaborate rituals and practices dealing with physical health; it is nevertheless true that Jesus spoke and acted from a consistent and well-developed point of view which was new and quite at variance with the mainstream of both Judaism and Olympian Greek religion.

Yahweh's Visitation

In the Old Testament generally there was little thought of any need for stop-and-go signals on God's power for life and death. Deuteronomy 32:39 pretty well summarizes the basic attitude of

33

most of the Old Testament: "It is I who deal death and life; when I have struck it is I who heal (and none can deliver from my hand)." This was essentially the same thing Yahweh had affirmed to Moses earlier, when he asked, "Who makes him dumb or deaf, gives him sight or leaves him blind? Is it not I, Yahweh?" (Exod. 4:11) This understanding of good and evil was practically the theme of the prophets. "Does misfortune come to a city if Yahweh has not sent it?" Amos demanded (3:6), while in Isaiah 45:7 it was Yahweh who declared: "I make good fortune and create calamity, it is I, Yahweh, who do all this." God, the giver of all good things, was seen equally as the dispenser of misfortune and pain, including sickness of all kinds.

The hostile and destructive reactions of Yahweh did not always have a reason that men could understand morally, and strange happenings were related. Jacob came away lamed from wrestling with the angel (or Yahweh himself) the night before he was to meet Esau on his journey home. (Gen. 32:32) Even more curious was the story of Moses coming directly from his encounter at the burning bush, when "Yahweh came to meet him and tried to kill him," and his wife interfered. Then Zipporah cut off the foreskin of their son and touched it to Moses' genitals, and God let him live. (Exod. 4:24–26) David was so displeased and fearful at seeing Uzzah struck down for merely steadying the ark as they were taking it to Jerusalem that he changed his plans and left it outside the citadel. (2 Sam. 6:7–10, 1 Chron. 13:10–13) But unlike these events, sickness was mostly seen as God's rebuke for man's sin.

Until very late in the history of Judaism there was so limited a conception of the afterlife that any reward or punishment coming to the individual had to be seen here and now. The shadowy existence of Sheol, or the Pit, was certainly no recompense for the disappointments of this life; as the psalmists reminded Yahweh on so many occasions, there was no praise for him from there.[1] Since God's goodness had to show in this life if it was to be felt at all, men were led to overvalue this world and its immediate rewards and punishments. In the book of Deuteronomy this point of view is clearly and consistently developed. Health and wealth are the rewards of God, and sickness and misfortune his punishments.

From the beginning the law went into detail about the kind of disease Yahweh would send upon those who did not live by his covenant. In Leviticus consumption, fever, and pestilence were enumerated along with a variety of other penalties (26:16, 25), and in Deuteronomy the list was greatly extended:

> "Yahweh will strike you down with Egyptian boils, with swellings in the groin, with scurvy and the itch for which you will find no cure. Yahweh will strike you down with madness, blindness, distraction of mind, until you grope your way at noontide like a blind man groping in the dark, and your steps will lead you nowhere." (28:27–29)

In fact, there was really no end to the ailments Yahweh could produce for the benefit of men who did not obey him to the letter. Besides these, burning fever, inflammation, all the diseases dreaded in Egypt, and every sickness 'not mentioned in the Book of this Law" were promised in payment for sin. (Deut. 28: 22, 59–61)

The connection between sickness and sin was borne out by the history. Beginning in Genesis, Pharoah's whole household was struck down by severe plagues because Sarah was taken into his palace. (12:17) When Abimelech unwittingly planned to take Sarah, Yahweh made all the women of his household barren. (20:18) Because Onan wasted his ability to procreate when it was needed, Yahweh caused him to die as Er had for his offense. (38:9–10) The plagues the Egyptians suffered for their hardness

1. Even to come near a corpse could produce uncleanness in the living. Lev. 21: 1–2.

of heart included physical illness and ended with the death of their first-born. (Exod. 9:8–10, 12:29) For her slander of Moses, Miriam was stricken with leprosy (Num. 12:10), and the same disease was inflicted on Gehazi for his avarice. (2 Kings 5:26–27) When quail were provided for the Israelites in the wilderness, their gluttony angered Yahweh so much that he sent a plague (probably a gastric illness), from which many of them died. (Num. 11:33)

After the Philistines captured the ark of God, wherever it was taken the townspeople suffered from tumors and were only relieved when the ark had been sent on its way. (1 Sam. 5:6—6:1–12) Because of his temerity in taking a census of the people, David was given a choice between famine, conquest, and plague. He accepted the last, and seventy thousand people died in Israel before God took pity on the country. (2 Sam. 24:10–15, 1 Chron. 21:7–14) There is certainly no question how sickness was looked upon in this major strand of the Old Testament; it was sent by Yahweh to punish men for breaking the ritualistic or moral law.[2]

Since the sick were tainted, no man could be a priest before

2. There are many more historical references to God's power to punish and direct men by striking them with sickness. For instance, Moses' hand was turned leprous and then restored. (Exod. 4: 6–7) Yahweh's angels struck the men blind who were threatening Lot's house. (Gen. 19:11) Yahweh threatened the people of Israel with pestilence when they were rebelling against Moses and Aaron, struck down a few and then many, and later inflicted plague upon them when they turned to Baal of Peor. (Num. 14:11–12, 36–37; 17:12–15; 25:3–9, 17–18; 31:16) The seventy sons of Jeconiah were struck down because they did not rejoice at the return of the ark. (1 Sam. 6:19) Yahweh determined the death of Jeroboam's child in order to wipe out the house of the unfaithful king. (1 Kings 14:10–14) Because he consulted Baalzebub, Ahaziah was refused healing by Yahweh. (2 Kings 1:16) In answer to Elisha's prayer Yahweh struck the enemy blind and later restored their sight. (2 Kings 6:18–20) Even though he had done what was pleasing to Yahweh, the king Uzziah was struck with leprosy. (2 Kings 15:3–5) The later editors considered that this had happened because of his pride. (2 Chron. 26:-16–20) Sennacharib's army was struck down in the night by the angel of Yahweh. (2 Kings 19:35, 2 Chron. 32:21, Isa. 37:36) For deserting Yahweh, Jehoram was struck down by an incurable disease of the bowels. (2 Chron. 21:14–15)

Yahweh who was deformed or ill. The effect of Leviticus 21:-18–23 is very clear:

... no man must come near [to offer the food of his God] if he has an infirmity such as blindness or lameness, if he is disfigured or deformed, if he has an injured foot or arm, if he is a hunchback or a dwarf, if he has a disease of the eyes or of the skin, if he has a running sore, or if he is a eunuch. . . . he must not go near the veil or approach the altar, because he has an infirmity, and must not profane my holy things; for it is I, Yahweh, who have sanctified them.

Sickness represented a breach between Yahweh and man. Those assigned to be priests were no longer worthy to approach holy things once illness or physical handicap had shown them to be profaned by sin.

This theory of illness was expressed in several ways in the Psalms. In those that cry to Yahweh for deliverance from enemies and foreign adversaries, sickness is included as one of the ills that seem to come from the Lord himself. Psalms 6, 22, 38, 39, 88, and 102 all express this despair about illness, praying for deliverance. Then there are the Psalms that call down a curse upon one's enemies, in which there are imprecations for disease as well as all other ills. In addition, Psalm 101 clearly spells out the thinking of Deuteronomy in theory, while 78 and 106 outline it in terms of history.

Throughout the book of Proverbs this basic theory runs like a recurring theme, warning that illness and misfortune follow upon sin. For example:

> Do not think of yourself as wise,
>   fear Yahweh and turn your back on evil:
> health-giving, this, to your body,
>   relief to your bones.
>
> .   .   .   .   .
>
> My son, do not scorn correction from Yahweh,

>do not resent his rebuke;
>for Yahweh reproves the man he loves,
>as a father checks a well-loved son. (3:7–8, 11–12)

Again and again one is told that to follow wisdom and the law will bring health and long life, while to do otherwise will result in misery, misfortune, sickness, and death.

Behind This Emphasis

Back of this concern with the disciplinary effect of disease rather than with healing were two most important factors. First was the stress upon the group. In much of the Old Testament there was so much emphasis upon the people of Israel as a whole that what happened to the individual was a secondary matter. For this reason the sin of David, for instance, was visited upon the whole people, and the Philistines all paid for the sin of their leaders in seizing the ark of Yahweh. Only in the latest developments of the Old Testament is the individual responsible for his own sins. Up to that time one had to suffer collective guilt as a matter of course.

The other principal reason for neglect of individual healing was the fact that any idea of evil spirits as the cause of sickness and harm was rejected. The belief was common among most peoples at the time of the early Hebrews. Both the Egyptians and the Babylonians held that sickness resulted from the demonic ill will of various gods or evil spirits. The Persians with their well-developed dualism looked on disease as one activity of the powers of darkness. In the Vedic writings it is sometimes even difficult to decide whether a noun refers to a sickness or to the demon who caused it, so closely are the two related. But much of the Old Testament was an attempt to bring the people of Israel to a worship of Yahweh alone, who was seen as the sole source of both good and evil, of sickness as well as health.

Demons had no place in the Old Testament, and its angels

were merely messengers to carry out Yahweh's will. Any idea of spiritual powers independent of Yahweh in their action came only in the postexilic time.[3] Then it almost appears as if the ideas of the Persians and Babylonians and Egyptians finally made inroads upon Hebrew thinking because the demonic power of their gods had to be recognized. Until this happened, there was no source from which sickness could come except Yahweh. And since real healing could come only from him, Hebrew ideas even of medicine were quite different in some respects from those found among other peoples.

While the secular practice of medicine was discussed in other ancient writings, it was barely mentioned in the Old Testament. For instance, the Persians and the Chaldeans recorded the separation of medical practice into surgery, medicinal treatment, and prayer, indicating that all three were considered and discussed. Among Egyptian writings there is at least one long account of the diseases treated, which even goes into the fees received by the physician. But in the Old Testament physicians are hardly mentioned except in a derogatory way. The only reference in the history is in connection with the death of King Asa, and here it is made quite clear that Asa died for a good reason. A disease attacked him from head to foot, "and, what is more, he turned in his sickness, not to Yahweh, but to doctors." (2 Chron. 16:12) This is most probably an allusion to pagan physicians, the only ones to whom the early Hebrews could turn.

Since secular and religious practices of healing were very closely tied together, it seems clear that both were discouraged among the Hebrews. Those who practiced medical healing were also versed in divination and magic and probably had relations with other gods, and so came in for the same condemnation as the foreign interpreters of dreams. With sickness the direct "gift" of

3. See Rivkah Schärf Kluger's *Satan in the Old Testament* (1967), on the Judaic concept of the origin of evil.

Yahweh, it is hardly logical that such secular means would be considered effective, or that healing of any kind would be much encouraged. For the most part it was spoken of only in connection with the priestly function of cleansing.

In fact, not until the apocryphal book of Ecclesiasticus, probably written in the century after Chronicles (about 190 B.C.), is there any other mention of physicians. In chapter 38 the first fifteen verses are devoted to the doctor. The sensible man will not despise medicines, according to this work, but since healing is a gift from the Most High, he will pay the doctor the honor and the fee that are due him. One is counseled, when sick, to cleanse himself from sin, offer incense and a gift of fine flour, and also as rich an offering as he can afford, and "then let the doctor take over." Thus the words of wisdom conclude with the cheerful thought: "If a man sins in the eyes of his Maker, may he fall under the care of the doctor."

The same attitude continued to be expressed in the rabbinic schools of later Judaism. In the Mishnah, and also later in the Talmud, we find the conviction that sin is the root cause of illness. Rabbi Johnathan, for one, is quoted as saying: "Plague comes for seven sins, for bloodshed, perjury, unchastity, pride, embezzlement, pitilessness, and slander." (*Babylonian Talmud, 'Arakin* 16a) Almost the same thinking is found in *Singer's Prayer Book* published in London around 1900, which lists the seven kinds of punishment meted out for the seven types of sins.

It is true that there was healing among the Jews in Jesus' time, in spite of the fact that these incidents were looked upon with great suspicion by the rabbis. Still, men sought some relief from their sufferings, and so a form was used in which the healer whispered words adapted from Exodus 15:26:

If you listen carefully to the voice of Yahweh your God and do what is right in his eyes, if you pay attention to his commandments and keep his statutes, I shall inflict on you none of the evils that I inflicted on the Egyptians, for it is I, Yahweh, who give you healing.

The main schools of Judaism considered the practice involved here akin to sorcery and magic and forbade it, but the Talmud attests to its use. In several places there are references to the fact that those who employ such measures will have no share in the world to come. (*Mishnah* 10[1]; *Babylonian Talmud, Sanhedrin,* XI and 101[a]) This is certainly consistent with the statement in the Talmud that Jesus was hanged on a tree on the Passover Eve because he practiced sorcery.

This whole attitude thus had its beginning in the teaching of the great prophets who first saw the righteousness of God. From being a theory which supported that concern for righteousness, it became part of the code in the book of Deuteronomy. As later editors who held to this view went through the sacred books, their sharpened pencils pointed up how this moral law was carried out in history. Now and then they did come across men whose lives did not fit the pattern—who were anything but moral, yet still kept health and wealth—but they slipped over these disconcerting facts as lightly as possible. After all, no one holds onto life and property forever, and the exception only proves the rule. It is not hard to see the origin of the English Office of the Visitation to the Sick, or of the idea for Dr. Wade Boggs's careful study; both express this Old Testament teaching.

Another Strand

But the amazing thing about the Old Testament in this conviction is the fact that the central belief set forth above is not the only one expressed in it. Another strand of experience and belief about healing was just as carefully preserved, though it did not become part of the code accepted as directing the people of Israel. There is no area where the difference between the Old and New

Testaments is more marked than in the teaching about healing. The people of Israel took one direction, and yet—here is the greatness of our religious heritage—they took care not to erase from their records the experiences and signs that pointed another way.

This other strand of belief about healing found in the Old Testament is not as wide or obvious as the teaching accepted by Hebrew leaders. It is expressed in certain healing stories, in some of the Psalms, in the hopes of certain passages of Isaiah, and in the gigantic protest of the book of Job. This element is the one upon which Jesus based his teaching, the base from which he acted.

As we have already seen, in the Old Testament there was no question, in theory, that Yahweh could heal. In several places remarkable instances were recorded. Some of the most touching and best-remembered stories are those in which children were given to women who were barren. Though barrenness was often considered the result of divine disfavor (Gen. 20:18, 30:2), a child was given as a particular gift of God to Sarah (Gen. 18:10, 14), to Manoah's wife, the mother of Samson (Judg. 13:5, 24), to Hannah, the mother of Samuel (1 Sam. 1:19–20), and to the Shunammite woman (2 Kings 4:16–17). There are also the beautiful stories of both Elijah and Elisha healing a child, which in so many ways carry the quality of the later healings of Jesus. No sin is imputed to the child or its mother, and these are acts of compassion through the power of Yahweh. (1 Kings 17:17–23, 2 Kings 4:- 18–37) Elisha's cleansing Namaan of leprosy is another example of healing where no sin is attributed to the sick man. (2 Kings 5:1–14)

There was also a strange story of raising from the dead, which took place just after the death of Elisha and involves the touching of relics, which in the Middle Ages became so prominent a theme. Some men were carrying a body out for burial, and as they came to Elisha's tomb a band of Moabite raiders appeared. The Israelites threw the body into the tomb and ran, and "The man had no sooner touched the bones of Elisha than he came to life and stood up on his feet." (2 Kings 13:21)

Instances are recounted of healing after the proper sacrifices are made. A bronze serpent was fashioned that saved anyone bitten by the fiery serpents Yahweh had sent. (Num. 21:9) The Philistines, to obtain healing, delivered to the people of Israel golden models of the tumors and rats Yahweh had inflicted on them. (1 Sam. 6:4–5) When Hezekiah prayed, he was saved from the death earlier decided by Yahweh; almost immediately Isaiah knew that Yahweh had relented and had a healing fig poultice placed on the king's ulcer. (2 Kings 20:1–7, Isa. 38:1–6, 21) Twice a plague was halted, once by Aaron's act of atonement, again by David's prayer. (Num. 16:47–50, II Samuel 24:10–25)

Finally, the apocryphal book of Tobit tells the delightful story of how Tobias, through the power of the angel Raphael, healed his father's blindness and defeated Asmodeus, the demon who was striking down Sarah's husbands. Except for Job, these few are all the references to incidents of healing up to the New Testament. Interesting as the stories are, they are peripheral to the main thought of Hebrew religion.

Yet the same theme is found scattered through the Psalms and the prophets. In Psalm 103 Yahweh is blessed for healing diseases, and Psalm 91 tells how he protects from all plague. Similar confidence in Yahweh as healer of mind, body, and outer condition is found in Psalms 41, 46, 62, 74, 116, 121, and 147. In certain Psalms healing power is simply implied; others, like 73 and 94, protest that Yahweh has failed to reward goodness with health and mercy. Hosea also made clear that Yahweh had power to save from evil—from plagues and death—but did not exercise it because of the people's wickedness. (6:1–11, 13:12–15)

Isaiah referred in certain passages to the days of Yahweh when all the ills of man would be healed. The dead would rise and the deaf and the blind would hear and see. (26:19, 29:18, 61:1–11)

> Then the eyes of the blind shall be opened,
> the ears of the deaf unsealed,
> then the lame shall leap like a deer
> and the tongues of the dumb sing for joy. . . .(35:5–6)

Although the day of Yahweh was seen by some as the end of time, when wrongs would all be righted, in the popular aspirations of the people it was also seen as the day of the Messiah—the one longed for—who would bring the kingdom of heaven with him. Ezekiel's story of the valley of dry bones (chap. 37) was also an expression of healing. Though told as an allegory, it conveys what Ezekiel apparently knew of the power of Yahweh to heal.

The great protest against the Deuteronomic theory of sickness and healing is found in the story of Job. One of the main purposes of the book was simply to challenge that theory. Job was a righteous man, of this there was no doubt. We are taken into the very court of heaven to discover why he should suffer. He was firm and sincere in his religious profession, but in order to convince Satan of this—Satan, who is seen as one of the Sons of God—Job is overwhelmed with suffering and privation, with rebuke and illness.

Because these outer symptoms obviously indicate disfavor with God, Job is treated with scorn by his neighbors and even by children—unthinkable among the Hebrews while a person was healthy. And so he ends up on the village dump, throwing ashes over his boils and scratching his sores with a potsherd. Even former friends turn upon him and plague him with their judgment, suggesting that he look for sins of which he knows he is not guilty. His wife leaves him with the comforting recommendation that he curse God and die. Unquestionably the reactions of Job's neighbors, children, wife, and friends represent the actual attitude of those days toward anyone struck down by adversity and serious illness. These were signs that a man had lost God's favor by his own fault and wickedness. But Job, maintaining his innocence, was in the end justified by Yahweh.

The whole book is a profound discussion of the problem of evil. Job's was a voice crying in the wilderness. So much did later copyists disagree with the presentation and its basic outlook that they altered the text to bring it a little more in line with the orthodox Deuteronomic theory of the origin of suffering and sickness. Thus this strand of teaching was not a final, accepted development of Jewish thought about healing. Its influence is seen in the less orthodox region of Galilee, where a rich demonology had grown up and sickness was understood, in part at least, as the result of evil spirits rather than as coming solely from Yahweh.

This, at any rate, was the strand of belief that Jesus brought forth—the understanding he developed even though it put him at odds with the official religion of his people. His own orthodox tradition did not have much to offer when it came to creating a new attitude toward sickness and sick human beings. In order not to be naive about Jesus' inspiration in regard to healing, let us look at possible antecedents very carefully.

Healing in the Hellenistic World

Did Jesus, then, receive the inspiration for his healing ministry as a package from the Hellenistic culture, which generally seems to us so mature and modern. If Greek paganism is looked at carefully, the answer is equally clear; although there *is* reason to see a kind of maturity in this culture, healing is not a significant part of its religious life. The early Greeks and Romans found ways to seek religious healing, just as the Hebrews did. There were several healing cults, including the well-developed cult of

Aesculapius, which reached many people. Formal medical study undoubtedly had its beginning in the great Hippocratic school of ancient Greece. And as we have shown elsewhere,[4] this school on the island of Cos evolved almost hand in hand with the growth of Aesculapian healing there.

Plato recognized the prime need for curing the soul in order to find real healing of the body, and he also saw the importance of healing as one of the ways in which divine creative energy seizes and possesses human beings. All through the *Dialogues* he variously stressed the necessity of getting at disease by treating the whole man;[5] in the discussion of divine inspiration in the *Phaedrus* he listed healing along with prophecy, art, and love as a way in which he saw the divine breaking through into the physical.[6] It is clear that Plato accepted the kind of healing that came to be experienced in the temples of Aesculapius. But there was little development of this basic understanding until after the Christian church had appropriated Plato for its own and this implication of his thought was realized.

Greek polytheism made it unnecessary to integrate this insight into a more central place in Greek thinking, and there was no

4. See my *Dreams: The Dark Speech of the Spirit* (1968), p. 71; also C. Kerényi, *Asklepios: Archetypal Image of the Physician's Existence* (1959), pp. 47 ff.

5. *Charmides* 156 f., *Symposium* 186, *Timaeus* 87 ff., *Republic* III 408. In the *Charmides* Plato wrote: "For all good and evil, whether in the body or in human nature, originates . . . in the soul, and overflows from thence, as if from the head into the eyes. And therefore if the head and body are to be well, you must begin by curing the soul; that is the first thing. And the cure, my dear youth, has to be effected by the use of certain charms, and these charms are fair words; and by them temperance is implanted in the soul, and where temperance is, there health is speedily imparted, not only to the head, but to the whole body. And he who taught me the cure and the charm at the same time added a special direction: 'Let no one,' he said, 'persuade you to cure the head, until he has first given you his soul to be cured by the charm. For this,' he said, 'is the great error of our day in the treatment of the human body, that physicians separate the soul from the body.' " (157)

6. *Phaedrus* 244. Josef Pieper in *Love and Inspiration: A Study of Plato's Phaedrus* (1965) discusses this very important point in Plato's philosophy, pp. 58 ff.

religious basis for it until the joining of Greek and primitive Christian experience in the church. With Aristotle, divine healing became impossible because of a metaphysics which rejected any elementary principle of evil in the world, and at the same time eliminated any other realm of reality which could intervene to offer healing. Here again Christianity picked up one strand of a culture and made it an integral factor of a new religious attitude which had its effect on the world for centuries.

In reality, there was only one major difference between the approach to sickness of the Greco-Roman world and that of Judaism. The Greeks looked upon disease as an affliction from the gods, and for the most part considered the sick unlucky, tainted people to be shunned and avoided, just as did the Jews. But they connected this more with fate or destiny than with sin. The idea of man's responsibility to God for his own actions—either as a whole people or later as an individual—was a Judaic one. The Greeks were subject to the gods, but not related to them by agreement or covenant. Thus sickness was seen as a matter more of luck or fate than as punishment for breaking an agreement—for misdoing or sin.

Throughout the literature of ancient Greece and Rome we find the idea that sick men were suffering from the displeasure of the gods. Like Yahweh, the same gods that brought disaster could sometimes turn about and bring healing. But there were only a few minor gods in whose shrines it was appropriate to ask for relief from sickness. There were the cults of Seraphis, Amphiaraus, Trophonios, and particularly Aesculapius.

It is true that the cult of Aesculapius, in particular, attracted many people in the Hellenistic period. The popularity of Aesculapian healing has been thoroughly demonstrated by modern archaeology. Yet there are few references in ancient writings to this cult, and it stood in contrast to the basic religious attitude of that world toward illness. The temples in which the god was worshiped were strictly places of healing. The sick person came there to sleep within the confines of the temple and to ask for a vision or dream from the god to heal him or show him the way to healing. All activity centered around this principal rite of "incubation."

Various symbolic acts seem to have contributed to the healings, such as the sacrifice of small animals in the rotunda (or mysterious labyrinth, at Epidaurus) near the altar. Ritual bathing and even stadiums and gymnasiums stressed the importance of the body. In great amphitheaters near the temples drama became part of the ritual, with healing effect. Certainly there was no lack of meaning for the individual in these rites, and it is even suggested that they offered the expectation of a culminating religious experience.[7] Still, there was little of specific religious commitment in the ceremonies, and their development was more a veneer on Greek religion than a foundation stone. In some ways the Aesculapeion was more like a mineral-water spa than a center of religious life.

In fact, the myth of Aesculapius itself reveals a great deal about the place given to healing in Greek religion. We are told that he was the son of Apollo and the human princess Coronis, who was killed by the sun god because she could not hide from him her desire for a mortal man. Apollo, however, saved his son and entrusted him to the care of Chiron, the wise Centaur whom Apollo himself had instructed in the arts. Aesculapius became a favorite pupil because of his preference for the gentle art of healing, and he surpassed his teacher as a physician, reputedly restoring even the dead to life. This drew the anger of the gods, and at Pluto's demand Zeus is said to have unleashed a thunderbolt and killed him.

Aesculapius came to be much honored by men, and in post-

7. Kerényi, *op. cit.*, pp. 38 f.

Homerian mythology was received among the Olympians—too late to become an equal of the gods. He remained specifically the healer. While the other gods were not particularly concerned with this, and still used their malicious powers, Aesculapius could be appealed to for relief of human misery. But his power was always subject to the higher authority of the other, greater Olympians.

Although his temples were widely popular, as shown by the numerous inscriptions telling of cures, they represent more the split in the Greek mind and culture than a central element of Greek religion. The period in which Aesculapius became a god, and his temples places of pilgrimage, was also the time in which the intellectual leaders of Greece withdrew into a world of their own and the people turned from the worship of their fathers to a variety of cults. Plato foresaw this and in his later writings made a bid to stave it off. But what he could not fully comprehend was the great need of the people for an inspired religion of caring about the whole man. Healing represented by the Aesculapian and other cults was an eddy alongside the stream of paganism. It could not rise to become such an inspiration.

Instead, these various separate gods of healing portray one of the most basic and imbedded ideas of ancient Greek culture. This is the notion of the dichotomy of mind and body, of *nous* and *physis*, known as Gnosticism. Out of this came a theory of the origin of man which held that men had been made when the *nous* somehow became entrapped in the grosser body, the *physis*. This material part was nonessential.[8] Later, as Gnosticism matured, the body came to be viewed as positively evil, and salvation was seen as the liberation of the mind-soul from it, so that the valua-

8. An excellent study of this theory of Orphism and its effect upon later Greek thinking is found in Walter Wili, "The Orphic Mysteries and the Greek Spirit," *Papers from the Eranos Yearbooks* 2, *The Mysteries* (1955): 64 ff. This paper draws together the evidence that supports the position above.

ble part of man might have freedom and bliss.

The combination of Greek thinking and Greek healing cults did not offer a resolution of this division in man. And so in Gnosticism a point of view emerged in which healing of the body was clearly a relatively unimportant matter. In some Gnostic asceticism the body was practically destroyed. Until the Council of Nicaea the church fathers were constantly fighting the influence of the Gnostic point of view on Christianity because its low valuation of the body resulted in a split in man's being. In a later chapter we shall consider how far the Gnostic point of view has crept back into the teaching and practice of the church.

Healing at the Greek shrines was one expression of the longing for a god who cared about the bodies as well as the minds and souls of men, a god who was soon to be a reality to them. These shrines became an important part of the Greek scene, accepted by some of the most sophisticated Greek thinkers as a natural part of life; beginning with Aristophanes references occur here and there in the literature. It is no wonder that the cults soon gave way to the vital practices of Jesus of Nazareth, who came among men to heal their bodies and minds along with their souls. Nor is it strange that Aesculapian shrines were so often transformed into Christian churches in the Greek world.[9]

Many of the Greeks believed that man's physical and mental health was influenced by spiritual powers. This attitude was expressed in medical practice, in literature, in popular Hellenistic religion, and also in the philosophy of Plato. Some Greeks put forward, with the most delicate understanding and finesse, the point of view of the whole religious way of life known as shamanism. This has been the form of religion of a vast number of

9. Mary Hamilton, *Incubation (or the Cure of Disease in Pagan Temples and Christian Churches)*, 1906, pp. 109 f. See also C. A. Meier, *Ancient Incubation and Modern Psychotherapy* (1967), p. 20. Dr. Meier offers evidence of the effectiveness of the practice of incubation (sleeping in these shrines).

human beings from the earliest days to the present time. The practices of some existing Siberian tribes still reflect the attitudes and practices of shamanism as clearly as any one ethnic ground. The customs of modern American Indians fall into the same category, as they are described by Carlos Castaneda in *The Teachings of Don Juan* and *A Separate Reality;* also by John Neihardt in *Black Elk Speaks.* The classic study of shamanism is Mircea Eliade's monumental work, *Shamanism.* Another work of the same compass is Violet MacDermot's, *The Cult of the Seer in the Ancient Middle East.* One might even say that in the writings of Plato one finds the philosophical statement of shamanism.

When we look at the ministry of Jesus, we shall see the contrast between his attitude and the official attitudes both of Judaism and the Olympic gods. We find that his life and acts, his teaching and practice, are rather akin to a shamanism based on an intimate relationship with a loving father god. In fact, an important study might be made comparing the ministry of Jesus with that of shamanism, but this is not the place for it. Those who are taken aback by his healing ministry and would disregard or excise it from the New Testament record or from present-day emulation simply are ignorant of the experiences of healing universally known—and in great numbers—in most forms of shamanism. The shaman is the mediator between the individual and spiritual reality, both good and evil, and because of this the healer of diseases of mind and body. In stepping into his healing role Jesus picks up the prophetic and shamanistic strand of the Old Testament tradition already mentioned. Thus Jesus brings to new focus an aspect of religious life which had been neglected in the official religions of the day.[10]

10. See Appendix B where I have discussed two of the recent Biblical critics, Norman Perrin and Günther Bornkamm, who support this point of view.

4

The Unique Healing Ministry of Jesus of Nazareth

Modern medicine has tended to look back to Hippocrates and Galen as the only ancient source and inspiration of modern medical practice. But this presents a very incomplete picture. As one physician recently pointed out,

It has become traditional to identify modern doctors in spirit with a long line of historic greats reaching back to the impressive Hippocrates. This notable Greek, a veritable pinnacle in ancient medicine, often called the "Father of Medicine," largely set the pattern for current professional attitudes and relationships. But sometimes it is forgotten that medicine owes its greatest debt not to Hippocrates, but to Jesus. It was the humble Galilean who more than any other figure in history bequeathed to the healing arts their essential meaning and spirit . . . Physicians would do well to remind themselves that without His spirit, medicine degenerates into depersonalized methodology, and its ethical code becomes a mere legal system. Jesus brings to methods and codes the corrective of love without which true healing is rarely actually possible. The spiritual "Father of Medicine" was not Hippocrates of the island of Cos, but Jesus of the town of Nazareth.[1]

Few religious leaders have had more influence on the basic ideas of modern man than Jesus of Nazareth. The effect of his teaching, his thoughts, is felt not only by several million avowed

1. J. W. Provonsha, M.D., "The Healing Christ," *Current Medical Digest* (December 1959): p. 3. See Appendix A for Dr. Provonsha's complete article.

Christians but among all peoples touched by Western civilization. Oddly enough, his thinking was in some respects the most materialistic of any of the important religious leaders, particularly in relation to health. The interest Jesus showed in the physical and mental health of men was greater than that of any other leader or religious system from Confucius through Buddha to Zen and Islam. There is no doubt about this, either in what he thought of the value of healing men's minds and bodies or in the way he put it into practice. The source material found in the New Testament is clear and consistent. Let us survey it briefly and then study certain aspects of it in detail.

The New Testament Record of Healing

In the first chapters of the Gospel of Mark the ministry of Jesus is characterized as threefold—a ministry of preaching, teaching, and healing. Similar passages are found in Luke and Matthew. An honest, unprejudiced reading of the Gospels makes it perfectly clear that this was the understanding of the writers and that it is a good summary of his total ministry. Jesus proclaimed, or preached, the Good News, the present reality of the kingdom of heaven, now accessible to men.[2] He taught his hearers how to relate their lives to God and his kingdom; his teachings showed them how the various aspects of their thinking, their devotional practice, and their behavior related to the God now breaking into men's lives and history in a new way. This new insight was

2. The kingdom, as Jesus proclaimed it, may be viewed inwardly as well as eschatologically. It is true that Jesus and his followers undoubtedly looked for the immediate coming of the kingdom in history. However, the statements about it may *also* be seen as referring to the kingdom within, or the kingdom breaking through now in history. In other words, eschatology need not refer only to the future; the ideas of God acting at present and in final things are not mutually exclusive. This understanding of the dual meaning of Jesus' preaching has been carefully developed by John A. Sanford in his book, *The Kingdom Within* (1970). In it he also shows that this was the understanding of the kingdom of God among the Greek fathers.

interpreted in the religious terms then current, the tradition of their Judaism. And third, he healed: he brought physical and mental health to the sick in body and mind, those possessed by physical affliction and what were known as demons.

Nearly one-fifth of the entire Gospels is devoted to Jesus' healing and the discussions occasioned by it.[3] Except for miracles in general, this is by far the greatest emphasis given to any one kind of experience in the narrative. It is startling to compare this emphasis on physical and mental healing with the scant attention given to moral healing. Very few examples of moral or ethical transformation are mentioned in the Gospels. There are the stories of Matthew, Zaccheus, the woman at the well of Sychar, and the woman of Luke 7:37 and John 8:3 which together originate the tradition of Mary Magdalene, and that is about all unless one considers the calling of the disciples as examples of moral conversion. A transformation of the apostles occurred at Pentecost after the ascension, but there is little in the Gospels which can be described as realization of "authentic being." There may well have been many moral transformations, but they are not recorded. Is it not possible that the belief in Jesus' moral healing has risen to take the place of those healings which have been allowed to be ignored?

Instead we find that everywhere Jesus went he functioned as a religious healer. Forty-one distinct instances of physical and mental healing are recorded in the four Gospels (there are seventy-two accounts in all, including duplications), but this by no means represents the total. Many of these references summarize the healings of large numbers of persons. Those described in detail are simply the more dramatic instances of this activity of

3. Out of the 3779 verses in the four Gospels, 727 relate specifically to the healing of physical and mental illness and resurrection of the dead. In addition there are 165 verses that deal in general with eternal life, and also 31 general references to miracles that include healing. Complete lists of these references are found in the appendix of my *Encounter with God* (1972).

Jesus—according to the record an extensive ministry, to say the least.

It is also clear that Jesus sent his disciples out to continue this basic ministry (Mark 6:7–13, Matthew 10:5–10, Luke 9:1–6). The book of Acts records how well they carried out this commission. It is difficult to see how Bultmann, on theological and philosophical grounds, can eliminate this entire ministry by calling it mythology. It is particularly difficult when we realize, on one hand, that these stories form one of the earliest levels of the Gospel tradition from the point of view of form criticism, and on the other, what a close relation modern medicine has shown between psyche and body and how much they interact with one another. In chapters 10 and 11 we shall deal with this subject in more detail.

The importance of this ministry is expressed in a very striking way in Ethel Banks's booklet, *The Great Physician Calling*. This is simply a collection of healing stories from the Gospels using the arrangement of Percy Dearmer's book, *Body and Soul.*[4] Mrs.

4. This tabulation of the healing works described in the Gospels is as follows, arranged in the order listed by Dearmer, pp. 137 ff.

No. Healing	Matthew	Mark	Luke	John	Method
1. Man with unclean spirit		1:23	4:33		Exorcism, word
2. Peter's mother-in-law	8:14	1:30	4:38		Touch, word; prayer of friends
3. Multitudes	8:16	1:32	4:40		Touch, word; faith of friends
4. Many demons		1:39			Preaching, exorcism
5. A leper	8:2	1:40	5:12		Word, touch; leper's faith and Christ's compassion
6. Man sick of the palsy	9:2	2:3	5:17		Word; faith of friends
7. Man's withered hand	12:9	3:1	6:6		Word; obedient faith
8. Multitudes	12:15	3:10			Exorcism, response to faith
9. Gerasene demoniac	8:28	5:1	8:26		Word, exorcism
10. Jairus' daughter	9:18	5:22	8:41		Word, touch; faith of father

	Matt.	Mark	Luke	John	
11. Woman with issue of blood	9:20	5:25	8:43		Touching His garment in faith
12. A few sick folk	13:58	6:5			Touch (hindered by unbelief)
13. Multitudes	14:34	6:55			Touch of His garment, friends' faith
14. Syrophoenician's daughter	15:22	7:24			Resp. to mother's prayer, faith
15. Deaf and dumb man		7:32			Word, touch; friends' prayer
16. Blind man (gradual healing)		8:22			Word, touch; friends' prayer
17. Child with evil spirit	17:14	9:14	9:38		Word, touch; faith of father
18. Blind Bartimaeus	20:30	10:46	18:35		Word, touch, compassion; faith
19. Centurion's servant	8:5		7:2		Resp. to master's prayer, faith
20. Two blind men	9:27				Word, touch; men's faith
21. Dumb demoniac	9:32				Exorcism
22. Blind and dumb demoniac	12:22		11:14		Exorcism
23. Multitudes	4:23		6:17		Teaching, preaching, healing
24. Multitudes	9:35				Teaching, preaching, healing
25. Multitudes	11:4		7:21		Proof to John Bapt. in prison
26. Multitudes	14:14		9:11	6:2	Compassion, response to need
27. Great multitudes	15:30				Faith of friends
28. Great multitudes	19:2				
29. Blind and lame in Temple	21:14				
30. Widow's son			7:11		Word, compassion
31. Mary Magdalene and others			8:2		Exorcism
32. Woman bound by Satan			13:10		Word, touch
33. Man with dropsy			14:1		Touch
34. Ten lepers			17:11		Word; faith of the men
35. Malchus' ear			22:49		Touch
36. Multitudes			5:15		
37. Various persons			13:32		Exorcism, and not stated
38. Nobleman's son				4:46	Word; father's faith
39. Impotent man				5:2	Word; man's faith

40. Man born blind	9:1	Word, touch
41. Lazarus	11:1	Word

Banks has combined stories that obviously tell of the same healing, listing them as one instance. As one reads account after
account in succession, they have an awakening impact. One begins to realize how much of the life of Christ was given to caring
for the physical and mental ills of people and how fully he expected his disciples to go on with the same work.

There is even evidence outside the Gospel narrative for this
aspect of the ministry of Jesus. In the Talmud (*Sanhedrin* 43a) we
find the tradition that Jesus of Nazareth was hanged on a tree on
the Passover Eve because he practiced sorcery; he was destroyed
because he healed by calling upon evil forces rather than upon
God. This tradition is confirmed in Mark 3:22.[5] When Jesus went
home to Nazareth, he was simply besieged by people who wanted
to be healed. His friends tried to seize him, saying that he was
beside himself, and the Pharisees claimed he was possessed by
Beelzebub and that it was by the prince of the demons that he cast
out demons. Even his opponents did not try to contest the fact
that Jesus healed but only to cast doubts upon the agency through
which he did it.

The ministry of healing of Jesus is certainly in line with the
constant emphasis in his teachings upon compassion and caring
about one's neighbor. Certainly it is not out of character with
that teaching. This stress on the importance of *agape*, love, is a
most basic aspect of his teaching. One of the most concrete ways
of expressing that love is through concern about another's physical and emotional condition, and the removal of torturing infirmities, physical hindrances, and mental or emotional illness. The
story of the good Samaritan is an excellent case in point, whatever the means of healing. Where sickness was so prevalent and
so little was actually known about curing it, those who cared

5. Parallel passages are found in Matt. 12:24 and Luke 11:15.

about people were drawn by this aspect of Jesus' teaching and practice. In effect they saw that God cared.

The healings of Jesus, far from conflicting with his preaching of the kingdom of God, were instead referred to as a direct evidence of it. He stated specifically that his healing was a sign that the kingdom of heaven was breaking forth. In answer to the charge that he was a sorcerer, he replied in Matthew 12:27–28, "And if it is through Beelzebul that I cast out devils, through whom do your own experts cast them out? Let them be your judges, then. But if it is through the Spirit of God that I cast devils out, then know that the kingdom of God has overtaken you."[6]

In much the same way Jesus answered the disciples of John when they came to inquire if he were the one who was to come or they should look for another. By quoting the essence of Isaiah 35:5 and 61:1, he pointed to Scripture and the messianic hope of both first and second Isaiah in these words: "Go back and tell John what you hear and see; the blind see again, and the lame walk, lepers are cleansed, and the deaf hear, and the dead are raised to life and the Good News is proclaimed to the poor. . . ." (Matt. 11:4–5)

According to this answer, the healing ministry was one basic credential and evidence that he was the Messiah, the long-awaited messenger of the kingdom of heaven. His healings were the sign needed by John, who languished in prison at the time, to believe that Jesus was indeed the one who was to usher in the new age. The message was given to comfort John, to make him realize that he had not preached and baptized in vain. This aspect of Jesus' ministry was thus certainly not considered incidental or unimportant by the Evangelists. They set down as one of his basic ideas that the power of God had broken through into our

6. Quotations of Scripture are from the Jerusalem Bible unless otherwise noted.

world and that these evil things were therefore being put to flight. In the final coming of the kingdom they would be eliminated entirely.

This theological attitude of Jesus marks one of the basic differences between the healings of Jesus and those in other ancient cultures, particularly in the Greek world. The Greek god Aesculapius was simply one divine power among many, a god who happened to be interested in healing. If Jesus saw himself as the Messiah, then he represented the essential nature of God himself and was his specific messenger, and his healings therefore sprang from the essential nature of God. Sickness and demon possession were considered prime evidences of evil in the world. By dealing with them as the Messiah, the agent of God, Jesus laid the attitude of God toward sickness out on the counter where all could see it. We shall have more to say about this in the next chapter.

Underlying this healing attitude was a view of man quite different from that of most of the ancient world. Jesus had a surprisingly modern theory of human personality. It was a unique and highly developed, if implicit, psychological point of view, consistent not only with his ministry but with his whole ethical attitude. His healing ministry was the natural result of this outlook.

The Psychology of Jesus

Everyone has a psychology, whether he knows it or not, whether he calls it by that name or not. Everyone has a pattern of acting toward other human beings; we show what we think about other people by the way we act toward them, even if we never verbally express the ideas embodied in our actions. While Jesus never expounded his psychological theory in so many words, it is not difficult to deduce from what he said and did. His teaching and his acts were of a piece, and both reveal a point of view very different from the popular attitude bequeathed to us by the rest of the ancient world. In order to see how different his outlook was, we must first of all sketch the view of personality which has been current in most societies from ancient Israel and Greece up to our own time.

According to this attitude the human personality is relatively simple and easy to understand. The basic assumption is that there is only one essential center to a man's being and personality, and each individual is in control of himself, able to determine his actions by his own conscious choice. If he has knowledge, therefore, of what is right or wrong, expedient or inexpedient, he will do the good or wise thing if his will is good, and the evil or foolishly inexpedient if his will is bad. *Therefore* (and this consequence is even larger than the first), if the human being does anything silly or evil or illegal with knowledge that it is so, it is because *he wants* to do the silly, evil, or illegal thing.

Thus evil action is the result of ill will, and ill will can be changed only by punishment. If you punish a person enough, he will change. If he does not respond to punishment, then it is because his will is irredeemably bad and there is no way to reach him. In a nutshell, this is the implicit attitude at the bottom of our ordinary social structure. The normally sane human being is understood to be a single integrated personality, knowing what he is doing and why, and capable of controlling himself at all times if he really wishes to. The task of society is to educate and to punish, and that is all. So long as one is not psychotic to the point of being unable to perceive reality, he is responsible for his actions.

What is never stated can hardly be questioned or criticized. This is the great danger of implicitly held beliefs. Because we do not set them forth in the open, in logical order, we simply cannot see their implications. This is what enables us to hold completely inconsistent or even contradictory views. The very fact that we keep so many of our beliefs unstated—until we express them in action—is what allows so many of us to live and act inconsistently, at times with such tragic effect. It would be better to say that an unquestioned, unstated belief holds us, than that we hold it. The unstated psychological theory sketched above is extremely significant, for it is upon this basis that we govern our actions and attitudes toward other people, both as individuals and as a society. It forms the very ground of our sense of our own being, as well as our relationship with our fellows.

Accepted from before the time of Christ down to the present, this basic view of man's essential nature is seldom challenged either by the man in the street or the average clergyman. It is simply taken as part of the social environment. Unless one has run into serious personal problems, has been faced with grave mental illness among those close to him, or has carefully studied the whole subject of emotional difficulties (and as a part of that study made clinical observations), few of us ever question our generally accepted psychological heritage. And the pity of it is that this idea of personality which is part of our *Weltanschauung* is quite inadequate.

On this theory "modern" legal practice is based. If it can be established that a person breaking the law was capable of "knowing" what he was doing, he then receives the full impact of the law's retribution. Because the law rests upon antiquated theory, persons who are clearly emotionally incapable, by any modern medical standards, of controlling their actions are sent to prison and to death by the courts.

The same inadequate theory of personality is the basis on which our ineffective penal institutions have been created and maintained, which do not pretend to reform the criminal personality but more often are mere schools for crime. The only penal institutions that have lowered the rate of recidivism are those that have broken entirely with the conventional psychological point of view. And this theory is no less responsible for many present-day mental hospitals, which have taken mentally ill persons out of society but which heal almost none of the inmates. Only as they have broken entirely with this rigid and ancient psychology have the persons under treatment had a chance to recover.

None the less, the very old psychology implicit in modern Western society has had great and noted advocates. It was the theory of Socrates. He stressed the fact that you must know before you can do, and so assumed that if you really knew, you would do the right thing unless your will was wrong. Nor did Plato ever come to grips with the question of how to change the basic core of human will. His theories apply only to the good will, which desired to do well. Eros or love which is capable of changing a person was seen by Plato to be an irrational gift which was given and not produced by the use of human will power. Hence the utter disillusionment of *The Laws*, where he relies only on law—almost dictatorship—to hold society together. Aristotle saw no basic change in the popular theory, which was also the personality theory of much of the Old Testament, reaching its ultimate expression in the book of Proverbs. Here wisdom is enough; if you get wisdom, and exalt wisdom, then you shall be brought to honor. For the Jews in general, morality was a relatively simple matter of education and good will, and fear a most useful instrument to enforce the right way when good will was not present.

Jesus, on the other hand, treated human beings as much more complex. He believed and taught that, up to a point, men do have conscious control of personality and that it should be exercised and developed. So much did Jesus stress the importance of conscious control, in fact, that it became one of the marks of a Christian society. In the societies which the teachings of Jesus have influenced, consciousness has grown more than anywhere else in our world.

In addition, however, Jesus clearly believed that men could be influenced by "spiritual powers"—i.e., by nonmaterial psychic realities. He was himself driven by the Spirit into the wilderness. He repeatedly referred to the angels of God or to the Son of man and his angels. While Jesus understood that men could be helped or enlightened and directed by these positive spiritual powers, he also believed that they could be possessed by alien powers, unclean spirits, evil spirits, demons, satanic forces. There is no evidence that he tried to change popular parlance in alluding to these things, some of which we might nowadays call by the name of "complexes." Demonic spirits made people sick physically, mentally, and morally. They could not be controlled by the conscious will of the individual, once it had been set aside by the alien power. The person's powers of knowing were not impaired; he knew that he was possessed but could do nothing about it. It was a matter of possessing the will, not of knowledge alone.

The whole subject of Jesus' perception of man's relation to subtle underlying modes of psychic or spiritual reality has been so completely ignored that one who begins to study it finds himself on virgin territory. It forms, however, such a basic part of Jesus' view of human personality that to ignore these references is to do violence to his psychological point of view and his whole awareness of the nature of man and of healing.

The interested reader is referred to the Appendix in my book *Tongue Speaking*, where all these nonphysical realities are carefully catalogued. We shall show later that Jesus' awareness of such realities in relation to man is not as absurd as was once believed. An understanding of the unconscious as explained by Carl Jung gives modern minds some grasp of what he may have meant. As the Dominican theologian Victor White has pointed out in *God and the Unconscious*, Jung's findings make good sense of these realities and of Jesus' knowledge of them. Apart from such an understanding it is certainly not possible to understand the healing ministry described in the New Testament.

Jesus also spoke of achieving the single eye, implying that human beings could be other than single-eyed, single-minded—that there might be various centers of personality, as well as more than one way of centering or orienting the self. He spoke again and again—it is almost the keynote of the Gospels—of losing one's life in order to find it. Whatever else this means, it certainly implies that there are various levels of personality, and that to gain one of them another has to be sacrificed. The importance of these concepts can hardly be overestimated in seeking an understanding of Jesus and the New Testament. One has to give up one's own will so that God's will, God's Spirit, the Holy Spirit can become the center of one's life and personality. The human will or ego cannot stand against demonic infiltration and possession unless one is endowed with the Holy Spirit. This again shows clearly the complexity Jesus saw in human personality.

Man by his own humanity, his own will, cannot deal with the depth and complication of the psychic life in which he participates; single-handed, humanity cannot stand against the demonic. One reason Jesus was so responsive to sickness and sin was his sense that they result from men's domination by alien spirits, to which his whole being was antagonistic. The only way to drive them out—to bring health of body, mind, and soul—was through the Spirit of God, the Holy Spirit. This is characterized by love, by agape. Thus the injunction of Jesus that we love one another as he loved is not just an ethical maxim. It also has healing implications. Only a life characterized by love can give hospitality to the Spirit of God. As this Spirit resides in a man, he builds up defenses against alien forces so that they cannot attack and possess him, at the same time helping others to mobilize their own personalities and so become free of similar domination. Love, as an invitation to God's Spirit and as an evidence of it, is one important agent which helps to free men from alien domination; it is healing to mind and body as well as moral in power.

Jesus' Point of View in Action

Jesus knew what was in man, and his attitude toward men who were caught in moral, mental, or physical illness was one of compassion. He was able to respond freely and directly because he knew that there were causes of sickness and suffering beyond human control. Nowhere in the Gospels is there any suggestion of Jesus asking a sick person what he had done or whether he had sinned before healing him. Instead he took direct action to meet the need. Even the healing of the Gentile child, the daughter of the Canaanite (or Syrophoenician) woman in Matthew 15:22–28, was given freely and without any strings attached.

Knowing the actualities that men encounter within the soul or psyche, Jesus had a clear point of view about them. He knew the reality of alien and evil "spirits" that can possess men (today we might often call this condition a mental complex) and also how the reality of God can touch an individual and not only drive out such a spirit but put something else in its place. According to his point of view, man cannot always by his own will fight off the infiltration of alien, evil personality constellations that somehow or other take possession of him. As Jesus describes in Luke 11:-24–26, a man can get rid of an evil spirit, but if that is all, the spirit returns to its old place, and "finding it swept and tidied, it then goes off and brings seven other spirits more wicked than itself, and they go in and set up house there, so that the man ends up by being worse than he was before."

Thus he made clear that men in their present condition do not deserve or need judgment and punishment, which only drive them further into despair and defeat. Only twice did he make any point of speaking to the sick about their sins, and the way he did

it was striking in itself. One was the paralytic whom Jesus for-
gave before healing him. (Matt. 9:2, Mark 2:5, Luke 5:20) The
other was the man he healed at the pool of Bethesda, whom he
then warned not to sin again or something worse might befall
him.[7] (John 5:14) Men who were sick and in trouble morally
needed understanding and compassion, not judgment and punishment. They were up against realities or forces which the human will could not handle on its own; they needed help, and
Jesus responded to their need. A recent account of possession and
exorcism is found in the bestselling novel, *The Exorcist*, by Wm.
Peter Blatty. The idea of possession touches something deep in
man no matter what his rational ideas may be.

He was also able to demonstrate the reality of his point of view
in opposition to almost the entire Judaic and Greek culture of his
time. At least six of his healings were done on the Sabbath to
show his own people how important it was to set aside statutes
of external observance when there was an opportunity to help a
sick or disabled person.[8] Thus Jesus' treatment of men was not
just his own unique approach. It was intended as a general way
for men to treat one another. As such, it was (and still is) a
radically new attitude toward men, with all sorts of implications
beyond the healing ministry.

7. Jesus' treatment of direct moral difficulty in Luke 7:48 and John 8:11 is the
same. These four are the only accounts of his dealing directly with the sins of an
individual. Judgment was for the establishment, for those in a position to take
care of themselves who kept the old order inflexible at the expense of other men's
moral, mental, and physical health. Jesus' judgment, in fact, was reserved for
those in a position to impose their ideas on others.

8. These are the healings in Mark 1:21–27 (Luke 4:31–35), Mark 3:1–6 (Matthew
12:9–13, Luke 6:6–10), Luke 13:10–13, 14:1–4, John 5:2–10, and John 9:1–14. The
account in Mark 1 also makes clear that the first recorded healing in the synagogue in Capernaum (1:23) was followed immediately by that of Peter's mother-
in-law (1:29–31), and that this demonstration by Jesus of his willingness to break
the law of the Sabbath for the sake of healing brought a crowd of sick people to
him. Because of his preaching, word about his ideas had already spread, and the
crowd came to his door after sunset when the Sabbath was over. The account in
Luke 4 is also parallel.

Jesus saw it was one of his major tasks as the Christ to defeat the realities of evil that could possess men and keep them from following his way. He saw himself in conflict with forces of evil. As Mark in particular shows in 1:24, 1:34, and 3:11, these demonic realities were equally aware that he was bent on dissolving their power. There was open warfare on a cosmic level, with physical and mental healing one of the things fought for. Failure to release man from these powers would have been unthinkable for those who saw man from Jesus' psychological point of view. And failure to heal if one had the power would have been just as unthinkable.

If Jesus had any one mission, it was to bring the power and healing of God's creative, loving Spirit to bear upon the moral, mental, and physical illnesses of the people around him. It was a matter of rescuing man from a situation in which he could not help himself. Jesus disclosed a new power, a ladder to bring him out of the pit of his brokenness and sin. Leaving man in his wretched condition so as to learn from it makes no sense in this psychological framework. Judgment and punishment only add to a burden already intolerable.

Jesus' healing actions flowed from his psychological awareness of man's nature and his experience of sonship with God. Modern medicine has adopted the same nonjudgmental attitude towards healing. The sick person is not to blame. Unless one understands the view Jesus had of man, it is difficult if not impossible to understand his healing ministry. It is also difficult to understand the kind of fellowship he formed around him and the injunctions he gave. The New Testament does not yield a wholly clear idea of when the end of the world was expected to come, but it is very clear that the disciples were to continue in their lives to manifest as much of God's healing Spirit as they could.[9] Present action and

9. One of the main gaps in the thinking of Barth and Bultmann is their neglect of this very fact that the disciples and the early church, as well as Jesus, did manifest the merciful action of God in a sinful and broken world by performing

eschatological hope were not inconsistent. The Spirit then manifested in a limited way, particularly in healing, would be manifest totally in the age to come. When that time came, the forces
of evil would be completely routed and sickness would disappear.

With this background let us now turn to a detailed discussion
of the healing ministry of Jesus.

physical and mental healing. This deliberate disregard of an element so emphati-
cally a part of the New Testament account—and in such bulk, with so many
ramified allusions—derives of course from their disbelief in the "mythology" of
the entire record of healings from beginning to end, even including Jesus' teaching *about* healing. On the other hand, if such things actually happened, then God
is not as far from the human condition as Barth and Bultmann insist. Once the
premise of man's absolute separation from God is denied, the structure of dialectic theology falls apart. Is one to take experience or reason as the final criterion
of truth—? This is the question.

5

WHAT, How, ANd WHy Did JESUS HEAL ?

When we actually look at the record of healing in the four Gospels, it is apparent that the writers were describing the effect of Jesus' actions on quite a number of different diseases. The words they used were of course different from those of modern clinical diagnosis, but even so, many of the conditions are well enough identified to compare with diseases we know today.

What Did Jesus Heal?

An element of interest in studying this ministry must be to know what the diseases were that Jesus healed. Probably the most common ailment dealt with was mental illness, generally described in New Testament times as demon possession. Many sources tell of the radically changing times of the first century and how the collective pattern of life was breaking up, much as it is in our time. Men found life without structure, without meaning to which they could cling. They could not cope with the uncertainties and complexities that faced them and so they disintegrated psychologically. Depth psychology shows how such factors contribute to mental illness. This kind of illness was described in the healings in Matthew 8:28–32, 15:22–28, and Mark 1:23–27, and their various parallels in other Gospels, plus Luke 8:2, as well as in the six references to the authority given the

69

disciples[1] and in nine of the many accounts of the healing of great numbers of people.[2]

In one instance what appears to have been epilepsy was healed —also viewed as a case of demon possession. This was the boy whom the disciples could not cure, described in Mark 9:17–27. (Matt. 17:14–18, Luke 9:38–42) Other physical illnesses appeared to those present clear examples of demonic possession, through psychogenic rather than physical causes. These are the instances apparently recognizable as cases of hysterical blindness or dumbness. In Matthew 9:32 and 12:22, where this is connected with demonic possession, and in Luke 11:14, where the demon itself is described as being mute, we find these physical healings distinguished from other instances.

Several persons were healed of "leprosy." Of course, it may well be that some "lepers" were suffering from a variety of other diseases. Because of the dread nature of leprosy and the difficulty of distinguishing it clearly from other afflictions in its early stages, all these healings were considered of great importance, and with good reason. Leprosy is a curse still to be feared. But there is nothing in the record itself to raise doubt about the curing of true leprosy by Jesus; there is suggestive evidence simply in the one story which tells of ten lepers coming to him in a group. These accounts of the healing of persons described as lepers are found in Matthew 8:2–4, Mark 1:40–42 (Luke 5:12–14), and Luke 17:12–15.

There are a number of examples of the healing of lameness, palsy or paralysis, and other crippling infirmities. It is easy for

1. Matt. 10:1 and 8, Mark 3:15 and 6:7, and Luke 9:1 and 10:17–20.
2. Matt. 4:24 and 8:16; Mark 1:32 and 39, 3:10–12, and 6:13; Luke 4:41, 6:18, and 7:21. The understanding of severe mental illness, schizophrenia in particular, as a reaction to the intolerable conditions under which men live is expounded in many of the writings of R. D. Laing. In *The Politics of Experience* (1968) he describes schizophrenia as the individual turning away from a disturbed, out-of-joint outer world to the inner world in search of healing and peace.

us to overlook the vital importance of these healings. There was no such thing as unemployment compensation or disability insurance, of course, and any crippling disease that kept a man from earning his living worked impossible hardship, often on family and friends as well as on the individual.

Perhaps the most striking story is that of the paralytic who was lowered by his friends through the roof into Jesus' presence because they could not bring his litter in through the crowds. This is related in Mark 2:3–4 and Luke 5:18–19. In John 5:2–7 the impotent man healed at the pool of Bethesda had apparently been lying there day in and day out, trying to get to the waters when they were said to be troubled by an angel. In Matthew 9:2–7 a paralytic was brought to him stretched on a bed. In at least one instance physical deterioration had taken place in the part that was restored; this is found in Matthew 12:9–13 (Mark 3:1–5 and Luke 6:6–10), where the man's hand is described as "withered" or "shriveled."

Some permanent damage might also be assumed in two of the women we are told Jesus healed. One was bent double; she had been disabled or "possessed by a spirit" for eighteen years. (Luke 13:10–11) The other had suffered from hemorrhages for twelve years (see Matt. 9:20–22, Mark 5:25–29, and Luke 8:43–44).

Two different accounts are found of sicknesses involving fever. The first is the delightful story of Peter's mother-in-law, who was healed so that she could get up and wait on the group of disciples —recorded in the three synoptic Gospels: Matthew 8:14–15, Mark 1:30–31, and Luke 4:38–39. In the incident of the nobleman's son in John 4:47–53. we know that the boy's illness was attended by fever since a report reached the father of the precise hour at which the fever had left him.

Blindness was another curse of the Roman world, as it has been of every culture not reached by modern medicine and hygiene. Since it was one of the greatest tragedies that could happen to a man, it is no wonder that so many examples are given of its healing. First of all the elaborate account of the man born blind in John 9, which takes the whole chapter—then the stories of the blind Bartimaeus in Mark 10:46–52 and Luke 18:35–42; of the two blind men in Matthew 20:30–34; of the man brought to Jesus at Bethsaida in Mark 8:22–25; of two blind men in Matthew 9:27–30; and finally of those who came to him in the Temple in Matthew 21:14. In Mark 7:32–35 we also find the homely story of how Jesus healed a man who was deaf and had an impediment in his speech.

In one instance there was a cure of dropsy or edema—in the case of the man healed on the Sabbath day in Luke 14:1–4. The single example of the healing of a wound occurred under most unusual circumstances: when one of the disciples resisted Jesus' arrest in the garden of Gethsemane, he struck out with a sword; in Luke 22:50–51 it is related that he injured the ear of Malchus, the high priest's servant, and Jesus healed it.

Stories even harder for moderns to accept are the three accounts of raising from the dead. These are told in some detail. There was the reviving of Jairus' daughter, found in Matthew 9:18 ff., Mark 5:22 ff., and Luke 8:41 ff. The raising of Lazarus in John 11 was a climactic event before the entry of Jesus into Jerusalem. And in Luke 7:11–15 an incident at Nain is related, when Jesus raised the widow's son from his bier. Nothing is said of the cause of death, however, in any of these instances.

Besides all these stories of individuals there are also nineteen places in the first three Gospels where it is said that numbers of people were healed, without much detail as to the diseases concerned. Very likely the healings described separately were the most dramatic occurrences. But there were also other cures of conditions that cannot be identified at all.[3] As the last words of

3. Nine of these passages simply say that Jesus healed "all kinds of diseases" or that he healed those who were sick: Matt. 4:23, 9:35, 12:15, 14:14, 14:35–36, 19:2; Mark 6:5, 6:55–56; Luke 9:11. In six of them similar wording is used, but demon possession is also included: Matt. 8:16; Mark 1:32–34, 3:7–12; Luke 4:40–41, 6:-

the Gospel of John suggest (21:25): "There were many other things that Jesus did; if all were written down, the world itself, I suppose, would not hold all the books that would have to be written."

There does not seem to be much question about the drift of these passages. Where great crowds gathered there were people with many different diseases, and—just as in the individual healings—a wide range of ailments was represented. Naturally we do not find modern descriptive terms such as carcinoma, sarcoma, leukemia, typhoid, rheumatic fever, gangrene, or the like, but this does not justify the inference that the conditions Jesus healed were any less serious or less varied than those we know today. On the other hand, neither can we attach modern labels to these illnesses, as some students have attempted to do. We have here only popular descriptions from an age which had far less specific information about human disease than our own, and it is useless to try to identify them by current laboratory definitions.

Still, there are broad medical categories which can be helpful in understanding the New Testament descriptions. Looked at in terms of the human organism itself, we find three basically different classes of human illness. First, there is organic disease in which the structure or tissue of the body is damaged in some way. Second are the functional disorders, in which sickness results because one organ or part of the body is not working properly. And third, there is psychic or mental illness, which shows up as a disturbance of the personality, and here brain disease is usually included, although there is some question as to how much ordinary mental illness can be blamed on brain damage. With an understanding of these three categories it is possible to under-

17–18, 8:2. There are also four similar passages that variously include demon possession, lunacy, paralysis, and healing of the blind, the dumb, the lame and crippled: Matt. 4:24, 15:30, 21:14, and Luke 7:21. In addition it is implied in Luke 5:15 that the sick among the crowds that gathered were being healed; Mark 1:39 tells that demons were cast out.

stand a good deal about the kinds of sickness spoken of in passages concerned with healing.

Under organic disease we find all the various disorders that cause actual physical alteration of the organism, resulting in direct damage to organic tissue. These disorders include wounds, foreign bodies, lesions, and resulting blood clots or hemorrhages; bacterial and viral infections, and growths of one kind or another. This group also embraces the deterioration that follows these invasions as well as that which results from long functional disturbance.

The second grouping comprises an almost infinite variety of disorders in which the malfunction of one part disturbs the whole organism. Nearly every organ may be affected: the heart or the entire cardiovascular system, the intestinal tract, the skin, the urinary system, indeed any part of the body. Many commonly recognized diseases, especially in their early stages, fall into this category : various heart diseases, high blood pressure, peptic ulcers, allergies, etc. It is also clear that functional disease which continues unchecked can so damage the affected organ that it is permanently changed, and organic disease results.

Finally, mental illness may manifest itself in various ways, as psychosis, neurosis, or in hysteria. In psychosis the mind retreats from reality and the ego no longer has direction; often the person cannot function as a human being at all, and his illness may be marked by states either of wild frenzy or catatonic stupors. Psychoneurosis, on the other hand, is the state of a troubled mind, one which has not broken with reality but is characterized by anxiety, compulsiveness, depression. The neurotic, it has been said, worries about castles in the air, while the psychotic lives in them. And then there are the hysterias: purely psychogenic physical states such as hysterical blindness or paralysis. The hysterical person can copy reliably nearly any disease syndrome. There is no organic damage, only the unconscious idea that one cannot use that particular organ—an idea so deep that the person is literally unable to do so. While hysterical patients can be suggested out of this state or tricked in various ways to reveal the psychic cause of the disease, still they are genuinely ill and cannot just snap out of it.[4]

It has become increasingly clear in recent medical practice that emotional causes or influences may play a part in any disease, whatever the class or immediate cause. Most of the work in psychosomatic medicine has been done in the area of functional illnesses; the psychic origin of many of these disorders has been revealed, and it is here that psychosomatic medicine has had real success in finding new methods of cure. For while emotional sources may directly cause many malfunctionings of the body, or its failure to resist disease, the effect is still that of physical illness.

It is perfectly clear that the healings of Jesus occurred in all three of these medical categories of disease. But even more interesting is the fact that they occurred predominantly in the first and last groups. According to the Gospel records Jesus did not heal many sicknesses that could be termed purely functional. We have no accounts of his healing headaches, backaches, stomach trouble, or muscular tension, although he undoubtedly must have, since these problems respond quite readily to suggestion and religious healing. It is quite possible that functional diseases were among those spoken of generally when it is said that he healed the multitudes.

The great majority of the recorded healings of Jesus were either psychological—i.e., of the mentally ill—or of physically damaged bodies and organic disease. It may be easier for us, because of the prevailing materialism of our time, to believe that

4. One occurrence of hysterical illness in recent times involved more than one hundred of the medical personnel of London's Royal Free Hospital, two-thirds of them sick enough to require hospitalization. The hospital had to be closed for over two months. "Mass Hysteria," *Time*, January 26, 1970, pp. 59 ff.

Jesus could heal mental illness than to accept his physical healings, but those who have had experience with it know that this
category of disease has been more resistant than any other to the
advances of modern medicine. It can be moderated or controlled
by drugs, but real healing is rare.

Recent studies indicate that one person out of every ten in the
United States suffers from a recognized psychiatric disorder.
There has been no great conquest of serious mental sickness, and
neurosis can be conquered only by long and costly treatment, nor
is this always successful. These healings are therefore just as
impressive and startling as the physical ones, if not more so.
Modern science has been able to care for and cure a great many
types of physical illness, but it has done little for mental illness
and many of its physical manifestations. For instance, although
it is known that certain allergic reactions have a basically emotional cause, and the symptoms can often be controlled or tempo-
rarily relieved, psychiatrists are embarrassed by the fact that they
can so seldom get at the psychic basis of the disorder and heal the
disease. Psychological illness is not in fact easy to heal. Nearly
half the hospital beds in the United States are reserved for the
mentally ill.

There have been many attempts to explain away the healing
ministry of Jesus as simply suggestion to relieve functional and
hysterical symptoms. I know this well, for it is the idea upon
which I was raised. We must recognize the fact, however, that
there is no basis for it in the actual records that have come down
to us, nor is there any basis (other than the interpreter's inclina-
tion) for rationalizing the healings as mere suggestion to psy-
choneurotics. This may suit the mind of modern man, but it does
not reflect the textual record. Most of the individual descriptions
point out a pertinent fact which clearly characterizes the disease
healed, such as the duration of bleeding in Mark 5:25, the crippling effect in Luke 5:18 and 6:6, or the severe psychotic state in
Mark 5:2–5.

There is also agreement between the descriptions of individual healings and the several passages which speak of the healing of numbers of people, both of which make a distinction between physical illness and demon possession. This is shown in Mark 1:34, Matthew 4:24 and 8:16, and Luke 4:40–41 and 6:17–19. Nor is it possible to understand "the lame, the crippled, the blind, the dumb and many others" who were brought to Jesus, according to Matthew 15:30, as simply neurotics or only functionally disturbed. The words of the Gospels are few, and they must be read as they are.

In fact, as we have shown, examples are given of the healing of physical disorders attributed to mental or psychic causes (demons), as in Matthew 9:32, 12:22 and Luke 11:14. When the disease was hysterical in nature, this seems to be how it was described. But purely hysterical illness is rather rare, and if Jesus' power was limited to alleviating this type of condition, he must have been on the lookout for such symptoms. Here there would be a certain implication of duplicity, and whatever else we may say about Jesus of Nazareth, this is patently absurd. It is out of character with the tone of the Gospel narrative. If it were true, it would mean the collapse of the whole structure of Christianity, both religious and ethical.

In addition, we have a tendency to look upon people living in the first century as quite simple and naïve, and to discount this ministry from our own superiority as men "come of age." But they were more sophisticated than we ordinarily realize. One has only to read Leviticus 13 to 15 with modern public health in mind to see the kind of medical insight that was the common heritage of this people. The authors of the Gospels seem to have been quite aware of the distinction between purely functional disorders and organic disease. It is clear that the healing incidents recounted in detail were selected out of a wide range of possible ones, and in the telling conveyed the amazement of those who witnessed them.

The fact is that the particular descriptions not only show that Jesus healed all kinds of disease, but stress the types that are especially resistant to either medical knowledge or religious healing practice, then as now. They omit any mention of purely functional ailments, sometimes relatively easier to cure. Instead, these passages emphasize what we know today as mental illness and organic disease, and they say again and again that those who saw these healings were amazed.

If we accept the stories at all, we must conclude that Jesus healed all kinds of disease and that we do not know how he did it, for we are still not able to follow in his steps. Most attempts to rationalize these miracles do not make sense for they are based more upon wishful thinking (in a negative sort of way) than on the facts as stated in the stories themselves. While there may be uncertainty in certain instances, the plain sense of the Gospels is that Jesus healed all kinds of ailments, and that what he did had the effect of true healing, not just of alleviating symptoms.

The modern rejection of the healing stories is mostly a *blanket rejection* which is theological and—over and above our own inexperience and sense of impotence in the matter of healing—entirely theoretical. The theologian may even take into account the newer understanding of recent medical practice and the fact that the stories themselves are most likely the earliest and most authentic in the Gospels. But he still considers the whole idea of them untenable because it is "mythological." By a circular reasoning he simply finds that God is unable to break through to man. As C. S. Lewis pointed out in his excellent essay "Modern Theology and Biblical Criticism," this kind of rejection is very questionable.[5] It denies the idea of an experience offhand and on pure theory, instead of dealing with the experience itself on a basis of actual knowledge of it. And the fact is that we have little

5. C. S. Lewis, *Christian Reflections* (1968), pp. 152 ff. In my *Encounter with God: A Theology of Christian Experience* (1972), I discuss this whole subject in detail.

reason in modern life for direct knowledge of this kind of experience; what seems impossible to us must therefore have been impossible long ago and is not to be taken seriously. We shall have more to say about all this later.

How Did Jesus Heal?

As Weatherhead indicates in his *Psychology, Religion and Healing*, Jesus used many different actions to heal the sick who came to him. He called upon the faith of the person who needed help, he touched the sick person, he uttered commands, he used various physical media. His healing ministry was as diverse in the methods used as in the kinds of disease he healed. And as one analyzes his approach, comparing it with other possible methods, it appears that the healing of Jesus was largely sacramental in nature.

His most common means of healing was by speaking words and touching the sick person with his hand. Often the two were combined, although at times he used them separately. The touch, in the later history of the church, became known as a "laying on of hands." In only two instances is this method referred to alone. When Jesus was in Nazareth, he was hindered by the unbelief of the people; yet he cured a few by laying his hands on them. (Mark 6:5) In the account of his healing of Malchus' wound, it is reported only that he touched it. (Luke 22:51)

The use of words or commands was also perpetuated in the life of the church in the practice of exorcism. A number of times Jesus appears to have used only words, as in the raising of Lazarus (John 11:43), the healing of the ten lepers (Luke 17:14), the freeing of the Gerasene demoniac (Mark 5:8), the healing of the nobleman's son at a distance (John 4:50), and the restoration of the impotent man at the pool of Bethesda (John 5:8). In most instances the two means were used together. Jesus touched the person—laid his hands upon him—and also spoke to him or to the

spirit that seemed to possess him. Nearly half the examples of
healing in the Gospel record are characterized by this approach.

There are three instances of the use of saliva, alone or mixed
with mud. Saliva was very common as a healing remedy at the
time, but Jesus used it not so much as a direct healing agent as
by way of a carrier of his personality and power. In the Gospel
of Mark we are told of the man who was deaf and dumb: Jesus
put his fingers in his ears, touched his tongue with his saliva, and
then spoke the word *Ephphatha*—"Be opened!" (7:33–34) Much
the same method was used for a blind man in Mark 8:23. In John
9:6–7 he mixes his saliva with earth, making a paste of it to rub
on the blind man's eyes, and then tells him to go and wash in the
pool of Siloam.

Although it is not stated that Jesus used oil in healing, the
probability is that he did. Mark says that the disciples used oil
when they were sent out by the Master; they "cast out many
devils, and anointed many sick people with oil and cured them."
(6:13) This was certainly a common healing practice from the
earliest times in the history of the church, and has continued
uninterrupted in Eastern Orthodox tradition.

Occasionally healing occurred as a person touched Jesus or his
garments. The story of the woman who suffered from a hemor-
rhage is one very clear example. (Mark 5:25–34) In Mark 6:56 it
is said that "wherever he went, to village, or town, or farm, they
laid down the sick in the open spaces, begging him to let them
touch even the fringe of his cloak. And all those who touched him
were cured."

In raising Lazarus Jesus prayed to God a prayer of thanks
before commanding Lazarus to come out. (John 11:41–44) In Matthew 15:25–28 it was the prayer of the Canaanite (or Syrophoenician) woman herself that initiated the healing of her daughter.
While people often begged Jesus' help, and healing was freely
given, in this instance the woman's humility and her own prayer

were involved. Jesus was quite harsh with her—indeed, she may at first have been noisy and importunate—but she accepted his rebuke and continued to ask for help. This persistent humility which obtained its goal was also stressed in the parable of the widow before the unjust judge. (Luke 18:1–5)

Several examples are given in which the faith of the individual was a potent factor in the healing. When Jesus spoke to the woman who had been healed of hemorrhaging, he told her, *"your faith has restored you to health."* (Mark 5:34—italics mine) When he restored the sight of the two blind men, he touched their eyes and said, "Your faith deserves it, so let this be done for you." (Matt. 9:29) Jesus put it up to the father of the epileptic boy that healing was possible for anyone who had faith, and the man cried out, "I do have faith. Help the little faith that I have." (Mark 9:23–24) In several instances the faith of a third person was the important factor. We see this in the stories of the court official's son in John 4:47–53 and the centurion's servant in Matthew 8:-5–13. Again, the faith of the friends who brought the paralyzed man and lowered him down through the roof was a determining factor in Mark 2:3–11.

As we have seen earlier, forgiveness of sins is twice mentioned in connection with healing. In the story of the paralyzed man brought by his friends Jesus said to him, "My child, your sins are forgiven." (Mark 2:5) And after the man had been healed at the pool of Bethesda, Jesus later saw him in the temple and told him, "Now you are well again, be sure not to sin any more, or something worse may happen to you." (John 5:14) We shall have somewhat more to say later about the connection between sin and disease.

Four times it is stated in the Gospel narrative that Jesus had compassion upon people and healed the sick. He felt sorry for the widow of Nain when he saw her standing beside the bier of her son. (Luke 7:13) In Matthew 14:14 a large crowd had followed him to a lonely place, and he took pity on them and healed their sick. When he went up to Jerusalem for the last time, and the two blind men sitting by the road heard that Jesus was passing by and told him what they wanted, he had compassion for them and healed them. (Matt. 20:34)

The fourth case was one of two strange instances in which anger was present at the time of healing. When the leper in Mark 1:40 came up to Jesus on his knees and said, "If you want to, you can cure me," Jesus was moved by compassion, by deep feeling apparently touched with sternness.[6] At least his final instruction to the man was direct and stern, as if he resented the man's doubt of his intention and desire to heal. Later he was clearly angry when he healed the man with the withered hand on the Sabbath (Mark 3:5), and it may be that this, and the reaction it evoked, contributed to both healings.

What, then, is the significance of these various actions of Jesus? In order to understand them in relation to the healing that resulted, one must look at them again from another standpoint, in this case to see his methods in relation to the various therapeutic practices of modern times. We have, first of all, healing which is purely medical and largely physical. This our age has developed to a fine art. It includes techniques to remove or repair an offending part, such as surgery, Xray and other radiation, or shock treatment for the mentally ill. Specific drugs help the body react favorably—digitalis for instance, or tranquilizers, hormones such

6. The Greek word here for compassion, pity, sorrow—*splagchnizomai*—means to be moved in the bowels, originally by anger; later with the connotation of other feelings. Jesus used it in the parables to express the feeling of the master toward the unforgiving debtor, the Samaritan toward the beaten man, the father toward the prodigal, and his own feeling for the crowds like sheep without a shepherd (Matt. 18:27, Luke 10:33, 15:20, Matt. 9:36). Zechariah used used a form of this word to speak of God's mercy in Luke 1:78. It describes Jesus' feeling toward the crowds when he provided the loaves and fishes (Matt. 15:32, Mark 6:34, 8:2) and at the time of these four healings (Matt. 14:14, 20:34, Mark 1:41, Luke 7:13). The father of the epileptic boy used it to ask compassion of Jesus (Mark 9:22).

as ACTH, even aspirin—as well as treatment by diet or rest. There are medicines, like the antihistamines and antibiotics, to aid in eliminating an offending substance. Finally, there is prevention, by isolating, cleaning up, or inoculating against the source of disease. While these methods intervene directly to change something in the body, they are all basically ways of improving conditions under which the body itself constantly resists or adjusts to disease. In essence, medical healing consists in methods of promoting the recuperative power of the body itself.

A second mode of healing is psychological, either by suggestion or through some form of psychotherapy. As Flanders Dunbar has pointed out so well, suggestion (of which hypnosis is only an extreme form) almost always plays an important role in getting well. A physician's negative suggestions as to the course of a disease may bring about a negative conclusion to it, while positive suggestion is usually an important factor in mobilizing the body's recuperative powers. The results of suggestion in arousing a patient's inner healing powers have been described recently by Jerome Frank in his fascinating book *Persuasion and Healing*, about which we shall have more to say in another chapter. Dr. Frank writes that "until the last few decades most medications prescribed by physicians were pharmacologically inert. That is, physicians were prescribing placebos without knowing it, so that, in a sense, the 'history of medical treatment until relatively recently is the history of the placebo effect' "—i.e., suggestion of some kind.[7] Suggestion does have healing power. However, suggestion seldom cures the more seriously neurotic or psychotic patient; instead its success lies often in merely suggesting away the symptom, leaving the underlying cause to pop up again in some other, often more serious guise. Nor is it possi-

7. Jerome D. Frank, *Persuasion and Healing* (1969), p. 66.

ble to tell exactly how suggestion or hypnosis works.

Psychotherapy does sometimes enable the seriously disturbed individual to relate to other people and adjust to his own inner psychic life and also to outer reality, both physical and nonphysical. Thus it removes anxiety and emotional conflicts and can have a positive effect upon the body, sometimes curing its illnesses. This method usually requires the cooperation of the patient and is a long and involved process, whose success, to say the least, is difficult to predict.

There is a third kind of healing which, for want of a better word, may be called psychic healing. It is a power which seems to inhere in certain people and to emanate from them with effects upon the lives of others. Since it apparently works at the level of unconscious images or attitudes (and perhaps at times even more directly), this kind of power may be present without conscious desire or realization of need for it. Jung has called attention to an interesting case history of such a person described in a work entitled *The Reluctant Healer*,[8] while some of the novels of Charles Williams also deal with this power in a fascinating way. Such healing has little relation to religion or morality and may come from persons with no religious faith and amoral lives. Since it takes place only unconsciously, the healing involves little wish for re-creation or transformation on either side. When one goes to a religious healer there is at least an implicit, if momentary, desire for religious change. Purely psychic healing is sometimes temporary in effect probably because it does not take deep root in conscious attitudes.

Finally, there is religious or sacramental healing, the result of the healer's conscious and deliberate relation to God. The healer as an individual is not viewed as the source of healing power.

8. William J. MacMillan, *The Reluctant Healer* (1952).

Rather he is seen as the agency through which the Spirit of God and his power, the very creative force of the universe, is transmitted. The acts of healing then depend, not on the personal powers of the individual but on the power of God, and are therefore sacramental. Spiritual healing is an outer and visible sign of particular grace, inward and spiritual, at work within both the healer and the one who seeks healing.

As we consider Jesus' actions in relation to each of these methods, the nature of his ministry becomes clear. He used almost no methods that could be considered medically or physically effective. He did use saliva and mud, but hardly as effective physical remedies. When Dr. Boggs states: "Rather, the prayer of faith combined with the use of oil (the best medicine available) will save the sick person *when it is God's will,*"[9] he does not deal with the facts. Most of the healings we know anything about have been accomplished without the use of any active outer physical agents at all. It was not the intention of Jesus to be a physician, nor to ask his disciples to meddle in matters of medical healing. This was simply not his interest or concern. There was no hostility (though there might well have been in view of the medical practices of the first century). Instead Jesus spoke of doctors quite positively in his important saying comparing those in good health who have no need of the physician with the sick who do. (Matt. 9:12, Mark 2:17, Luke 5:31) This suggests a more sympathetic attitude toward secular healing than was shown by most of contemporary Judaism.

Of course, Jesus used some psychological methods, but not in the general sense of modern practice. Undoubtedly he made use of suggestion in some way, but with permanent effect, while ours usually is not. He did not employ hypnotism or psychotherapy,

9. Wade H. Boggs, Jr., *Faith Healing and the Christian Faith* (1956), p. 158.

always a lengthy process. His contacts with people were brief, and according to the record most of the healings appear to have been instantaneous. The only possibility of psychotherapy would concern the disciples, who were not ill, or perhaps some of the women among his followers. The continual companionship and discourse with Jesus may well have been a kind of group therapy, but this was not used for healing the sick. The latter, instead of joining his company, were usually told to return to their homes.

Thus there is little in modern psychological practices to compare with Jesus' method, and where such unusual effects do occur, they are as much a mystery to the therapist as many of the actions of Jesus are to us. As a matter of fact, we do not have any clear idea of how psychological healing comes about, either through suggestion or psychotherapy. In the last analysis we actually know very little about how the mind affects the body, and how the psychic affects the physical. We can call the methods of Jesus psychological, but in so doing we are more or less describing one unknown in terms of another and are not moving very far toward understanding what went on in Jesus' healings.

A personality of such power as Jesus would unquestionably have a psychic effect whether he intended it or not, but there is little evidence that he used personal psychic powers as such. He continually turned attention away from himself and toward the power that came through him. He spoke of himself as an agent —"if it is by the Spirit of God that I cast out demons. . . ." He tried to keep people from spreading news of him as a healer, and constantly referred to something within the healed individuals which had been effective. At no point is personal psychic power spoken of as contributing to the healings.

Instead, the methods Jesus used with such effect upon the sick were actions which appear to have done two things. They awakened the spirit that lay deep within these people, waiting to be touched.[10] And at the same time his actions, words, and attitudes brought contact with the Spirit of God, the creative force of reality, which sets men's minds and bodies aright and recreates them. Deep spoke to deep, through sacramental action. The nature of his healing, its essential method, was sacramental, religious. Through him the power of God broke through into the lives of men, and they were made whole. There is little more that one can say.

The belief of certain healing sects that Jesus taught a detailed method of mental healing is unfounded in the Gospel record. It is true that he taught men about God, but his healing did not follow as the result of his sermons or teachings. His acts of healing did not reveal spiritual laws by which the individual might live and so escape from physical ills. Seldom in the four Gospels did Jesus speak of spiritual laws in relation to physical healing. The latter was usually accomplished by something other than getting the right ideas about reality or morality into people's heads. It was not accomplished by *knowledge of reality*, or *laws*, or *occult science*. There was little Gnosticism in Jesus.

While so much modern religious healing is based upon the idea of discovering and living by spiritual laws, this is generally quite different from the spirit in which Jesus healed. He was dealing with a dynamic reality, a spiritual personality, a living God. He was not concerned with a mechanical spirituality, to be used as one follows the textbook laws of physics or mathematics. Such a conception of reality is far from the mind and attitude of Jesus. His way was to bring people into a faith relationship to God by the various methods of touching, speaking commands, compassion, and forgiveness, so that the power of the living God might

10. It has been suggested to me that sacramental actions perhaps opened the individual so that the Spirit of God dwelling within him was released or drawn out. The laying on of hands would then appear to be a drawing out process as much as flowing in.

break through upon them and restore them. Then he set about teaching them.

In order to start the process, to break through any hindrances to healing, Jesus drew upon the faith of the individual and those around him, and on his own compassion and power to forgive. He combined these attitudes with various physical media—a touch or a word—to convey his concern and also God's sacramental action. Through the complex medium of his own concern and the sick person's faith, a physical event became a sacrament of God's creative power. If one can fully explain sacramental acts then one may be able to explain Jesus' healing. Somehow, through his actions and attitudes the power of God made effective contact with the individual. When there was utter disbelief or lack of faith in a large group of people, such healing was kept from taking place, as when he went home to visit in Nazareth. (Mark 6:5)

Why Did Jesus Heal?

Still, the most important of these several questions is not what Jesus healed, or how he did it, but *why*. Some very important things can be learned about this question from a careful reading of the Gospels, and there is a most cogent reason for Christians to find them out. For if as a Christian one believes in the incarnation, then Jesus' attitude toward illness will reveal the attitude of God toward it. Certainly no Christian discussion of God's attitude toward sickness and suffering is complete without taking this into account. I am well aware of the difficulty proposed by modern Biblical criticism, of trying to plumb the mind of Jesus. However, if we are careful we can come to some understanding of what seemed to be Jesus' rationale in healing.

The most important reason that Jesus healed was that he cared about people and suffered when they did. The root meaning of compassion is just this: to know suffering together. He could not care without wanting to show mercy and to help. He was opposed to sickness because it caused needless suffering. It is the same spirit that rises to indignation when one hears of a sick person being turned away from a hospital because he could not pay. In cultures where the spirit of Christ has not been felt, this compassion is often conspicuously lacking. The healing ministry is the logical result of the incarnation: God so loved the world that he gave his only begotten Son; Jesus so loved that he healed. His healings were the authentication of his mission and his person. They flowed naturally from him because he was what he was.

Another of Jesus' reasons for healing seems to have been that he was somehow hostile to what made people sick. He rebuked the forces that seemed to possess the mentally ill, and expressed the same antagonism towards physical illness. In the Gospel of Mark the story of Jesus' ministry begins with his rebuking and casting out an unclean spirit (1:25). His attitude was the same in the story of Gerasene demoniac. (Mark 5:8) When he finally healed the epileptic boy, "he rebuked the unclean spirit. 'Deaf and dumb spirit,' he said, 'I command you: Come out of him and never enter him again.' " (Mark 9:25) In the Sabbath-day healing of the woman who had a spirit of infirmity, Jesus answered the indignant Pharisee, "And this woman, a daughter of Abraham whom Satan has held bound these eighteen years—was it not right to untie her bonds on the sabbath day?" (Luke 13:16)

Jesus' underlying attitude was that the demon-possessed and the physically ill were under the influence or control of an evil power. Some evil source—demons, Satan, something destructive and uncreative, the very opposite of the Spirit of God or the Holy Spirit—seemed to have gained control or at least a partial influence over the sick person. Since Jesus by his very nature was opposed to this power and hostile to it, he wanted to bring it into subjection and in that way to free men.

He made clear in various ways the destructive and deteriorating effect of sickness on human beings: that it tears life down rather than building it up. Experience bears this out. More dispositions are soured and lives warped by illness than the contrary. Personally I am well aware of how much harder I have to work at being halfway decent to live with, and how often my wife and children have to take cover, if I am sick too long. It is well and good to talk of the brave, patient souls who have developed through suffering, but the fine border-line at which disease ceases to be a destructive force and becomes a blessing is very hard to see.

Perhaps God can turn evil to good, but this does not change the fact that many are simply destroyed by illness. For instance, the mentally ill who have disintegrated as egos cannot possibly benefit. And men who have been great in spite of illness might well have been even greater had they lived out their lives as whole persons. What the world would have lost, had Paul been a helpless invalid or had Francis of Assisi died prematurely!

The "Christian" attitude that glories in sickness is completely alien to that of Jesus of Nazareth; it is aligned on the side of what he was fighting against. I very much suspect that anyone who glories in the benefits of illness has either known little of it in himself or those dear to him, or else has serious masochistic tendencies. Sickness is a destructive and evil phenomenon, and Christ as the incarnation of creativity was dead set against it. Modern medical practice is a monument to the attitude of Jesus; it practices in his way as the churches often do not.

Healing was also a good work. It was like pulling an ox or an ass out of a pit—important and valuable enough to break the Sabbath so as to accomplish it. The equally valuable laws of the Sabbath, made to protect men from being overworked, could and should be broken to show mercy and healing.

When Jesus entered the synagogue on a Sabbath and found there a man with a withered hand, the authorities watched to see whether he would heal him, for evidently he seldom let sickness come his way without dealing with it. Jesus called the man and then turned to those who hoped to catch him breaking the Sabbath and said, "Is it against the law on the sabbath day to do good, or to do evil; to save life, or to kill?" But they said nothing. Grieved to find them so obstinate, he looked angrily round at them and said to the man, "Stretch out your hand." (Mark 3:4–5) The first of the healings recorded in Mark, that of the man with an unclean spirit, also took place on the Sabbath. (Mark 1:21–26)

The obvious implication of all this is that it is a good thing to heal human beings—important enough so that ritual laws should not stand in the way. Just as the ox has a "right" to live, the human has a right to be well. Man is valuable, and whatever contributes to his restoration and health is also valuable. You will also note that this was independent of whether the man was good or bad, rich or poor. These questions are not found here. Healing, per se, was good. There is no other sense that can be made of the Gospel narrative.

When men came to him with faith and humility and courage, as did the centurion, the nobleman, and the Canaanite woman, Jesus healed as a response to this trust. These are the qualities that bring a man to God. They were to be encouraged. When men came with these attitudes, Jesus did not let them down. He healed to build up and strengthen such qualities. In the same way, when the father in Mark 9:24 was torn between doubt and belief, it appears that Jesus healed in part to help the man believe. The healing was his response to the man's request: "Help the little faith I have!"

There is the strange passage in Mark 1:40 where Jesus is strongly moved by the leper's begging: "If you want to you can cure me." Could it be that Jesus was angry, and healed because the man doubted that he wished to make him well? Then there is the passage quoted above from Mark 3:4 in which he is angry at those who would stand in the way of a healing act; their hearts are hard because they are more interested in religious rules than in human beings. Again we see real hostility toward sickness and the forces that cause it, including those who obstruct healing.

In the story of the man born blind Jesus said quite specifically that he healed so that the works of God might be displayed in men. He wanted men to know the kind of God they had and to glorify him. Blindness was an obstacle to a man's glorifying God; sight in one who had been blind enabled him and others to turn to God in thanksgiving and worship. Healing, then, is one way of opening men's eyes to the wonderful nature and power of God, so that men who are healed or see healing performed begin to take God and the religious life far more seriously. This has been my own experience. Men who feel the power of God through physical healing often become more religious men.

Third and finally, Jesus healed to help men toward repentance. He was quite conscious of the relation between sin and sickness and of man's need for a spur toward wholeness. We have seen that at least twice—when he healed the paralyzed man in Mark 2:5 and after healing the invalid who could not get to the waters in John 5:14—Jesus expressly related sickness with sin. He never made sin the sole or most important cause of sickness.

Sin and Sickness

If sin is understood as turning aside from God's way, failing to follow the way of wholeness or individuation,[11] there is good

11. Churches have so often taken an opposite view of sin that it is well to stop and consider just how this other, moralistic view relates to the ideas of Jesus about sickness. Where the major emphasis is on keeping a moral law, the needs of the group or of society take first place. The individual is expected to find fulfillment through the social order. In contrast, the New Testament looked upon fulfillment of the individual, his *wholeness*, as God's way of fulfilling society's needs and the

reason for believing that this leads to illness. Men who lose their religious way, or have found none to follow, find themselves exposed to destructive spiritual forces that often trigger emotional disturbances. Thus they are open to fear and hate; to mental distress, meaninglessness, and despair; to destructive emotions that are almost a catalogue of the cardinal sins. There is good evidence, as we shall see, that such emotional disturbances often produce or contribute to a variety of mental and physical illnesses.[12] There is clearly a very direct connection between sin and sickness, particularly if sin is understood as missing the spiritual mark.

moral law. The first, of course, is the older idea of Judaism, the second the specific way of Christianity.

When keeping the moral law becomes the main religious goal, the individual has certain choices. So long as he can accept the particular law religiously (as the final prophetic word of God for the particular group), he can either live within it rigidly, or, when the law conflicts with his own needs or desires, divide his thinking and actions between conscious morality and less conscious individuality. But once there is doubt about either the origin or the finality of the moral code, then the individual is left to shift for himself, consciously and unconsciously. He can attempt to live a self-centered existence, essentially some kind of hedonism; or, if he has what it takes, he may start out on the quest for a new religious way. Whatever route the individual follows, it seems clear that moralistic or legalistic religion leaves him to take the consequences of individual action and thought and belief on his own. The tension between individual needs or desires and the codified solutions of the group has to be borne by each one alone. Thus, where the particular moral code is still seen as God's final word, the individual's deviations from it must be seen as sin. He must either use up the tension of individuality as best he can, or else take it out on other people and himself, his mind and body. When the tension becomes destructive, particularly if the individual "sins" unconsciously, the result is often sickness. And so there is reason for moralistic religions to consider sickness the punishment of God for sin. This kind of religion may try to offer healing, but too often it defeats itself.

In contrast, Jesus put the stress on God's way of wholeness for the individual. Instead of a direct emphasis on moral law, Jesus looked upon the conscious goal of love as the embodiment of the essentially moral life. In Christian terms genuine morality is found where each individual is trying to make his life whole as God would have it and seeking to love in the way Jesus commanded. Of course Christianity also produces its own tensions, but they are expected. The Christian is directed to pick up his own cross and follow, and in the church and the fellowship he is given support. Healing is then a possibility.

12. See chap. 10, pp. 243 ff. for the medical evidence.

Yet although some illness is caused by sin, Jesus did not have any illusion that therefore it all originates in sin. Nor did he hold that once a man had stepped off the way and was suffering for it, he ought to be made to endure the full burden of his mistake. Let us examine these two ideas that Jesus avoided. They are very important if we are to understand the current popular outlook, modern behavior based on it, and how the attitude and actions of Jesus differed.

Deuteronomic Judaism affirmed that all sickness was the result of sin—that it was one of God's punishments for disobedience to his will. Hellenistic thinking came to much the same conclusion: sickness was the direct result of the anger of the gods against men who got in their way or took liberties with divine prerogative. This idea of chastisement by disease, which we have already discussed at some length, was also basic to the paganism that overwhelmed the church from the sixth on into the tenth century.

While it is easy to see how men arrive at the idea that sickness *can* be caused by sin, this is no reason, as the book of Job so ably shows, to enter upon a one-way street in the matter. But men hate to have incomplete knowledge, and their partial, incomplete statements often become transformed into final, unquestioning conclusions. Jesus did not fall into this error. He specifically rejected the theory that all that ails man is caused by sin.

In Luke 13:2–5 in speaking to a large group, where people came to tell him about the Galileans whose blood Pilate had mingled with their sacrifices, Jesus responded:

"Do you suppose these Galileans who suffered like that were greater sinners than any other Galileans? They were not, I tell you. No; but unless you repent you will all perish as they did. Or those eighteen on whom the tower at Siloam fell and killed them? Do you suppose that they were more guilty than all the other people living in Jerusalem? They were not, I tell you. . . ."

How could this be stated any more clearly? There is no mistaking the sense: the man who suffered tragedy was no *more* sinful than other people. And when the disciples questioned him in the same way about the man born blind, Jesus answered, "Neither he nor his parents sinned"—adding, ". . . he was born blind so that the works of God might be displayed in him." (John 9:3)

When he saw a need to speak of sin in connection with a healing, he did not go on to say that this was the sole cause of the person's trouble. Jesus seemed to believe that a primary cause of sickness was a force of evil loose in the world which was hostile to God and his way. He believed that men were sometimes in the hands of this power, so that it exerted a baneful influence in their lives. You may call this force Satan, the devil, evil spirits, demons, autonomous complexes, or what you will; its exact source was never fully accounted for. But this understanding, this knowledge of the reality, the fact of such errant destructiveness is shot through the teaching and life of Christ.

Perhaps sin does leave an individual more open to the invasion of this power. Jesus did not discuss this relationship except when he suggested that it was emptiness that allowed a man, after he was healed of an unclean spirit, to be possessed by seven other devils. (Matt. 12:44-45) The man's defenses were nil. In fact, the way Jesus treated men who were beyond the pale suggests that sin itself may be the result of an intrusion of the power of evil into the personality of men, so that the sinning and the sick man equally need God's conversion and help.

The older attitude is still very much alive among today's Christians, however. As we have indicated, this attitude—the modern feeling that most sickness must result from some basic error or fault on the part of the sick person—comes to us directly from the Reformation. This is one area of medieval thinking the reformers didn't reform. Instead they firmly preserved the medieval idea about man and his need for healing. The thirteenth-century church, for instance, carefully kept a sick man from seeing a doctor until after the priest had come to hear and forgive his sins. Church authorities in nineteenth-century England still thought this decree "wisely made."[13] And English clergy were given detailed instructions, based on references to Calvin, on how to bring a sick man to realize God's purpose in making him suffer. Today many sincere Christians assume that somehow illness, borne properly, makes stronger and better Christians, without questioning why they believe such a thing (though this need not prevent them from having the doctor and doing their best to get well).

Yet this is uncomfortably close to the conclusion that, if sickness can be caused by sin, it must be God's will for man and therefore relieving it is vaguely contrary to God's will. Behind this conclusion is the basic premise that God enjoys a very human anger against men and loves them only when they are good, hating and punishing them when they are bad.[14] God must then be seen as interested not so much in keeping men corrected as in

13. *Visitatio Informorum: Or, Offices for the Clergy in Praying with, Directing, and Comforting the Sick, Infirm, and Afflicted,* 3d ed. (1854), p. 323.

14. Many churchmen in the eighteenth and nineteenth centuries seem to have concluded that God liked them best when they were dead. The English book of prayers for visiting the sick, the *Visitatio Infirmorum* referred to in note 13, above, suggests this in service after service. It is particularly clear in the three-page exhortation "to a Child dangerously ill," which begins, "My dear Child, do not be afraid of death. . . . To wicked people, indeed, to die is a very dreadful thing, for it takes them to those torments which await them in another life; but to the pure and good, death is only the way to pleasures so great, that if you could now plainly and clearly see them, you would, I am sure, be quite willing to leave this naughty world. For your soul, whenever it leaves this body of yours, will immediately return to GOD. . . . Who loves you much better than even your dear parents here on earth. . . ." And "your body will not be long kept from these great pleasures, which GOD made it fit to enjoy," on and on to the minister's last words: "And now tell me, my child, when you thus think of the joys of the next world, and the miseries of this, whether you would not willingly change this present life for that happy one which is to come; and whether it will not be better for you, if GOD so require it, to hasten immediately to the presence of GOD, rather than by staying longer in this life to expose yourself to the danger of losing all these great delights, by falling into sin." *Ibid.,* pp. 394 ff.

punishing them for punishment's sake. Sickness becomes a weapon he reaches for in anger because men overstep the way he has set for them. Not many people today put this into words or consider how completely Jesus avoids this attitude.

The coming of Jesus, if indeed he was the incarnation of God, wipes out once and for all the notion that God puts sickness upon men because he is angry with them. Jesus' ministry of healing embodies the exact antithesis of this idea. He did not inquire whether a man was good or bad, whether he had repented or was reforming, *before* he healed him. He loved men just as they were and wanted to help them out of their misery. If sin had caused that misery, Jesus' attitude appears to have been: once this man is healed, perhaps he will reflect and come to his senses, but as long as he is sick it is difficult for him to come into a relationship that makes sense.

With essentially this point of view, Jesus acted to express God's compassion toward men caught up in sin and sickness; he healed both. There was no hint of sitting back to wait for suffering to teach a man his lesson and bring him back into relation with God; Jesus knew that healing could accomplish God's will in men far better. God through Christ is interested in whole, redeemed men, not in using them to satisfy divine anger. This is one of the fundamental conceptions of Jesus and vital Christianity.

All the Wrong Reasons

Reasons are sometimes given for Jesus' healings, however, for which there is little if any support in the Gospel record. We have discussed some of these in chapter 2. Let us now look at them in the light of the material we have unearthed. One is the notion that illness is the best time to catch a man off base and get him on the path toward his greatest spiritual development; one way God uses to trip men up when they are going astray. There may be some truth in this. In time of illness men are sometimes more open, and those who are more or less conscious can, by reflection, let disease or emotional problems help to show them where they have wandered from the track. But while this may be found to happen in both psychological practice and under religious direction, it does not mean that sickness itself is God's will. The first task is to get over it, not to bear it patiently. As Jesus demonstrated in helping people on their way toward wholeness, it is not the illness itself but the *healing* that is a steppingstone toward repentance and change. Jesus first healed. And if healing failed in that effect—well, converting men *is* a challenge.

There is also the idea among Christians that Jesus came to provide a do-it-yourself manual for man; that his primary purpose, so to speak, was to teach ingenuity, self-reliance, and the one right method of healing. This does not tally with the record as a whole. Jesus helped men to enjoy the diversity of God's handiwork; he did not show them how to make all things and all men shape up to one uniform mold. As we have seen, his healing practices varied, and he made no explicit suggestion that men should learn to get along without physicians. Nor, of course, did he recommend that they do without God's healing and rely entirely on science. Instead Jesus dignified both men's intelligence in dealing with their problems, and also their reliance upon God.

The notion that his healings were intended only to point the way to salvation—to ultimate wholeness in another life—has even less foundation in the Gospel story. This is sometimes the net result of theological study. But this completely ignores the fact that healings actually occurred, and that they were effective in bringing new life right then, as well as in confirming the expectation of life to come. Essentially everything we know of Jesus of Nazareth underlines the importance of this present life, both in its own relation to God and as a way of touching his kingdom in preparation for the future. Jesus certainly did not seem to be healing in order to make an allegorical statement of something quite different.

Finally, some churches believe that Jesus healed merely to help people take his mission seriously. They are persuaded that his purpose was to reveal his spiritual authority, confirm his divinity. Hence the church continued to heal until this was well established, and then the power was withdrawn from man. Many Christians seriously hold this theory which, as we have seen, is one doctrine of dispensationalism.

This is seldom the attitude of Jesus. Far from using his healings as signs of power, he seemed embarrassed by them and told people not to speak of them. At times he even gave the impression that he would rather not have performed miracles, from a tactical point of view. But it was his nature to be hostile to illness and to have mercy on the sick; it appears almost as if he could not help himself. As the representative of God, he had the authority and power to heal; it was his task—very nearly the obligation he had to accept, if he was to fulfill and be himself.

We also know that in his temptation Jesus rejected once and for all the idea of using miracles as a come-on—a proof positive to make people take spiritual reality seriously. He repelled the suggestion of the devil to jump from the top of the Temple where everyone would see and believe, and so demonstrate that he would be held up on the hands of angels. (Matt. 4:5–7) His healing miracles were not done just so that men might witness them and believe; they were rather the natural reaction of his spirit to sickness and suffering in the world and his desire for God's grace to be known in those he touched. When the Pharisees, on the other hand, wanted him to produce a sign, he replied, "It is an evil and unfaithful generation that asks for a sign! The only sign it will be given is the sign of the prophet Jonah." (Matt. 12:39)

Practical Conclusions

What were the reasons, then, that Jesus used so much of his ministry to heal sick people, and what conclusions can we draw from this?

He was the son of God, filled with the Spirit of God and fully expressing God's nature for men. He knew what it is to be a man and to care about one's own value and dignity and reason for being, and he cared about men whom God had created in his own image. He was hostile to anything that marred that image— particularly the destructive aspects of spiritual reality which resulted in sickness. Illness hampered men in being what they ought to be, and he wanted them to have life, and that abundantly, so that they might "glorify God and enjoy him forever."

There is more than just academic interest in this. The attitude of Jesus and his healing ministry offer some very practical considerations for the life of the church. Our analysis suggests four principal conclusions for Christian groups, which we shall consider further as we look at healing in the history of the church.

1. The Christian who goes around saying that sickness is God's will has not fully understood the life and teaching of Christ. A large part, perhaps even the major part, of Jesus' ministry was devoted to healing the sick just because it was indeed God's will that they should be well and not ill. God in Christ was opposed to sickness and to what makes men sick; he was in the world to heal it.

2. Health of mind and body and Christianity cannot be separated. It may be possible to separate health of mind and body out from other religions, but not from Christianity; they are in a corporate relationship. Whether God wants perfect health for all men at all times one cannot be sure, but it is certain that he wants

wholeness, salvation for each individual. He sent Christ into the world in order to give men a better chance at wholeness, at Life with a capital *L*. It is dangerous, if not downright deadly, to judge of any other person that his sickness is good for him; in fact it is even dangerous to judge this about oneself. Instead, the task of Christians is to use whatever means they can to bring wholeness and health without first judging—in other words, with just about the same interest and concern that any good medical doctor brings to those who need him.

Can you imagine Jesus of Nazareth saying to anyone, "Oh, go your way and make something of your sickness! It is better for you than the mischief you have been getting into"—? Although he could be quite harsh when it was needed, this was not his tone toward the sick, or even toward individuals generally. Instead, his judgment was directed to the people as a whole. But toward the sick he took religious action. In the next chapter we shall look at Paul's actions, and also what he said and did not say about having a thorn in the flesh. Later we shall compare these things with some of our own opinions and our actions or lack of action.

3. For all practical purposes the aim in founding the church was to make it possible to carry on the ministry of Christ while they waited for the coming of the Kingdom. On one hand Christians who are actually followers of Christ—in whom his Spirit is still working—have good reason to want that ministry and its healing activity to continue. And on the other, there seems to be only one good way to keep this Spirit alive in people, and that is to be touched by and to help carry out that same activity and ministry.

Jesus gathered together a band of disciples to carry on his work after he was gone. While he was still with them, he started them out with the same ministry as his own. In Mark 6:7, Matthew 10:5–8, and Luke 9:1 we have the account of his sending out his disciples and giving them authority to cast out demons, preach, heal the sick, cleanse lepers, and raise the dead. The disciples returned ecstatic with joy and amazement because of their success. In Luke 10 we are told that Jesus selected seventy-two others and sent them out with similar instructions. They too reported phenomenal success, and Jesus said:

"I watched Satan fall like lightning from heaven. Yes, I have given you power to tread underfoot serpents and scorpions and the whole strength of the enemy; nothing shall ever hurt you. Yet do not rejoice that the Spirits submit to you; rejoice rather that your names are written in heaven." (10:18–20)

One can write this off as mythology and say that Jesus and his followers were *only* interested in eschatology—but not without doing real violence to the text.

In John 14:12–14 Jesus expressed the same essential attitude when he said:

> I tell you most solemnly,
> whoever believes in me
> will perform the same works as I do myself
> he will perform even greater works,
> because I am going to the Father.
> Whatever you ask for in my name I will do,
> so that the Father may be glorified in the Son.
> If you ask for anything in my name,
> I will do it.

It is hard to see how followers who really accepted such a commission could come back later and ask whether it was God's will or not that men be healed in this way.

4. Jesus' ministry was to preach, teach, and heal. It was to be the same ministry for his disciples, for his church. The appendix to Mark (16:17–18) summarizes the last aspect of this threefold ministry of the early church in these words:

These are the signs that will be associated with believers: in my name they will cast out devils; they will have the gift of tongues; they will pick up snakes in their hands, and be unharmed should they drink deadly poison; they will lay their hands on the sick, who will recover.

In other words, they were to proclaim the present coming of the kingdom of God. They were to share the implications of the kingdom for living at that present time. And finally, in some very specific ways they were to bring the healing power of God to bear on the mental and physical illness of their time. The commissions would seem to be the same for the church in our time, unless the words of the New Testament have been superseded by later authority.

Beyond all the embroideries and inventions that must have crept into so large and long a tradition, the core of real expectation and experience seems undeniable. As we shall note presently, when Paul wrote to the Galatians reminding them of healings they had already witnessed, he had nothing to gain in his missionary labors by pointing to something false and unconvincing which would at once discredit him. No—the core of reality is there beyond all obscuring by legend or imagination; and we shall see it reappear abundantly in our own day, even also in terms of modern medicine and psychiatry.

6

Signs, Wonders, and Mighty Works

We turn now to the first organized group of Christians to see what they actually did about all this. The books and letters that contain the record of the first Christian churches, taken together, do not make a very long work. But besides the record of persons and places and experiences, of specific problems that arose and were solved, these books contain some of the most important thinking that has been done by Christians. As the apostles carried the new faith to the centers of the Gentile world, Paul and others set down for the new churches much of their basic understanding of Christian experiences, including healing. The passages about healing are brief and to the point, and one has to know where to look to put the whole story together.

Any serious study of healing in the early church should begin with three brief references in the letters of Paul. They occur in three of the earliest letters to different congregations: the Galatians, the Corinthians, and the Romans. No modern scholar denies Paul's authorship of these letters. They are authentic, firsthand accounts of what was happening among Christians twenty to thirty years after the resurrection, written by a leader who left his imprint on all organized Christianity from then on. In his exegesis on 2 Corinthians 12:12 in the *Interpreter's Bible*, Floyd Filson has remarked significantly:

Writing to churches that would have challenged him had he falsified the facts, Paul refers unhesitatingly to such miracles [as healing]; he knows that even his enemies cannot deny their occurrence. In other words, the study of miracles must begin by accepting the fact that many such remarkable events happened. Moreover, this verse implies clearly that other true apostles were doing similar MIGHTY WORKS.[1]

Although the word "healing" itself is not used in these three places, there is essential agreement among scholars, as Filson suggests, that this is the plain meaning of the Greek. Let us look at these passages in which healing is referred to as one most important seal of the true apostle of Christ.

Writing to the Galatians who were turning away from his teaching, Paul asked, "Does God give you the Spirit so freely and work miracles among you because you practice the Law, or because you believed what was preached to you?" (3:5) To the Corinthians, who were in conflict with him on many subjects, Paul was opening his heart about what it meant to be an apostle; toward the end of this second letter he stated one of the clearest confirmations of his authentic ministry: "You have seen done among you all the things that mark the true apostle, unfailingly produced: the signs, the marvels, the miracles." (12:12) In the following year he put together his careful reasoning about Christian experience in a letter to the Romans, in conclusion commending his ministry to them and saying, "What I am presuming to speak of, of course, is only what Christ himself has done to win the allegiance of the pagans, using what I have said and done by the power of signs and wonders, by the power of the Holy Spirit." (15:18–19)

Paul used here the Greek word *dúnamis*, translated as miracle and power, *semeîon* or sign, and *téras*, marvels or wonders. All three were also used again and again in the Gospels and Acts to

1. *The Interpreter's Bible*, 10:411. Emphasis from the original.

refer to the miracles done by Jesus and later by the apostles, very often miracles of healing. The translation of these words is not consistent, particularly in the King James version, and it is worthwhile to look at their meaning in the original Greek.

Words and Acts of Power

Dúnamis (δύναμις), which means power or ability, is the word from which "dynamite" and "dynamic" are both derived. Any power may be implied, from the power of money to that of medicine or of mathematical exponents. It is that essential force or energy which can effectively accomplish some result; something of the same sense is conveyed by the English word dynamics. It is also commonly used in the phrase "the power of God" (or of Christ, or the Holy Spirit), and in this sense it refers to divine or spiritual power, as in the doxology of the Lord's Prayer.

Since the same word *dúnamis* may also refer to the action accomplished, it often means "miracle"—the action or deed that has been accomplished by some extraordinary power, in Paul's words "by the power of God," or of Christ or the Holy Spirit. The miracle, in other words, is the concrete expression of the particular power. The Gospels, Acts, and Paul's letters all used this word in the same way to speak of the more than ordinary happenings, the "mighty works" or signs and wonders, particularly healings, by which divine power manifests itself.[2]

Semeîon (σημεῖον), or distinguishing mark, carries much the same significance as the English word sign. In the New Testament it is used almost exclusively to speak of unusual events that

2. *Dúnamis* in the sense of miracle, a mighty or wondrous work that is a sign of divine power, occurs in Matt. 7:22, 11:20*, 21*, 23*, 13:54*, 58*; Mark 6:2*, 5*, 14*, 9:39*; Luke 10:13*, 19:37*; Acts 2:22*, 8:13*, 19:11*; 1 Cor. 12:10, 28, 29; 2 Cor. 12:12*; Gal. 3:5*; 1 Thess. 1:5; 2 Thess. 1:11, 2:9 (satanic power); Heb. 2:4*. The starred verses refer either to specific healings or to miracles in general, including healing.

display divine, or sometimes demonic, power.³ Particularly in the Gospel of John the healing miracles are spoken of as signs of Jesus' divine calling and mission. In these passages and also throughout Acts, this word is used to refer to healings as the significant evidence of divine power breaking through into the human realm. In a few places it was also used to describe portents in the heavens, as in Luke 21:11, or in the simpler sense of an ordinary sign, like the kiss given by Judas as a sign for the soldiers to act in Matthew 26:48.

Téras (τέρας) is used only with the word sign *(semeîon)* in the New Testament, in the phrase "signs and wonders" or "marvels."⁴ Basically it means a portentous event or prodigy, a happening that excites wonder and awe. This word is particularly interesting because the specific way it is used in the New Testament reveals how a meaning in classical Greek was given a new Christian sense. To the Greeks an event in nature—a thunderbolt, a snake, the wind—rightly timed, could be a prodigy in itself. A god had caused the wind to rise before their ship, a serpent to drop onto the altar at the sacrifice. To Christian writers a prodigy was not separate from its significance as being a sign of Christ or the Holy Spirit. "Wonders" were spoken of, not as wonders in themselves, but in conjunction with the signs and evidences that Jesus gave, and those the apostles continued to perform in his Spirit. And except for two references to Old Testament events and those to false Christs, the wonders described were all miracles of healing.

3. *Semeîon* as a miracle, a sign of divine intervention, occurs in Matt. 12:38, 39, 16:4; Mark 8:11, 12, 16:17*; Luke 11:16, 29, 30, 21:7, 11; John 2:11*, 18, 23*, 3:2*, 4:54*, 6:2*, 14, 26*, 30, 7:31*, 9:16*, 10:41, 11:47*, 12:18*, 37*, 20:30*; Acts 4:16*, 22*, 8:6*; in conjunction with *téras*, marvel or wonder, it is found in Matt. 24:24; Mark 13:22; John 4:48*; Acts 2:19, 22*, 43*, 4:30*, 5:12*, 6:8*, 7:36, 8:13*, 14:3*, 15:12*; Rom. 15:19*; 2 Cor. 12:12*; 2 Thess. 2:9 (satanic sign); Heb. 2:4*. The starred verses refer specifically to healings or to works of divine power which include healing.

4. See note 3, above.

Thus it is clear what Paul was speaking of when he wrote simply about miracles in Galatians and with the emphasis of signs and wonders in Romans and 2 Corinthians. Healing, he told these congregations, is the sign by which they could know that the divine Spirit had broken in upon them; it was one important test of a true apostle of Christ.

Then in his first letter to the Corinthians Paul referred directly to the ministry of healing as a special *charisma* or gift of the Holy Spirit. Twice in the twelfth chapter he catalogued the gifts. To some people, he wrote, "gifts of healing [are given] by the one Spirit" (12:9, RSV), and again in conclusion,

And God has appointed in the church first apostles, second prophets, third teachers, then workers of miracles, then healers, helpers, administrators, speakers in various kinds of tongues. Are all apostles? Are all prophets? Are all teachers? Do all work miracles? Do all possess gifts of healing? (12:28–30 RSV)

Here Paul specifically relates the ministry of healing through sacramental or spiritual means to the power of God. Healing, representing the Spirit's presence, has the dignity of a Christian profession.

In this discussion Paul used one of the common words for healing or remedy *(íama)*, found in medical literature as well as other writings. He spoke of gifts *(charísmata)* of healing in much the same way that Luke wrote about miracles or signs of healing, using the word *semeîon* with *íasis*, a word from the same root as *íama*, in Acts 4:22. In Paul's writing the word *charísmata* (χαρίς-ματα) was used to signify those divine gifts which give Christians special powers beyond ordinary human capabilities. In the case of gifts of healing an ordinary word for curing or restoring to health was given a special, Christian sense, and this was one of four such basic words which we should recognize. All four, given here in the verb form, were used in an essentially similar way throughout the Gospels and Acts.

Iáomai (ἰάομαι), to heal or cure, was almost exclusively a medical term in Greek usage. Like such words in our own language, however, it could extend to the healing of moral wounds or sickness. Indeed, as far as the Greek language goes it may have had a peculiar application to sin in pagan usage, since sin itself was seen as a kind of sickness, rather than as one separate and discrete thing that causes another separate and distinct condition (physical or mental) known as sickness.

Therapeúō (θεραπεύω), from which our English word therapy is derived, was another common word for medical treatment and healing. The original meaning was to give care or service of various kinds, including serving the gods. By adoption it came to mean heal, restore, or cure.

Hugiaínō (ὑγιαίνω), to be in good health, was taken from the name of the goddess of health, Hygeia, and has given us the English word hygiene. This word could be used to refer to a healthy or sound state either of the body or of political or religious affairs; it was a basic word in Greek medical usage.

Sōzō (σώζω), to preserve or keep from harm, to rescue, save from death, was used in a variety of senses, including the medical, in classical Greek. It carried the meaning of healing in the sense of saving a person from illness or death. Since in the Greek mind the saving of the body implied moving one step on the way toward salvation of the entire being, this word was related by implication to the whole idea of salvation. From it the theological word soteriology, or the study of salvation, is derived. The compound word *diasōzō* (διασώζω, combining the meanings of "through" and "preserve"), to bring safely through some danger or preserve through danger, was similar in meaning and usage.

These, then, are the words used all through the Gospels and Acts to say that where Jesus, and later other men, brought his

ministry there was healing.⁵ Such miracles were spoken of simply as healings or cures, being made whole and healthy, saved
from sickness and disease. They were stated in the same words
Hippocrates and Galen used, both in description of the incidents
themselves and also in the discussion of gifts in 1 Corinthians and
in the instructions about healing in the letter of James. The fact
that these events were supernatural or religious in nature is
known simply from the accounts of what was said and done at
the time they were happening, and because they were spoken of
as "miracles," "works of power," or "signs and wonders."

Besides these specific references to healing and gifts of healing,

5. These words used in the sense of healing disease, are found in the following
places in the New Testament:
Íáomai, íama, íasis: Matt. 8:8, 13; 15:28.
  Mark 5:29.
  Luke 5: 17; 6:17, 19; 7:7; 8:47; 9:2, 11, 42; 13:32; 14:4; 17:15; 22:51.
  John 4:47; 5:13.
  Acts 3:11; 4:22, 30; 9:34; 10:38; 28:8.
  I Cor. 12:9, 28, 30.
  James 5:16.
Therapeúō, therapeía: Matt. 4:23, 24; 8:7, 16; 9:35; 10:1, 8; 12:10, 15, 22; 14:14; 15:30;
17:16, 18; 19:2; 21:14.
  Mark 1:34; 3:2, 10, 15; 6:5, 13.
  Luke 4:23, 40; 5:15; 6:7, 18; 7:21; 8:2, 43; 9:1, 6, 11; 10:9; 13:14; 14:3.
  John 5:10.
  Acts 4:14; 5:16; 8:7; 28:9.
Hugiaínō, hugiés: Matt. 12:13; 15:31.
  Mark 3:5; 5:34.
  Luke 5:31; 6:10; 7:10; (healthy) 15:27.
  John 5:4, 6, 9, 11, 14, 15; 7:23.
  Acts 4:10.
Sózō, diasózō: Matt. 9:21, 22; 14:36.
  Mark 5:23, 28, 34; 6:56, 10:52.
  Luke 7:3; 8:36, 48, 50; 17:19; 18:42.
  John 11:12.
  Acts 4:9; 14:9.
  James 5:15.
In addition, in raisings from the dead, it was simply said that the dead arose, and
the implication is that they were then whole. The command Jesus gave to the
daughter of Jairus was "Wake up," and to Lazarus "Come out," while Peter
simply said to Tabitha "Arise."

there are a number of other statements in the Epistles of the conviction that mankind has been under the influence of various forces of evil. Paul spoke of these forces as demons or idols, sovereignties, elements, powers, the flesh, the law, sin, death, dominions, etc.[6] One of the primary results of their domination over human beings was sickness. And one of the reasons for the coming of Christ in Paul's theology was to rescue men from this domination and set them free both from evil forces and from the illness—moral, mental, and physical—that came in their wake.

This idea of sickness is suggested in Galatians, where he wrote:

Formerly, when you did not know God, you were in bondage to beings that by nature are no gods; but now that you have come to know God, or rather to be known by God, how can you turn back again to the *weak* and beggarly elemental spirits, whose slaves you want to be once more? (4:8–9 RSV—italics mine)

Paul used here the Greek word *àsthenés* ($\dot{\alpha}\sigma\theta\epsilon\nu\acute{\eta}\varsigma$) to speak of elements that are weak, sick, or diseased. This is the same word that occurs in various places in his own writings and in the Gospels and Acts to describe people who were sick.[7]

Other statements of this basic conviction are found in 1 Corinthians 15:24, Romans 6:11 and 8:38, while in Colossians Paul wrote:

He has overridden the Law . . . he has done away with it by nailing it to the Cross; and so he got rid of the Sovereignties and the Powers, and paraded them in public, behind him in his triumphal procession. (2:-14–15)

6. See Appendix A in my book on tongue speaking for a complete listing of these colorful names (*Tongue Speaking: An Experiment in Spiritual Experience* (1964), pp. 237 ff.).

7. As in Mark 6:56; Luke 4:40; John 4:46, 11:1 and 3; Acts 9:37, 19:12; and in Paul's letters in Phil. 2:26, 1 Tim. 5:23, 2 Tim. 4:20, and 1 Cor. 11:30; also in James 5:14, (including noun and verb form). In translating Gal. 4:9, for some reason the Jerusalem Bible omits the specifically descriptive words and refers only to "elemental things . . . that can do nothing and give nothing."

Whoever wrote the letter to the Ephesians expressed the same doctrine.

> For it is not against human enemies that we have to struggle, but against the Sovereignties and the Powers who originate the darkness in this world, the spiritual army of evil in the heavens. (6:12)

In Hebrews it was also held that:

> Since all the children share the same blood and flesh, he too shared equally in it, so that by his death he could take away all the power of the devil, who had power over death, and set free all those who had been held in slavery all their lives by the fear of death. (2:14–15)

As we shall see, these ideas of metaphysical evil make a good deal more sense than the modern world at one time considered. Basically it was the contention of Paul and the other writers that there were forces of evil which could not be grappled with physically and which sapped and destroyed human life. The Christian as a follower of Christ had a means to oppose these damaging forces.

Another Point of View

The only passages in the letters that suggest any other point of view about the value of healing are the famous "thorn in the flesh" passage in 2 Corinthians 12:7 and the references to illness in 1 Corinthians 11:29–30, Philippians 2:26–27, 1 Timothy 5:23, and 2 Timothy 4:20. Let us look at the simpler references to illness first and then turn to Paul's description of his own trouble, which is quoted by nearly everyone who believes that the healing ministry should not be a part of Christian practice today.

Paul gave a stern warning to the Corinthians about the casual way they were partaking of the Lord's supper. He told them that any one who shares in it "without recognizing the Body [of Christ] is eating and drinking his own condemnation. In fact that

is why many of you are weak and ill and some of you have died."
(1 Cor. 11:29–30) He then went on to say that the reason for
punishment like that was "to correct us and stop us from being
condemned with the world." Irreverence toward the sacred was
seen here as resulting in sickness, which could only be relieved
by reforming and getting back into God's good graces. This is the
most pointed such judgment in the New Testament outside the
book of Revelation and the story of Ananias and Sapphira in
Acts.[8] Sickness is tied to irreverence much as it was in most of
the Old Testament. In Acts, however, the illustration is even
more graphic. After Ananias and Sapphira had defrauded the
Christian community, each came in separately, lied about it, and
there in front of the apostles fell down dead. As it says in Acts,
"This made a profound impression on the whole Church. . . ."
(Acts 5:11)

Then there are three places in which Paul speaks about the
illness of men close to him. He reports to the Philippians that his
"brother" and fellow worker Epaphroditus has recovered after
being so sick that he almost died. The congregation had had news
of his illness and were worried; Paul reassures them that he will
soon be back with them. (2:25–28) There is no contradiction here,
for as far as I know no one seriously suggests that Christians are
perfect and never fall ill, but only that they can often be healed.
The means of healing are simply not mentioned in this instance,
and we have no way of knowing whether they were religious or
medicinal.

In another letter Paul advises Timothy, who often had trouble
with his stomach, to drink a little wine to relieve the ailment and

8. These deaths appear to be examples of taboo deaths, a phenomenon which
is studied and discussed by scientists today. For instance, Dr. Jerome D. Frank,
who teaches medicine at Johns Hopkins, has included a discussion of the subject
in his *Persuasion and Healing* (1969), giving references to both anthropological and
physiological studies of similar deaths pp. 39 ff. See also Herman Feifel, ed., *The
Meaning of Death* (1959) pp. 302–313.

help his digestion.[9] (1 Timothy 5:23) There is nothing here of contradiction to Christian healing. Paul simply recommends a remedy of long standing. If one believes that God heals directly by contact with his Spirit, this in no way implies that he may not also heal by thoroughly physical and medical means. In the second letter Paul tells Timothy that he has left Trophimus sick in Miletus. (4:20) There is no reason to suppose that he was not in the process of getting well.

The passage in 2 Corinthians is important enough to quote in full. Paul wrote:

> In view of the extraordinary nature of these revelations, to stop me from getting too proud I was given a thorn in the flesh, an angel of Satan to beat me and stop me from getting too proud! About this thing, I have pleaded with the Lord three times for it to leave me, but he has said, "My grace is enough for you: my power is at its best in weakness." (12:7–9)

Twice he repeated that the trouble, whatever it was, was given him because he became too proud or puffed up, and it kept his feet on the ground so that he would not be carried away by his own importance. It was a messenger of Satan which prevented self-inflation, itself a malady that resulted in ego-centeredness rather than letting his experiences keep him God-centered.

Thus Paul did not say that God sent it or that it was a good thing. He only made clear that God did not take it away because it gave Paul the weakness, humility, and poverty of spirit which he needed for God to be manifest in his life. I am sure that God would have preferred Paul minus his pride *and* his thorn. But even if it is assumed from this passage that God was responsible for the ailment, this did not keep Paul from healing other people and commending the healing ministry. It is therefore not an

9. The question of whether or not Paul was actually the writer of these letters does not matter greatly; they are early Christian documents and represent some of the concerns of the early church, whoever the writer was.

argument for others to shy away from the ministry of healing in the Christian church; it cannot be generalized as a basis for Christian action.

The Classic Healing Text

In the letter of James we find the classic New Testament text on spiritual healing. The church has pondered and studied it for centuries, and the later practice of anointing the sick was largely based on it. But outside of the Pentecostal and some fundamentalist churches it is not considered much today, and students in seminary hear very little about these words. James wrote, probably to Jewish Christians all over the empire:

> If one of you is ill, he should send for the elders of the church, and they must anoint him with oil in the name of the Lord and pray over him. The prayer of faith will save the sick man and the Lord will raise him up again; and if he has committed any sins, he will be forgiven. So confess your sins to one another, and pray for one another, and this will cure you. . . . (5:14–16)

For centuries the Roman Catholic Church officially interpreted this passage to mean the act of saving a person from spiritual death, and supported this meaning with the translation from the Vulgate. It was upon this understanding that the practice of extreme unction was based. Instead of the Latin words *curo* or *sano*, which commonly meant to heal or cure medically, only the word *salvo*, to save, was used in the Vulgate to translate "save" or "heal" and "cure" in this passage. This was a word that came into Latin only in Christian times and carried the peculiar modern meaning of salvation, rather than the ordinary meaning of the words in common usage.[10] The idea of being "saved from spiritual death" cannot be supported, however, by the original

10. The latin word *salvo* was probably first used by Lactantius in the third or fourth century, A.D.

Greek text. The sense of the words in Greek is "healed, cured, saved from illness or death," and modern Roman Catholicism is returning to this meaning. While there may be some question as to who was the actual author of this letter, there is no one who doubts the early Christian inspiration and authorship of the passage.

It is worth considering carefully. First we notice that Christian healing has added a different character. It is no longer limited to a special gift, a unique *charisma* which God gives to certain individuals; it now becomes the official action of the church officer as such. Thus what was once exclusively a *charisma* is now a sacrament which any qualified churchman may administer. Second, anointing for healing was given a firm foundation in this passage, and in the West the practice did continue as an integral part of the church's ministry for nearly a thousand years. In the Orthodox church it is still a central religious practice. Finally, not only was anointing directed, but this was done in a certain relation to forgiveness of sin. The anointing and healing came first; confession and forgiveness might well go along with the healing actions or follow them, but they were not necessarily prerequisite for the healing itself.

In at least one official modern document an attitude toward healing has been expressed that is very similar to this passage from the letter of James. The Anglican report on healing at Lambeth in 1930 took the following position:

Within the Church. . . . systems of healing based on the redemptive work of our Lord . . . all spring from a belief in the fundamental principle that the power to exercise spiritual healing is taught by Christ to be the natural heritage of Christian people who are living in fellowship with God, and is part of the ministry of Christ through His Body the Church.[11]

11. *The Ministry of Healing: Report of the Committee Appointed in Accordance with Resolution 63 of the Lambeth Conference, 1920* (1924), p. 13, and *The Lambeth Conference, 1930* pp. 61 f., also pp. 182 f.

The Anglican bishops assembled at this Lambeth Conference commended the statement to their church without a dissenting vote. The resolution still called for "a fuller understanding of the intimate connexion between moral and spiritual disorders and mental and physical ills," but it stressed a ministry for the whole man. For the first time that I know of, a modern mainline church acknowledged in an official pronouncement that unction and laying on of hands can have a direct effect on the body.

In contrast, the letter of James represented the practice of the whole church. As Luke says in Acts by way of preface to what the apostles did after Pentecost, "The many miracles and signs worked through the apostles made a deep impression on everyone. . . . Day by day the Lord added to their community those destined to be saved." (2:43, 47)

The Healing Ministry of the Apostles

The healing practice referred to in the letters of the New Testament is borne out all through the book of Acts,[12] which is to say wherever Christianity was taken during all the early years of the church's life. Since there is no work available at present which discusses this record as a whole, we present a complete summary of the examples given in Acts.

This ministry of the apostles began after Pentecost with the healing of a man who had been lame all his life. As Peter and John were going into the Temple for prayers, he begged them for money. They told him, "Look at us," and when he did, Peter said,

"I have neither silver nor gold, but I will give you what I have: in the name of Jesus Christ the Nazarene, walk!" Peter then took him by the hand and helped him to stand up. Instantly his feet and ankles became firm, he jumped up, stood, and began to walk, and he went with them into the Temple, walking and jumping and praising God. Everyone

12. Percy Dearmer's excellent work, *Body and Soul* (1909) offers a very fine analysis of the healing ministry recorded in Acts; see chap. 19.

could see him walking and praising God, and they recognized him as the man who used to sit begging at the Beautiful Gate of the Temple. They were all astonished and unable to explain what had happened to him. (3:6–10)

A similar healing of a cripple who had never walked occurred in Paul's ministry in the town of Lystra. While Paul was preaching this man managed to catch his eye, and Paul realized immediately that he had faith to be cured. He simply called out in a loud voice, "Get to your feet—stand up," and the cripple jumped up and started to walk. The crowds were so amazed that they thought Paul and Barnabas must be gods disguised as men, and called them Zeus and Hermes. The two had all they could do to keep the people from offering a sacrifice to them. (14:8–12)

In two instances details are given about the healing of particular diseases, one paralysis and the other dysentery. When Peter came to visit the Christians in Lydda, he found there a man named Aeneas who had been paralyzed and bedridden for eight years. Peter said to him, "Aeneas, Jesus Christ cures you: get up and fold up your sleeping mat," and the man at once arose. Everyone who lived there, and in the next town as well, saw him, and they were all converted to the Lord. (9:32–35)

In the other instance the healing came through the actions of Paul. This was after their shipwreck on the island of Malta. Publius, the chief official of the island, took them into his home, and when Paul found that his host's father was in bed suffering from feverish attacks and dysentery, he went in to him and prayed. Then he layed his hands on the old man and he was healed. (28:8)

Twice Paul himself was miraculously saved. Just before this healing, when they had got safely to shore, Paul was putting sticks on a fire and a poisonous snake, attracted by the heat, fastened itself on him. The natives saw the creature hanging from his hand and decided he must be a murderer; he had escaped the sea, but divine vengeance had caught up with him. Paul shook the snake off, and they waited a long time for him to swell up and die. When nothing happened, they changed their minds and concluded instead that he was a god. (28:3–6) These last two stories come from the "we" section of Acts and are probably eyewitness accounts.

Again in Lystra, some Jews hounded the apostles and turned the townspeople against them. Paul was stoned and dragged outside the town, apparently dead. But when the apostles gathered close around him, he got up, and on the following day he and Barnabas went on to the next town. (14:19–20)

One story is told of the healing of demon possession, and on another occasion the negative power of the demons is referred to. In Philippi the apostles met a slave-girl who had a spirit of divination and made a great deal of money for her masters by telling fortunes. She annoyed Paul by following them everywhere and shouting, "Here are the servants of the Most High God; they have come to tell you how to be saved!" Paul finally faced her and ordered the spirit in the name of Jesus Christ to leave her, and it came out and left her whole. As a result she lost her soothsaying ability and her masters lost their profit. They took Silas and Paul into court and had them flogged and jailed. (16:16–24) Demons or evil spirits are also mentioned three times in passages telling how the apostles healed large numbers of people.

There is a refreshing reverse twist in the story of the demon and the seven sons of Sceva. Jewish exorcists were going about casting out demons "by the Jesus whose spokesman is Paul," and these sons of the High Priest had found how effective this was. But one day an evil spirit answered back, "Jesus I recognize, and I know who Paul is, but who are you?" Instead of coming out of the man, the spirit made him jump on them and beat them until they ran from the house naked and mauled. (19:13–16) These men found it was dangerous to imitate apostolic methods without the apostolic Spirit and power. This is the difference between magic and healing; trying to control nature or spiritual powers, rather than relating to them, often leads to destruction. Modern science comes perilously close to magic when it seeks to control nature without an accompanying spirit of humility and awe: the result is a bomb, either psychic or atomic.

The healing of blindness is represented by the story of Paul and Ananias, almost too well known to need discussion. Whatever the cause of his blindness on the Damascus Road, Paul was completely restored when Ananias, somewhat reluctantly, laid his hands upon him so that he might receive his sight. (9:17) There is also a negative instance of blindness, which happened as the governor of Cyprus was about to be converted to Christianity. The sorcerer Bar-Jesus tried to interfere, and for this was struck blind. (13:6–11) In its implications this incident parallels the story of Ananias and Sapphira, and also Paul's warning to the Corinthians about punishing themselves with sickness for their misuse of the Lord's Supper. While this account is the opposite of a healing, it does represent graphically the intimate connection between religion and health.

Once, and perhaps later in a second instance, a person was raised from the dead. The first of these was Tabitha, or Dorcas, who died in Joppa where she had done so many kind things for people. The widows who prepared her body for burial were even wearing clothes she had made for them. When the disciples there heard that Peter was nearby in Lydda, they sent for him to come in a hurry. He came immediately, and putting the mourners outside knelt down and prayed; then he turned to the dead woman and said, "Tabitha, stand up." She opened her eyes, and when she saw Peter she sat up, and Peter helped her to her feet. (9:36–41)

The other incident is that of Eutychus, who was sitting in a third-story window listening to Paul preach when he fell asleep and tumbled out to the ground. This story, not really clear as to whether the young man was dead or how badly he was injured, must be a warning for those who sleep through sermons. It relates that the people rushed down and picked him up as dead. But Paul embraced him and then said, "Don't get so excited. His life is in him." The group then ate and talked until morning, and happily took Eutychus back home with them alive and well. (20:8–12)

In addition to these specific healings, described in some detail, there are ten places in Acts which refer to the healing of large numbers of persons by the apostles. Most of these passages simply seem to reinforce, as briefly as possible, what everyone was aware of already. The statements occur as follows:

> Acts 2:43: Awe came upon every soul, and many signs and wonders took place through the apostles.

> Acts 5:12: And many signs and wonders happened among the people by the hands of the apostles.

> Acts 5:15: The sick were brought out on beds and couches into the street so that at Peter's coming his shadow might fall on some of them. And a crowd from the cities around Jerusalem also came together bringing their sick and those beset by unclean spirits, and they were all cured.

> Acts 6:8: And Stephen, full of faith and power, worked great miracles and signs among the people.

> Acts 8:6: And the crowds with one mind listened to the things Philip said when they heard and saw the miracles he did. For unclean spirits, crying with a loud voice, came out

of many who were possessed by them, and many that were paralyzed and lame were cured. And the joy was great in that city.

Acts 8:13: And Simon also believed, and having been baptized, stayed by Philip, because he was amazed to see the signs and great works of power being done.

Acts 14:3: Therefore . . . [Paul and Barnabas] stayed there a long time, speaking boldly with reliance on the Lord, who gave witness to the message of his grace by causing signs and miracles to be done through their hands.

Acts 15:12: The crowds kept still and heard Barnabas and Paul telling what signs and miracles God had done among the people through them.

Acts 19:11: And God worked unusual works of power by the hands of Paul, so that if even handkerchiefs or aprons from next to his skin were brought to the sick, the diseases left them and the wicked spirits came out of them.

Acts 28:9: [After the healing on Malta], all the rest on the island who had diseases came and were cured.[13]

All of One Piece

Reading one after another the stories of these events in Acts, one is struck by the same quality of expectation, the same experience of power as is found in Paul's letters and in James. Those of us

13. We have made our own translation of these statements from the Greek. The reader not familiar with Greek may consult; *The Interlinear Literal Translation of the Greek New Testament* by George Ricker Berry (1960).

who would take the New Testament seriously must deal with these experiences which the apostles professed to have. The person who ignores them, or thinks of them as unimportant later additions to the text, can hardly consider the letters of Paul as they were written, using precisely the same words about miracles of healing. Nor can the events themselves be studied seriously if they are dismissed as mythology, pure and simple, on philosophical and theological grounds. The apostles, in actuality, seem to have started with a positive approach to such things—particularly to the experiences which continued the ministry Jesus had commended to them.

As Geddes MacGregor has stated in his exegesis on Acts in the *Interpreter's Bible*, "There can be no question that the first Christians lived in daily expectation of 'miracles,' and may therefore well have experienced them; and Luke is just as likely as any alleged later editor to record miracles in full good faith."[14] While this is scarcely an all-out plug for spiritual healing, it is an honest effort to face the facts as given in the text.

Indeed the evidence of the early church is of one piece. In a simple, almost offhand way it affirms that the ministry carried on by Jesus was continued among his followers. They did not go out of their way to make a point of the matter. It just *was*. Of course it was important, for it offered the credentials that the Holy Spirit was working through them. It means something to a sick man to get well, and large numbers of pagans who were healed turned with joy and amazement to the church. Not all were converted, any more than all of the ten lepers returned to give thanks to Jesus after their healing, but this ministry was one means of evangelization. After all if simple, ordinary people have access to divine power, it is impressive; and on the basis of Acts and the Epistles, taken together, we can come to no other conclu-

14. *Interpreter's Bible* 9:53.

sion. These men seemed to have a power and Spirit more than their own, which worked through them and gave them uncommon resources to deal with the physical and mental illnesses of men.

There are two somewhat different views of how the Spirit was given to men. In some sources the power to heal was viewed as bestowed directly on certain people as their vocation—a nontransferable grace or charisma. This view prevails in Paul's letter to the Corinthians. Elsewhere it was considered a function of the church as a corporate entity. The individual then mediated the spiritual power of the church. In this case any ordained member of the group had the power; perhaps any Christian did, simply by virtue of being a part of the redeemed and Spirit-filled group or community. This is the general idea expressed in the letter of James.

Whatever the theory about how the gift of healing was received, we find the apostles using the same basic sacramental approach to it as Jesus. Some word, a touch, or a material element such as oil was believed to convey the power that passed through the healer. The words or touch were important as an outward and visible sign of an inner grace, a spiritual energy. It was not magic. The sacramental acts were only outward carriers of something nonphysical, something of the Spirit. The healer's contact with the Holy Spirit had to be maintained or the action became meaningless.

We have seen examples of exorcism and other commands; of invoking the name of Jesus; of touching, laying on hands, and anointing. There are also examples of men healed by contact with the clothing of an apostle. As in the healings of Jesus, the faith of the sick person is sometimes mentioned, and we must also assume that the compassion of the healer was involved, although these factors seem to play a lesser part in the actions of the apostles. As time went on there was apparently less and less of the personal element in the healings, and less psychological emphasis or understanding. They became more stereotyped, more strictly sacramental; yet from the records there is little evidence that they were any less effective.

There is no indication, as some authors suggest, that sacramental healing was implemented by the apostles through medical means. But neither is there any suggestion that medical means of healing were discouraged. There is no evidence for the contention of some healing groups that Christians had to avoid medicine or other external methods if they were to receive spiritual healing. As far as we know, the church in those early years never suggested that spiritual healing was a higher method and other methods of a lower order. It had been commissioned by its Lord to heal, and so it healed. It distilled the essence of Jesus' actions and perpetuated them, and this continued to work even through people who had no special healing gift.

If we ask *why* the apostles healed, we find one very simple answer. The first reason was most likely obedience. Their master had told them to do it, and so they did. Undoubtedly the natural thing for them was to continue the ministry they had seen in their teacher and learned from him, of which healing was a part. It became one aspect of being a Christian. Beyond this the apostles themselves do not seem to have questioned. It did not occur to them to ask, "Is it God's will that this person should be healed, or not?"

An *attitude* of good will (which may prove relatively little about performance) is so normal in modern Western civilization that we seldom realize what a new thing it was in ancient times to wish to help others—just anybody. Basically these men had learned to love, and to care for themselves and others by being cared for in a new way, which they had learned was God's way. They had been in contact with God's Spirit, and when they became filled with the Holy Spirit themselves, they were then filled with love, agape. These words are practically interchangeable in the letters of Paul; love or agape and the Holy Spirit can be substituted for each other with practically no change in his meaning. The Spirit that had touched the disciples and the Holy Spirit that now filled them were the same, and they continued to express it. As Jesus had shown love by healing and ministering to people, finally offering his life as a sacrifice for the souls of men —just so they wanted to continue the same kind of caring. The misery of men's sickness touched their hearts as it had their master's, and they wanted to relieve as much of the suffering and sin and lostness of men as they could.

The apostles did not pause to consider whether they *should* heal —any more than they stopped to ponder whether they should bear love toward other men, or question whether they should relieve the distress of widows and orphans. From the actual text it does not appear that a choice ever occurred to them. Nor does it appear that they reasoned about any failure to heal; if the question was raised, they must have faced it within themselves. Very likely they wondered at times about their own inadequacy, as in the story of the epileptic boy in Mark 9.

It is also clear from the record what a great difference there was between Jesus and his disciples in their relation to God. In the pages of Acts the apostles who carried on the ministry of healing are revealed as ordinary men. When they stretched forth their hands to heal, these men who had known Jesus were trying to share with other men like themselves the gift they had received from God—the priceless gift of his Spirit, freeing and yet directing body, mind, and soul to work together in health toward his goal for them. The story in Acts 3 shows their basic approach.

It is also clear that these men who were sent out by Jesus to heal had an understanding of ministering his Spirit to others which is as relevant to our lives today as it was then. If the same Spirit is in the church today as in that time, then the same things can happen once again. Unless one disputes the entire record as fact, or restricts it by some framework like dispensationalism, there is no other conclusion possible. Looking what facts we have straight in the eye, we see that a major part of the Gospel account is devoted to healings. Aside from the many individual incidents related, we are told that great crowds gathered around Jesus from the earliest moments of his ministry, so that he was hard pressed to find time to sleep or pray, and—again and again—that he healed them; that the people came from all the region around, both city and country, from the sea to the eastern mountains, even considerable distances, sometimes at the cost of fatigue and exhaustion; that he took refuge at times on the hillsides, across the lake, or in the middle of the night to find privacy; that he healed a great variety of ailments; that he repeatedly commanded his disciples to heal, and instructed them in how they should go out to do so; that his answer to a deputation from John in prison involved mention of extensive healing; that what Herod had heard about him was along this line, making him want to see a "miracle" at Jesus' hands.

It is rather hard to believe that this person was, on the contrary, merely a charismatic lecturer on ethics and religion, about whom a tremendous and complex legend grew up quite specifically at odds with what he really was and did. If we find in modern life any experience that bears out the possibilities of healing so abundantly set forth in the Gospel record (and down the centuries), we must think ourselves rather silly not to look into it.

It is true that in Acts and the Epistles the moralistic theory of health found in the Old Testament began to be reintroduced in small doses. There is no doubt that Paul and the author of Acts attributed certain sicknesses to man's transgression. Paul's blindness on the Damascus road, the blindness of the sorcerer Bar-Jesus, the sicknesses and deaths of the Corinthian Christians, the

deaths of Ananias and Sapphira, and Paul's thorn in the flesh are
seen in this light. Yet there is no suggestion that, because this was
the case, Christians should cease their healing activity. No other
examples of sickness make this connection. Whether these afflictions were due to a demonic agency to which these people had
exposed themselves or to the action of God is not stated clearly,
and the door is opened once again to the less compassionate
theory of the Old Testament, a possibility not found in the acts
or sayings of Jesus. In his own healing ministry Jesus was apparently perfectly consistent with his principle: judge not lest you
be judged. The more moralistic attitude toward healing was undoubtedly one way of reinforcing authority. But only after many
more generations would the older attitude fully re-emerge and
begin to blot out the whole healing ministry. Instead, this ministry continued as the church grew.

The disciples of Jesus attracted other men like themselves into
the fellowship of the risen Christ. These men and women went
out to the far corners of the Roman Empire and even beyond it,
preaching, teaching, and healing. No small part of the impression
Christianity made upon that empire came from the healing ministry of these earliest ambassadors of Christ.

7

The Expectation of Every Christian

To trace what actually happened about healing in the history of the church involves research enough to fill a book rather than a chapter or two. Because of the skepticism mentioned earlier, the subject has simply been ignored by the scholarly world in modern times. Even the New Testament record of healing in the apostolic church, where it was so obviously important, has rarely been discussed, and except for one careful study done about thirty years ago, there has been no effort that I know of to discover whether similar experiences were recorded by the later writers. Since there are a great many later works, some of them still only to be read in Latin and Greek, and since references to various incidents are scattered all through them, not many people have really known for sure whether healing continued in the church or not.

The one study that has been done is the very important *Christian Healing* by Evelyn Frost, which covers the earliest records of the church after the New Testament, from about the year 100 to 250.[1] Dr. Frost's work has made the whole approach to the

1. Evelyn Frost, *Christian Healing: A Consideration of the Place of Spiritual Healing in the Church of To-day in the Light of the Doctrine and Practice of the Ante-Nicene Church* (1940). This book is a necessity for anyone who wants an understanding of the original place of healing in the Christian church. It shows clearly that the practices of healing described in the New Testament continued without interruption for the next two centuries.

129

history of healing practices in the church easier. She has not only examined piece by piece the several thick volumes of this early literature, turning up a quantity of valuable references, but has helped to show the reality of the ideas of healing in that period.

These first accounts, however, are far fewer and less detailed than the records that were to come later. Men who were drawn to the early church produced the kind of writing that circumstances demanded—largely theological reasoning. They did not talk very much about their own experiences. To understand the importance of such elements as healing in the Christianity of that time, one needs to know why these men wrote as well as what they wrote.

Allowance must be made, of course, for the strong human tendency to invent, embroider, and circulate tales of wondrous happenings, especially in a rustic ancient world which had as yet no faintest inkling of such a thing as electronic news media, with their almost instant verification or debunking of events simply by being so formidably on the spot. But on the whole, the sober quality and the large number of healings recorded in the New Testament and by early Christians stands firm against any attempt to turn this body of experience into myth or mere fancy —to say nothing of the fact that healing continues in modern times, a perpetual reminder of man's potentialities in relation to God.

The witnesses we have selected are careful writers, as different from the superstitious tale tellers of the ancient world as the New Testament is from the overblown accounts found in the apocryphal Gospels, Letters, and Acts of the various saints. (As has sometimes been remarked, the sobriety and sanity of the New Testament by comparison with much of this literature is astounding when the two are set side by side. A compelling trait of the New Testament, in great contrast with much contemporary writing, is its very simple and mature seriousness of tone.)

Undoubtedly there has been some elaboration in the material before us, and many of the stories of healing will in any case seem fantastic to readers brought up in a rationally materialistic modern world. Yet, then as now, the witness is there. We give the record of that time as it comes down to us, with its flaws and strangeness.

Let us look, then, at Christian life in that world where Christianity was becoming a universal religion.

A Vital Church

The church experienced a time of great vitality during the two hundred years after the apostolic period. Starting from small bands of Christians, usually centered in the big cities, it grew to a vast spiritual fellowship reaching into nearly every corner of the Roman Empire. Evidences of Christianity dating from this era are found in Britain, Switzerland, North Africa, along the Danube, and far into the east, carried by the ambassadors of Christ wherever the Romans went and even beyond. Part of the vital faith these Christians brought with them was the conviction that their God was a healing God who expected a healing ministry from his followers.

Christianity spread in spite of the fact that it was a proscribed religion up until the Edict of Milan in 313. It was probably made illegal during the time of Nero, about the middle of the first century, and from then on a Christian was always in danger if he were discovered. It was not a continuous persecution, however. For years Christians were tolerated, until one emperor or another, needing a domestic scapegoat on whom to project current fears and anxieties, would settle upon the Christians. They served the purpose the Jews did in Nazi Germany, and anything might happen to an individual Christian. One person might suffer minor legal penalties while another was condemned to torture and death, or had his property confiscated and his wife and children sold into slavery. For nearly three hundred years anyone who took part in the new religion lived with danger, almost from day to day. In spite of this the church grew and flourished. Indeed, as we shall see, torture and death gave Christians an opportunity to manifest an important form of both spiritual and physical poise and strength, which—if not healing —was nevertheless an expression of wholeness and inner joy that roused the wonder and envy of those who saw them die.

Obviously one did not become a Christian during this period merely from intellectual curiosity or fanciful whim. It required real conviction. In return the church was careful to screen newcomers to the fellowship. It was vital not to betray the secrecy of meeting places and rites, and there was constant danger that someone might be accepted who, carelessly or for money, would become an informer. As a result few asked or were accepted who were not deeply moved to become Christian.

For much of this time Christians were also the target of personal hatred and ridicule—a by-product of persecution and the necessary secrecy. Almost anything evil was believed of them. Stories were circulated about sexual orgies and drunken brawls, of how they sacrificed babies for the strange feasts they held. It is no wonder that the earliest groups separated themselves from the world, often actually underground. Records of this period are almost nonexistent. Much of the knowledge we have of the church from the day of Pentecost for a hundred years or more depends on archaeological findings and a few references in the Talmud and contemporary Roman writers. Both the New Testament and the seven or eight authentic documents that remain from around the year 100 were written to inform and instruct the Christian community itself, rather than for the outside world. For a long time, in fact, the church stayed apart in the belief that the world itself was about to end.

But as persecution continued year after year and the end of the world still did not come, Christians began to turn to the pagan world in an effort to justify their position. More and more pagans were drawn into the church, and for them the change of outlook was much greater than it had been for converts from Judaism. For most pagans Christianity demanded an about-face in moral point of view as well as deep religious conviction. One of the real tasks of church leaders was to develop a method of training new converts. As late as the third century, three years of training as catechumens was often required in preparation for baptism. Consequently, few people came into the church in this period who were not both well trained and deeply convinced.

The result was that the church retained the vitality of the apostolic age. It also prepared men to take the lead who knew at first hand what Christianity could offer to pagan life and saw ways of reaching the pagan world. From about the middle of the second century on these early fathers, now termed "apologists," began to express the Christian message in ways that the outside world—the pagan world and its philosophers—would understand. From the earliest time, writings were preserved and have come down to us which show that the healing ministry was continuing in much the same way as in apostolic days. These works show that healing was part of a total framework in which all Christians were educated: a reality of religious experience in which all participated, either directly or indirectly. And indeed, if they were to follow the teachings of Christ as handed down, it is hard to see how they could do otherwise. Materialistic disbelief was not yet—by many centuries—a norm in the world.

There was trouble, however, and not only from the outside. Along with persecution, the church was also soon faced by heresy within, and it took some of the most important efforts of new Christian thinkers to combat these Gnostic departures. Early in the second century Greek Gnosticism was already attracted to the figure of Jesus. Groups of Gnostic Christians, known as Docetists, began to preach a Christianity quite at variance with the Gospels. The entire physical world was seen as the creation of an evil demiurge, directly opposed to the God of Christ; from this point of view man's body itself was an evil. Thus any idea of incarnation appeared unthinkable. The physical Jesus was seen as an illusion, and there could have been no crucifixion in the real sense. Christ had come to give a teaching, a system of knowledge or *gnosis* through which man could save himself, and so any idea of atonement also disappeared in these systems.

Some of the Gnostics were thinkers and leaders of first caliber. The writings of Valentinus and the excerpts we have of Basilides still make interesting reading today as one follows the intricate maze of speculation that captivated the intellectuals of the time. But the early fathers saw how people were allured by these ideas, as was Augustine at a later date,[2] and actually came to feel that what one did with his physical self made no real difference. According to this line of thought the body had so little value that it did not need to be considered morally or in any significant way. Thus Christian thinkers were forced to argue with vigor to defend the value of the body and the idea of the incarnation, the resurrection of the flesh, and the atonement. To these men who had found new meaning in life, this was as much a matter of life and death as persecution from the outside.[3]

Let us first look briefly at these leaders whose thinking was so crucial for the church's life and growth and how they spoke of experiences of healing, and then see the understanding that de-

2. For nine years Augustine stayed with the Gnostic Manicheans as a reader, and after he finally broke away and entered the church it took some of his best thinking to refute their ideas.

3. For the reader who wishes more detailed information on this period, an excellent study of the background and the struggle that resulted is found in Hans Lietzmann's *A History of the Early Church*; see particularly (1963), chap. 15: 264 ff. Also, for an interesting study of some later, contrasting source material, see E. R. Dodds, *Pagan and Christian in an Age of Anxiety* (1965).

veloped as they began to explain the reality of their faith to a hostile world.

The Early Christian Thinkers and Their Evidence

The first of the Christians who produced formal defenses of their faith, or apologies, were converts who lived and wrote in Rome: Quadratus early in the second century, and Justin Martyr, who taught philosophy there until he was accused and killed about 165. At Carthage in North Africa Tertullian and Cyprian became two of the church's most influential converts, writing until well into the third century. During the same period two other men came to similar stature in the great intellectual center of Alexandria: Clement had been drawn there from a pagan background in Athens, while his brilliant follower Origen was a native, born into a Christian home. Irenaeus, originally from the church in Smyrna, lived in Gaul and wrote voluminously through the latter part of the second century.

These were educated men, often drawn to Christianity after wide experience in the pagan schools and world. Indeed, they were men of culture, even intellectual sophistication. While it may be easy to think of the New Testament writers as intellectually naïve (far as this is from the truth), the same idea cannot be made to fit these leaders of the church. Tertullian, for instance, was a first-rate jurist and wrote as polished Latin as any of his most cultivated contemporaries. Origen had one of the best minds of his day and was admired by non-Christians as well as Christians, while the Christian school in Alexandria at that time was one of the most respected intellectual centers in the entire empire.

We have many of the writings of these men which show quite clearly the way they approached the idea that God, one God, was known among them. They wrote about all kinds of experience that showed how God had acted and continued to act in Christian lives, including much that was lively and down-to-earth. Healing and the ability to relieve "demon possession" is spoken of again and again in the more important works and referred to in some way by all these writers. Justin Martyr, for example, wrote in his "apology" addressed to the emperor in Rome, referring to the significance of Jesus as man and Savior:

For numberless demoniacs throughout the whole world, and in your city, many of our Christian men exorcizing them in the Name of Jesus Christ . . . have healed and do heal, rendering helpless and driving the possessing devils out of the men, though they could not be cured by all the other exorcists, and those who used incantations and drugs.[4]

Origen wrote his great treatise *Against Celsus* to take pagan thinking apart piece by piece, and here he spoke in several places of how Christians "expel evil spirits, and perform many cures" —many of which he had himself witnessed. Or again, "the name of Jesus can still remove distractions from the minds of men, and expel demons, and also take away diseases."[5] Several such statements occur in this work, which was written especially for the top-level pagan community. Cyprian told in one of his letters how baptism itself was sometimes the means by which a serious illness was cured, and that there were Christians living on and giving their lives to the church because of such an experience.[6]

In a telling protest written to the proconsul in North Africa during the persecutions there, Tertullian cited facts even more specifically:

4. Justin Martyr, *Second Apology: To the Roman Senate*, 6. Unless otherwise noted, references to the works of these fathers are taken from *The Ante-Nicene Fathers* (various dates).

5. Origen, *Against Celsus* I.46 and 67.

6. Cyprian, *Epistle* 75.15.

All this [that is, the number of times Roman officials simply dismissed charges against Christians] might be officially brought under your notice, and by the very advocates, who are themselves also under obligations to us, although in court they give their voice as it suits them. The clerk of one of them, who was liable to be thrown upon the ground by an evil spirit, was set free from his affliction; as was also the relative of another, and the little boy of a third. And how many men of rank (to say nothing of common people) have been delivered from devils, and healed of diseases! Even Severus himself, the father of Antonine [the emperor], was graciously mindful of the Christians; for he sought out the Christian Proculus, surnamed Torpacion, the steward of Euhodias, and in gratitude for his having once cured him by anointing, he kept him in his palace till the day of his death. . . .[7]

Thus there is no question that the ministry of healing continued in the church. These men, whose evidence we shall consider in more detail later, were writing for a skeptical public who made no bones about their attitude toward Christianity: that the world would be better off if these annoying Christians were simply eliminated. The Christian writers were well aware of this. They were also well informed for their time—well enough to be sure of the facts they presented. From all parts of the church and out of their many different backgrounds, they spoke of healing in much the same way. It was simply a fact of Christian experience which pagan officials could verify if they wished.

At the same time they did not talk very much about individual healings, or give names very often. Of course, there were not many emperors whose names could be produced as "Antonine" was by Tertullian, and most ordinary citizens were not anxious to have their names connected with the Christians. Origen once

7. Tertullian, *To Scapula* 4. Severus until his death was coemperor with his son Caracalla, who was often called "Antonine" because he tried to pattern his rule after Marcus Aurelius Antoninus. Severus was vilified by contemporary historians, and the picture we have of Caracalla was probably created in part in the same way.

commented that there were many instances he could set down
from his own experience, but he saw no point in giving non-
believers another chance to ridicule Christians for imagining
things like healing;[8] while Irenaeus, who offered the most impressive list of kinds of healing to be seen in the church, said
explicitly that Christians were not practising deception on people. The followers of Gnosticism, for whom he was writing,
simply did not believe such things were possible.

In different ways, the thinking of both pagans and Gnostic
Christians shut out the idea of healing accomplished directly by
God. Magic they could accept, but the idea and experience of
what is simply a divine gift was as effectively blocked as it is for
most people today. And so Christian thinkers tackled this problem, for there was no point in talking about experiences that
people could not even see. They set out to provide an approach
that would bring both the superstitious materialism of most pagans and the overspirituality of most Gnostics into focus. What
they did in the end was to produce the theological and philosophical foundation on which Christians would build and the Christian world would expand for a thousand years. Let us look carefully at this approach as it relates to various ideas men have held
about the human body and soul.

Theology and Healing in the Early Church

Christian theology as it is now understood first developed during
the second century in a joining of philosophy and Christian
experience. Theology, both then and now, is an attempt to relate
religious experience to the rest of one's experience and knowledge. This effort to fit religious experience into the total framework of life and thought usually does not take place until a man's
religion is questioned—until he tries to explain to someone who

8. Origen, *op, cit.*, I.46.

disagrees with him what he really believes and tries to practice. There is little developed theology in the New Testament. It contains, instead, the raw material of theology: that is, the experience upon which a theology is based. In describing it the New Testament writers all express an implicit theology, but its explicit development came with the effort of the apologists to justify and explain their faith to a hostile world and a divided church.

Justin Martyr was the first to unite the intellectual method and world view of Plato with the life and experience he had discovered in the Christian community. The importance of Plato to Christian theology is not always recognized today. It is well to remember that the philosophic framework was provided by Plato's carefully expressed notion of a nonphysical and eternal world which shapes and directs the physical world. He refined and stated the belief commonly held in most cultures that man is caught between two worlds—a physical one, which he reaches through his senses, and a nonphysical one that breaks in directly upon his nonphysical or spiritual nature, or soul. Platonic philosophy tried to show how the tangible world, of which man's body is a part, constantly interacts with a world of Ideas, spirits, demons, and deities. In this framework the Old Testament descriptions of man's direct dealings with God made good sense, as did the dreams and visions, the healings, prophecies, and angels and demons of the New Testament.

From his knowledge of Plato and his Christian experience, Justin saw that what Plato had conceived intellectually the fellowship of *the Way* now knew in concrete reality, though without realizing its full philosophical and theological significance. The fathers who came after Justin took the same basic approach, and together reached quite a consistent body of theological conclusions. This basic understanding of two worlds in interaction was the philosophic foundation of their ideas, as well as of the rest of

Christian thinking for the next thousand years. Four of these central ideas are directly connected with healing; indeed these are so significant that they make a healing ministry practically imperative for the Christian church.

All four ideas originated in the experience of the apostles with the man Jesus, which continued to be expressed in relationships within the church. This experience of Jesus had struck deep into their lives and minds. Although they were unprepared for the resurrection, they could look back to intimations they had had of Jesus' more than human nature. The living, resurrected Christ continued to appear to them. They believed first of all that this man had *truly incarnated* the God of the Hebrew people. Second, because of this and their Hebrew background they saw *man's flesh and body as essentially good*; as a result the realization grew that man's body had eternal significance.

Again, the early church valued at the same time things remembered and its own fresh experience, so that in the second century the early creeds began to state formally the idea (our third here) of *the resurrection of men's bodies*. Finally, the concept of *the atonement* was also developed at this time, comprehending Christ's incarnation, life, death, and resurrection as the sequence that defeated the forces of evil which had dominated men. Each of these ideas represented an utter rejection of the Gnostic speculation of the time. Their importance for a theology of healing can hardly be overestimated. Let us look at the effect they had upon the theory and practice of the church.

As Dr. Frost has pointed out, the early church inherited the high valuation of the body from Hellenistic Judaism.[9]This belief was almost unique in the ancient world. To both Greek and Oriental thinkers the soul was the only salvageable part of man. We have already suggested the Greek understanding, expressed

9. *Op. cit.*, pp. 20 ff.

in the myth of a cosmic catastrophe or explosion of the pleroma which trapped the soul in pieces of evil matter.[10] Hellensim for the most part saw little real value in the body itself. The soul was so separated from it that what men did with their bodies in this world—their morality—had little effect on what happened to their souls.

The elaborate embalming rituals of Egypt expressed the same essential thought in a somewhat different form. The religion of the Egyptians was almost entirely otherworldly in its emphasis. While that future life was viewed in a very physical way, still it was quite separate from this physical life and infinitely more important. Thus the kings of Upper Egypt spent much of their lives and substance erecting temples and tombs to prepare their way out of this life, whose value was small compared with that of the next.

The idea of interdependence of soul and body grew up in Judaism. Until very late the Hebrews had little belief in a worthwhile afterlife. If good were to be experienced, it had to be known in the here and now. Those who contributed to the earthly misery of their fellow men came under the severe censure of the prophets. Later Judaism codified these insights, and we find a value placed upon this world, the physical body, and morality—upon human relationships and material things—that is found in few religions which have not sprung from the Judeo-Christian heritage. Man's body and his existential, physical life in the world shared in the value of man as a creature of God.

It was, then, not by chance that morality, man's way of acting toward his fellow man in the physical world, assumed such an important place in the thinking of this people. The moral emphasis was one the ancient world was hungering for, and all over that world Gentiles flocked to the Hebrew synagogues. Although

10. See our discussion pp. 49 f.

they did not embrace the ritual law, these "God-fearers" took seriously the ethical side of Judaism. Such groups provided ready-made congregations to which the Christian teaching appealed.

Nor was it by chance that among these people, with one foot in Judaism and the other in the pagan world, the idea of the incarnation took hold. They were at least aware of the Hebrew sense of the value of the body, while the Greek notion of the gods consorting with men was certainly not foreign to them. If the incarnation was true, then the body was good and valuable enough to incarnate—to enflesh—not only the human soul but God himself. Tertullian put it well in his treatise on resurrection when he wrote:

For, whatever was the form and expression which was then given to the clay [by the Creator], Christ was in His thoughts, as one day to become man, because the Word, too, was to be both clay and flesh, even as the earth was then. . . . To what purpose is it to bandy about the name *earth*, as that of a sordid and grovelling element, with the view of tarnishing the origin of the flesh, when . . . it would be requisite that the dignity of the Maker should be taken into consideration. . . . It was quite allowable for God that He should clear the gold of our flesh from all the taints . . . of its *native* clay, by purging the original substance of its dross.[11]

It is not flesh or earth that is evil, but something that happens to it when it falls under the domination of "death" and the forces of evil. The soul is even more subject to this evil than the body, and passes its corruption on to the latter.[12]

11. Tertullian, *On the Resurrection of the Flesh* 6.

12. Evelyn Frost (*op. cit.*, pp. 71 ff.), cites a great number of passages from the ante-Nicene fathers relating to the ideas here discussed. Among them, those that deal primarily with the value of the body, and also how it becomes subject to evil, are *The Epistle of Barnabas* 6; Justin Martyr, Fragments of the lost work *On the Resurrection* 7 f., and Fragment found in Leontius, *Against Eutychians* II; Theophilus of Antioch, *To Autolycus* II.25; Irenaeus, *Against Heresies* III.23.5 ff.; Tertullian (besides the above passage), *Against Marcion* II.4 ff.; Methodius, *Discourse on the Resurrection* I.11; and also the references in note 13, below.

The incarnation gave tremendous significance to the physical body, a significance which carried over to the afterlife. The result was the doctrine of the resurrection of the body. But this was not held naïvely as in some of the more fundamentalist sects today. We tend to laugh at the belief and to prefer the Greek idea of immortality of the soul, which is quite different as Oscar Cullmann has pointed out in his provocative *Immortality of the Soul or Resurrection of the Dead?* Some of the notions we impute to the thinkers of the early church are really quite funny. I remember, for instance, a housekeeper in our family who worried about the resurrection of the body because her husband had lost a leg in France, and she wondered how the Lord would get him together again. But these ancients were sophisticated men whose understanding was very different. Their main point was that the body has eternal significance and that out of it a resurrected form arises, not physical as we know it, but somewhat as a seed germinates and grows into a plant.

The implications of this thinking for Christian healing were great. The body had real intrinsic value, not merely because it was associated with the soul, but in its own right. Thus healing the body was a valid act; it became a good work whether the soul was influenced or not. (How different from the official position of the church in the Middle Ages!) It should be noted, however, that healing of the body was seen to have almost inevitably an effect upon the soul, while healing the soul had its effect on the body; the two were inextricably joined. The sharp sense of separateness which is current today (when we can hardly say that we *have* such a thing as a soul), and was current in the pagan world, simply did not exist for early Christians.[13]

13. The close relation between body and soul was stressed by most of these writers, as in Clement of Rome, *First Epistle: To the Corinthians* 26; Ignatius, *Epistles to the Magnesians* 13, *to the Smyrneans* 13; *The Pastor of Hermas* III.5.6 f.; Clement of Alexandria, *The Instructor* I.2 and III.12; Athenagoras, *Treatise on the Resurrection of the Dead* 15; Irenaeus, *Against Heresies* IV.20.4, V.3.3, 6.1 f., 8.1. Also in discus-

Equally important for healing was the understanding of evil
and the saving work of Christ. It was believed that man's
disobedience in Adam resulted in "death," which was more than
simple physical dissolution of the body. In this first falling away
an alien and destructive spirit entered men's lives, which gained
power over them, corrupting both body and soul. The term
"death" referred to this metaphysical entity as well as to the
resulting condition. It was an uncreative, disintegrating force
directly opposed to God. Through men's disobedience it could
and did possess human life. This spirit, "death," obtained control
over men and turned them away from God and the Holy or
creative Spirit. Its power was expressed in man's life spiritually
by sin and mental illness, and physically in bodily disease which
led eventually to physical death. Illness was not in fact the will
of God, but directly and antagonistically opposed to it.

Then on Golgotha Christ met the forces of "death," submitted
to them and conquered them. Through his cross and resurrection
the power of "death" (the Evil One) was defeated, so that by
following his Way men could find rescue from *both* sin and sickness. The early church knew these forces which Christ defeated.
They had dominated mankind up to that time and still ruled most
men. They were described in the New Testament, particularly
by Paul, as "dominions," "thrones," "principalities," "spiritual
wickedness," "the dragon," "death," and a variety of colorful
names.[14]

To the thinkers of the church these forces were not merely
concepts; they were concrete and powerful entities. As Gustav

sions of the resurrection pointing up the importance of the body and of healing,
Justin Martyr, *The First Apology* 18 f. and Fragments of the lost work *On the
Resurrection* 4 f. and 9 f.; *The Second Epistle of Clement* (An Ancient Homily) 9;
Tatian, *To the Greeks* 6, 16, and 20; Theophilus of Antioch, *To Autolycus* I.7 and
II.26; Origen, *Against Celsus* V.19 and VII.32; Methodius, *Discourse on the Resurrec-
tion* I.12 f.

14. For a complete catalogue of these passages, see Appendix A in my book
Tongue Speaking: An Experiment in Spiritual Experience, pp. 237 ff.

Aulén has shown conclusively, up to the seventh century the atonement was seen by nearly all the church fathers in terms of a victory over just such actual spiritual beings of some sort.[15] And as we shall see, even for later thinkers the idea of spiritual entities or elements outside the personality that affect men's minds and bodies is not quite so absurd as most people feel. The studies of Dr. Jung have helped us to take a fresh look at these things.

With the understanding that the effect of these forces in the actual physical world was disease, corruption, and dissolution (death) of both body and soul, healing was the natural result of Jesus' having lived. In the words of that time,

How can they maintain that the flesh is incapable of receiving the life which flows from Him, when it received healing from Him? For life is brought about through healing, and incorruption through life. He, therefore, who confers healing, the same does also confer life; and He . . . [who gives] life, also surrounds His own handiwork with incorruption.[16]

Jesus by his nature had brought life and healing to the people he encountered. He had also shown that the power of his being was greater than the power of the Evil One by rescuing men from it, and finally by defeating it on the cross. Ultimately it was

15. Gustav Aulén, *Christus Victor: An Historical Study of the Three Main Types of the Idea of the Atonement* (1951). This understanding of "death," of its effect, and of the Christian attitude toward it was developed by one after another of the church fathers. It is found in Clement, *The First Epistle: To the Corinthians* 3 ff., 9, 24, 44 f.; *The Epistle of Barnabas* 16; Ignatius, *Epistle to the Ephesians* 19; Polycarp, *Epistle to the Philippians* 10; the *Epistle to Diognetus* 10; Justin Martyr, *Dialogue with Trypho* 124; Tatian, *To the Greeks* 12 ff.; Irenaeus, *Against Heresies* III.19.1, 23.6 f., IV.33.4, 38.3 f., 39.1, V.7.2, 12.1 ff., and 24.4; Tertullian, *On the Soul* 52, *On the Flesh of Christ* 6, 17, *On the Resurrection of the Flesh* 47 f., 54, *Apology* 50, *Against Marcion* I.22, *Antidote for the Scorpion's Sting* 6, *On Idolatry* 14, and *Ad Nationes* I.19; Clement of Alexandria, *Exhortation to the Heathen* 11 f., *Stromata* II.9, IV.7, and VI.9; Origen, *Against Celsus* VI.36, 44, and VII.32; Hippolytus, *Refutation of All Heresies* IX.19; Cyprian, *On the Lapsed* 26 ff., *Epistles* X.2, XX.2, XXVI.1, and LIV.17; Lactantius, *The Divine Institutes* II.13, 16, and IV.27.

16. Irenaeus, *Against Heresies* V.12.6.

thought, when the spirit of God gains complete control in the world, these forces of evil will be ruled out entirely and illness will disappear. In the meantime,

As He suffered, so also is He alive, and life-giving, and healing all our infirmity . . .[17]

He freely bestows life on you . . . He Who expels destruction and pursues death . . . He Who builds up the Temple of God in men, that He may cause God to take up His abode in men. . . .[18]

. . . without hesitation accept . . . what you have seen already on every side; nor doubt that God, Whom you have discovered to be the restorer of all things, is likewise the reviver of the flesh.[19]

Within the church the Spirit of Christ still lived. It was available to Christians, ready to indwell those who followed him. The first and major battle with the forces of evil had been won. If the devil was still around, particularly in the dark corners, the church had ways to continue the fight. It could also offer healing for the bodies and minds as well as the souls

17. Irenaeus, *Fragment* from the lost writing 52.
18. Clement of Alexandria, *Exhortation to the Heathen* 11.
19. Tertullian, *On the Resurrection of the Flesh* 12. There are a great many of these passages about the saving action of Christ, the atonement, and the effect on man here and now, his flesh, and his diseases, bodily and otherwise. They are also found in *The Epistle of Barnabas* 16; Ignatius, *Epistles to the Smyrneans* 5, *to the Ephesians* 3, 7 f., and 17, *to the Magnesians* 1 and 5, *to the Philadelphians* 9, *to the Trallians* 9; the *Epistle to Diognetus* 9; Justin Martyr, *The Second Apology* 13, *Dialogue with Trypho* 17 and 30, Fragments of the lost work *On the Resurrection* 10; Theophilus of Antioch, *To Autolycus* I.7; Athenagoras, *A Plea for the Christians* 10; Irenaeus, *Against Heresies* III.18.4, IV.20.2 and 4 ff., 33.4, 38.1, V.3.1. ff., 6.1 f., 11.2; Tertullian, *Of Patience* 15, *To His Wife* II.3, *On the Flesh of Christ* 6, *On the Resurrection of the Flesh* 34, 47, 54, and 57 f.; Clement of Alexandria, *Tractate: Who Is the Rich Man That Shall Be Saved* 37; *Stromata* IV.7, V.11, and VII.11; Hippolytus, *Treatise Against Boron and Helix*, esp. Fragment 2, *Discourse on the Holy Theophany* 7 f.; Origen, *Against Celsus* VII.32; Cyprian, *An Exhortation to Martyrdom* 10, *Epistles* 74.2 f. and 76.2; Methodius, *Oration Concerning Simeon and Anna* 1 and 5, *Homily on the Cross and Passion of Christ* 1.

of men, just as Jesus had done in his time.

Naturally the early church sought out the sick to care for them and heal them, just as it sought out sinners and tried to convert them. Healing was rescuing men from the domination of the enemy. This was the natural function of Christians as members of the body of Christ. It was not by chance that Christian churches came to be regarded as healing shrines competitive with the shrines of Aesculapius. It was also natural that in many places the Christian churches should take over the function of those temples as the pagan religion died out, and that a Christian shrine often appeared on the site of a former pagan temple.

In confrontation with the pagan world, the uniqueness of Christianity was clear. Celsus, who warned second-century pagans about the dangers of the new religion, sneered at Christians because sick and sinful people were acceptable to their God, who would not cast them off, and who indeed had sent his son to serve them.[20] Almost two centuries later the emperor Julian the Apostate gave much the same picture of fourth-century pagans and Christians when he wrote:

These impious Galileans give themselves to this kind of humanity: as men allure children with a cake, so they . . . bring converts to their impiety. . . . Now we can see what makes Christians such powerful enemies of our gods. It is the brotherly love which they manifest toward strangers and toward the sick and the poor.[21]

These men represent well the attitude toward the human body discussed above. It was the underlying outlook of the Hellenistic world in which Christianity grew up, expressed in the mystery cults, philosophies like the later Pythagoreanism and the Docetism and Gnosticism both inside and outside the church. They

20. Origen, *Against Celsus* III.71 ff. Much of the work of Celsus is extant because Origen refuted it point by point, quoting whole sections.
21. Juliani Imperatoris, *Quae Supersunt Praeter Reliquias apud Cyrillum: Omnia*, 1:391 f.

were all views which separated out the mind or soul from the grosser body, concerning themselves only with the part of man that was considered valuable and finding some assurance that it would live on. These approaches to life—involving either *(a)* secret rites and union with a bodiless god, or *(b)* a passing to higher and higher stages of esoteric knowledge—found no particular value in the healing of the body; they concentrated rather on freeing the soul from its prison, the physical world.

The church stood firm against both of these efforts. It continued to see salvation as the redemption of the total man, not just his liberation from the body. The Hebrew idea that God created the world and it was good, and was meant to be good, was never lost to the mainstream of Christian thought. The value of the body and the saving action of Christ for both body and soul remained a cardinal doctrine of the early church. (Since one's thinking is likely to have quite an influence on one's ultimate behavior, the actual theology of the body in today's church would be an interesting study.)

In the second and third centuries, at any rate, Christians acted upon their belief that the spirit of God would work through them and through the sacraments to save men both physically and spiritually. As a result, what they had to say theologically kept alluding to experiences of healing then happening in the church. Practically every one of the writers set down at least some fact or a general view of the healing he himself had seen.

The Facts about Healing

The prevailing acceptance of healing as a norm in the Christian church appears from many sources. In the very early and imaginative *Shepherd of Hermas* we find a fascinating reference to those who did *not* undertake to relieve illness and distress in the Christian way. "He therefore," Hermas wrote, "that knows the calamity of such a man, and does not free him from it, commits a great sin, and is guilty of his blood."[22] Indeed the healing of physical illness was seen in this period as telling evidence that the Spirit of Christ was actually present and at work among Christians. Since both bodily and mental illness were a sign of domination by some evil entity, the power to heal disease was prime evidence that the opposite spirit—the Spirit of God—was operating in the healer. Thus the healing of "demon possession" was often spoken of in conjunction with curing illness from other causes.

Quadratus, one of the earliest apologists, wrote in Rome that the works of the Savior had continued to his time and that the continued presence of men who had been healed left no question as to the reality of physical healing. Justin Martyr tells in several places how Christians healed in the name of Jesus Christ, driving out demons and all kinds of evil spirits. Writing about the charismata, the gifts God pours out upon believers, he calls attention to the power to heal as one of the particular gifts that was being received and used.

Theophilus of Antioch specified the physical healing of human beings he had witnessed as particular evidence that the resurrection was beginning to work in them and death being put to flight; he also spoke of the fact that demons were sometimes exorcised and confessed their demonic nature. Tertullian, as we have seen, explicitly identified persons who had been healed and testified to their great number and the wide range of physical and mental diseases represented. Elsewhere he also says that God could, and sometimes did, recall men's souls to their bodies.[23]

22. *The Shepherd of Hermas* III.X.4 in *The Apostolic Fathers*, trans. Archbishop William Wake (1909), 1:299.

23. References to healing by these various writers are found in Quadratus, *Apology*, (fragment); Justin Martyr, *Second Apology: To the Roman Senate 6, Dialogue with Trypho* 30, 39, 76, and 85; Theophilus of Antioch, *To Autolycus* I.13 and II.8; Tertullian, *To Scapula*, 4, *The Soul's Testimony* 3, *The Shows* (or *De Spectaculis*) 26 and

In the *Acts of S. Eugenia,* who is portrayed as being so close to God that she could cast out devils, it is told how a certain noblewoman of Alexandria was healed of a recurring fever when Eugenia prayed over her. And Minucius Felix, who wrote about the end of the second century, describes the exorcism of demons in these words:

Since they themselves are the witnesses that they are demons, believe them when they confess the truth of themselves; for when abjured by the only and true God, unwillingly the wretched beings shudder in their bodies, and either at once leap forth, or vanish by degrees, as the faith of the sufferer assists or the grace of the healer inspires.[24]

Perhaps the most interesting discussion of healing among the ante-Nicene fathers came from Irenaeus in Gaul, who undoubtedly wrote more freely through being somewhat removed from the danger of persecution that faced most of these men. In *Against Heresies* one of his telling points was that heretics were not able to accomplish the miracles of healing that Christians could perform. They did not have access to the power of God and so could not heal. One wonders what he would say of modern Christianity, liberal and fundamental.

Irenaeus attested to almost the same range of healings as we have found in the Gospels and Acts. All kinds of bodily infirmity as well as many different diseases had been cured. The damage from external accidents had been repaired. He had seen the exorcism of all sorts of demons. He even describes the raising of the dead. His pagan readers were well aware of these miracles of healing, as he makes clear, since this was often the path to conver-

29, *Apology* 23 and 27, and *On the Soul* 57. Also Tatian, *To the Greeks* 17 f. and 20; while in the earliest Clementine literature an instruction is found for Christians to visit the sick as bearers of the Holy Spirit and healing, *First Epistle Concerning Virginity* 12.

24. Minucius Felix, *The Octavius* 27. Also *Acts of S. Eugenia* 10 f.—cf. Edgar J. Goodspeed, *The Story of Eugenia and Philip* (1931), pp. 80 f.

sion for pagans, as well as the means of bringing bodily health
to both Christians and non-Christians. It is interesting that he
also mentions the fact that no fee was charged for healing performed by Christians, a practice quite different from the pagan
temples of healing such as the famous ones in Epidaurus and
Pergamum.[25]

There is no indication that Irenaeus viewed any disease as
incurable or any healing as against God's will. Indeed the whole
attitude he voiced was that healing is a natural activity of Christians as they express the creative power of God, given them as
members of Christ. But fifty years or so later Cyprian was com-
plaining that the church lacked strength in prayer because it was
growing more worldly and so giving power to the enemy. Appro-
priately enough, this passage comes from his book *On the Lapsed*.
Even so, Cyprian discussed in other passages the means by which
healing continued to take place within the church.

At the same time Origen also showed that the gift of healing
extended even to Greeks and barbarians who came to believe in
Jesus Christ, and these men sometimes performed amazing cures
by invoking the name of Jesus. "For by these means," he wrote,
"we too have seen many persons freed from grievous calamities,
and from distractions of mind, and madness, and countless other
ills, which could be cured neither by men nor devils."[26] Origen
saw that the name of Jesus (or a man's belief) could bring about
a complete change even in his body, by removing a diseased
condition. In one place he adds that demons were sometimes
driven even out of the bodies of animals, which could also suffer

25. Irenaeus' discussions of healing are found in *Against Heresies* II.6.2, 10.4,
31.2, 32.4 f., and III.5.2.

26. Origen, *Against Celsus* III.24; also I.6, 25, 46 f., and 67, II.8 and 33, III.24,
28, and 36, VII.35 and 67, VIII.58. References in Cyprian's works occur in *On the
Lapsed* 6 f.; *On the Vanity of Idols* 7; and *Epistle* 75.12 f. and 15 f. There are similar
statements in Hippolytus, *Scholia on Daniel* X.16; Dionysius of Alexandria, *Epistle
XII, To the Alexandrians* 4; and Clement of Alexandria, *Who Is the Rich Man That
Shall be Saved?* 34.

injury inflicted on them by evil spirits.

Finally, at the beginning of the fourth century both Arnobius and his pupil Lactantius wrote about healing. While Arnobius spoke mainly of Jesus and his apostles, his point was that none of Jesus' healings were so miraculous or astonishing that he did not freely put them within the power of the humble and rustic men who followed him. Arnobius' implication is clear, and Lactantius added what he had seen in the church in his time, writing:

As He Himself before His passion put to confusion demons by His word and command, so now, by the name and sign of the same passion, unclean spirits, having insinuated themselves into the bodies of men, are driven out, when racked and tormented, and confessing themselves to be demons, they yield themselves to God, who harasses them.[27]

Several methods of healing are mentioned in the various writings cited, and we find practices very similar to those recorded of Jesus and the apostles. Prayer along with laying hands on the sick is specifically mentioned; undoubtedly oil was used. Sometimes prayer alone was effective; or again, the result was obtained by calling on the name of the Lord or even mentioning some fact of his life. In one place Irenaeus speaks of the prayer and fasting of an entire church as effective in raising a person from the dead.

Nearly all the ante-Nicene fathers note the successful use of exorcism. During those powerful years of the church's life the Christian group was recognized for its ability to treat the mentally sick or "demon-possessed." The church, as its early writings show, was the place to which people came to find this help. Exorcism was so much a part of its life that the writers of the time

27. Lactantius, *Epitome of the Divine Institutes* 51—cf. also *The Divine Institutes* II.16 and V.22; Arnobius, *Against the Heathen* I.48 ff.; Victorinus of Petau, *On the Creation of the World*. Many stories of healings also occur all through the apocryphal works and religious romances of this time. While these do not give firm evidence of healings, they do give a picture of the mental horizon of the time as to the fact of healing and its prevalence.

give little thought to defending it; they mostly write about the results. It appears, however, that it was performed in several ways. One method was to rebuke the evil spirit in the name of Jesus Christ. Another was to touch or lay hands upon the possessed person; a third way was to breathe upon him. Sometimes stories of Jesus may have been told, and holy water was probably used.[28]

This was not only a priestly function, but in the third century specially selected laymen were trained for it. In fact, the order of exorcists soon grew so large that one bishop in Rome complained that they outnumbered the priests.[29] During this period candidates for baptism were all exorcised, and vestiges of this practice are found in the Roman order of baptism today.

Indeed, the sacraments themselves were a direct source of healing. Cyprian, discussing the fact that wicked spirits no longer found a home in the bodies of Christians who were coming to know the Holy Spirit after baptism, wrote, "This, finally, in very fact we also experience, that those who are baptized by urgent necessity in sickness, and obtain grace, are free from the unclean spirit wherewith they were previously moved, and live in the Church in praise and honour. . . ."[30] The same direct effects were known to flow from the forgiveness of sins and from the Communion itself—spoken of as a renewal of flesh and blood. Besides the sacramental actions of exorcism and laying on of hands, the sign of the cross (the *sphragis*) was also generally used, in renewal

28. Aside from aspects of mental illness and other phases of the self which we shall consider in chap. 11, exorcism may have more relevance for our day than most of us have considered. One should look at the evidence from recent times presented by Leon Christiani in his *Evidences of Satan in the Modern World* (1962); and in *Demonism Verified and Analyzed*, written by Hugh W. White, a missionary in China, in 1922 and reprinted in 1963. Wm. Peter Blatty mentions other standard sources in *The Exorcist*, (1971).

29. About the end of the fourth century, abuses made it necessary to abolish the order and transfer this function to the priesthood.

30. Cyprian, *Epistle* 75.15 f.

of protective and authoritative healing power when one felt danger from evil spirits. Evidence for this effect of sacramental action—conveying grace to body as well as soul—is found in most of these works[31] and also in the liturgies which we shall discuss later.

The Victorious Christians

For nearly three centuries this healing, centrally experienced, was an indispensable ingredient of Christian life. The same strengthening force was at work, not only in dealing with physical and mental disease, but in meeting persecution. The power, the same profound experience, was given to these men and women to meet agonizing death, often by slow degrees, without yielding to save themselves by repudiating Christianity. Thus the martyrs, too, stood as continuous evidence of a power able to strengthen them beyond normal expectations of human life, and of the Christian's relation to the source of that power.

There are many examples of the belief that the Spirit of God enabled the martyrs to withstand and overcome the torture to which they were subjected by the pagan world. Ignatius on his way to martyrdom testified to the amazing resource upon which

31. For instance, *The Epistle of Barnabas* 6 and 16; Justin Martyr, *Dialogue with Trypho* 14, *The First Apology* 66; Irenaeus, *Against Heresies*, various places, particularly IV.18.5, V.2.2. f. and 11.1; Tertullian, *On Baptism* 5, *To His Wife* II.5; Clement of Alexandria, *Stromata* I.20 and II.11; Origen, *Against Celsus* VI.48; Hippolytus, *Discourse on the Holy Theophany* 8; Cyprian, *Demonstration of the Apostolic Preaching* 97, *On the Dress of Virgins* 2; Vincentius of Thibaris in *The Seventh Council of Carthage under Cyprian (A.D. 258)*; and the *Recognitions of Clement* II.71 and IV.17. A story is also told by Gregory of Nyssa—a careful writer—about a deacon in this period who arrived at a certain city late one day and insisted on taking a bath. He was told that a demon visited the public baths at night and inflicted incurable diseases or other harm on anyone who entered. Finally he was given the key and went in to meet the terrifying visions of the demon; but in each room he made the sign of the cross, and the demon left. When he came out unharmed, the guard could hardly believe his eyes. S. Gregorii Nysseni, *De Vita S. Gregorii Thaumaturgi*, in Migne, *Patrologiae Graecae* 46 (1869), col. 951.

these men drew in their trials. The author of the *Epistle to Diognetus* expressed the conviction of almost all contemporary witnesses: "Dost thou not see men cast to wild beasts in order that they may deny their Lord, and yet they are not conquered? . . . These seem not to be the deeds of man, these things are the power of God; these are the signs of His Presence."[32]

Cyprian, writing during the Decian persecutions, told of instance after instance of the power of Christians to stand above and be victorious over torture and death. Gregory Thaumaturgus, an eyewitness of these martyrdoms, wrote in *A Discourse on All the Saints*, "And if any one believes not that death is abolished . . . let him look on the martyrs disporting themselves in the presence of death, and taking up the jubilant strain of the victory of Christ. O the marvel! Since the hour when Christ despoiled Hades, men have danced in triumph over death."[33]

One finds the same conviction, the same power, in the specific accounts of martyrdoms. The pagans who witnessed them were amazed—stunned—by the casual way in which Christians met death, not just stoically but with a joyous abandon. Undoubtedly this power, vividly evident, was a crucial factor in drawing many pagans to the Christian church. These people had such conviction, such strength and joy, that not even death affected them— or torture either. And the men and women who saw it, and hungered for such authority, such serenity and conviction, were drawn to the group which could give these gifts. The blood of martyrs was indeed the seed of the church, for here was manifest the reality of a power over agony of mind and body, and joyful equanimity in death.

Strength given by God was both reality and necessity for these

32. *The Epistle to Diognetus* 7, *Apostolic Fathers*, 2:187.
33. Gregory Thaumaturgus, *A Discourse on All the Saints*, as translated in Evelyn Frost, op. cit., p. 55. There is, however, some question as to the authenticity of the work.

men and women who outlived and outdied the ancient world. But the era was ending. What place would this great power find in everyday life as Christianity moved out into a newer world that was trying to be friendly?

8

HEALING IN THE VICTORIOUS CHURCH

With the victory of Constantine and the Edict of Milan in 313, persecution of the church almost ceased, and this freedom opened up a new era in the church's life. In a very short time the tables were turned and Christianity became, first an accepted religion, then the established religion of the empire. Religious freedom seems to act as an intoxicant on some people, and elements within the church reacted to Constantine's acceptance with a rash of heretical doctrines and ideas. Besides the Arians, who wanted to make doctrine about Christ more rationally acceptable and less paradoxical, there were dozens of other groups, now almost forgotten, each intent on proving it had the right line of reasoning to explain Christian experience. Great leaders arose to bring order out of this theological chaos. There was a burst of activity and creativity which brought a flow of new literary work.

Although few clergy and fewer lay Christians are acquainted with these leaders or their writings, most of them are preserved in the magnificent edition of J.-P. Migne. There is no lack of firsthand evidence. Letters, sermons, theological studies, and biblical commentaries lie hidden for the most part in the more than three hundred volumes of this library of the fathers. Only a small number of these works have been translated from the original

Greek and Latin in which they were printed in the nineteenth century.

Anyone wanting to know the theological ideas of the men who set the mold for all later Christian thought can find hundreds of works by scholars who have combed much of this rich material. Its theological content is well known. If, however, one is looking for evidence of the attitudes of this time toward healing or dreams, visions or demons, one looks in vain. Until my book, *Dreams: the Dark Speech of the Spirit*, no one in recent years had examined the experience or thought of these church fathers with regard to dreams and visions. Yet they believed that God used these means to touch the lives of men. Dr. Frost's study covers interest in healing in the church before the victory of Constantine, but there her record comes to an end. No one has continued her work, and the modern explorer of the subject is on his own, in virgin territory. The prejudices of the nineteenth century against healing in the church did not encourage patristic scholarship in these areas. Indeed, when scholars came upon passages which told of healings, they either ignored them or wrote condescending notes.

As one plunges into the voluminous literary remains of the victorious church, one finds there the same essential practice and theory that began in the New Testament and continued through the dark days of persecution. One change may be observed, however. The church was now flooded with nominal Christians who found that membership brought favor rather than disfavor. This was hardly the climate for militant enthusiasm, commitment, or works of healing. Such Christians did not, one must suppose, produce healings, but where vitality of faith and dedication were found, the record shows that healing continued as in the preceding age.

The materials on the subject from this period might well be the substance of an entire book. We shall try to present the evidence of the Christian empire and its writers at this time in one chapter, as briefly as possible, selecting only those acknowledged as the greatest thinkers and avoiding the religious romances in which fact and fancy are intermixed—of which there were many. Exhaustive reference to the sources is required throughout, since the material is not gathered together anywhere else.

The Doctors of the Church

The Christian church, emerging from underground life to become one of the most important institutions in the Byzantine Empire, now produced some of its greatest minds. There were a host of problems. In addition to theological confusion, the new position in the empire posed several insistent questions. What was to be the relation of the church to the imperial government? What was the Christian's role as a legal citizen or servant of the empire? How did he reconcile himself to the world? If Christianity was to survive its adoption by emperors it had to rework its theology, its ethics, its educational methods, and its political theory and thus develop a secure intellectual base.

The great Athanasius broke ground for other thinkers and laid the foundation for all subsequent Christian thinking. Almost single-handed he stood against emperor and Arian bishops as defender of the Trinitarian faith. His long life span, from 296 until 393, saw orthodoxy solidly accepted. In the East he was followed by four men of culture, intellectual power, and saintliness. Together they forged the structure of dogmatic Christianity, which has changed but little in the East since their time. Three were known as the great Cappadocians: Basil the Great (329–379), his brother Gregory of Nyssa (331?–396), and their friend Gregory of Nazianzus (329?–389). All were theologians—they were considered the finest minds of their time, Christian or

pagan. John Chrysostom (345–407), known as "the Golden-
mouth" for his eloquence, was the greatest preacher of the time
and popularized the ideas of the other three. All four were bishops and directed the practical affairs of the church as well. We
shall see that they recorded the practice of healing in the church
and had a place in their theology for it as well.

Meanwhile the West produced four men in the same general
period who were later acclaimed as doctors of the church. The
saintly Ambrose (340?–397) laid the foundations for the papacy as
well as interpreting the conclusions of Eastern orthodoxy for the
West. He was followed by Augustine (354–430), whose education
was second only to Basil's and his intellectual contribution to
Christianity scarcely second to any. His voluminous writings set
the direction of the western church for the next thousand years.
Jerome (340–420) was one of the less attractive figures of this
period, although he was the scholar among doctors of the church,
translating the Bible into Latin —the Vulgate—and thus leaving
his imprint on all western Christians. The fourth illustrious doctor of the West, Gregory the Great, came nearly two centuries
later—born in 540 and living into the early part of the seventh
century. Although we find accounts of healing among these various men, they viewed it from disparate angles, and eventually
this made a great difference. We shall also consider at some length
the teachings and records of two other figures who came from
roughly the same early stretch of time: Sulpitius Severus, the
biographer of St. Martin of Tours, one of the most popular of all
wonder-workers, and John Cassian, who set forth much of the
thought behind Western monasticism.

These ten men started from a common intellectual point of
view. All built upon the theological foundations of the post-apostolic thinkers described in the last chapter. They believed in a
basically Platonic world view. They saw man as subject to both
physical and spiritual powers. They believed in the destructive

elements of the spiritual world which they called demons, as well as in the positive, angelic aspects of it. Seldom did these men project such ideas into physically absurd concreteness. They believed that demons attacked men's psyches directly, bringing physical and mental illness. They accepted the crucifixion and resurrection as events indissolubly linked, through which the demonic host was defeated, and believed that those who were filled with the Spirit of Christ had power to turn back demonic attack and to bring healing.

Healing itself was considered one of the evidences that creative spiritual powers were working through human beings. These men accepted Plato's basic thinking on the subject, which I have outlined in an earlier chapter; his thought is indeed quite in line with much of modern science, as we shall see presently. In fact, one psychiatrist who read this manuscript remarked that it might well serve as an historical introduction to the study of psychosomatic medicine.

Many of the incidents these men relate will be very difficult for the modern reader to accept—particularly those who are still immersed in the almost wholly materialistic world view of the nineteenth century. Those, however, who have gone out of their way to witness and verify the healings of an Agnes Sanford or a Kathryn Kuhlman will realize that they are seeing the same kind of thing as was observed and recorded by these sophisticated and brilliant men who laid the intellectual foundations of all mainline Christianity.

Four historians are responsible for recording the events of the first six centuries of the church's life. None of them draw any particular attention to the healings they describe, but all occasionally include them in their histories. Eusebius was the first of the four; his work is a sober and careful account of the first years in the life of the church. Without his record we would know but little of the earliest centuries of Christian history. He was a

contemporary of Constantine as well as a friend of that first
Christian emperor, and tells in some detail of Constantine's conversion experience. The historians Sozomen and Socrates Scholasticus continue the record of Eusebius, building upon his narrative and adding materials from the following centuries. Finally
Theoderet draws upon them all and carries the account on into
his own time. These successive writers show no particular fasci-
nation with the miraculous, but occasional healings are a part of
the history they record. They are certainly no more credulous
than the secular historians of their age.

Socrates, for instance, tells how Maruthas, the Bishop of
Mesopotamia, cured the Persian king of headaches which the
Magi had not been able to relieve, and that Maruthas was permitted in consequence to establish churches wherever he wished in
Persia.[1] In the great church built by Constantine in his new
capital, on the other hand, an attorney was healed whom Sozomen had known when he was practicing law there. This man was
unable to retain any food, and his physicians were baffled; half
dead (as Sozomen tells it), he had his servants carry him into the
church, praying earnestly either to die or to be freed of the
illness. In the night a divine power appeared to him and told him
to dip his foot in honey, wine, and pepper. Quite against the
opposition of his physicians, he did as he was told and was cured.[2]
These two instances are more or less typical of those that recur
in the historical tradition.

1. Socrates Scholasticus, *Ecclesiastical History* VII.8. Unless otherwise noted,
references to the historians and fathers of the church are found in *A Select Library
of the Nicene and Post-Nicene Fathers of the Christian Church* (various dates).
2. Sozomen, *The Ecclesiastical History* II.3. The following references locate all
the healings we have found in these historians: Eusebius, *The Church History* I.13;
IV.3; V.7; VII.18; Socrates Scholasticus, *Ecclesiastical History* I.17, 19, 20; IV.23, 24,
27; and VII.4; Sozomen, *The Ecclesiastical History* II.1, 6, 7; III.14; IV.3, 16; V.21;
VI.16, 20, 28, and 29, VII.27; Theodoret, *The Ecclesiastical History* I.17, 23; IV.14,
16, and 18; also, *The Sayings of the Fathers* V.37, and *History of the Monks of Egypt*
6, in Helen Waddell, *The Desert Fathers* (1936), pp. 66 and 115 f.

Healing and Desert Solitude

Discouraged with the worldliness of the church, increasing numbers of men went into the deserts of Egypt to recover the quality of life of the first Christians. Along with the greater intensity of inner life one finds also the expectation that healings would take place.

The beginnings of Christian monasticism in Egypt are not very well known today. Monastic orders in the West soon took quite a different direction. Even the eastern tradition, under the direct influence of the "desert fathers," came to look back more to their interpreters than to the men themselves. Until the present century the "histories" that recounted these beginnings were published only in versions rewritten, rearranged, often interpolated or interwoven, and so confused that they appeared to have little if any relation to actual fact. Most students simply scoffed at the experiences set forth; even Antony was assumed to be a fictional character, whose life could not have been written by the great Athanasius.

About the end of the last century, however, the most important of these histories was taken apart with a fine-tooth comb by Cuthbert Butler at Cambridge University.[3] This was the *Historia Lausiaca* of Palladius. Once its text had been extricated from other source materials, most of the problems about dates and the movements of persons were soon resolved. Palladius himself was authentic enough. He was in Egypt for about twelve years and after that went to Bithynia, where he was consecrated bishop. He was present at a synod in Constantinople in 400, and for his support of Chrysostom—particularly in Rome

3. The story of this painstaking research is found in vol. 1 of his work, *The Lausiac History of Palladius*(1967), and the resulting reconstructed text makes up vol. 2. The material that follows comes largely from this work.

in 405—he, too, was exiled for several years.

Palladius came to Alexandria as a monk in 388, and after some time there joined one of the colonies in the Nitrian desert for over a year. Twenty years later he set down what he remembered of these first monks or had been told by their disciples.[4] The stories he related were homely, often earthy, sometimes derogatory. He did not dwell much on beliefs, or dramatize their experiences, but recounted what these men did to try to conquer all desire for physical satisfaction, and how they knew another world of visions and healing and power over demons. There were both men and women who stayed alone for years praying and working, sometimes in cells like tombs; who kept themselves from sleep or fasted for long periods, ate only dry bread or raw things, wore only rags, or never bathed (so that they would not be reminded of the sexual practices that went on in the public baths). As he told it, some of them found complete dependence on Christ and the Spirit given by God. Some became so tenderhearted that they spent all their time caring for the needs of others; some were given powers of healing or prophecy.

Palladius described a number of healings in detail, including at least three that had happened in his presence. One of these occurred after he had been in the inner desert for some time, when a young boy possessed by an evil spirit was brought to Macarius there.[5] The latter put a hand on the boy's head and the other over his heart, and prayed; the boy's body became inflamed and swelled, until he seemed suspended in air. Suddenly he cried out, water poured from his body, and it returned to normal size. Macarius put him in his father's arms, cured, with a caution not to give him meat or wine for forty days. Similar occurrences are

4. The name "Lausiac History" came from Palladius' dedication of his book to Lausus, an official of the empire.
5. This was Macarius of Alexandria, a monk who was apparently the mainstay of those who lived in this area.

reported in many cultures, however difficult for many moderns to believe.

The old monk then revealed to Palladius his own temptation at one time to go to Rome and show off his gift for curing the sick, and how he had struggled to resist it, wearing himself out by carrying heavy loads across the sand. There were countless instances of his ridding people of demons; one was a noble woman brought from Thessaly who had been paralyzed for several years, and was cured when he anointed her with oil and prayed over her for twenty days. On another occasion Palladius begged Macarius to help a certain priest, who had sinned; he healed a cancerous growth on the man and also induced him to promise that he would live differently.[6]

The stories of several other monks who had power to heal and cast out demons are included in the *History* of Palladius.[7] He did not glorify the lives of these men, but showed that for most of them the struggle in dreams, or with "demons" who even did them bodily mischief, or with an inflated ego, was constant. He tells of hearing the old Macarius in his cell muttering to himself, "What do you want, you old man of evil? . . . Come, you white-haired old glutton, how long shall I be with you?"[8] He tells of quarrels and weaknesses; there were failures and near-failures, and some fell ill in the desert. Isidore of Scete, for instance, took care of a certain convert, Moses, who had given up a life of temptation and getting into trouble. He was sick for a year, but finally regained strength.

The great Isidore said then: "Stop contending with demons and do not bother them, for there are limits in bravery as well as in ascetic prac-

6. Butler, *op. cit.*, 2: 58 ff.
7. *Ibid.*, pp. 48, 79 ff., 83, 119, 104, 121, 113, 57, 55. Besides these there are other references to healing and casting out demons on pp. 47, 51, 57 f., 108, 115, 131, 132, 152, and also 89 f. (the story of a demon or temptation cast out in a dream).
8. *Ibid.*, p. 66.

tice." He replied: "I shall not stop before my fantasy of demons ceases."

Isidore said: "In the name of Jesus Christ, your dreams have vanished. Now receive Communion confidently. You were subjected to this for your own good, so that you might not boast of overcoming passion." And he went back to his own cell again. Later . . . [Moses] said he no longer suffered anything. He was deemed worthy of power over demons; we have a greater fear of flies than he had of demons.[9]

In their own way, these desert fathers tried to do as they felt Jesus Christ wanted men to do. Their lives left a record of healing and of prophetic encounters which deeply penetrated the Christianity of their age, an influence felt throughout the eastern church, and also in the West for a long time. The record of Palladius is difficult to accept, but it cannot be totally dismissed as mere fancy. Other reliable authors have set down the same kinds of things, and experiences similar to these are recorded today.

Convincing support for these accounts is found in the writings of Athanasius himself. It was late in life before he took time from his political and theological labors to write specifically on the desert monks and healing. He had taken refuge earlier with the monks in the Egyptian desert and was asked to write about Antony after his death. His *Life of St. Antony*, set down about 357, was soon referred to as "a rule of monastic life in the form of a narrative."[10]

In this deeply perceptive work Athanasius quoted, quite casually, the words of the old saint about his own healings and those of the other monks:

We must not boast of casting out devils, nor be elated at the healing of diseases, nor should we admire only the man who casts out devils, and account that one useless who does not. . . . To work miracles is not ours;

9. *Ibid.*, p. 70.
10. Gregory of Nazianzen, *Oration XXI*, On the Great Athanasius, Bishop of Alexandria 5, quoted by Johannes Quasten, in his *Patrology* (1960), 3:40

that is the Saviour's work. At any rate, He said to His disciples: "But do not rejoice in this, that the spirits are subject to you; rejoice rather in this, that your names are written in heaven."[11]

For this pillar of the church, as for the desert fathers who were considered the founders of monasticism, healing was simply one expression of men's devotion to Christ, to be used as he gave opportunity. He took for granted that such things happen, as did other Christians of his time. But Athanasius was in a peculiar position to appreciate it, for he had been called to a different profession, and his life was filled with doing things he had not expected to do.

Healing Among the Leaders

Few serious modern Christian theologians would lightly reject the theological reasoning of St. Basil or his close friend, Gregory of Nazianzus, yet these men also wrote of Christian healing. Is there any sound reason to ignore their thinking on the subject? Both had a good knowledge of medicine for their time—Basil, indeed, had some medical training—and with health none too good, both had a direct interest in practical medicine.[12] Gregory also had reason to be aware of the brilliant medical career of his brother Caesarius, while Basil founded and maintained a large hospital outside Caesarea—probably the first public institution devoted to care of the sick. At the same time, the two men were equally committed to the reality of healing through Christ. In place after place Gregory showed his understanding of the "deep roots" of disease and how closely the church's task with people

11. St. Athanasius, *Life of Saint Anthony* 38, in Roy J. Deferrari, ed., *Early Christian Biographies* (1952), pp. 169 f.
12. Numerous references to both medicine and religious healing in Gregory's writings are found in Sister Mary Emily Keenan's article, "St. Gregory of Nazianzus and Early Byzantine Medicine," *Bulletin of the History of Medicine* 9 (January 1941): 8–30.

was allied to the job of the medical practitioner.

He relates two incidents of healing in Basil's public life. The first occurred when he was about to be exiled by the emperor Valens, whose small son was suddenly sick and in pain. When physicians could not help the baby, the emperor had a change of heart and called for Basil, who came immediately; according to the reports of those present, the boy began to improve at once, but later died because his father was overanxious and asked the physicians to try their treatment again. The other incident also occurred during a personal conflict, this time with the Bishop Eusebius, who was then taken ill and called for him. He went willingly, and Eusebius confessed that he had been in the wrong and asked to be saved. According to Gregory his life was indeed restored, and Eusebius never ceased to wonder at Basil's power.[13]

Gregory also recounts some remarkable healings in his immediate family. One instance was widely known locally. His sister Gorgonia was dragged by a team of mules and so frightfully injured that no one thought she could recover; she was saved by the prayers of the congregation. Years later she had a second experience, which was understandably not spoken of outside the family while she lived. Gregory describes her illness as a burning fever alternating with periods of deathlike coma, with only brief remissions. He recounts how it continued in spite of prayers and all that several physicians could do. One night, in the middle of the night, she somehow made her way into the church and in despair took some of the reserved sacrament in her hand and knelt, grasping the altar. Crying out that she would hold on until she was made whole, she rubbed the precious substance on her body, and at last stood up, refreshed and stronger; she knew she was saved, and again a miraculous recovery had begun.[14]

Another account describes a similar healing of his father. On

13. Gregory Nazianzen, *Oration XLIII*, The Panegyric on S. Basil, 54 f.
14. Gregory Nazianzen, *Oration VII*, On his Sister Gorgonia, 15 ff.

Easter eve one year the elder Gregory was dangerously ill. The church was filled with people praying for his recovery as his son began the service. Just as the bread and wine were set out and all was quiet for the prayers of consecration, the old bishop suddenly woke and called out to his servant, who came running. He asked to be helped to his knees, and there beside the bed joined his people in celebration of the great rite. After pronouncing the final thanksgiving and blessing, he asked for food and then went to sleep quietly. On the next Sunday he was at the altar again to join his clergy in offering thanks for the miracle of his recovery and renewed vigor. As Gregory says, summing up the qualities of his father's life and the kind of events that filled it, "What wonder if he was thought worthy of the miracles by which God establishes true religion?"[15]

Several other events of this kind appear in Gregory's writings,[16] and in his theological poems the healing miracles of the Bible are made vividly alive. This fascinating family was so deeply at home in the reality of the spiritual world that healing could be sought and received naturally as a gift from God. It is no wonder that Gregory of Nazianzus was in so many ways the pivot on whom the establishment of an orthodox faith depended.

In telling how Gregory of Nazianzus took over in Constantinople at the end of the Arian controversy, the historian Sozomen adds an account of the healing of a pregnant woman in Gregory's church. He concludes that at least in this Orthodox church, "the power of God was there manifested, and was helpful both in waking visions and in dreams, often for the relief of many dis-

15. Gregory Nazianzen, *Oration XVIII*, On the Death of His Father, 27 ff.
16. One of the few times Gregory could remember his mother being ill she had a dream of his bringing her a "basket of pure white loaves" which he blessed at the altar and then fed to her. The vision was so real that when he stopped by in the morning to ask how she was, she was surprised; he must know very well how much better she felt. With the kindness that seems spontaneous in this family, Gregory conspired with her maids to keep her from knowing it had been a dream, lest the knowledge throw her back into depression. *Ibid.*, 30.

eases and for those afflicted by some sudden transmutation in their affairs."[17] This kind of healing was not often reported among the Arians whom Gregory replaced, and the Orthodox made the most of this apparent deficiency.

St. Basil was interested in practical matters and therefore in healing. In *The Long Rules,* one of the most important treatises on monastic life, he considered the question of "whether recourse to the medical art is in keeping with the practice of piety." His thinking has a modern ring to it. Medical science has been given to men by God, he contended, to be used when necessary, although not as the only decisive factor. Just as the Lord sometimes healed merely by uttering a command and sometimes by physical touch, so "He sometimes cures us secretly and without visible means when He judges this mode of treatment beneficial to our souls; and again He wills that we use material remedies for our ills."[18]

He discussed the various natural remedies provided by medicine, implying that these are also gifts for which God is to be thanked, and remarking that "to reject entirely the benefits to be derived from this art is the sign of a petty nature." On the other hand, there were reasons why a man might suffer sickness or fail to be healed. In considering them Basil did not deny either kind of healing to anyone, except possibly a saint like Paul. It might be necessary, he said, for a saint to suffer some infirmity to know that he was human, but "those who have contracted illness by living improperly should make use of the healing of their body as a type and exemplar, so to speak, for the cure of their soul."[19] In other words, saints and sinners alike might expect to suffer for getting off the beam, but redemption—for sinners at least—was very much like the healing of physical illness. The expectation

17. Sozomen, *Ecclesiastical History* VII.5.
18. Saint Basil, *The Long Rules* Q. 55, in his *Ascetical Works* (1950), p. 332.
19. *Ibid.,* pp. 333 and 336.

of healing as a normal Christian phenomenon apparently continued throughout Basil's active life. In his late sermon on "The Forty Holy Martyrs," for instance, he instructed his people: "Here is found a pious woman praying for her children, the return of her husband, his recovery when sick: let your prayers be made with the martyrs!"[20]

A Theology of Healing

The rest of the reporting of actual events by these men came from Gregory of Nyssa, younger brother of Basil the Great, whose preparation was quite different from the others'. Because of poor health Gregory remained at home. Fortunately his intellectual capacity made it possible for him to direct his own education. But he did not choose a career. Then came his famous conversion experience,[21] which did not immediately show fruit. He backed away, apparently, and became a rhetorician as his father had been. Basil protested. Then Gregory of Nazianzus also expressed strong concern, and the younger Gregory took his place in the church. The thinking of these three men—Basil, his friend Gregory of Nazianzus, and his brother Gregory of Nyssa—is so similar that one can practically speak for another. Indeed, Gregory of Nyssa finished his brother's important work, *Hexaemeron*, after Basil's death.

In *The Making of Man*, his thorough discussion of the healing miracles of Jesus revealed his understanding of the way man's faith and theology develop, starting from basic facts such as healing. Then in three very interesting subsequent works he had occasion to describe certain healings quite carefully. One was a sermon also telling about the dream that first brought him into

20. S. Basilii Magni, *In Sanctos Quadraginta Martyres* 8, J.-P. Migne, *Patrologiae Graecae* 31 (1885), col. 523.

21. This is described in chap. 6 of my book, *Dreams: The Dark Speech of the Spirit*, p. 135.

the church. This occurred at the shrine of the forty martyrs: Christians in the last major persecution who had stood by their faith even when the Roman army forced them into an icy pond to freeze to death.

Gregory told how the soldiers from a nearby base would bring their sick and injured men to the shrine. One night a lame soldier was in the shrine with several other men. He poured out prayers to God and to the martyrs, and in the night had a vision of a fine-looking man who said to him, "Lame one, do you need a cure? Give me your foot that I may touch it." As the soldier dreamed of dragging his leg forward, there was a wrenching noise and then a sound of violent impact that roused the others; and the soldier awoke and stood up cured. This was a man whom Gregory knew and had stayed with, who told everyone he met about the kindness of the martyrs and of his fellow soldiers.[22]

Soon after Basil died in 379, Gregory made a trip to their sister's retreat to find comfort. But she too was near death, and so, with the urging of those close to her, he began to write the *Life of St. Macrina.* This beautiful story was almost finished when a man, a military leader of the area, came to him to say, "Let me tell you what kind of good came out of her life, and how much there was of it." And he went on to tell what happened when he and his wife were visiting Macrina's convent, and

"there was with us our little girl who was suffering from an eye ailment resulting from an infectious sickness. It was a terrible and pitiful thing to see her as the membrane around the pupil was swollen and whitened by the disease. . . . I went to the men's quarters where your brother Peter was Superior, and . . . [my wife] went to the women's quarters to be with the holy one. After an interval of time . . . we were getting ready to leave

22. S. Gregorii Nysseni, *In Quadraginta Martyres,* in Migne, *Patrologiae Graecae* 46 (1863), col. 783. Gregory preached three sermons on the "forty martyrs," showing how he knew that they were still alive and active in people's lives. In his *Oratio Laudatoria Sancti Ac Magni Martyris Theodori* he invoked the help of St. Theodore again and again.

. . . but the blessed one would not let my wife go, and said she would not give up my daughter, whom she was holding in her arms, until she had given them a meal and offered them the wealth of philosophy. She kissed the child as one might expect and put her lips on her eyes and, when she noticed the diseased pupil, she said: 'If you do me the favor of remaining for dinner, I will give you a return in keeping with this honor.' When the child's mother asked what it was, the great lady replied: 'I have some medicine which is especially effective in curing eye disease.' . . . we gladly remained and. . . . started the journey home bright and happy. Each of us told his own story on the way. . . . [My wife] was telling everything in order, as if going through a treatise, and when she came to the point at which the medicine was promised, interrupting the narrative she said: 'What have we done? How did we forget the promise, the medicine for the eyes?' I was annoyed at our thoughtlessness, and quickly sent one of my men back to ask for the medicine, when the child, who happened to be in her nurse's arms, looked at her mother, and the mother fixing her gaze on the child's eyes, said: 'Stop being upset by our carelessness.' She said this in a loud voice, joyfully and fearfully. 'Nothing of what was promised to us has been omitted, but the true medicine that heals diseases, the cure that comes from prayer, this she has given us, and it has already worked; nothing at all is left of the disease of the eyes.' As she said this, she took our child and put her in my arms and I, also, then comprehended the miracles in the gospel which I had not believed before and I said: 'What a great thing it is for sight to be restored to the blind by the hand of God, if now His handmaiden makes such cures and has done such a thing through faith in Him, a fact no less impressive than these miracles.'"[23]

As Gregory noted, this was but one of several such miracles in Macrina's life that were talked about locally.

Gregory Thaumaturgus (the "Wonder-worker") came to Cappadocia in the days of persecution. His life and power made a tremendous impression, particularly on the families of the three

---

23. Saint Gregory of Nyssa, *The Life of St. Macrina*, in his *Ascetical Works* (1967), pp. 188 ff.

great Cappadocians. No wonder Gregory of Nyssa wrote a life of the saint. In it he told an eyewitness account of the casting out of a demon that was tormenting an adolescent boy, who then stood quiet and whole before a crowd of country people. In addition, his power against sickness of all kinds was known throughout the region.[24] Basil gives much the same account of this Gregory in brief form in his work *On the Spirit* (XXIX.74).

Gregory of Nyssa was the only one of the Eastern theologians who made a definite statement relating healing to his total theology. In two of his most important works, *The Great Catechism* and *On the Making of Man*, he referred to it as the main door through which a knowledge of God reaches men. First, in considering "the way Deity is mingled with humanity," he proposed unequivocally that, although the subject was unapproachable by the processes of reasoning, yet "the miracles recorded permit us not to entertain a doubt that God was born in the nature of man."[25] As he went on to show, this is so because healing is as much a divine gift as life itself. Later in the same work he considered how one can be certain that deity is present when called upon to enter into the elements used for baptism. And again he concluded that the ability to perform miracles is one evidence that the baptismal water has indeed conferred grace upon the baptized.[26]

On the Making of Man describes in graphic terms a number of the healings of Jesus, showing how central they were to faith in his resurrection. In other words, they opened people's eyes to knowledge that the resurrection was a possibility.[27] Thus healing

24. S. Gregorii Nysseni, *De Vita S. Gregorii Thaumaturgi*, in Migne, *Patrologiae Graecae* 46 (1863), cols. 942 f.; also 922 f. and 950 f., where these healing powers are also considered.
25. Gregory of Nyssa, *The Great Catechism* XI.
26. *Ibid.*, XXXIV.
27. *On The Making of Man* XXV.6 ff. Similar reasoning is presented in *On the Soul and the Resurrection*.

miracles were in the same category as the most important event in Christian history, only a little lower in the scale.

Healing from Another Perspective

A few years later, John Chrysostom in Antioch brought into the eastern church a different experience and contribution. He was as well educated as possible under pagan teaching and became the favorite of his teacher, the renowned Libanius.[28] Before the age of twenty he was a successful lawyer in the city, already earning his appelation of "golden-mouth." Then Meletius was made Bishop of Antioch, and apparently Chrysostom and the older man were drawn to each other. The youth abandoned the law and turned his life entirely to the church. Without leaving home, he had been found where the church needed him: in the city— first in Antioch and later in Constantinople—where not even Christians were very deeply concerned about morality.

From then on his consuming interest was to see the gospel lived—primarily in his own monastic life, and then, when his health prevented, in the lives of others—through moral commitment to it. This he constantly preached as the only base from which Christian experience could spring. And people came to listen, many of whom were far more at home in the theater than in church. When he applied the same truths to the empress and was banished for speaking out, they even followed him to his place of exile. He preached with sympathy, but never avoiding hard conclusions, and there was no question about the response. To this day Eastern Orthodox thinking still bases its doctrine on points he scored, particularly moral ones.[29]

28. This was the great classical scholar, friend of the pagan Emperor Julian, who had returned to Antioch after years in Athens and Constantinople.

29. See, for instance, *The Pedalion* (or "Rudder"), trans. Cummings (1957). This basic reference book of Greek Orthodox faith alludes to Chrysostom again and again.

At the same time, Chrysostom did not overlook the reality of healing or the expectation of actual miracles in his own time. He expanded on the healings of Jesus and the apostles as few other writers did. In discussing the miracles in Acts he never lost sight of the fact that they were performed, and continued to be done, not by men but by God, whose power is always the same. The healing at the Beautiful Gate, he held, succeeded because these men called upon God for the things they ought to ask of him.[30] In his work written to comfort the monk Stagirius, who was suffering from severe depression with psychotic episodes, he put the emphasis entirely upon "demons" as the cause of the illness.[31]

Chrysostom never tired of mentioning the miracles he had known personally at the shrine of St. Babylas the martyr, near Antioch. In his treatise on the power of the martyr against the actions of Emperor Julian, he spoke of "the miracles . . . performed daily by the holy martyrs."[32] Once in a while he also gives details of a healing he knows of, such as the boy who was saved more than once by God's direct help. Left inarticulate after a fever, nothing the physicians did helped him. Finally when his mother was in despair and prayed, God loosed the cord that held his tongue useless. Another time the boy's eyes were so affected by thick discharge that no hope was held for saving his sight; and again out of despair, through prayer, God alone produced a miraculous recovery.[33]

But looking for the immediate action of the divine in a life next

30. St. Chrysostom, *A Commentary on the Acts of the Apostles*, Homily X. Also, for instance, *ibid.*, Homily I; *The Homilies on the Statues* X.7 and I.5 ff., where the illness of Paul and others are considered, first as proving their fully human nature and second as *permitted* (not caused) by God; finally, as no hindrance or even embarrassment to them. They went right on healing and doing other works without becoming indifferent or powerless.

31. S. Joannis Chrysostomi, *Ad Stagirium a Daemone Vexatum* I.1, in Migne, *Patrologiae Graecae* 47 (1863), col. 425 f.

32. S. Joannis Chrysostomi, *De S. Babyla, Contra Julianum et Gentiles* 12, in Migne, *Patrologiae Graecae* 50 (1862), col. 551.

33. St. Chrysostom, *A Commentary on the Acts of the Apostles*, Homily XXXVIII.

door was not Chrysostom's strongest point. He was more likely to complain, as he once did, of finding the sanctuary lamp empty when someone had run out of consecrated oil and wanted to anoint a sick friend. Or he might mention how much trouble the physicians were sometimes saved because simply sleep and prayer itself seemed to free a patient from his sickness.[34] Chrysostom knew almost too much about carelessness of both Christians and pagans in dealing with spiritual concerns.

In a lecture on the holy martyrs to men and women preparing for baptism, Chrysostom makes reference in passing to healing. The bodies of the martyrs have been left on earth so that Christians may reach out to them and so receive the greatest possible healing for either soul or body. The martyrs do not require the time and money it takes to procure the services of a physician, for

. . . if we stand beside them with faith, whether our sickness be of the body or the soul, we will not leave their tombs without the healing of which we stood in need . . . here we need none of these things, neither the long journey, nor the trouble, nor the going back and forth, nor the expense; it is enough that we bring a loyal faith, that we shed warm tears and have a sober soul, for us to find forthwith a cure for our soul and healing for our body.[35]

Chrysostom goes on to note prayers that have been answered— a husband brought back from far away, a frightfully sick child made healthy.

These four men, combining the intellectual, practical, moral, and intuitive approaches, worked together to produce a theology of healing that has remained alive in the eastern church through the centuries. We shall see that this belief was enshrined in the records of public worship which have come down to us.

34. St. Chrysostom, *The Homilies on the Statues*, Homily VIII.1.
35. St. John Chrysostom, *Baptismal Instructions* VII.5 f., (1963), p. 106.

Liturgy and Healing

The forms of worship used by the early church may not seem an exciting study, but if we are to understand Christian life at that time it is essential. The importance of healing is clearly underlined in the liturgy of the church. The words and motions of the Eucharist carried the meaning of atonement and resurrection, of joining soul and mind and body in a kind of health that would last into life after death. With the comparatively recent discovery of the *Apostolic Tradition of Hippolytus* from about the year 215, we now have a good picture of how the idea of healing developed in early liturgies and how much it was an ingredient of ordinary life.

The early church orders of service were practical handbooks of Christian worship and often a good deal more. They are one of the principal sources we have for knowing what went on in the early churches, and not only describe the local forms of worship but also suggest the meaning then attached to these forms. They include a certain amount of moral instruction, and some are even presented as the picture of an ideal Christian community. Except for the earliest—the *Didache*, which grew out of a Jewish instruction for converts to Judaism—all give specific directions as to healing practices in connection with the central acts of Christian worship.[36]

36. Careful studies of Christian rituals to the present time, particularly in relation to healing, are found in W.K. Lowther Clarke's *Liturgy and Worship* (1954). The section on "Visitation of the Sick" is especially valuable, and we are indebted to this study for many of the references that follow. See also Jean Daniélou, *The Bible and Liturgy* (1956), for important insights about healing in connection with the biblical origins of various Christian rites.

The various service books are discussed by Burton Scott Easton in *The Apostolic Tradition of Hippolytus* (1962), pp. 9 ff. See also Bernard Botte. O.S.B., ed., *La Tradition Apostolique* [Hippolyte de Rome]: *D'Après Les Anciennes Versions* (1968), and Gregory Dix, ed., *The Treatise on the Apostolic Tradition of St. Hippolytus of Rome* (1968).

From the first the sacraments were expected to bring life and
health. Even in the *Didache* the formal prayers offering the bread
and wine for the Eucharist offer thanks first for life, and then for
life eternal. A century later, when Hippolytus came to set down
the tradition in Rome, oil reserved for the sick could also be
offered at the Lord's Supper, and thanks were given

. . . as at the offering of the bread and wine . . . in the same general
manner, saying, 'That sanctifying this oil, O God, wherewith thou didst
anoint kings, priests and prophets, thou wouldest grant health to them
who use it and partake of it, so that it may bestow comfort on all who
taste it and health on all who use it."[37]

As other liturgies became fixed, the same expectation was
found in the words of the Eucharist in widely scattered areas
from Gaul to Egypt, and the sacrament itself was offered as
"the specific medicine of life unto the healing of every illness."[38] As we have seen, this expectation might also attach to
baptism, and preparation for baptism became closely associated with healing.

At first the commission to heal was seen as a special gift or
charisma, much as Paul had spoken of it. The individual who
received this gift did not need to be ordained, as the *Apostolic
Tradition of Hippolytus* clearly shows in the direction: "If anyone says, 'I have received the gift of healing,' hands shall not
be laid upon him; the deed shall make manifest if he speaks
the truth."[39]A century later it was apparently common for
persons who received the gift of healing to ask to become
priests, and the later *Canons of Hippolytus* directed that the
facts be definitely proved before a healer was ordained. (53 f.)
The *Apostolic Constitutions* also provided for the ordination of

37. *Apostolic Tradition of Hippolytus* I.5, in Easton, *op. cit.*, pp. 36 f.
38. *Bishop Sarapion's Prayer-Book* I.I.c. ed. John Wordsworth, Bishop of Salisbury (1923), p. 63.
39. *Apostolic Tradition of Hippolytus* I.15, Easton, *op. cit.*, p. 41.

exorcists and healers.[40] (VIII.26)

By this time the clergy were instructed in the importance of visiting the sick, which Hippolytus had only mentioned. The *Canons* point out that visits by the bishop are "a great thing for the sick man. . . . He recovers from his disease when a Bishop comes to him, particularly if he prays over him." (199) While the *Canons* suggest that it is best for the sick to be present for public prayers, visits by the clergy are directed, with the clear intent that they should be able to heal. (219)

This intention is also found in the prayers for ordination, from deacons to bishops. There were prayers for a deacon to have power over demons, and that a presbyter be "filled with the gifts of healing," (*Apostolic Constitutions*, VIII.16), as well as the following specific prayer for either a presbyter or bishop: "Grant to him, O Lord, a mild spirit, and power to remit sins, and grant to him power to loose all bonds of the iniquity of demons [i.e., by exorcism], and to heal all diseases, and to beat down Satan under his feet quickly." (*Canons*, 17) Thus it was more and more understood that the gift of healing was conferred by the sacramental action of the church. What had been a charisma given to individuals was becoming a part of the priestly office, to be sought and used through the sacraments.

Lay Christians still continued to heal, but on a different basis. Besides services for visiting the sick, there were also prayers for sanctifying the oil and other objects which might be used to convey healing. *Bishop Sarapion's Prayer-Book* (IV.17) and the *Apostolic Constitutions* (VIII.29) both provided special prayers at the Eucharist for blessing oil, bread, or even water for the sick, which were then taken to sick persons to heal them. Oil in particular was a "sacramental" that could heal when power was given through the prayers and sacraments of the church. And, the

40. References to the *Canons of Hippolytus* are from Clarke, *op. cit.*, pp. 475 ff.; those to the *Apostolic Constitutions* are taken from *The Ante-Nicene Fathers*, 7 491-94.

shrines of the martyrs, both in the eastern church and in North
Africa, had come to have the same power, for in the remains of
a martyr holiness and therefore healing were seen as being still
implicit, by the sacrament of their devotion and death.

It is clear that people took the consecrated oil (or other things)
home to use when there was need. This practice caused enough
controversy by the fifth century for Innocent I to write to one
of his questioning bishops that Christians not only had the definite right, when sick, to be anointed by the clergy with holy oil,
but also "to use it themselves for anointing in their own need, or
in the need of members of their households." Three hundred
years later in England, when the Venerable Bede came to discuss
the needs of the sick in his exegesis on the letter of James, he
supported the same practice for his people, citing the pope's
letter as confirmation.[41]

This use of consecrated oil by ordinary Christians became
fixed in the Western liturgy through the forms for preparing
candidates for baptism. In Hippolytus' time new Christians, who
had been exorcised daily during their final preparations, were
anointed twice on Easter Sunday, the day of baptism. The "oil
of exorcism" was used first, and then the "oil of thanksgiving"
or chrism. As the rituals developed in Rome, these oils and also
oil for anointing the sick were blessed by the pope (or in other
places by a bishop) at the Chrismal Mass on the Thursday before
Easter. As Mgr. Louis Duchesne has described so carefully

Towards the end of the Canon the faithful brought small vessels of oil
to be blessed for their own use. This was the oil for anointing the sick,
and the faithful could make use of it themselves. It served also for

41. Innocentii I Papae, *Epistola*, XXV.8 in Migne, *Patrologiae Latinae* 20 (1845),
cols. 560-61. Also, Venerabilis Bedae, *Super Epistolas Catholicas: Expositio Super Divi
Jacobi Epistolam* V, in Migne, *Patrologiae Latinae* 93 (1862), col. 39. For further
evidence of this practice, see Hastings' *Encyclopedia of Religion and Ethics*, Vol. 5:
672 f.

extreme unction. The vessels containing it were placed on the balustrade
. . . and brought to the altar where the Pope blessed them, using the
following formulary:

"Send forth from the heavens, Thou who art our Lord, Thy Holy
Spirit, the Comforter, into this fat oil to bring forth, as from green wood,
things worthy for restoration of mind and body; let Thy Holy blessing
protect in mind and body, in soul and spirit, all who are anointed, all
who taste or carry it away, doing away with all pain, all infirmity, all
sickness of mind and body, blessing them as Thou didst anoint Thy
priests, kings, prophets and martyrs with Thy perfect unction, O Master, bringing it to continue permanent in our flesh, in the name of our
Lord and Master Jesus Christ."[42]

After the Communion the greater vessels of oil were blessed, as
is still done on Holy Thursday. This Mass has been celebrated
with high ceremony since about the sixth century, and with its
inclusion in the *Pontifical*—the service book for Catholic bishops
—the basic idea of anointing for healing was given a place in the
liturgy, where it remained for several centuries.

There was another form for healing, however, also found in
the oldest service books that have come down to us from the
Roman tradition. This was a form for visiting, anointing, and
laying hands on the sick, undoubtedly originating from the early
church orders of service. The eastern liturgy, starting from the
same forms of Hippolytus, provided a similar service, and we
shall see still provides such a service for use today. But in the
West the healing element or meaning was gradually laid aside,
and the service itself, while continuing in use, was transformed.

The oldest copy at present known of a western service for
visiting the sick comes from the library of a monastery in north-
ern France. It is part of a fairly complete service book dating

42. Mgr. Louis Duchesne, *Christian Worship: Its Origin and Evolution* (1919), pp.
305 f. The prayer is given in our translation from the Latin used by Duchesne.
See also Michel Andrieu, *Les Ordines du Haut Moyen Age* (1931–1948), 3: 468 f.

from before the reign of Charlemagne, and varies greatly from the later versions.[43] The contrast reflects the gradual change from healing to a service to speed the dying, of which more will be said later. Until at least the eleventh century the intention was definitely to heal. This earliest version called for several priests and members of the congregation to take part and pray with the sick man. They began by exorcising and blessing water and salt, which were mixed and sprinkled over the house. The prayers that follow call to mind the fact of healing in the New Testament and leave no doubt that health of body is what is being asked for.

The sick person then knelt for laying on of hands, suggesting that his recovery had begun. He was anointed on the throat, breast, and back, "and also," the service reads, "let him be more thoroughly and liberally anointed where the pain is more threatening." Besides general prayers of thanksgiving, he was told to pray for his own recovery; only after all this did he make any confession he had to make and receive Communion. Finally, priests and "ministers" were directed to come back for seven days to bring Communion; they were to repeat any part of the office that seemed advisable until the sick person was up and around.

It is hard to understand how this service could become a preparation for death, and in the East this did not happen. Instead the healing practices and attitude of the primitive church continued in the eastern liturgy. The *Euchologion*, the service book for most Orthodox churches, which had its beginnings in the early centuries of Christianity, still today provides a congregational healing service, performed if possible in church and by seven priests. But in case of necessity whoever is present represents the whole

43. This copy of the "Orationes ad visitandum infirmum" is found in the *Liber Sacramentorum* (Sancti Gregorii Magni), in Migne, *Patrologiae Latinae* 78 (1895), cols. 231-36. There is a preface, written by Hugo Menard about 1645, carefully describing the various manuscripts, and four variations of the service, down to the tenth century, are compared in detail (cols. 15-24 and 519-42).

assembly. Anyone seriously ill may be anointed whether in danger of death or not, and the service is performed as many times
as needed.[44] In practice the eastern rite of unction has been neglected and sometimes mixed with local superstition, but the
understanding still remains that the Holy Spirit, operating
through the body of the church, can heal the sick. There is no
essential difference between the understanding of Greek service
books and the thinking of the early doctors of the eastern church;
they are of one piece.

Healing in the West

The development of Augustine's thought holds special interest
for the understanding of Christian healing. He was the undis-
puted theologian of the West for nearly a thousand years. In his
early writings he stated quite specifically that Christians are not
to look for continuance of the healing gift. Then something happened, his skepticism gave way to belief in Christ's healing
power, and he frankly admitted that he had been wrong. In the
Confessions (VIII. (6).14) he acknowledged the important part
played by Athanasius' *Life of Antony* in his conversion. At that
time, however, physical healing among the desert fathers or elsewhere did not seem very important to him. Nearly forty years
later in 424, when his greatest work, *The City of God*, was nearing
completion, his outlook changed.

He took one of the important final sections of that work to
describe miracles of healing in his own diocese of Hippo Regius,
and how he instituted the recording and attesting of miracles
there. This was done, he wrote,

44. See the *Service Book of the Holy Orthodox-Catholic Apostolic Church* [*The Euchologion*, Tikhon ed.] (1922), pp. 332 ff.; also Aimé Georges Martimort, *L'Église en
Prière: Introduction à la Liturgie* (1961), p. 96. Richard and Eva Blum, *Health and
Healing in Rural Greece* (1965), pp. 208 ff., also offer most interesting present-day
confirmation of these facts.

... once I realized how many miracles were occurring in our own day and which were so like the miracles of old and also how wrong it would be to allow the memory of these marvels of divine power to perish from among our people. It is only two years ago that the keeping of records was begun here in Hippo, and already, at this writing, we have nearly seventy attested miracles.[45]

The City of God was completed in 426. The following year, three years before he died, Augustine wrote in the *Retractions* (more properly the "Revisions"):

I also said, *These miracles are not allowed to continue into our time, lest the soul should always require things that can be seen, and by becoming accustomed to them mankind should grow cold towards the very thing whose novelty had made men glow with fire. (De Vera Religione,* cap. 25, nn. 46, 47) It is indeed true: that not everyone today who has hands laid on them in baptism thus receives the Holy Spirit so as to speak in tongues; nor are the sick always healed by having the shadow of the promise of Christ pass across them; and if such things were once done, it is clear that they afterwards ceased.

But what I said should not be taken as understanding that no miracles are believed to happen today in the name of Christ. For at the very time I wrote this book I already knew that, by approaching the bodies of the two martyrs of Milan, a blind man in that same city was given back his sight; and so many other things of this kind have happened, even in this present time, that it is not possible for us either to know of all of them or to count up all of those that we do have knowledge of.[46]

What had happened to change his view? The story, which must be pieced together partly from sources still in Latin, begins with the discovery in 415 of the bones venerated as relics of St. Stephen the martyr. One of several shrines containing these relics

45. Saint Augustine, *The City of God* XXII.8 (1954), p. 445.
46. S. Augustini, *Retractationum* I.13.7, in Migne, *Patrologiae Latinae* 32 (1877), cols. 604 f. Another section (*ibid.*, I.14.15, col. 607), referring to *On the Advantage of Believing* 16.34, retracts a similar statement about miracles in much the same way. The miracle mentioned above as occurring in Milan is told in the *Confessions* IX.(7).16 and is described on p. 188, below.

was placed in Augustine's church in Hippo. In 424, two weeks before Easter, a brother and sister came to Hippo, both suffering from convulsive seizures. They gave a sad account of parental rejection and came each day to pray at the shrine for healing. On Easter morning before the service the young man was in the crowded church, praying as he held onto the screen around the reliquary.

Augustine was still in the vestibule, ready for the processional, when the young man fell down as if dead. People near were filled with fear. But the next moment he got up and stood staring back at them, perfectly normal and quite cured. When one after another had run to tell Augustine about it, the church finally quieted down for the service. In his sermon the bishop did little more than mention what had happened, but the young man stayed with him for dinner and they talked at length.

On the following days Augustine preached about St. Stephen, the healing, and also other martyrs and healings. On the third day after Easter he read the young man's statement, while both brother and sister stood on the choir steps where the whole congregation could see them—one quiet and normal, the other still trembling convulsively. Augustine then asked them to sit down, and was giving his sermon about the healing when he was interrupted by loud cries. The young woman had gone straight to the shrine to pray, and exactly the same thing had happened to her. Once more she stood before the people, this time healed, and in Augustine's own words, "Praise to God was shouted so loud that my ears could scarcely stand the din. But, of course, the main point was that, in the hearts of all this clamoring crowd, there burned that faith in Christ for which the martyr Stephen shed his blood."[47] In this last section of his final great work Augustine paid his dues, all at once, to the reality of healing. It

47. *City of God*, p. 450.

was one of the ways, he now saw, that men find how true the gospel really is, particularly the resurrection.

These facts can be read in *The City of God*, but the sequence and the connection with Augustine's understanding of healing must be followed in other places, particularly in his day-by-day sermons recorded at the time.[48] He continued to preach about healing, and by the time *The City of God* was completed in 426 he had witnessed another remarkable instance—also observed by the physicians of the man concerned, who had been preparing him for an operation which then was not required. Augustine likewise knew personally and in detail of several incidents. Some occurred in Uzalum, where his friend Evodius was bishop, others in Calama, where attested records had been kept for a number of years; in both places shrines had been dedicated to St. Stephen.[49] Just before his death Augustine himself, it was recorded, became a healer of others who came to him. The incident occurred during his last illness, after *The City of God* was completed and Hippo itself was under siege. His biographer Possidius mentions how he prayed with tears and supplication for certain demoniacs, and they were freed from possession. He then relates that after Augustine fell ill

a certain man came with a sick relative and asked him to lay his hand upon him that he might be cured. Augustine replied that, if he had any such power, he certainly would have first applied it to himself. There-

48. S. Augustini Episcopi, *Sermo CCCXVII-CCCXXIV* in Migne, *Patrologiae Latinae* 38 (1841), cols. 1435–47. See also F. van der Meer, *Augustine the Bishop: The Life and Work of a Father of the Church* (1961), pp. 549 ff., for a complete but critical account. In addition, in 425 Augustine sent some relics of St. Stephen to another bishop and wrote him suggesting that they be honored as they had been in Hippo. *Letters (204–270)* 212 (1956), pp. 51 f.

49. *City of God*, pp. 433 ff. The discovery of Stephen's relics through the vision of Lucian is told in *Epistola: Luciana ad Omnen Ecclesiam*, and several of the miracles at Uzalum are described in *De Miraculis: Sancti Stephani Protomartyris*, written for Evodius by an unknown author, Migne, *Patrologiae Latinae* 41 (1900), cols. 807–818 and 833–54.

upon, his visitor replied that he had had a vision and in his sleep had heard these words: "Go to Bishop Augustine, that he may lay his hand upon him, and he will be healed!" When Augustine learned this, he did not delay doing it and immediately the Lord caused the sick man to depart from him healed.[50]

Again with this great man as with Gregory of Nazianzus, dreams were closely associated with healing.

The very first healing mentioned by Augustine was also linked with a visionary experience. This was the vision that revealed to Ambrose, Bishop of Milan, where he would find the hidden bodies of the martyrs Gervasius and Protasius. When they were found, he had them placed in his new church, and a service was held in their honor. As the bodies were being laid on their biers, Severus, who had been blind for many years and was well known in Milan, begged to touch his handkerchief to the biers. He did so, and put it to his eyes, and his sight was immediately restored. At the same time many people who were possessed by unclean spirits were cured.

These events, which took place in Milan before Augustine's baptism, are recounted both in *The Confessions* and in the *Life of St. Ambrose* by Paulinus, who had been Ambrose's secretary as well as his friend and protégé.[51] Paulinus recorded several other healing miracles connected with Ambrose, including bringing a dead child to life again. His great power over unclean spirits is described, and there is one delightful story of Nicentius, a notary who was so crippled by pain in his feet that he was rarely seen in public. But when he came to church one day and had come up to the altar to receive the sacrament, the bishop accidentally stepped on his foot. He cried out with the pain and heard Am-

50. Possidius, *Life of St. Augustine* 29, in Deferrari, *Early Christian Biographies* (1952), p. 111.

51. St. Augustine, *The Confessions*, IX (VII). 16 (as well as in *The City of God* XXII.8, and in certain later sermons); Paulinus, *Life of St. Ambrose* 5.14, in Deferrari, *Early Christian Biographies* : 41.

brose say, "Go, and be well henceforth!" At the death of Ambrose he came weeping to say that from then on he had had no more pain.

Another incident was told of a healing involving the remains of martyrs and a vision of Ambrose after his death. A blind man dreamed of seeing men in white disembark from a ship, and of learning that one of them was the dead bishop and praying to him to be cured. In the dream Ambrose told him to go to Milan on a certain day and contact his "brothers" who were coming there. The man went, and on that day the bodies of Sisinius and Alexander, who had died in a recent persecution, were being carried to the church. He touched the bier and was given his sight.[52]

Far to the north in Gaul there was another man in this period whose remarkable healing powers are described. This was St. Martin of Tours who, almost single-handed, was responsible for establishing monasticism and thus education in the heart of what is now France. Martin's biographer, Sulpitius Severus, was almost equally interesting. He was a lawyer known for his accomplishments, and at the peak of his career, after the death of his wife, he withdrew from the active world to become a follower of the saint. His little *Life of St. Martin* dwells far more on the miraculous than most of the eastern records to which we have referred, and its emphasis on this aspect of the saint's life is difficult for the modern reader to accept. It is as if our Gospels had recorded healings and little else; one wonders in fact if the author's enthusiasm did not sometimes run away with him. On the other hand the actual accounts of healing are not very different from those of New Testament times.

Martin had been a soldier in the Roman army—an unusual one, who desired to live a Christian life. Probably the best-known incident of his career is his cutting of his only garment in two

52. Paulinus, *Life of St. Ambrose* 8.28, 9.44, 10.52; other healings are told in 3.10, 6.21, and 9.44. In Deferrari, *op. cit.* 50, 60, 64, 38 f., 45 f., and 60.

to share with a freezing beggar, and the dream that night in which Christ appeared to him clad in the half of his cloak he had given away. But when he was released from the army and became attached to a church, he did not feel worthy of serving at the altar. His bishop wisely appointed him to be an exorcist and thus learn in a more humble position.

His whole story is remarkable, simply because he cared so deeply about both God and men. His healings, miraculous as they were, seemed to flow naturally from this depth of spirit. On one occasion, returning to the monastery of which he had become head, Martin found the brothers mourning for a young follower who had died after a brief fever. Sulpitius relates that at first he wept.

> Then laying hold, as it were, of the Holy Spirit, with the whole powers of his mind, he orders the others to quit the cell in which the body was lying; and bolting the door, he stretched himself at full length on the dead limbs of the departed brother. Having given himself for some time to earnest prayer, and perceiving by means of the Spirit of God that power was present, he then rose up for a little, and gazing on the countenance of the deceased, he waited without misgiving for the result of his prayer and of the mercy of the Lord. And scarcely had the space of two hours elapsed, when he saw the dead man begin to move a little in all his members, and to tremble with his eyes opened. . . . Then indeed, turning to the Lord with a loud voice and giving thanks, he filled the cell with his ejaculations.[53]

There was a similar quality to the other stories. In one of them he maintained contact with a paralyzed girl until, little by little, her body gained strength and she walked. On another occasion, to get control of a demoniac who tried to bite anyone who came near, he put his own fingers into the man's mouth, saying to the demon, "If you have power, devour these," and the man drew

53. Sulpitius Severus, *Life of St. Martin* VII.

back as if burned, without hurting him. Then the cure could
begin.[54]

According to Sulpitius, pagans who were healed by Martin
often went away believers; they usually returned to prepare for
baptism, and regarded him with extraordinary affection. But
apparently there were some in the church who did not. Later, in
his *Dialogues of Sulpitius Severus,* he found it necessary to defend
Martin's gifts and to emphasize again his patience and the interest and love he showed for others. Sulpitius saw the gift of healing denied, and seemed to sense that it might be lost and the
experiences forgotten. He continued to describe the incidents he
knew, comparing them to what was being said of the monks in
the Egyptian desert and insisting that this kind of experience
should be listened to.

Beginning of a New Attitude

Despite the parallel experiences in the western church, understanding did not develop around them as it did in the East. The
events witnessed by Augustine in his own church, which
brought home to him the reality of healing, came near the end
of his life. They are reflected in only two of his writings, and he
does little more than present them as facts. Elsewhere his discussions of miracles, important as they were, often turned more
upon the wonders of the natural world than upon the effects of
the divine on physical man.

Writing about the same time, Jerome dealt with the subjects of
healing and monasticism, but not through any conscious development in personal experience. Because of his own great talents
he moved in a different direction, and together with his fiery
temper this probably did not encourage the occurrence of direct
incidents of healing around him. Yet he certainly felt the reality

54. *Ibid.*, XVI, XVII; other healings are told in XVIII, and XIX.

of such experience, and his letters referred again and again to the miracles of Jesus and others as if he were seeing them as he walked with the disciples on sacred ground. But healing as a present possibility got through to him mainly through the lives of others.

Jerome early became interested in the desert monks. We have a letter written to his friend Rufinus congratulating him for having gone to visit the famous desert monk, Macarius.[55] Soon Jerome retired to a nearby colony himself for five years, and in this period his *Life of Paulus the First Hermit* was written, an account of certain wonderful things that happened because St. Antony in his old age crossed the desert to take care of Paulus when he died. The monks in Egypt stirred Jerome's imagination, and finally after ten years, spent first with Gregory of Nazianzus and then in Rome, Jerome, too, made a visit to their abodes.

His party included Paula, who was to be his friend and helper for the rest of her life. Through her eyes perhaps more than his own, he saw "the Lord's glory manifested in . . . the Macarii" (Macarius of Egypt and Macarius of Alexandria, whose gift of healing was, if anything, even better known) and these "other pillars of Christ." Nearly twenty years later he wrote vividly of how they sought out each cell, finding Christ himself in these men.[56]

After leaving Egypt they went directly to Bethlehem, where Jerome and Paula founded a monastery and convent side by side, and a few years later Jerome wrote the book that expressed his

55. St. Jerome, *Letter* III.2, To Rufinus, the Monk. This was Macarius of Egypt whose story was told in various works, one of them the *Historia Monachorum* translated by Rufinus. See Butler, *Lausiac History* 1: 15 ff. and 2: 54 f.

56. St. Jerome, *Letter* CVIII, To Eustochium, written in 404. There is a statement in his *Life of S. Hilarion* which also makes one suspect that the closer Jerome got to things the less good he saw in them. Hilarion became a monk as a follower of Antony, but left after two months because he could not stand the crowds of sick and demon-ridden people who sought out the latter. It was "a strange anamoly that he should have to bear in the desert the crowds of the cities. . . ."

knowledge of the reality on which monasticism was based. This was the *Life of S. Hilarion,* who was born in Palestine, became a disciple of Antony, and returned to the desert near Gaza. Jerome tells how, after years of solitude and withstanding all kinds of demonic visions, Hilarion's reputation spread and people who needed healing began coming to him. There was a wife who had been childless for fifteen years; he told her to have faith and wept for her, and within a year she came to show him her baby. There were the three little boys consumed by fever, for whom he had to leave his retreat; he made the sign of the cross over their beds, and almost immediately they began to sweat and to recover. There was a demon who seized a man and made him rigid; when the man signified to Hilarion that he would live as a Christian, he was left free and healthy.

There are many other stories. Soon, Jerome recorded, crowds began to find Hilarion wherever he went. "Even the blessed Antony" gladly corresponded with him and told sick people about him. As his followers increased, monasteries were founded all over Palestine, and miracle after miracle continued in his life and even after his death. Jerome warmed to his subject as he remembered what had happened, and the account of miraculous gifts did not lose anything in the telling. For Jerome, too, was paying his dues to the reality of healing all in one fell swoop. But unlike Augustine's *City of God* his story was of events in the lives of others rather than any that left a deep imprint on his own life. It is a secondhand account by a man for whom the miraculous is central; this alone is enough to make the modern reader wary.

There were difficulties in Jerome's personal life which may well have made him afraid of the whole subject. His most vital contribution to Christianity was the Vulgate—that great work of scholarship which made the Bible available in the common tongue of the western church. In it his use of the strictly theological word *salvo* to translate both "save" (and thus heal or make whole) and "cure" in James 5:14 was strangely similar to the way he turned the Old Testament prohibition against "soothsaying" into a command to pay no attention to dreams.[57] Whatever his personal reasons, Jerome helped to turn the church's attention away from healing itself, focusing it on what healing represented symbolically.

Yet Ambrose, from whose presence healing seemed to flow naturally, also took this approach in his writings. In his work on the sacraments he describes Namaan's healing in the Jordan, not to show that healing is possible for Christians but to demonstrate the sanctification and curing of sins available in baptism.[58] For the most part Ambrose did not touch on healing.

One writer of some importance in the western church at this time, did express his ideas about healing. John Cassian spent several years among the monks in Egypt and also around Bethlehem, and he interpreted the thinking of the desert fathers for western Christians. His works had a significant influence on the

57. See pp. 115 f.; also my book *Dreams: The Dark Speech of the Spirit*, p. 159n. In the case of dreams, Jerome had had hot words with his former friend Rufinus over his own failure to adhere inflexibly to the literal direction of his great conversion dream. It seems very likely that he suffered real guilt over the accusations of Rufinus and allowed this to determine, more or less unconsciously, his translation of the particular Old Testament passages.

In the matter of healing, it would seem that Jerome had run-ins with some of the desert monks. Palladius tells of a Theban named Posidonius who had spent some time in a monastery outside Bethlehem, and expressed his opinion of Jerome quite freely. Palladius had a high regard for this Posidonius, with whom he lived for a year there near Bethlehem; he reported: "I knew of this prophecy made by this man: A priest, Jerome, dwelt in the same place; he was a man of good birth and well gifted in Latin letters, but he had such a disposition that it eclipsed his learning. Posidonius had lived with him a goodly number of days and he whispered into my ear: 'The fine Paula who takes care of him is going to die and escape his meanness, I believe.' " *Lausiac History* 36.6, also 41.2, in Butler, *op. cit.*, 2:104 and 118.

In addition, Jerome's first work on desert monasticism, the *Life of Paulus the First Hermit*, was not well received. Interestingly enough it did not even mention miracles of healing.

58. St. Ambrose, *The Sacraments* I.5.13 ff., in his *Theological and Dogmatic Works* (1963), p. 274.

growth of monasticism in the West; Cassian's *Conferences* was one of the books specified by St. Benedict, for example, to be read aloud each day to the assembled brothers. A discussion of the divine gift of healing occurs in it, based on three accounts of miracles among the desert monks. These are prefaced by the statement that "we have never found that those works and signs were affected by our fathers; nay, rather when they did possess them by the grace of the Holy Spirit they would never use them, unless perhaps extreme and unavoidable necessity drove them to do so."[59]

These miracles, as Cassian saw it, were performed to demonstrate the power of the Lord to heretics or scoffers, or because a monk was "pestered" for healing. He thus expressed the most correct theology—the works were accomplished by the compassion of the Lord and not the merit of monks—but he himself seemed to have learned little about compassion. From this point on, the purpose of his discussion is clear. It was necessary to warn the church about the dangers of using the gift of healing. If one were not fully aware of them, he might lose not only his humility but his inward purity and perfect chastity. Indeed, the implication was that one could lose his very soul by too much attention to healing men's bodies.

We cannot be sure, of course, what lay behind this drift of reasoning, which continued in the church. Perhaps it sprang, in part, from an obscure contradiction between severe ascetic practices, so widely recognized as necessary to produce purity and humility, and the deep response to the ordinary needs and suffering of people—"the compassion of the Lord," which alone opens the way for divine healing to become a natural event in human life. Desert and monastery alike perhaps to some extent removed the devout Christian unwittingly from fertile contact with the

59. John Cassian, *The Conferences*, The Second Conference of Abbot Nesteros XV.2.

common needs of his contemporaries. Where mortification of the flesh was highly valued (a theme nowhere emphasized by Jesus), the ready healing of it must have been increasingly felt as an anomaly. Nor do we know, either, how far the growing climate of vague disapproval toward easing the pains of the flesh served as an alibi for something much more profound and hidden: sheer loss of ability—and back of that any deep desire—to be a channel for divine compassion to do its healing work.

At any rate, the attitude of which Cassian is typical grew in the monasteries until it was picked up and enshrined by the last notable doctor of the western church, Gregory the Great, in his *Book of Pastoral Rule*. This was one of the finest works on pastoral care to be found in the West. It was highly admired in Gregory's time. His special emissary to England, Augustine of Canterbury, took it with him as the basis for the new church there. Three hundred years later Alfred had it translated into the West-Saxon tongue, and a copy was sent to every bishop in the kingdom. By the command of Charlemagne in successive councils, this book was already studied by every bishop in Gaul along with the New Testament and the canons of the fathers. There is evidence from the end of the ninth century that a copy of the *Pastoral Rule* was put into the hands of bishops at the altar during their consecration, along with the *Book of Canons*.

This Gregory, who was Bishop of Rome from 590 to 604, lived in a difficult period. Civilization had begun to crumble. Italy had been conquered and overrun by barbarians and partly reconquered by Byzantium. The eastern regent resided at Ravenna—not Rome—and travel between them depended on the whims of the Lombard invaders. Life was uncertain at best, and God's wrath seemed more apparent than his love. Men could hardly dream of the pleasant days of the fourth century.

In such times it was no wonder that Gregory saw illness as one more way in which God chastises his faithful sons. "The sick are to be admonished that they feel themselves to be sons of God in that the scourge of discipline chastises them." He understood illness as one more blow of the hammer in shaping the stones of humanity be placed in the heavenly wall on the other side. Sickness brings a man to himself so that he can ponder his sins and repent. Gregory compared the flesh with Balaam's ass, which stopped in its tracks because the angel of God stood in the way; just so the body, slowed by affliction, reveals the presence of God which the mind does not perceive. And last of all, "who with sound understanding can be ungrateful for being himself smitten, when even He who lived here without sin went not hence without a scourge?"[60]

Gregory's letters suggest that he practiced what he preached. He wrote to Marinianus, Bishop of Ravenna, about his own agony from the gout that plagued the last years of his life, and asked the bishop to

implore for me the compassion of divine loving-kindness, that it would mercifully mitigate towards me the scourges of its smiting, and grant me patience to endure, lest . . . my heart break out into impatience from excessive weariness, and the guilt which might have been well cured through stripes be increased by murmuring.[61]

He attributed the sickness of Venantius to his having left the monastery. In a letter to Rusticiana in Constantinople he told several tales of the demons that persecuted monks who thought of leaving their vocation, and even how a horse revealed two runaway monks by refusing to pass the tomb in which they were hiding. On the other hand, he enjoined Marinianus to follow his physician's advice during an illness, even at the cost of pastoral duties or fasts and devotions, and also sent relics to help abate the ravages of an epidemic in Ravenna. Gregory, as we shall see, was

60. Gregory the Great, *The Book of Pastoral Rule* II.13.
61. *Epistles* of St. Gregory the Great XI.32; also XI.30, 33, 36, 40, and 46.

well aware of divine intervention, but saw it as unleashed for
wrath more often than for love, which was only for the penitent.
And when he did describe miracles it was with little discrimina-
tion: reasonably possible stories appear next to tales which the
most credulous would have difficulty in believing. One does not
find in him the intellectual depth and critical understanding of
Augustine or Basil.

With Gregory's point of view and practice, western thinking
about healing had come full circle. Sickness was no longer understood as the malicious work of "demons" or the Evil One, to be
countered in every instance. Instead, it was a mark of God's
correction, sometimes inflicted by the negative powers with his
approval, to bring moral renewal. There was no question about
God's *power* to heal or his ability to intervene, but only of his
will to heal. Only the righteous were likely to find healing. We
find in Gregory's attitude the theme that grew more and more
prevalent in the West until it was fully expressed in the English
Office of the Visitation of the Sick. Here the Old Testament view
of sickness largely displaced that of Jesus, the apostles, the early
church, and the eastern church.

Yet even with Jerome, Cassian, and Gregory there was no
question whatever as to the *possibility* of healing through the
Spirit, but rather of its advisability. Along with nearly all other
church fathers, these men shared the implicit Platonic view of
the world in which it was perfectly natural for the spiritual realm
to influence the physical one.

Augustine of Hippo, in particular, did some thinking about
miracles that was followed until Aquinas and Scholasticism took
over nearly a thousand years later. To him the miracle was not
a hypothetical intervention of God contrary to his own natural
law, as later thinkers held. For the whole world is sustained by
the immanent power of God; but because man becomes too accustomed to this wonder, God breaks through in a more unusual

way in miracles to bring attention back to his immanent sustaining grace. Although western thinkers did not spell out the specific implications of their world view for healing, miracles were no problem to Augustine or the other church fathers, since they continued to live in a world where such things were expected. He did not in point of fact, say very much in his writings about healing miracles—probably (as noted above) because of his late appreciation of their frequency and value.[62]

Thus, with almost no clear emphasis on the importance of healing from a theological point of view, the western church moved into the turmoil and confusion of the seventh and eighth centuries dominated by the pervasive influence of Gregory, who saw illness largely as a scourge of God. There were also other forces at work, which we shall examine briefly as we try to discover what the approach has been to healing in our own part of the Christian world since that time.

62. A careful study of Augustine's treatment of miracles, with exhaustive references, is found in Louis Monden's *Signs and Wonders* (1966), pp. 41 ff. Father Monden sketches the difference between this point of view and that of Aquinas, showing how much more congenial the Augustinian framework is to an appreciation and understanding of healing miracles.

9

Modern Christianity and Healing

As already suggested, there is a great gulf between the modern Christian attitude toward healing and that of the early church and the renowned eastern doctors of the church. Indeed, the difference is so pronounced that one wonders how two such divergent views could have developed within the same institution. This is even more puzzling when one realizes that the point of view of the early church was largely a simple continuation of the understanding found in the New Testament in the practice of Jesus and his immediate followers. How did so great a change in attitude toward Christian healing come about? What historical influences produced it? We have seen the beginnings of these causes—we must now examine them in more detail.

Finding even some of the answers to such questions has been a fascinating pursuit over many years. If we are to see whether healing has a place in modern Christian activity we must understand how the change took place. If the influences that led to the gradual elimination of a ministry of religious healing grow out of the essence of the gospel, then this Christian practice should be discouraged or rejected. If, however, the factors responsible for the change are peripheral or contrary to the central meaning of the gospel, then an effort should be made to reintroduce healing as a part of present-day Christian theory and practice.

Three Reasons for Change

Any tracing of historical development over a period of a thousand years is a complex and difficult task. After years of work the pieces have come together in a pattern and we venture to offer some tentative answers. Three main factors seem to have produced the change. (1) First of all, there was a subtle and gradual alteration in popular views of the nature of God and of man. This was associated with the decline of civilization in the West and the barbarian conquests. (2) There was a major shift in theological thinking, in which Plato's world view was replaced by that of Aristotle; this resulted in a rationalistic outlook which had little place for any direct contact between God and man, hence little room for healing. (3) Throughout these years there continued at the same time a popular, often superstitious thread of belief in the miraculous which supported a lively and uncritical interest in healing miracles. Separated from theological understanding and criticism, this became more and more fanciful until it was difficult to believe any of the stories brought forward.

It is difficult for most of us to imagine living in a profoundly disintegrating civilization. The worst historical disasters of recent times have been followed by some kind of restoration and rebuilding. It was not so as western civilization began to crumble in the sixth and seventh centuries. Disaster followed disaster, and there was no renewal. Great cities of several hundred thousand people, like Aquileia, simply ceased to exist. Hundreds of other prosperous cities, from Italy to Britain and from Switzerland to Spain were deserted and remained only as piles of rubble, soon totally forgotten.

From the time of Constantine and even before, the barbarians —some pagan, some Arian—hammered away at all sides of the western Roman Empire. Rome was plundered and finally fell.

For a while the emperors based at the nearly impregnable city of Byzantium tried to resist the incursions of semicivilized tribes in the West, but soon their attention was diverted elsewhere. Shortly after the death of Pope Gregory the Great the Arabs came to a sense of national and religious identity and swept away much of the Roman Empire, all of Asia Minor and North Africa, and most of Spain. Arab pirates gained control of the Mediterranean, and commerce simply disappeared, as did the urban civilization based upon it. The collapse was nearly complete. Indeed, the church was the only major institution to survive the chaos.

In such conditions it is not strange that men should become less confident of God's love and mercy and think more vividly of the wrathful aspect of the Godhead. We saw the beginning of this tendency in Cassian and Jerome, then even more markedly in Gregory the Great. As things grew worse, people all but forgot the sense of God's love and concern for man, so much the essence of the message of Jesus. As education disappeared, few could read the gospels even enough to hear what the teaching had been. The liturgy was often in a language unknown to the worshiper. With the end of persecution under Constantine, less committed Christians flooded the church. Imagine what changes were wrought, when mass baptism of entire tribes followed the conversion of the chiefs or kings! The Christianity of such converts can hardly compare with the committedness of those who had followed Jesus or who spent three years as catechumens before being allowed full membership in the church. The faith of many of these people was little more than their pagan religion with a new label. It is difficult to generalize about all the gods whom the barbarian invaders brought with them, but the Teutonic religions as we have records of them did not present man with gods of a pleasant demeanor. As far as I have been able to discover there were but few shamans within these religious groups, to ameliorate the effects of the stern gods. And so the Lombards, Goths, and

Franks came in and took over a dying civilization, only to be soon overrun by other groups: the Normans and the Danes. Life was grim. When the course of life itself appears in such dark colors, of what use is a little bodily healing? Even death is not so horrible under these conditions.

Within this total context a new view developed of the relation of healing to God. The important thing was not to find some comfort in this life—that could hardly be expected—but rather to insure a good existence after death. Care of the soul became much more significant than care of the body; a saved soul brought one to the bliss of heaven—the body and this life were relatively unimportant. Since sickness was the result of God's wrath at the sins of man, it was actually a valuable indicator of one's inner state, and from this viewpoint it was downright stupid to cure the physical body without finding out what was wrong in the soul and healing that. In addition, suffering was seen as sharing in the crucifixion, and the removal of it questionable. Curing the body without curing the soul was valueless, if not dangerous. Any kind of healing began to be treated with suspicion, whether secular or religious: the idea of compassion for a man afflicted through no fault of his own was nearly lost.

With the emphasis on the next life, a profound change took place in the sacrament of healing. Its meaning shifted gradually to healing of the soul in preparation. Unction for healing became unction for dying—a final cleansing which practically guaranteed (at least in the popular mind) that one would arrive in good condition and on the right path when he reached the other side. Following Jerome's translation of the word "heal" as "save," the medieval church developed its understanding of the sacrament of extreme unction, which remained until Vatican II in 1962. Evidence of this will be offered in more detail presently.

As against these trends and quite independent of them, there was meanwhile a transformation in the intellectual climate of

western Europe. The philosophical base of many influential
western thinkers shifted from Plato to Aristotle. Even the best-
educated men in western Europe could not read Greek; even a
genius like Aquinas never read most of the Platonic dialogues—
they were not available in Latin. Any understanding of Plato's
thought came largely from popularizers like Chalcidius, who
presented a one-sided and otherworldly version of it.[1]

Whole generations of men forgot that Plato had stressed the
importance of this life as well as the next, and they needed a point
of view which gave value to the present world. There was no
doubt in anyone's mind that Aristotle provided such an outlook,
and so, as medieval civilization pulled out of the Dark Ages it
turned more and more to the thinking of Aristotle, which had
already formed a foundation for the brilliant Arab culture to the
south.

Several Neoplatonic writings were accepted at this time as the
work of Aristotle, and this made him far more palatable to the
church. Boethius had translated his logic (the *Organon*), providing an educational curriculum for western Europe for centuries
to come, based largely on Aristotle's thinking. Many of the converted barbarians were not pure pagans, but Aristotelian Arians.
Conditions were ripe and a new world view emerged, based on
the thinking of Aristotle—a view which came to dominate the
outlook of all western Europeans: prince and scholar, tradesman
and pauper alike. Some scholars have called it Scholasticism, but
it is more correctly defined as the Aristotelio-medieval world
view. All of life and experience were part of a logically certain
system ranging from a geocentric astronomy to the logical necessity of the Sermon on the Mount. Any deviation from this total
view or any part of it was considered heresy, for it had the full
support of an authoritarian church. At the same time, a schism

1. The importance of Chalcidius and others like him is described in my book,
Dreams: The Dark Speech of the Spirit (1968), p. 155.

developed between the eastern and western churches, and anything Greek was viewed as practically heretical. Fertilization by
sophisticated Platonic thought ceased. Instead of learning from
the East, western crusaders sacked Constantinople and occupied
it to bring the heretics to the true faith!

The most gifted exponent of this world view was St. Thomas
Aquinas. Man has produced few greater geniuses, and he made
an heroic attempt to build Christian thought and practice upon
an Aristotelian foundation. And this made a great difference in
attitude toward healing. If God is known primarily through intellectual activity rather than experience, there is little place for
any gifts of the Spirit. As described by Paul, they fit more easily
into a Platonic world view than an Aristotelian one. The medieval church developed a final and certain total outlook based on
past revelation elaborated by man's reason; it needed nothing
more. There was no need for God to continue to break through
into the lives of men. One might expect no further revelations or
healings as the natural interaction of man and God, but only
under extraordinary supernatural conditions. Thus the theologians supplied good reasoning to back up the more general shift
away from the practice of religious healing, discussed above. A
closer look at the thinking of Aquinas and his followers will show
how pervasive this change in attitude toward it really was.[2]

Meanwhile, however—and paradoxically—healings continued
to occur throughout most of this period. As James Michael Lee
once said, the Catholic Church has an Aristotelian head and a
Platonic heart. The two do not always operate in concert. From
the time of Gregory reports of healings continue. In the end,
several attested miracles, usually healings, were required before
a person could be declared a saint. As Chaucer reminds us in the

2. I have described this development of thought in detail in *Encounter with God:
A Theology of Christian Experience* (1972). The reader who wishes to pursue the
change from Platonic to Aristotelian thought is referred to this work.

Canterbury Tales, pilgrimages to shrines developed into a universal pastime. The trade in relics was brisk and profitable. It has been suggested that enough fragments of the one true cross were available by the end of the Middle Ages to construct a fair-sized church. Cut off from critical scrutiny, the miracles of healing proliferated, and it became difficult to tell the genuine from exaggerated or picturesquely fabricated instances. Books containing the most outrageous stories have circulated in every century down to our own.[3] No wonder many serious Christians have doubted the existence of genuine healing at all. In fact, a good many people who otherwise consider themselves Christians have been driven to a point of view, even about the "miracles" of Jesus, very similar to the fundamental position of the humanists.

Can we however, looking back over the whole perspective, assume that all these accounts and the entire phenomenon of healing are fanciful? Again and again life has a way of bringing us up short with the reality. Aside from any firsthand experience of my own, within the last several months one very critical Roman Catholic priest and two highly educated Anglican ones, on being informed of my interest in this subject, have told me of the most amazing healings in their own lives—adding that usually they did not speak of these things. Let us look a little more closely at the forces which have lead to a disregard for religious healing, and then see how persistent the gift has been throughout the ages, among most trustworthy and reliable Christian witnesses.

3. For instance, in *The Dialogues on Miracles*, written by Caesarius of Heisterbach about 1220 to 1235, trans. H. von E. Scott and C. C. Swinton Bland (1929), there are many stories of miracles occurring in outer, physical substances. Two centuries later when the Dominican priest Johannes Herolt (Discipulus, ca. 1440) compiled the *Miracles of the Blessed Virgin Mary*, trans. C. C. Swinton Bland (1928), his emphasis was even more on tangible aspects of the miraculous. Many stories of this kind, down into the nineteenth century, are found in E. Cobham Brewer's *A Dictionary of Miracles, Imitative, Realistic and Dogmatic* (1885), republished in 1901.

Once more, since the reader cannot be referred to any single source, I must go into some detail.

From Healing to Forgiveness of Sins

By the time of Charlemagne, as we have seen, the western church was beginning to transform unction for healing into unction as preparation for death.[4] We can trace this change step by step. A similar restriction also applied to visiting, exorcising, and laying hands on the sick. The Council of Chalon-sur-Sâone in 813 reserved the administration of unction to priests and priests alone. At Metz in 847 and Pavia in 850 the idea was clearly expressed that unction had more to do with forgiveness of sins than with bodily healing.[5]

The service soon reflected the change in thinking. In two copies from the ninth and tenth centuries almost the first words of the priest as he walked into the sick man's house were to remind him of his sins. One of them called for confession first of all, while in the other the first act was to make a cross of ashes on the sick person's breast and cover him with a hair shirt. One or more of the seven penitential Psalms was read to him. The holy water was no longer blessed in his presence. He was anointed— not where there was pain, but indicating each of the five senses, with a prayer to expiate and repair anything illicit, offensive, or harmful. The priest was to return with Communion, but out of five variations of the service only one retained the direction to "repeat any other rite"—perhaps fortunately for the patient.

Strangely enough, the words still expressed an intent to heal.

4. Charlemagne's ecclesiastical adviser, Theodulf, who was Bishop of Orleans about 815, seems to have been the first to issue a general instruction which stressed the administration of unction as a preparation for death, putting this aspect before healing. Theodulfus Aurelianensis Episcopus, *Capitulare*, in J.-P. Migne, *Patrologiae Latinae* 105 (1864), cols. 220–44.

5. Cited by Percy Dearmer, *Body and Soul* (1909), pp. 220 f.; also W. K. Lowther Clarke, *Liturgy and Worship* (1954), p. 492.

Even in the eleventh-century service the priest might begin by
stressing the healings in the New Testament to remind the person of God's love and kindness, and then, just before his Communion, ask God to free him of sickness so that "confirming him
in strength, upholding him in power, you may restore him to the
altars of your holy church with no good thing lacking for full
health."[6] But in this same version, as in all others of the period,
the motions that had shown care for the person in his immediate
illness are replaced by those that negate healing—by emphasis on
sin and penitential Psalms and anointing for faults of the senses.
The final act was to lay a hair shirt on the floor, place the person
on it, and sign him with ashes, asking him to think how he would
return to ashes. With the question, "Are ashes and hair cloth
pleasing to you as evidence of your penitence before God in the
day of Judgment?" and the sick person's formal response, "They
are pleasing," the priest turned his back and the service ended.

Certainly by this time the change was nearly complete. Most
of the order for visiting the sick was better calculated to produce
anxiety and tension than to awaken forces for healing. Before
long it would be given the name of a final sacrament for the
dying. There is no doubt concerning the origin of the rite of
extreme unction or its original meaning, but this was soon forgotten. Sin and sickness were linked together in what was almost
an a priori connection. No one considered the different tack
taken by Jesus of Nazareth who had expressly denied an exclusive connection.

In all the records we have scanned, we find no mention of a
formal sacrament of healing. Instead, by the thirteenth century

6. Migne, *Patrologiae Latinae* 78 (1895), cols. 1017–23; also 138 (1880), cols. 987–
1002 *(Monumenta Liturgica)*. The evolution of the rite of extreme unction from
these various services for the sick is detailed by Aimé Georges Martimort, *L'Église
en Prière: Introduction à la Liturgie* (1961), pp. 580 ff. The later manuscripts are also
listed by Michel Andrieu, *Les Ordines Romani du Haut Moyen Age* (1931–48), 1 (see
Index under *infirmus*).

the order for visiting and anointing the sick was becoming known as *Unctio Extrema*, one of the seven sacraments named by Peter Lombard in 1151.[7] The healing effect of unction was never denied; there may well have been, and still may be, innumerable cures as a result. But the church was fast coming to the position that it was to be administered principally (or *only*) at the point of death, for the purpose of securing "a spiritual advantage."[8]

The theologians finished what the councils started. Those who completed the *Summa Theologica* for Aquinas added this final touch: "Extreme Unction is a spiritual remedy, since it avails for the remission of sins, according to James 5:15. Therefore it is a sacrament. . . . Now the effect intended in the administration of the sacraments is the healing of the disease of sin." (III-Supp. 29.1) Since the other sacraments took ample care of the sins of the living, the only purpose of anointing the sick was that "it prepares man for glory immediately" at the time of death. The chance that healing might happen could not be entirely denied, but there was no expectation that the spiritual could affect the physical body.[9] In 1551 the Council of Trent legally made unction a service only for those in danger of death, and healing ceased to exist as an official rite of the Catholic Church until very recent times.

Much the same attitude toward other gifts of the Holy Spirit continued up until the Second Vatican Council in 1962. As far

7. Around 1150, it appears, the first pronouncement about seven sacraments that included a sacrament of extreme unction was made in Peter Lombard's *Sentences*, which was one of the principal works studied by all theological students at the time of Aquinas. Petri Lombardi, *Sententiarum* IV.23.1 f., in Migne, *Patrologiae Latinae* 192 (1880), col. 899.

8. As John Peckham, Archbishop of Canterbury, for instance, held in his *Constitutions of 1281*; quoted from Lyndewode's *Provinciale* by Dearmer, *op cit.* pp. 221 f.

9. Any more than there is today. A good friend in the Catholic Church has told me how puzzled her parish priest was after he had been called and had administered unction on two occasions to an uncle who was dying, and immediately the old man's condition improved.

as the gifts described by Paul are concerned, there was a special rule for saints (a gift like healing might be a sign of extraordinary holiness). But for ordinary people, some of these gifts were even considered, without qualification, a mark of demonic possession.[10] Certainly the Spirit had little room to operate in the church during these centuries. And during this period the church did not confine itself to liturgy; it began to legislate about medical healing as well.

The Church and Medical Healing

In the beginning of the twelfth century several decrees were laid down which in the end would put a damper even on medical healing. The first general council in the West, the First Lateran in 1123, was faced with the growing power of the monasteries. As a solution, monks were forbidden to hold public Masses or offer penance, with a further proviso that they must not consecrate holy oil, administer unction, or even visit the sick. (Canon 17) Henceforth, in the church a single, authoritarian approach to sickness could be encouraged.

Then, as monks began to study medicine and law to make money on the side, this too was soundly condemned. The Second Lateran Council in 1139 held not only that the cure of souls was being neglected, but that the monks "thus make themselves physicians of human bodies. Since an impure eye is the messenger of an impure heart, those things about which good people blush to speak, religion ought not to treat."[11] (Canon 9) But in the meantime there were some in the itinerant orders who found that

10. "Signs of possession are the following: ability to speak with some facility in a strange tongue or to understand it when spoken by another; the faculty of divulging future and hidden events; display of powers which are beyond the subject's age and natural condition. . . ." Section on Exorcism, *The Roman Ritual*, trans. and ed. Rev. Philip Weller (1952), 2: 169.

11. Rev. H. J. Schroeder, O.P., *Disciplinary Decrees of the General Councils* (1937), pp. 201 f.

surgery could be practiced profitably, even without training, on a hit-and-run basis. The Council of Tours handled this problem in 1163 by simply prohibiting churchmen from practising surgery at all, on the ground that "the church abhors the shedding of blood"; consequently, as medicine developed, surgery was left behind to become a barber's trade. The separation of medicine and surgery hindered the growth of both disciplines.

Medicine cannot develop without the study of anatomy. Medieval physicians forbidden to practice human dissection cut up pigs to find out how the human system worked. Galen, the ancient medical authority, had asserted that man's anatomy was similar to that of pigs. The reason for prohibiting dissection was strange indeed. During the Crusades the peculiar practice developed of boiling and macerating the bodies of men who died far from home so that their bones could be brought back for burial. In 1300 Boniface VIII issued a papal bull prohibiting the practice. Since about this time human bodies were beginning to be used for medical dissection, the similarity was almost too striking to avoid. Human dissection was forbidden, and even when the ban was eventually relaxed, schools had to fight to obtain one or two bodies a year to teach (or even learn) a little about human anatomy. No wonder there was antagonism between physicians and the church; the wonder is that it did not linger on.

For there was more. In 1215 the Fourth Lateran Council, on the premise that "bodily infirmity is sometimes caused by sin," decreed that when a physician was called to take care of a sick person, his first duty was to call for the priest. The decree explained that after spiritual health was restored, bodily medicine might be applied beneficially, "for the cause being removed the effect will pass away." It then went on:

We publish this decree for the reason that some, when they are sick, and are advised by the physician in the course of the sickness to attend to the salvation of their soul, give up all hope and yield more easily to the danger of death. If any physician shall transgress this decree after it has been published by the bishops, let him be cut off from the Church till he has made suitable satisfaction for his transgression. And since the soul is far more precious than the body, we forbid under penalty of anathema that a physician advise a patient to have recourse to sinful means for the recovery of bodily health. (Canon 22)[12]

From this time on, doctors ran a personal risk in caring for the sick at all.

The worst was yet to come as the Catholic Church backed up its moral thinking on the subject of illness by putting the burden on physicians to enforce penance on the sick. From 1566 on, to obtain a license to practice medicine, doctors were required to swear that they would stop seeing a patient on the third day unless he had confessed his sins and had a statement signed by his confessor to show for it. The Roman Synod renewed this decree in 1725 with added penalties. For continuing to care for patients who had not confessed their sins, the eighteenth-century Catholic physician was permanently removed from the practice of medicine, ejected from medical societies, and bore "forever the stigma of infamy."[13] Small wonder that psychiatrists have so often pointed to religious and moral tension as a major cause of mental and other illness.

And is it any wonder that medicine looked with suspicion on the church and its attitudes and went its own way, viewing man as merely another material thing? We shall take up this theme in the next chapter. Obviously, this kind of thinking has little relation to the Christian idea of wholeness of soul and mind and body, or to the acts of Jesus. It is hard to see how the church ever reconciled it with the original Christian theology. But then,

12. *Ibid.*, pp. 263 f.
13. *Loc. cit.* We have read of a French physician sentenced under this canon in the 1700s, but have not discovered the original reference.

through the efforts of a very singular man theology itself was changed, and the way most Christians thought of their relation to God was altered.

Aquinas and Healing

Many people find theology dull, and Scholastic theology even duller. The interminable questions and answers, the dialectical subtlety and the hair-splitting distinctions tax the patience of the general reader and many modern theologians as well. However, when a theology finally takes hold in a culture it has deep and pervasive influence. Sooner or later the basic ideas of men usually result in action.

Thomas Aquinas was not the only theologian to write from an Aristotelian base, but he was the best, and his thinking finally became standard for the Catholic Church. His influence was so great that it can hardly be measured. His work affected the secular world as well as the religious; in fact, his writing was one of the factors that made possible the development of science in the Western world.

However, Aquinas had no real place for religious healing in his systematic thought, and his basic ideas gradually gained acceptance among Protestant thinkers as well as Catholic theologians. It is impossible to understand the intellectual rejection of the healing ministry in modern times without following his reasoning closely. There is again no study of the subject to which to refer the reader, and so of necessity we must present some rather uninspiring prose to reveal the conscious reasons for this rejection.

St. Thomas lived and wrote in the golden age of medieval civilization, in the latter half of the thirteenth century. He died at the age of forty nine, after producing an incredible quantity of work. He began to teach and write just as the church was coming to realize that the "new" philosophy of Aristotle was in the Western universities to stay. When the general writings of Aristotle began to appear in Europe, around 1200, the church at first tried to prohibit entirely the study of his physical (including psychological) and metaphysical works,[14] because they were so clearly inconsistent with the Christian understanding of the world. Aristotle had concentrated on the outer forms of things, and in the end set up a closed, naturalistic system in which Christianity could have little or no effect, as many theologians apparently saw.

But by Aquinas' time students and faculties alike were finding a whole new way of observing and thinking about the world in Aristotelian terms, and Aquinas began almost immediately to teach and work with these ideas. Besides commentaries on them, he wrote his two main religious treatises to show—not that Christianity and Aristotle each offered valid descriptions of the world from different viewpoints—but that, by rational under-standing, Christianity could fit into a world just about as Aris-totle described it. He first wrote a book devoted to converting the Aristotelian Arabs, the *Summa Contra Gentiles*. But the theology of his day was not fit for that task. He then produced a handbook of religious knowledge which would be relevant to the Aris-totelian thinking of his time, and this was the *Summa Theologica*: his legacy to modern Western man.

In it, step by step, he developed an understanding of God, of creation, and of man's nature within a natural order of cause and effect. Actual experiences of God's power, or anything else outside this natural order, were pushed out of sight. Again and again Aquinas referred to medical healing in all kinds of ana-

14. F. C. Copleston's *Aquinas* (1961), pp. 59 ff. gives an interesting account of this period and the opinions of various theologians about the "pagan philoso-pher." But Aristotle's works on logic, known as the *Organon*, had been available in Latin and used all through the Middle Ages; there was no objection to these or to his *Ethics*.

logies,[15] but he never once mentioned Christian healing in the
present tense, as any part of Christian life after the time of the
apostles. In the last part, when he finally came to the manifestation of Christ and the sacraments of the church, he did discuss
the miracles of Christ and referred to such events in relation to
penance. But here, as we shall see, there is a story to tell.

In part III, in the two questions on Christ's miracles, Aquinas
said practically everything he had to say about healing. His interest was very limited. The main question he asked was why miracles occurred at all, and his explanation was that Christ worked
them primarily in order to prove his teaching to men. Because
his doctrine was supernatural, it surpassed human reason, and
therefore the show of divine power was required so that men
would take this teaching on faith. And second, the miracles were
needed to demonstrate the divinity of Christ. This was essentially Aquinas' whole point about the healings and other miracles; the rest of his thinking in this section came through on the
same wave length. It is strange that Aquinas, who wrote with
such perception about the primacy of love and compassion, did
not see that Christ's healings were inspired more by love than as
instructive demonstrations.

It is equally strange that Thomas allotted such a brief portion
of the *Summa* to the consideration of healing and exorcism, in
sharp contrast to the treatment accorded these phenomena in the
four Gospels, Acts, and the Epistles (one is reminded of the
treatment given these experiences in the *Interpreter's Bible*, already referred to). In one of the briefest statements in the entire
Summa Theologica, he does approve the miracles "worked in

15. The references that follow are taken from St. Thomas Aquinas, *The "Summa
Theologica,"* literally translated by the Fathers of the English Dominican Province
(various dates), in which the purely physical causes of healing by medical or
"natural" means are alluded to at I.13.2, 5, 6, 16.6, 57.3, 62.4, 87.2, and 117.1;
II-I.5.5, 8.3, 9.4, 12.3, 19.8, 33.4, 51.1, 79.4, 87.6, 101.3, and 109.5; II-II.1.1, 20.1,
24.10, 27.3, 6, and 33.7; III.15.6, 60.1, and 65.1; as well as other places.

spiritual substances" (exorcism or the casting out of demons) and those "worked on men" (physical healing). (III.44.1) In the next breath he remarks that Christ came especially for the salvation of man's soul. "Consequently, He allowed the demons, that He cast out, to do man some harm, either in his body or in his goods, for the salvation of man's soul—namely, for man's instruction." (44.1, Ad. 4) This is quite a change from the Christ who came to combat the Evil One and his forces and died in his battle to defeat him.

While it was also "fitting that Christ, by miraculously healing men in particular, should prove Himself to be the universal and spiritual Saviour of all" (44.3), Aquinas took a great deal more trouble to show that Christ did work miracles on the soul, because "in man the soul is of more import than the body." He cited several passages to demonstrate that Christ changed the minds of men, not only by giving them righteousness and wisdom "which pertains to the end of miracles, but also by outwardly drawing men to Himself, or by terrifying or stupefying them, which pertains to the miraculous itself." Finally he cited Chrysostom to specify again: "By how much a soul is of more account than a body, by so much is the forgiving of sins a greater work than healing the body; but because the one is unseen He does the lesser and more manifest thing in order to prove the greater and more unseen." (III.44.3, Ad. 1 and 3)

Aquinas and the Gifts of the Spirit

One wonders what difference it might have made in our present thinking about healing if Augustine had been struck by the experience of healing earlier and had built his theology from the beginning on its importance. For Aquinas, Augustine was *the* theologian, as Aristotle was *the* philosopher. If Aquinas had been forced to consider over and over again the amazement and conviction of which Augustine wrote in the final chapters of the *City of God*, it might have occurred to him that something was missing from the careful philosophic tower he was building.

Instead, western thinkers had developed a theology based largely on experiences other than healing, and along the way a new idea emerged about the gifts of the Holy Spirit. Gregory the Great in his *Morals on the Book of Job* suggested that there were seven of these; beginning with wisdom, science, understanding, and counsel, he then added fortitude, piety, and fear in place of the healing, miracles, prophecy, and others described by Paul in 1 Corinthians.[16] When Aquinas came to his one main discussion of the subject, he chose the list suggested by Gregory. (II-I. 68–70) These gifts, he held, were the perfections that disposed man "to be moved by God" (II-I.68.1) toward "the Divine good which is known by the intellect alone." (II-II.24.1) He then turned to look at evil habits, vice, and the law, which finally brought him to a separate section on grace.

At this point the ideas of Paul about the Holy Spirit could not be avoided. But Aquinas partitioned them off. There was first sanctifying grace, which was noble because it made man pleasing to God. Then there was gratuitous grace, including the charismata or gifts discussed by Paul. (II-I.111.1) The real purpose of these gifts was to produce an effective teacher, for one could only lead another person to God by instructing him. (II-I.111.4) Certain outer equipment was needed to teach. Perfect knowledge of divine things was necessary, so there were "faith," "the word of knowledge," and "the word of wisdom." To provide proof when argument failed, there were "the grace of healing," "miracles," "prophecy," and "discerning of spirits." Finally, to supply the proper idiom and expression of meaning, there were "tongues" and "the interpretation of tongues."

16. S. Gregorii Magni, *Moralium Libri, sive Expositio in Librum B. Job* 1.27 and 2.49, in Migne, *Patrologiae Latinae* 75 (1902), cols. 543–44 and 592–94.

It was difficult for Aquinas within his world view to see that man can be influenced in other ways than through the intellect and sense experience. The complexities of the teaching process and the importance of emotions and the unconscious in meaningful communication were beyond his grasp. He believed that the saints performed true miracles, but not so much out of compassion for man's suffering as to confirm his knowledge of salvation.[17] (II-II.178.1) And this was practically, although not quite, the final word Aquinas had to say about healing, or indeed any other way in which spiritual power could work through man.

As "the Philosopher" demonstrated so clearly, man in this life was a part of the physical world, and his experiences, even his dreams, were pretty well limited to it.[18] Man was given his senses and the ability to reason from sense experience because these were his natural capacities for receiving experience. If God or any supernatural experience touched him, it had to come intellectually or else through some physical and sensory means. Unquestionably this was the kind of experience Aquinas knew.

He then came to the sacrament of penance. (III.84–90) He had worked almost steadily for six years on the *Summa*, and here he was faced with a question that had to be wrestled with personally as well as intellectually. First of all, the validity of penance did not operate through any corporeal thing: there was no water, or bread and wine, or even oil, that was made divine by the priest's

17. It is at this point that the modern reader has the greatest trouble in understanding Aquinas. It is difficult for most of us to comprehend how concern with our soul's salvation would not also involve care for our suffering human bodies. It is impossible for most of us to separate mind, body, and emotions, and the idea of touching one of them without touching and affecting the others is nearly unthinkable. Aquinas was, however, more at home in discussing immutable essences than process. The idea that mind and spirit, emotion and body, were in constant interaction and flux was beyond him. It is for this reason that his ideas seem so foreign and unreal to many moderns, whether Catholic or Protestant.

18. See my book *Dreams*, pp. 173 ff. for a more complete discussion of the effect of Aristotelian philosophy upon man's understanding of the processes by which he receives knowledge. Also *Encounter with God, op. cit.*

action. There was no substance inside a person that was supposed to react and still remain if the penance was effective. Instead of consecrating something or using hallowed matter, this sacrament consisted in the removal of something.

More important, the priest obviously did in fact *do* something, if sins were removed when he simply said: "I absolve thee." By a simple human action, speaking ordinary words, the priest accomplished the work of God himself. Aquinas knew what it meant to be a priest and—with nothing holy in his hands to carry the power of Christ—to face a person who needed help. And so he looked again at the healings accomplished by the apostles simply through a word of command. He realized that penance and healing had much in common, and discussed the healing of the man at the Beautiful Gate (Acts 3:6) in this light. (III. 84.4) He even considered whether the laying on of hands would make the words more effective. He then took up the healing efficacy of the human touch, particularly the touch of a "sanctified man's hand," and asserted that such a touch might heal the physical body. (III.84.5)

For the first time Aquinas came close to suggesting that men might share the Spirit with each other in a nonintellectual way. But he skirted the idea and went back to penance. It was not meant to confer grace, but only to eliminate sins. Here he arrived at questions even closer to home. Did penance restore a man to ecclesiastical dignity? What effect did it have on works conceived without charity? And then on the morning of December 6, 1273, while saying Mass, Aquinas experienced something which made him from that moment leave his own monumental work where it stood, unfinished. "I can write no more," he told his friends. "All that I have written seems like so much straw compared with what I have seen and what has been revealed to me."

Many writers have spoken of this experience. But we know of no one who has looked at it in relation to Aquinas' understanding of how we know God and the realm of the Spirit. No one, as far as we know, has asked why the experience was so important, or why it came at just that time, only a few days after he had expressly stated that there was no connection between forgiveness of sins (penance) and the direct experience of the grace of God. Our suggestion is that once he had begun to look directly at the question of man's desire and need for direct awareness of God's grace, he was given an immediate vision of the healing and love which God offers to any who truly desire him. This was bestowed, not because God wanted to save his soul, but just because he loves and wants to express that love. There is more communication in love than in any intellectual process.

Unquestionably something of the grace, love, and healing of God spoke directly to Thomas from within. Whether one calls it the Self or the Holy Spirit or God breaking through, certainly a revelation from beyond his intellect or field of sense perception came through to him. Is this supernatural, or is it the natural way in which God responds to men when we give him a chance? Where would Aquinas put this experience in his system? He had met that of which he could not speak. Three months later, starting on a mission for the pope, he fell ill and died. The *Summa* was finished and its Aristotelian view of man rounded out by other Scholastics. Gradually its ideas were accepted, until for modern man the separation from God seems complete—unless one has an experience like that of Aquinas himself.

The Reformers and Healing

The Protestant reformation changed many aspects of church life and practice, but it never attacked the problem of the world view of the Scholastics against whom it revolted. Among Protestants this has not changed much since.[19] It did not occur to the Protes-

19. I have discussed the similarity between the reformers and the Scholastics in the matter of basic philosophy in some detail in *Tongue Speaking*, pp. 186 ff. Those interested in the evidence will find it there.

tant leaders of the Reformation that anything was required but to get rid of superfluous practices such as unction and indulgences. They did not realize that the whole base of Christian theology needed to be rethought if Christian experience was to be central to church doctrine. Then, too, Calvin and Luther were almost as much concerned to offer religious certainty as the Scholastics of the Council of Trent.

Luther clearly believed that the great miracles like healing were given in the beginning simply so that church people could later do "greater works than these" by teaching, converting, and saving men spiritually. Writing for parents about the fine things that could be expected of a son who entered the church, he went on:

Thus Paul says in Romans 8 that God will raise up our mortal bodies because of his Spirit which dwells in us. Now how are men helped to this faith and to this beginning of the resurrection of the body except through the office of preaching and the word of God, the office your son performs? Is this not an immeasurably greater and more glorious work and miracle than if he were in a bodily or temporal way to raise the dead again to life, or help the blind, deaf, dumb, and leprous here in the world, in this transitory life?[20]

In fact, Luther rarely missed an opportunity to show that the "real miracles" were not visible ones.

Calvin, as we have seen, was even more explicit when he came to discuss unction. There was simply no way it could be a sacrament of any miraculous power such as healing. These gifts, he said, were only temporary to begin with, because they were needed to make the preaching of the gospel wonderful. Calvin was intent on limiting human authority in the church, and he

20. "A Sermon on Keeping Children in School," *Luther's Works* 46, ed. Robert C. Schultz (1967) 224 f. There is an interesting discussion of this problem by Louis Monden, S.J., in *Signs and Wonders: A Study of the Miraculous Element in Religion* (1966), pp. 295 ff., with various references. Also in other volumes of *Luther's Works*, 8: 182 f., 23: 220 f. and 375 f., 37: 76f.

spared no argument to show that extreme unction was "neither a ceremony appointed by God, nor has any promise."[21] Men were partly to blame for the fact that healing had ceased, since they performed the rite too late to cure or even to bring solace. But this was secondary to the image of an authoritarian God who had no interest in keeping the power to heal alive on earth.

In fact, neither Calvin nor Luther had much interest in *how* a relation comes about between God and man. Despite Luther's interest in Plato and Augustine and his outspoken rejection of Aristotle, philosophy was not the long suit of the Protestant leaders any more than psychology. For the most part they simply accepted the growing view that man's experiences of the ordinary world were in one category and his experiences of God and the spiritual world in another. While God had worked at one time in the ordinary physical world, and could enter it at any time, this was no longer necessary. The coming of Christ had made the salvation of man's soul available in the spiritual world, and the rules had been laid down for the physical world. The two sacraments of baptism and Holy Communion provided a bridge, and no other miracle was needed. Faith in the saving power of Jesus Christ was more noble than asking for experience or evidence. (Though we shall see [p. 233] that, like Augustine and perhaps Aquinas, Luther too seems to have changed his mind about the healing love of the Holy Spirit in his final years.)

On the other hand, there was no lack of divine action in the external world if men refused to abide by the rules or turned away from the sacraments. In England, as we have seen, where the break was more with the discipline of Rome than with Roman tradition, sickness came to be viewed as a particular punishment given by God for man's good. There was probably no worse place in the Christian world to be sick and destitute than in

21. John Calvin, *Institutes of the Christian Religion* IV.19.20, trans. Henry Beveridge (1953), 2: 638.

England in the seventeenth and eighteenth centuries. The monasteries—which had provided healing and also physical care for the sick—declined in numbers and support on the Continent; but in England they were wiped out entirely when money was needed for a navy and political advantage. Luther's followers were at least told to visit the sick, while Calvin made the hospital in Geneva a major responsibility of his local church. In England, however, the sick were not only left to private care, but in 1552 annointing was dropped from the Order for Visitation, leaving English Christians with the idea firmly planted that even their peccadilloes would bring on gout, if not something much worse!

Healing in Modern Churches

Since the time of the reformers innumerable practical actions have been taken by Christians and church groups to deal with sickness, both physically and medically. Christian hospitals and clinics and medical schools have been established wherever Protestant missionaries have gone. By a strange quirk of logic it is permissible to remove medically the results of man's sins, but it is not quite correct to believe that God will do it himself if asked in prayer or invoked through sacraments.

It is true that some groups do meet to pray for the sick, and here and there individual ministers use unction or the laying on of hands sacramentally for healing.[22] In five of the principal Christian bodies official studies have even been made of the effectiveness of religious healing and the need for it today.[23] The

22. These churches are listed from time to time in *Sharing*, the journal published in San Diego by the International Order of St. Luke.

23. These are *The Relation of Christian Faith to Health*, United Presbyterian Church (1960); *Anointing and Healing: Statement*, United Lutheran Church in America (1962); *Christian Faith and the Ministry of Healing*, American Lutheran Church (1965); *Handbook on the Healing Ministry of the Church*, Church of Canada (n.d.); and the *Report of the Bishop of Toronto's Commission on the Church's Ministry of Healing* (1968). There are various reports also from the Church of England,

reports all offer a good understanding of facts and ample reasoning, and all recommend the practice of healing by the Christian church today. Yet each report hedges in some way—in varying degrees—about the ability or willingness of God to heal men directly, except through strictly material, physical means.

There is no theology which is accepted or approved by any major modern church which has a place for the direct action of God in any of the gifts of the Spirit, healing included. In a later chapter we shall sketch a theological framework in which healing has an integral place. This is also the purpose of my book, cited above, *Encounter with God: A Theology of Christian Experience.* The church speaks of miracles like a public exhibition once staged, but overlooks the desire of God to be sought and his ability to step into the immediate physical world specifically, creatively, with healing. The almost unbelievable power of God to love, to care for the created world, has been pushed further and further out of the picture. The Scholastic solution is still with us.

Two leaders of twentieth-century theology convey this very plainly. Barth, who speaks for the more fundamentalist and orthodox believers, has written:

It is strange but true that fundamentally and in general practice we cannot say more of the Holy Spirit and His work than that He is the power in which Jesus Christ attests Himself . . . creating in man response and obedience. We describe Him as His awakening power. Later we will have to describe Him as His quickening and enlightening power. . . . How gladly we would hear and know and say something more, something more precise, something more palpable concerning the way in which the work of the Holy Spirit is done![24]

including *The Ministry of Healing* (1924), sections on spiritual healing in *The Lambeth Conference: 1930;* and *The Church's Ministry of Healing* (1958). In addition, there is a study by the Standing Liturgical Commission of the Protestant Episcopal Church, *Prayer Book Studies III: The Order for the Ministration to the Sick,* (1951).
    24. Karl Barth *Church Dogmatics* 4, *The Doctrine of Reconciliation* (1958), pt. 1:648.

Bultmann puts it somewhat more bluntly for liberal and existential theology. He questions the reality of the healing experiences contained in the New Testament. They are examples of myth, the breaking through of a more than physical order into the physical world. Such impossibilities must be eliminated from the New Testament narrative if Christians are to get on with the task of authentic living in the here and now. Speaking about actual experience of the Holy Spirit and how it fitted into his system, he said to a friend: "In my entire life I have never been able to get to first base so far as the Holy Ghost is concerned." (Ich habe in meinem ganzen Leben mit dem Heiligen Geist nichts anfangen können.)[25] Even the magnificent and influential Dietrich Bonhoeffer writes, in *Letters from Prison*, that since man has come of age and can understand and manage the physical world so efficiently, he no longer needs a God who works directly in the physical world to help him in his helplessness.

In spite of all this, individual Christians throughout the ages have attested to the healing power of God. This is true of nearly every age and every part of the divided church. Let us look at the evidence.

A Persistent Gift

For the first several centuries after the fall of Rome there is little difference between the western record of healing and what we have described as occurring around the leaders of the eastern church. Not many accounts survive of elaborate sacramental healings, although exorcism is often mentioned and oil was certainly used by individuals for anointing.

One of the earliest descriptions of an incident was written at the beginning of this period by Ennodius, the Bishop of Pavia,

25. From a personal letter written by the friend to whom Bultmann was speaking.

to tell a friend of his own healing. About the year 510 he was desperately ill with a fever, and his physician told him there was no remedy. He says, "My hopes increased when the help of man failed. I addressed myself with tears to the heavenly physician, and anointed my dying body with some blessed oil as a remedy against the fever . . . and in that instant the fever left me. . . . God had heard my prayer. . . ."[26]

Apparently the oil for anointing often came from the shrine of a saint—from the lamps kept burning in those places. Gregory of Tours wrote of several healings produced by oil from various shrines of St. Martin.[27] This Gregory, who was Bishop of Tours from 573 to 594, is one of the best sources of information as to practices connected with these shrines. He was carried to Tours for the first time when critically ill to find healing at the tomb of St. Martin, and also describes many other healings of those who kept watch and prayed at the shrines of saints. Several of these stories concern his own experience or that of his family, and there are other accounts of the effective power of relics and the need to care for them properly.[28] The matter of relics is particularly difficult for modern man to swallow, since we like to avoid the fact that the placebo effect, or medical relic (in the form of a sugar pill) produces amazing cures in our own time, as we shall see in the next chapter. This operates on suggestion and faith in the doctor, and how it goes about actually affecting the body is a matter still shrouded in nearly total mystery.

26. Ennodii Felicis, *Epistolarum* VIII.4, Ennodius (ad) Fausto, in Migne, *Patrologiae Latinae* 63 (1882), col. 141.

27. *De Virtutibus Sancti Martini* I.15 and II.32; *De Gloria Beatorum Confessorum* 9; in Georges Florent Gregoire, *Les Livres des Miracles et Autres Opuscules*, (1860), 2:48 f., 146 ff., and 360 ff. Other references to the same practice are cited by Percy Dearmer, *op. cit.*, pp. 256 f.

28. *Libri Miraculorum* II.9, Gregoire, *op. cit.*, 1: 323. The personal accounts are found in the *Libri Miraculorum* II.24 f., *De Virtutibus Sancti Martini* I.32 f., II.1 f., II.60, III.1 and 10, and IV.1 f.; *ibid.*, 1: 350 ff.; 2: 74 ff., 92 ff., 188 ff., 196 f., 208 f., and 274 ff.

Gregory also mentions that sleeping in the shrines of saints and martyrs—incubation—was practiced quite frequently. We have mentioned that such a practice was common among the Greeks in Epidaurus, centuries before Christ; also [p. 50n] a study by a Swiss psychiatrist which suggests that there may be some significance in the practice. Gregory tells how a woman who had lain paralyzed for eighteen years was brought to the basilica of St. Julien in Vienne, hoping that she might at least beg during the vigils. But in the night she dreamed of a striking figure of a man who asked why she was not keeping watch with the others. As she explained, he seemed to pick her up and carry her right up to the tomb, . . . "and there she made her prayer, still quite asleep; at the same time it seemed to her that many chains fell away from parts of her body. Awakened by the noise, she saw that she had recovered the fullest health. Immediately she got up and began to offer thanks in a loud voice, to the amazement of everyone."[29] For Gregory, who knew the experience of healing himself, such happenings were simple facts of Christian life.

Meanwhile in Rome where Gregory the Great was pope, we have seen that a different understanding was planted. In the *Dialogues* this more famous Gregory makes clear that he also personally knew the experience of healing. He tells of a severe illness and of begging one of the monks to pray for him; it is one of the many examples of healing he mentions. Some are plausible, while others stretch the imagination.[30] Healing, according to this Gregory, came from a power given directly by God to certain individuals. But he did not see restoring a sick man to health as

29. It is interesting that Gregory came from an influential senatorial family, that had also produced many of the bishops for this area. As a small child he had dreamed, during an illness of his father, of the remedy that would cure the ailment (*De Gloria Beatorum Confessorum* 60, *ibid.*, 2: 420 ff.).

30. These stories are found in Saint Gregory the Great, *Dialogues* (1959) I.2, 4, 10, 12; II.11, 16, 26, 27, 30, 32, 38; III.2, 3, 5, 6, 14, 17, 21, 22, 25, 33 (including his own healing); IV.6, 11, 40, and 42. (Pp. 11 f., 17 f., 41 ff., 50 ff., 76 f., 81 f., 95 ff., 100 f., 108, 116 ff., 130 f., 145 f., 152 ff., 158, 170 ff., 199 f., 201 f., 244 f., 249 f.)

very different from any other extraordinary happening: say, the miraculous replenishing of a supply of grain or oil. Either power, he concluded, was obviously a sign of God's personal favor and an indication of moral perfection. To claim such power was dangerous for ordinary men; even a pope, with his mortal imperfections. This thinking is found all through the *Dialogues* and is implied elsewhere. Informed that his special emissary to England, Augustine, Archbishop of Canterbury, had healed a blind man by his prayers in the presence of a large assembly, he wrote a special letter to warn him of the need to temper such miraculous gifts with fear.

Rejoice [he wrote] that the souls of the English are, by the means of outward miracles brought to a participation of inward grace. But fear, lest amidst the wonders that are wrought, the mind, which is but weak, should be puffed up to presumption, and incur the inward guilt of vain glory, on account of that exterior honor.[31]

Gregory the Great, so far as we have been able to find, was the last major writer in the church until modern times to describe himself as healed by God's power. Apparently it was not quite cricket to be touched by divine power; it is not consistent with proper humility. But at the same time as Gregory, others in the West were writing of healing: John of Bobbio and Bishop Ouen among them.[32]

Two of England's bishops at the end of the seventh century were known for their healing powers. The Venerable Bede described these miraculous gifts first in his *Life and Miracles of Saint Cuthbert*, the Bishop of Lindisfarne. Then in his *Ecclesiastical History of the English Nation*, which is not supercharged with the

31. Sancti Gregorii Magni, *Epistolarum*, Lib. XI.28, Ad Augustinum Anglorum Episcopum, in Migne, *Patrologiae Latinae* 77 (1896), col. 1139.
32. Ionas, *Vitae Sanctorum Columbani* II.24, Scriptores Rerum Germanicarum (1905), pp. 286 ff. S. Eligii Episcopi Noviomensis, *Vita*, in Migne, *Patrologiae Latinae* 87 (1863), cols. 482–594.

miraculous, he recounts two incidents that occurred after Cuthbert's death.[33] Bede also gives a number of eyewitness accounts of healings by John of Beverley, who was Bishop of York until he retired to found a monastery. The wife of an earl had lain acutely ill for over a month. When John came to consecrate a church near their estate, he sent some of the holy water to the woman with instructions that she drink part of it and be washed with the rest where her pain was greatest. The earl finally pressed him to stay for dinner and bless their home, and while they were eating the woman got up, perfectly recovered, and came down to serve the bishop herself.

In another instance a friend lay dying after a fall from his horse. John spent the night alone praying for him; in the morning he went in to him, spoke his name, and the man regained consciousness; later that day he sat up, able to talk and ready for the surgeon to bind his skull. Others were healed whom John simply touched and blessed, saying, "May you soon recover."

On another occasion John took a dumb boy, whose head was covered with scabs, to live with him during Lent. In the second week he called the boy and told him to put out his tongue. Making the sign of the cross on it, he asked him to say the word "yea." The boy's tongue was immediately loosed, and the bishop had him repeat letters, then syllables and words; during the rest of the day he hardly stopped speaking. Rejoicing, John ordered the physician to take care of his scurvied head, and with the help of the bishop's blessing and prayers a good head of hair grew as the flesh healed. Instead of a deformed beggar, a handsome, articulate boy was returned to his family.[34]

These stories, set down by the "father of English history," seem to reflect more the idea of Christian love and concern than the magic and superstition usually associated with medieval

33. *Bede's Ecclesiastical History of the English People*, IV. 30 ff. (1969), pp. 444–49.
34. *Ibid.*, V.2 ff., pp. 456–69.

miracles and miracle-workers. At almost the same time another Englishman was becoming known for his healings among the Frisians in the Low Countries. This was the missionary Willibrord, who became Archbishop of Utrecht and whose miracles were later celebrated by Alcuin. In his life of Willibrord the great medieval scholar also tells of many wonderful works still being done in his time (about 800) through the relics of the saint. Alcuin describes particularly how people were healed by anointing themselves with oil from the lamps kept burning at his shrine. The equally famous Boniface, who spent three years with Willibrord, was also known for the miracles he performed by means of relics he had obtained from Rome. He was likewise renowned for arranging the condemnation of Adelbert, a Frankish bishop, for the sale of fraudulent relics, which he claimed to have received direct from the angels.[35]

A Change in Healing Experiences

As the church shifted its emphasis from healing to forgiveness we find fewer and fewer records of healing by living people. While there was undoubtedly good reason for a new emphasis on moral responsibility, at the same time, as we have seen, the sacred and profane were becoming separated in a way not contemplated in either Judaism or early Christianity. As a result there was a gap between abstract ideas about God and the actual experience of men. Something had to flow in, as into a vacuum, and the idea closest at hand was that of an emotional and angry deity, of divine vengeance. The image of the compassionate Mary took the place of the sterner, judging Christ. As the church gave up the experience of divine love and concern expressed in healing, the

35. *The Life of St. Willibrord* by Alcuin, *The Life of St. Boniface* by Willibald, and *Acts of the Synod of 25 October 745, Condemning Adelbert and Clemens,* in *The Anglo-Saxon Missionaries in Germany,* trans. and ed. C. H. Talbot (1954), pp. 19 ff., 60, and 107 ff.

words of the liturgy came to say one thing while the actions involved in it expressed another: the propitiation of a God who punished naughty people with sickness.

God became more abstract and further removed from ordinary men, and it apparently became easier to see the divine in special individuals: the saints, who could receive almost magic power to heal because the perfection of their lives was pleasing to God. Some of their healings were probably genuine; men generally do not become saints without evincing a good measure of divine love and care. Meanwhile the whole idea of healing became more restricted to special instances, more superstitiously regarded and further from the center of officially accepted Christian life. The records in this ongoing period, which are numerous, describe healing almost entirely in connection with the relics of saints.[36]

About the year 1100 several of the most illustrious saints of the Middle Ages made their appearance. Around each of these, and the other notable saints who were to follow, appeared the same kind of miraculous events, usually healings. In Lyons people took the leavings from Anselm's plate to heal their sick, and some attested to healing simply by hearing him bless the sacrament at the altar. Innumerable people were cured by eating bread blessed by Bernard of Clairvaux. Around 1200, many healings were attributed to Dominic, founder of the Dominican order, and St.

36. Often, as with the miracles of Saint Benedict, there were various reports by different writers from several different shrines. For instance, *Les Miracles de Saint Bénoit, écrits par Adrevald, Aimoin, André, Raoul Tortaire et Hugues de Sainte Marie* (1858) covers only the miracles associated with Benedict that happened in France from about 825 to 1100.

See also *Vita Sancti Anselmi*, Auctore Eadmero I.6, II.5 and 7 in Migne, *Patrologiae Latinae* 158 (1864), cols. 76–80, 104–106, and 114–16; *Sancti Bernardi, Abbatis Clarae-Vallensis, Vita et Res Gestae*, bk I, Auctore Guillelmo IX.44, X.46, XI.53 f., XII.57 ff; bk VI, Auctore Philippo I-V, in Migne, *Patrologiae Latinae* 185 (1879), cols. 253–54, 256–60, and 373–86; *The Miraculous Powers of the Church of Christ asserted through each Successive Century from the Apostles down to the Present Time* (1756), pp. 250 ff.; Thomas of Celano, *Tractatus de miraculis S. Francisci Assisiensis* (1928); also Paul Sabatier, *Life of St. Francis of Assisi* (1938), pp. 192 ff.

Francis of Assisi. Indeed, St. Francis had to be buried hurriedly to keep his body from being dismembered by people who wanted even the smallest relic which still carried the healing power he had in life.

Each of these men apparently healed many persons individually by touch or prayer and the sign of the cross, and these incidents, well attested by eyewitnesses, often occurred in the presence of numbers of people. Bernard, for instance, wrote the life of Malachy, the primate of Ireland, and recounted not only the acts of his life, but told of the crowded funeral where Bernard himself, noticing a boy with a withered hand, placed it on the dead saint's hand and saw it healed.[37] There were other men not quite so famous, such as Antony of Padua, disciple of St. Francis, and in England Thomas of Hereford, Edmund of Canterbury, and Richard of Chichester, whose miraculous powers were also renowned.

Healing Among Catholics and Protestants

The gift of healing has continued to be given to those who have been most dedicated in their service of God, particularly persons working in physical ways to comfort the sick and poor. Those who are genuinely and deeply interested in caring for the misery of their fellow men seem to have less resistance to healing them

37. S. Bernardi Abbatis Clarae-Vallensis, *De Vita et Rebus Gestis S. Malachiae* XVII.40 f., XX.45 f., XXII.49 ff., XXIV.53, XXXI.75, in Migne, *Patrologiae Latinae* 182 (1879), cols. 1095–96, 1099–1100, 1101–1104, and 1117–18; also James Cotter Morison, *The Life and Times of Saint Bernard, Abbot of Clairvaux* (1901), pp. 56 ff., where some of the miracles are described with the comment that, "No expression of disgust or of contempt is required now with reference to such a stage of human belief. The great majority of mankind have ever held opinions similar to or identical with the above. The exception is to hold the reverse, and to substitute for Miracle a reliance on Law. Intrinsically, then, these groundless beliefs are nothing but silly tales, with little merit of either variety or invention. But, regarded historically, as stages in man's mental development, they assume quite a philosophic importance."

through spiritual ways. St. Francis Xavier, for instance, had studied medicine and put it to good use in the Far East, yet his letters give clear details of more than one miraculous healing; others have been related directly by eyewitnesses. St. Vincent of Paul, who was able to heal by the power of God, is better known for his practical labors as founder of a hospital and groups to care for the sick. The healings of St. Catherine of Siena, somewhat earlier, are no more amazing than her life of service to the sick, combined with political service to the church. Yet she was slandered again and again because she followed God as an individual, rather than keeping to her place within her order.[38] John Wesley, who later told of healings through prayer, also wrote an enormously popular book on practical medicine which helped many, many people in England.[39]

Luther, who had denied the gift of healing for his time, lived to see his friend Melanchthon visibly brought from the point of death through his own prayers. Five years later in 1545, the year before he died, when asked what to do for a man who was mentally ill, Luther wrote instructions for a healing service based on the New Testament letter of James, adding, "This is what we do, and that we have been accustomed to do, for a cabinetmaker here was similarly afflicted with madness and we cured him by prayer in Christ's name."[40] Like the two great saints of the church before him—Augustine and Aquinas both—he seems to have learned in his mellower years to value, rather than to disregard, this gift from God.

38. Henry James Coleridge, *The Life and Letters of St. Francis Xavier* (1881), I: 65 f., 147, and 215 f.; *The Miraculous Powers of the Church of Christ, op. cit.,* pp. 266 f.; Josephine Butler, *Catherine of Siena: A Biography* (1878), pp. 96 ff. and 191; [Margaret Roberts], *Saint Catherine of Siena and Her Times* (1906), pp. 51 ff.

39. *Primitive Physick, or an Easy and Natural Method of Curing Most Diseases,* published in 1747, went into nearly fifty editions and reprints by 1850.

40. W. J. Kooiman, *By Faith Alone: The Life of Martin Luther* (1954), p. 192; letter to Pastor Severin Schulze, June 1, 1545, *Luther: Letters of Spiritual Counsel* (1955), pp. 51 f.

About this time, too, there were St. Philip Neri, St. Francis de Sales, and St. Jean François Regis, whose healings by prayer or touch and the sign of the cross were widely known. One of the most famous of the many cures by means of relics also occurred in this period. Pascal's niece was healed at the dedication of a shrine when the nun who was her teacher was inspired to touch her with the relic of our Savior. Pascal added to his crest the symbols of this healing with the words *"scio cui credidi"* (What I once believed, I now know).[41]

George Fox, founder of the Society of Friends, knew the power of God to heal and recorded its use. Fox set down straightforward, concrete facts all through his *Journal*, and he also left a "Book of Miracles" in bound manuscript form, which was never published. All that remains of it today are the title and an index of brief notes about the experiences. Not even the record of the Society's discussion about publishing it was kept, as with other works.[42] Apparently the Quakers had had their fill of ridicule and painful accusations of demonism, blasphemy, and glorifying Fox as a magic-worker. Englishmen generally were interested in any kind of miracle worked by spirits, "touch doctors," and even angels, but not in the direct power of God working through man himself.

Yet the king's touch was sought for healing, so much that tickets had to be issued for the ceremony. By anointing he was given divine power, and until 1715 the Prayer Book ordered a special prayer for his healing power. The early Baptists in England and America practised anointing for healing and recorded

41. Marcel Jouhandeau, *St. Philip Neri* (1960), pp. 55 ff.; *Miraculous Powers*, pp. 268 ff. Pascal quoted by Dearmer, *op. cit.*, pp. 359 ff., from a contemporary source published in Paris in 1656.

42. Henry J. Cadbury, ed., *George Fox's 'Book of Miracles'* (1948), pp. 65 f. and 39 f. The editor has reconstructed parts of the "Book of Miracles" from the *Journal*, letters, and other sources. Healings are recorded in *The Journal of George Fox* (1911), 1: 58, 61, 108, 140 f., 199, 201; 2: 22, 226 f., 229, 234, 243, 310, 437 f., and 466 f.

their success, particularly with mental illness.[43] John Wesley described numerous miracles of God's healing, many of them through his own prayers, and also told one of the most delightful and down-to-earth stories of the time. He was on his way to an important preaching mission when his horse suddenly became lame. Quite naturally he placed his hand on the horse and prayed that he might be well. When it was time to go on, the animal had recovered, and both arrived in good spirits.[44]

In 1815 Prince Alexander of Hohenlohe began his priesthood during an epidemic in Germany, and only later found that something happened to sick people if he touched them with faith, asking God for healing. Father Mathew in Ireland was bringing thousands into the temperance movement when his healing powers were discovered by a sick woman who begged only for his blessing and a prayer. Dorothea Trüdel, who ran a home factory in Zurich, was worried when four of her workers became ill and medical treatment did not help; as she asked God what to do, the prayer of faith popped into her mind, and she was startled to find that it worked.[45]

In 1842 another amazing story of healings began in a village at

43. *The Records of a Church of Christ Meeting at Broadmead, Bristol 1640–1687*, quoted by Cadbury, *op. cit.*, pp. 2 f.

44. Again and again in his *Journal* Wesley described experiences of healing. See *The Journal of the Rev. John Wesley*, Vol. 1, Feb. 21, 1736; May 19, 1738; Feb. 9, Sept. 3, 28, and Oct. 13, 1739; Nov. 16, 1740; Feb. 15, 19, 21, May 8, Nov. 20, 1741; Mar. 31, Dec. 20, 1742; Nov. 2, 1745; Mar. 17, Oct. 12, 1746 (pp. 24, 95, 172 f., 223, 228, 232, 291, 304 ff, 310, 348, 365, 407, 433 ff., 547, 572 f.). Vol. 2, May 24, 1749; Apr. 8, Sept. 19, 1750; Apr. 27, 1752; Sept. 7–11, 1755; Apr. 6, June 22, Sept. 22, 1756; May 5, 1757; Feb. 23, 1758; May 12, July 1, 1759 (pp. 100 f., 145, 173, 225, 309, 326 f., 339 f., 353, 373 f., 405, 448 f., 461). Vol. 3, Dec. 26, 1761; Oct. 19, 1762; Oct. 1, 1763; Mar. 19, 1766; June 21, Oct. 30, 1767; May 2, 1768; May 18, June 26, 1772 (pp. 77 f., 117, 149 ff., 248, 289 f., 308, 325, 471, 483). Vol. 4, Oct. 16, 1778; Sept. 5, 1781; Apr. 24, Sept. 3, 1782; May 23, 1783; Apr. 12, 1784; May 31, 1785; Oct. 24, 1787; Oct. 7, 1790 (pp. 142, 220 231 f., 240, 253, 277, 320, 413, and 512 f.).

45. Dearmer, *op. cit.*, pp. 363 ff., cites the original German, Austrian, and English sources for Prince Hohenlohe; John Francis Maguire, *Father Mathew* (1864), pp. 529 ff.; *Dorothea Trüdel, or the Prayer of Faith* (1865), pp. 10 and 52 ff.

the edge of the Black Forest, where Johann Christoph Blumhardt had come as pastor. The clergyman needed to help a girl in his church who was seriously disturbed and whose illness was accompanied by unexplained and frightening psychic phenomena. He found himself face to face with a power that was working to split one personality and destroy others both physically and mentally. With every tactic of the Spirit, he was able in the end to help her regain mental and physical health, and won her lifelong loyalty to the church. But this was only one of the results. Blumhardt himself found the power of the Spirit through this confrontation, and both he and his parish were changed by it.

People began coming to him to confess things they had done. Because he knew the satanic forces that were pitted against God, he could offer forgiveness in a way unorthodox for Lutherans. He also had to meet the same satanic forces in himself and ask God to hold off judgment for a while. His parish came alive; people flocked to church, looking and acting younger, and suddenly healing was occurring. A physician who came to investigate recognized in one healthy woman a patient who had been declared incurable at the clinic at Tübingen. As Blumhardt's church became crowded with people from other parishes, the church also came to investigate. In 1846 he was forbidden to make physical healing a part of his spiritual ministry. His reply, however, made it clear that he could not stop healings from happening if he continued this ministry, and he was allowed to go on within his own parish. Six years later he left the church to give full time to working with the sick at Bad Boll.[46]

This ministry did not escape notice by the theologians. When Karl Barth came to the gift of healing, he criticized Bultmann for remarking that "The stories of Blumhardt are an abomination to

46. Friedrich Zündel, *Johann Christoph Blumhardt* (1967); also *Pioneer of Divine Healing: Jon. Chr. Blumhardt,* author and date unknown, published by the Order of St. Luke the Physician.

me!" Barth did not have much trouble in accepting that Blumhardt's idea of a struggle with the devil offered "new light" on healing in the New Testament. But he did not have any more to say. Instead, he went right on to consider how the manful struggle against sickness reveals a final kernel of truth: "that it is good for man to live a limited and impeded life. . . ."[47]

Francis Thompson, who knew the need for healing and salvation, in 1905 wrote his little book *Health and Holiness* as a plea for understanding that "we can no longer set body against spirit and let them come to grips after the lighthearted fashion of our ancestors."[48] In the Catholic Church, to which he was speaking, one way was still open for a direct healing relation between body and spirit. This was the healing shrine, which has taken on a new form in modern times.

When the crypt was built in Chartres Cathedral in the twelfth century, it was so constructed that it could easily be washed down after the sick pilgrims had left. This tradition of coming to sleep at a shrine or at least to visit it was common throughout Europe. In the eighteenth century the practice received new attention. From Lourdes and Fatima to Ste. Anne de Beaupré in Canada, these new shrines have sprung from a spontaneous contact with the Spirit, from visions given to a living person. From 1860 on, the number of pilgrims has increased until more than two million people go to Lourdes alone each year. In 1882 a medical bureau was set up at which close to 100,000 persons now register annually, with well over a thousand nonmedical cures carefully examined since 1918. Procedure now includes the requirement of a full preceding medical record as well as follow-up information at stated intervals, for recognition of a genuine cure. By 1957 fifty-four specific healings had been accepted as miracles

47. Karl Barth, *Church Dogmatics* 3, *The Doctrine of Creation*, pt. 4 (1961): 371 and 374.
48. p. 30.

(i.e., impossible by any natural means).[49]

There have also been healings in Germany through Theresa Neumann, whose spiritual gifts have been examined from all sides, particularly the visions she had so frequently, her fasts, and the stigmata she bore at special times. It is interesting that one of the most perceptive and thoughtful of these studies, written after two visits there, brings out her effect on the life of the parish, pointing to just the kind of situation in which such gifts as healing do break through.[50] Dorothy Kerin in England was another such gifted person.

The Healing Sects Influence the Church

In our own country healing has had a lively history in the past hundred years, starting with the teaching of Phineas P. Quimby and the development of Christian Science and New Thought. Quimby became interested through mesmerism and clairvoyance. As the Quimby Manuscripts show, his knowledge of the power of the mind came from his experiences with hypnotism. He also found how easily a clairvoyant under hypnotism could pick up what a sick person had told about his condition, and then offer a simple remedy that often produced a cure.[51] He came to believe that disease resulted only from mental error, and all healing from right belief or wisdom. He found that he was able to reach the need of individuals below the surface of the mind and suggest wisdom based on the New Testament and his own practi-

49. Francois Leuret and Henri Bon, *Modern Miraculous Cures: A Documented Account of Miracles and Medicine in the Twentieth Century* (1957), pp. 107 ff. and 205; also Monden, *op. cit.*, pp. 194 ff., for information from various sources and an excellent presentation of selected cases.

50. Neil G. McCluskey, S.J., "Darkness and Light over Konnersreuth," *The Priest* 10 (September 1954): 765–74.

51. *The Quimby Manuscripts*, ed. Horatio W. Dresser (1961), pp. 29 ff.; also a section on Mrs. Eddy up to her publication of *Science and Health* in 1875, pp. 152 ff. The 1921 edition contains a number of her letters to Quimby.

cal good sense, but he could see no good in organized Christianity, which only perpetuated error.

Mary Baker Eddy came to him as a patient in 1862 and was soon well enough to begin treating other people by his methods. The inspiration for Christian Science came after his death. Again she experienced healing, while alone reading the New Testament, and the idea grew of a church that would reject illness and even the reality of the body entirely. In 1879 the church was organized. After this Unity, with its ministry of "Silent Unity," and Religious Science and other New Thought groups were founded by others who tried to follow Quimby's thinking. In spite of their philosophic approach, these sects have had a real insight into the historic ministry of Christianity to the bodies of men, and numbers of healings have unquestionably occurred in these groups, as did not happen in the traditional church of the time.

A. J. Gordon, the great Baptist minister in Boston, pointed out in his *Ministry of Healing* in 1882, that the book would not be popular with either theologians or most Christians; their embarrassment was only too obvious if someone spoke of God's answering a prayer. Yet Dr. Gordon took the trouble to describe the history of healing and even mention examples in his own ministry, remarking, "So far as our observation goes, the most powerful effect of such experiences is upon the subjects themselves, in the marked consecration and extraordinary spiritual anointing which almost invariably attend them. We can bear unqualified testimony on this point."[52]

Indeed, as others have realized, conservative Christianity has reason to thank these new groups for opening a door which its own philosophic approach had closed. Had the mainline

52. A. J. Gordon, *The Ministry of Healing* (1961), p. 206. In his remarkable ministry Dr. Gordon brought to reality the dream he had had of Christ coming unknown into his church; see my book *Dreams*, pp. 186 ff.

churches been more open theologically, the healing movement might have been integrated in them. But in view of their hostility toward the subject, the movement had to go forward on its own or come to an end. In a sense the theological rigidity of the popular churches was directly responsible for the development of these sects.

Since that time a new spirit has been moving both in the church and in medicine. The pioneer movement started in Boston in 1905 by Dr. Elwood Worcester, his colleagues at Emmanuel Church, and several physicians and psychiatrists in his congregation, brought results for many persons who had not been helped by either approach alone. At St. Mark's-in-the-Bowery Dr. Loring W. Batten, who also taught Old Testament literature at General Theological Seminary, carried on the same work and helped to spread the ideas of Emmanuel. At the same time the Guild of Health—now still active—was organized in England to practice and encourage healing in cooperation with medicine. A few years later the Order of the Nazarene was formed in this country.

With a gradual growth in medical understanding, two of the most influential groups in this country were started in the 1930s. The Camps Farthest Out, established by Glenn Clark, have introduced a great many lay people and clergy to the reality of spiritual healing; the two camps held particularly for healing have continued to grow. Dr. John Gayner Banks, founder of the Order of St. Luke, emphasized the need for lay people to practice healing, and the order is now active in several countries. As noted earlier, in the monthly magazine *Sharing* a directory of healing services appears from time to time, which shows dramatically the great increase in interest in recent years.

Through the Schools of Pastoral Care the healing ministry of Agnes Sanford is known personally to numbers of people in this country as well as abroad. Her books, beginning with *The Healing*

Light, offer an excellent introduction to the subject, and her novel *Lost Shepherd* is essentially a story of healing power. Alfred Price, Louise Eggleston, Tommy Tyson, and Olga Worrall are others whose lives are deeply involved in ministering healing through the Spirit. There is also the very remarkable ministry of Kathryn Kuhlman, which has touched so many lives and focused so much attention on the possibility of spiritual healing. In the Pentecostal churches, along with other gifts of the Spirit, a renewal of healing has occurred which was quite unexpected when these churches were beginning. The ministry of Oral Roberts has touched yet another group of people, and friends who have known him well have told me of his genuineness. The ministry of healing need not be hampered by good public relations.

There have been two excellent studies of the experience of healing in our time. In *The Case for Spiritual Healing* Don H. Gross has presented the reality of these experiences with enthusiasm and deep understanding. Bernard Martin, who has also written *If God Does Not Die,* offers a framework and a practical point of view very similar to our own in his book, *The Healing Ministry in the Church.* In addition, a recent issue of the *Journal of Pastoral Counseling* was devoted entirely to spiritual healing, treating various aspects from experimentation to the charismatic movement.[53]

We have already mentioned the action of the Anglican Bishops meeting at Lambeth. Finally, Vatican II made it quite clear to Catholics that healing is to be expected in the church. The Decree on the Apostolate of the Laity (I.3 f) not only directs the use of gifts received from the Holy Spirit, including the special gifts outlined by Paul in 1 Corinthians 12, but the Constitution on the Sacred Liturgy (III.73 ff.) specifies that

53. Don H. Gross, *The Case for Spiritual Healing* (1958); Bernard Martin, *The Healing Ministry in the Church* (1960); *Journal of Pastoral Counseling* 6 (Fall-Winter, 1971–1972).

"Extreme Unction," which may also and more fittingly be called "anointing of the sick," is not a sacrament for those only who are at the point of death. Hence, as soon as any one of the faithful begins to be in danger of death from sickness or old age, the appropriate time for him to receive this sacrament has certainly already arrived.

In addition to the separate rites for anointing of the sick and for Viaticum,* a continuous rite shall be prepared according to which the sick man is anointed after he has made his confession and before he receives Viaticum.

The number of the anointings is to be adapted to the occasion, and the prayers accompanying the rite of anointing are to be revised so as to correspond with the varying conditions of the sick who receive the sacrament.[54]

*The last communion given to the dying, or "provision for the journey."

This new emphasis on healing in the Christian churches is anything but an isolated phenomenon. It is world-wide, extending to places like India, for instance, with the healings of Shai Baba, and Japan, where dozens of new religions have been founded since World War II, of which healing is often the principal aspect.[55] My friend Jean Willans tells the same story of Hong Kong and the healings among agnostics, Protestants, and Catholics there, with other gifts of the Spirit often accompanying them. Clearly, a new spirit is moving among men, which speaks of their need for healing. Let us now see how this can be understood—medically, psychologically, and in terms of the deepest insights of Christianity.

54. *The Documents of Vatican II* (1966), pp. 492 ff., and 161. Italics mine.
55. Thomas Wayne Johnson, "Japan's New Religions: A Search for Uniformities," *Kroeber Anthropological Society Papers*, University of California, no. 42, pp. 112 ff.

10

Body, Emotions, and Healing

There was a time not too long ago when the medical profession felt quite confident that the nature of disease was fully understood. There was reason for the confidence. Within scarcely a hundred years, some of the most dangerous diseases have been almost eliminated, and medical men have found ways to repair or reduce the damage of a great many others. We have gained an understanding of the human body and some of its inter-relationships in ways that could hardly be dreamed of at the beginning of this period. And in the process a new understanding has been growing among medical men.

All these advances were realized as medicine took the one-way approach to disease discussed in chapter 2. There is no question that the approach was needed; but gradually it became the total understanding. The human body was seen as a mere complex aggregation of atoms reacting to physical laws like any other organization of matter. The sick person was even treated like a reaction in a sterile test tube, and hospitals were often run this way. But as one friend in the medical profession—a man whose quiet concern and humor have helped bring many to health— recently remarked to a group of students, "You cannot cure an ulcer patient by performing a partial gastrectomy, or an asthmatic with an injection of aminophylin, or even an ulcerative colitis victim with a removal of the sigmoid colon. The separation of the psyche and the soma can only be effected by a removal of the cerebrum, and that has not been medically accepted."

Even mental illness came to be considered the result of some damage to the brain or nervous system. In 1913 when Noguchi discovered the syphilitic origin of general paralysis, hopes were high for finding a similarly concrete cause of other mental disturbances. But neurologists were able to account for only a few, like those of speech or body movements; they did not point up very often that under the microscope a psychotic brain looked just about the same as a normal brain.

An autonomous and nonphysical soul or psyche could not be a part of this closed mechanical system and neither could such a psyche—or even God—affect it. Mind and body together, man was only one part of a vast system of matter, a machine which had been programed and sealed. There was no room for argument. This basic assumption was accepted, not only by physicians, but alike by philosophers, theologians, and ordinary Christians. Only as men such as Einstein, the Curies, Heisenberg, Freud and Jung, and Teilhard de Chardin began to uncover a very different structure in the actualities they worked with, and new facts poured in from all sides, did a shift occur in this assumption of the mechanistic naturalism of the universe.

Within medicine itself, the tension about basic assumptions returned as it was realized that certain psychoneuroses were simply being "talked away." The brain was still the same cellular organism, but the mind could be freed from sickness by a mental understanding of itself in a new light. Not only that, but obviously physical conditions such as hysterical blindness and paralysis—conditions that could closely simulate almost any organic malady—were cured at the same time, as well as functional diseases of the intestines, heart, and other organs.

Freud made his first *public* address on psychoanalysis in 1909, at Clark University in Worcester, Massachusetts. To his great surprise he found it possible to discuss freely and scientifically what was so objectionable in ordinary circles, and he gained important backing and interest at Harvard. Within fifteen years clinical psychiatry was adopting a psychosomatic view, keeping the *psyche*, or mind, and the *soma*, or body, separated by almost apologetic explanations to medicine. Then in 1935 a young woman teaching in the medical school of Columbia University published an exhaustive survey of all the research on psychosomatic interrelationships. This was Dr. Flanders Dunbar, whose book *Emotions and Bodily Changes* laid a firm base for further investigation. Four years later the journal *Psychosomatic Medicine* was founded, which has remained an important source of information and communication for those on this growing edge.

Meanwhile World War I had put psychoneurosis into the headlines and polite conversation with the colorful term "shell shock," and the first textbook on psychosomatic medicine, published in 1943, pointed out that this country had already spent a billion dollars for physical care of veterans with neuropsychiatric disorders.[1] The authors quoted from several sources to make a strong plea for psychotherapy, so that these veterans and their families could return to normal life. They made clear that the problem of neurosis is a general one and that war merely offers a wider opportunity for it to be outwardly expressed.

World War II showed the importance of psychiatry as a general medical tool. W. C. Menninger, then chief of the Army division of psychiatry, explained that "every army physician was confronted with a far greater number of patients having physical complaints in which no organic pathology could be found, than he saw in civilian life."[2] In the medical and surgical wards as high as a quarter of the men suffered from purely functional disturb-

1. Edward Weiss and O. Spurgeon English, *Psychosomatic Medicine: The Clinical Application of Psychopathology to General Medical Problems* (1943).
2. *Ibid.*, 2d ed. (1949), p. 54.

ances, particularly among the heart and gastrointestinal cases, while two-thirds of the psychiatric patients surveyed had physical complaints. The neurotic or emotionally disturbed organ was a startling reality.

The medical profession is divided in its theory and practice. Development of a fantastic array of new drugs, among them a series which can produce symptoms of mental illness in normal persons, has helped to keep the simpler view of a purely physical medicine alive, if somewhat beleaguered and bewildered. But the physician himself is rarely allowed to forget that his stock of remedies includes a good deal more than exclusively physical treatment. Dr. Jerome Frank, professor of psychiatry at Johns Hopkins, has written that a fresh review of man's religious life with today's understanding

emphasizes the profound influence of emotions on health and suggests that anxiety and despair can be lethal, confidence and hope, life-giving. The modern assumptive world of Western society, which includes mind-body dualism, has had difficulty incorporating this obvious fact and has therefore tended to under-emphasize it.

And in concluding his study, *Persuasion and Healing*, he wrote,

The question of how far a physician should go to meet a patient's expectations is a thorny one. Obviously he cannot use methods in which he himself does not believe. Moreover, reliance on the healing powers of faith, if it led to neglect of proper diagnostic or treatment procedures, would clearly be irresponsible. On the other hand, faith may be a specific antidote for certain emotions such as fear or discouragement, which may constitute the essence of a patient's illness. For such patients, the mobilization of expectant trust by whatever means may be as much an etiological remedy as penicillin for pneumonia.[3]

3. Jerome D. Frank, *Persuasion and Healing* (1963) pp. 61 and 233 f. This understanding has spread widely in recent years. For instance, an article by William A. McGarey entitled "Healing 'Round the World" was published by *Arizona Medicine* in the October 1971 issue (pp. 752–9), telling about spiritual healing and

Medical minds are wrestling with the whole materialistic medical theory. Foremost among them have been Dr. C. G. Jung and his followers. It is only recently, however, that the same questioning has been taken up by philosophers and theologians. We shall have more to say about this in a later chapter.

Specific Medical Puzzles

Perhaps the best way to illustrate the changing medical attitude is to look at the thinking in certain specific medical areas: for instance, tuberculosis. This is a physically communicated disease, caused without exception by the presence of *Bacillus tuberculosis* in the affected area. It has been controlled, in that it is a comparatively negligible cause of death today in this country; whereas in 1900 it was the leading cause. Yet among communicable diseases tuberculosis still leads as a chronic disabler. While the rate of new cases continues to fall, this classic ailment still strikes more people by far than any other communicable illness except measles, venereal disease, or streptococcal sore throat. In short, it is a specifically physical disease about which medicine has a great store of knowledge, and yet, as with every other disease of every kind, in its etiology and pathology there is still a blank page.

In a time when one-seventh of the world's population was dying of tuberculosis, Sir William Osler, the greatest medical teacher of his day, warned his profession that the fate of the tubercular depended more on what they had in their heads than on what was in their chests. It was known then that 90 percent of the world's city dwellers who died from other causes had small tuberculous lesions in their bodies. Today's wide use of X ray has

particularly the experiences of Edgar Cayce, whose many years of documented diagnosis and prescription combine physical means with (often) emotional recommendations and—so far as one can make it out—a spiritual source.

proven that almost no one escapes infection at some time in his or her life.

Allen K. Krause, who was probably the leading writer on tuberculosis in this country, faced this problem in terms of the "lung block." The bacillus lives and breeds persistently in just the dirt and darkness found in tenements. In his book *Environment and Resistance in Tuberculosis,* he pointed out that the lung-block dwellers nearly all had live tubercle bacilli in them and seemed to keep them. But by far the greater number of these refractory subjects never developed a symptom, and they lived to die of other things. Dr. Krause gave a real place to personality disturbance in the environment that either nourishes or retards disease. He wrote:

When, sick with angina pectoris and aware of the influence of psychic disturbance upon his physical condition, John Hunter said that his life was in the hands of any rascal in London who chose to take it, he simply indicated the possibly more disastrous effects of an environment about which our books on general medicine are strangely or perversely silent, yet which drives thousands of us mortals to our practitioners. This is the environment of personal association—of antagonistic personal association, in particular. . . . Until recently, when psychiatrists again brought this type of environment into prominence and coined a new nomenclature to speak intelligibly to one another of "repressions" and "conflicts," and the morbid results of these, formal medical instruction, given to more material and mechanical views of disease, was apparently oblivious to its existence and influence.[4]

This was written in 1923; fortunately it is less true today. Several years ago a good friend of mine went into the West's leading university hospital for diagnosis of his third bout with pulmonary tuberculosis. The university radiologist, a neighbor and close friend of his, grimaced over the pictures and, pointing to

4. Allen K. Krause, *Environment and Resistance in Tuberculosis* (1923), p. 11.

his own temple, remarked, "It's time you got things straight up here." As soon as he was able my friend followed this advice, and has remained in good health since that time.

The other leading permanent destroyer of health among communicable diseases is syphilis. The total reliance on penicillin, which seemed possible only a few years ago, now appears illusory since the unit dosage has gradually had to be stepped up. Recently venereal disease was declared pandemic in this country. Public health measures are being pushed and research is continuing. But in spite of all that has been learned, the unexplained fact remains that over half the cases of untreated syphilis are spontaneously cured or show no sign of a third stage except for a positive blood reaction.

A wound that heals slowly, or is infected and fails to respond to treatment, poses direct questions about varying recuperative power. As physicians have reminded me on several occasions, it is not what they do that actually heals. Without the body's recuperative power they could do next to nothing—no surgery or suturing, for instance, would be possible. What the physician does is to remove the roadblocks so that the forces within the individual are freed to work for healing and restoration. Yet these forces that heal in one individual are slow to respond, or fail entirely, in another.

These are questions raised by physicians themselves in the areas of medicine's greatest successes. They come up precisely because of those successes. No one any longer has to touch and bury the victims of black smallpox, or fear having a baby in the hospital because of puerperal fever, or see a child die of diphtheria. Since so many external and tangible causes of disease have been met and prevented, medical science itself has turned to inner questions. Endocrinology has revealed the indispensable functions of the internal secretions; work on allergy has shown the body's own production of indisposing histamines; various fields are studying the maze of complex chemicals produced to keep the body's economy going; while psychiatry, finally, is glimpsing how the mind relates to the whole.

Perhaps it is not so much medicine that is bewildered. Both doctor and patient have time today to worry about illness that disables or incapacitates, and there is enough to worry over. Recent Public Health surveys show that nearly two-thirds of the adults outside of institutions in this country suffer from one or more chronic conditions.[5] These are mainly diseases whose causes are unknown, or arise within the body itself. It is recognized today that emotional factors play a large part in them. While it may be easier for us to believe that the doctor has a pill of just the right color and size to cure the part that pains us, or that the surgeon could simply remove it, physicians have had to face the results of this kind of practice. As Adolf Meyer, who became world-famous in psychiatry during his many years at Johns Hopkins, once reminded the medical profession, "It is sad that we still do get patients who arrive practically eviscerated, for a last trial, which very often ought to have been the first— namely, that of getting the life adjustment within the range of socialized health offered while it can be fully used."[6]

It is odd how often commonly used folk sayings speak of emotions in terms of physical symptoms. Without stopping to think, one says, "I can't stomach it!" "It took my breath away!" "I was scared stiff." Or he speaks truthfully of an "angry throat," or tells someone, "You give me a pain in the neck!" When we stop to think (and perhaps we should do so more often), we see how common the knowledge is that emotions and feelings have a real physical effect on our bodies. Stage fright, or blushing, or waking

5. *Limitation of Activity and Mobility Due to Chronic Conditions: United States–July 1965–June 1966* (May 1968).

6. Adolf Meyer, "The Psychiatric Aspects of Gastroenterology," *American Journal of Surgery* 15 (March 1932): 508 f.

up afraid in the night bring actual physiological changes in the body, only a part of which are sensed by the mind. The same kinds of changes in muscular tension, blood pressure, and glandular secretion going on inside a sick person's body can have a decisive influence on how he reacts to an illness.

Sociological studies have shown clearly that when white men have brought their culture patterns to primitive areas, deaths among the natives have been due not only to the disease the whites brought, but also to the disruption of social life that occurred. Robbed of their culture and deprived of meaningful existence, native people have died like flies. As John Cowper Powys shows in *The Meaning of Culture*, life cannot exist without the matrix of a culture. It must be remembered, however, that those who profess to have no purpose in life often have an unconscious will to live, while others who say they want to live may be unaware of their deep meaninglessness. Still, it is a safe conclusion that life unsupported by meaning seldom lasts long; it is terminated in one way or another.

A dramatic experience brought this home to me several years ago. It happened in a small hospital where a member of my family had been confined for months with a heart condition. As usual, one gets to know a great deal about other patients and their troubles. We were visiting one day when we heard that a woman with a similar condition had just been admitted, and later in the week I was amazed to learn that she had died. The physician commented to us that she had not been particularly sick, but had no desire to live. Then he made a point of telling me quietly, "If your aunt had as sound a heart as the dead woman had, she would be out playing golf right now."

The studies of taboo deaths among primitive peoples, and also of certain deaths in prisoner-of-war camps, indicate a close parallel. Dr. Jerome Frank has gathered together this work, as well as relevant research on animals, showing that when terror or despair strikes either man or animals, deaths actually occur from no other cause.[7] Recently I was told much the same thing by a surgeon to whom I happened to mention these studies. He said that he never initiated surgery when a patient was fearful if it could be postponed, because he had seen so many unfortunate results from operating under those conditions.

Assuming that these things are true, how can something as intangible as emotion have such effect on the physical body?

A Bridge Between Mind and Body

One of the principal ways that emotions produce direct physical changes in the body is through the autonomic nervous system. This remarkable mechanism, which enables the human physique to organize its own processes without conscious direction, actually consists of two systems. The parasympathetic part sees to building up the body and storing energy. It stimulates the organs that digest and assimilate food; by dilating the blood vessels that supply them, it slows down the heart and lowers blood pressure. It also has protective functions such as contracting the pupils of the eyes against light or the bronchial tubes against foreign matter.

The sympathetic system, on the other hand, prepares for a quick release of energy, organizing the whole body to meet an emergency. It works mostly in opposition to the parasympathetic system and countermands its directions. The impulses are sent out all at once, changing the blood supply and ordering new secretions and chemicals needed for exertion.[8]

Both of these parts of the nervous system originate in the

7. Frank, *op. cit.*, pp. 38 ff.; also Herman Feifel, ed., *The Meaning of Death* (1959), pp. 302 ff.

8. We are describing the principal and general function of the sympathetic system; these nerve pathways also carry specific messages to individual organs—for instance, to dilate the pupils of the eyes to adjust to darkness.

hypothalamus, a part of the midbrain near the head of the spinal column which evolved early in vertebrate life. Unlike the cortex, which can be consciously activated, it is not under ordinary conscious control. Once an impression is received in the hypothalamus and the autonomic nervous system is set in action, one can rarely if ever just switch it off.[9]

To see this clearly, let us suppose that we are driving a car along at a reasonable rate, in a thoroughly law-abiding manner. Suddenly there is a siren and/or flashing red light in the rear-view mirror. As we come to a stop we find our breathing heavy, our hearts pounding, our bodies tense. It makes no difference whether we want to have these reactions or not; we may not feel any conscious fear of authority figures at all; but when the officer looms up, these reactions occur. Once we perceive something that is alarming, the body is activated by the sympathetic nervous system. Whether we like it or not, it cannot be directly controlled. One may be quite unaware that anything is frightening him; his unconscious fear still triggers this system. In fact, if one constantly reacts from sympathetic stimulation without seeing a reason, he may be quite sure that it comes from some situation he does not know he fears. There is no point in telling him to "snap out of it"; the person who has such reactions cannot do so. Only as his fear is removed can his reactions be controlled.

The sympathetic system organizes a "fight or flight" response to danger. When there is anger—call it resentment, hostility, hatred, or whatever name you give to the aggressive emotion—the sympathetic nervous system is set in motion. Equally, when there is fear—call it concern, apprehension, anxiety, or whatever name you give to the emotion of active withdrawal—the sympa-

9. James Hillman has made an excellent study of the whole subject of emotion from a phenomenological point of view. In his book *Emotion* (1964), pp. 214 ff., he calls attention to the studies by M. Choisy of a group of rigorously disciplined yogis who were able to resist physiological reaction when presented with cobras and scorpions. This is extremely rare, however.

thetic system is set in action. Anger and fear are strangely similar; indeed they are opposite sides of the same coin. Both are reactions to a threatening situation. In anger one feels that he can meet the threat by attack, while in fear he feels that he is inadequate to deal with it and must run away or freeze.

What happens, then, when the sympathetic system is activated? A tiny chemical produced in the hypothalamus, which has only recently been identified, starts a chain reaction. A message goes first to the pituitary, which then alerts the adrenals and other glands to start the chain of commands. Immediately the blood vessels to the stomach and intestinal areas are shut down. Digestion, assimilation, and elimination all halt, and blood driven away from these areas is sent to the brain, lungs, and external muscles where energy is suddenly required. A flow of adrenalin speeds the tempo. Both heart and lungs are stimulated to move fuel and oxygen faster. The bronchial tubes relax, admitting more oxygen. The liver and other storage depots are directed to release carbohydrates as quickly utilizable blood sugar. Blood pressure rises; the clotting time of the blood decreases as the body prepares itself for a possible wound.

What an admirable system this is for the caveman suddenly confronted by a bear or another angry caveman! Immediately his whole body is mobilized for action. Energy is concentrated for release. All his vegetative tendencies are inhibited, and a spurt of adrenalin spurs him to instant decision and action. Even his blood will clot faster if he is hurt. Without any conscious thought he is ready to put maximum energy into a fight, or turn and run for the nearest tree. The sympathetic system works magnificently in the face of real physical danger. But it is a bit superfluous if the anger, resentment, or fear is directed toward the stock market or one's mother-in-law, toward government spending or the inefficiency of an airline, or just a threatening world. Yet these things can produce the same physical reactions as facing a charging bear or a berserk caveman.

One does not even have to be consciously holding these fears or resentments. They may be attitudes tucked away in an over-looked corner of the mind and still touch off the entire reaction just as if one were constantly confronted by a raging beast. But if the "beast" is an unconscious worry, one's energy is not di-rectly drawn upon. Instead, his entire body is constantly ordered to prepare for what does not happen. The parasympathetic im-pulses, directing his organs to return to their natural functions, are constantly contradicted. Unconscious fear simply defeats the autonomic system in its seeking for balance between hunger and exertion.[10]

Perhaps it seems implausible that a man who may even appear calm and controlled can have these pronounced physical reac-tions going on in his body, produced by fear of which he is not aware, or anger he does not consciously know he feels. It is easy to see that the "adrenalin addict," as Aldous Huxley has called the man who cannot hold his temper, must be hurting himself. But *unconscious* fear and anger can react incessantly on a man's heart and kidneys, his stomach, or his entire circulatory system without his knowing it, until the structure of one organ or an-other has been changed enough to cause him pain. The lie detec-tor functions on exactly this principle, recording physical reac-tions to memories a man wants to conceal. A medical "lie detector" has shown clearly that the same reactions occur in patients who may not know they are angry or afraid.

This technique has been used to study hypertension or high blood pressure.[11] While the physician talked with a patient about

10. There may also be a withdrawal reaction that results in constant overstimu-lation of the parasympathetic system, as we shall see.

11. Hypertension is still the greatest disease problem of adult middle life. Its deadly effects on the eyes, brain, heart, and kidneys are caused by constriction of the peripheral arteries, which cuts down the blood supply to certain areas. Nearly a fourth of all deaths after fifty are still due to this disorder, most of them

everyday things, the blood pressure and flow of blood in the kidneys were recorded. When the patient was led to discuss very personal matters, often things about his close family, blood pressure rose even though he showed little or no emotion outwardly. At the same time the blood vessels in the kidneys were constricted practically enough to account for the increased pressure in his whole body. This renal blood flow fell off by as much as 25 percent. By letting the patient then talk about things that made him feel secure, his blood pressure went down and kidney circulation returned to a more normal level as the small blood vessels were allowed to dilate again.

And if this is an everyday occurrence, with emotional pressure continually producing physical pressures, what happens? Somewhere in the body a chemical is apparently produced that further constricts the arterial system, damaging other organs. Unless the cycle is interrupted, the blood vessels can thicken and become inelastic; functional high blood pressure becomes organic high blood pressure, with irreversible damage to heart and kidneys

resulting immediately from stroke, heart failure, or kidney failure.

A great deal has been learned about its cause. While a tendency seems to be inherited, in practically every case there is also a direct relation to emotional tensions. It is generally associated with damage to the kidneys from severe limitation of the blood supply caused by the sympathetic nervous system. This first began to be understood about 1933, when an ingenious silver clamp was applied to a dog's renal arteries; the kidneys deteriorated, and the dog developed persistent high blood pressure. He then remained diseased even though the nerves were severed so that the sympathetic nervous system no longer functioned. The researchers suggested that the starved kidney releases a chemical into the blood stream that continues to constrict feeder arteries all through the body, further damaging the kidneys so that the hypertensive reaction thus becomes self-perpetuating. The later work of Hans Selye at Montreal University has shown that this may well be the case, cf. "The General Adaptation Syndrome and Diseases of Adaptation," *Journal of Clinical Endocrinology* 6 (February 1946): 217 ff.

In addition, hypertension is almost entirely a disease of Western civilization. The American Negro has no racial inheritance of it. Yet the Negro in this country has a tendency to develop this disorder two and a half to three times as great as the white American, and statistics show that it generally runs a severer course in the Negro than in his white brother. Weiss and English, *op. cit.*, 2d ed. (1949), pp. 303 ff.

and brain. The magazine *Fortune*, in a hard-hitting article in January 1972, laid these facts on the line to show business executives the imperative need to deal with stress before anything else. This important article, "What Stress Can Do to You," was condensed in the April 1972 *Reader's Digest.*[12]

Any organ can become the target of the autonomic system when the body is continously misused as an emotional outlet. If the blood vessels in the stomach keep being overconstricted and then dilated, a pocket can form in the lining and burst. And if this is followed by overstimulation of the parasympathetic system, with plenty of acid and no food, the stomach may go to work on itself, and an ulcer results. In the days before the now popular acid-absorbing pills, physicians at Mayo Clinic devised the eating method of controlling an ulcer. If one had been upset or angry during the evening, he got up in the middle of the night and ate a large meal of beefsteak, cottage cheese, or some other protein that used up any extra hydrochloric acid. (Rebecca Beard has commented that this was a fine thing for a man to do just because he could not keep his temper.)

In much the same way, high blood pressure over a long period can cause a stroke or heart failure; as the body responds to continuous threat with new secretions, the artery muscles thicken and pressure builds up until a weakened spot in the system gives way. Or fear and anger can simply start a clot moving toward a constricted artery in the brain and suddenly cause the whole body to die, or destroy a bit of brain tissue. It is fine for a man faced with a wild beast to have his blood-clotting time decreased and the pressure raised. But for the man on Wall Street, faced instead with a ticker tape, this physical response to anxiety increases the possibility of angina, or of a break or a clot causing all sorts of physical effects from coronary thrombosis to cerebral

12. Walter McQuade, "What Stress Can Do to You," *Fortune* (January 1972), pp. 102–7, 134–41.

accidents. As one New York physician remarked to a friend, the cardiologists made their money on Wall Street when the ticker tape went down and heart disease jumped.

The remark of John Hunter, the famous English surgeon, who died of angina pectoris, has been quoted earlier. Osler used to repeat it to his students: "John Hunter," he told them, "used to say that his life was in the hands of any rascal who chose to worry him—and his fatal attack happened during a fit of anger." To put over the same point Dr. A. M. Master, consulting cardiologist at Mt. Sinai Hospital in New York, recently told a postgraduate group of heart specialists[13] that angina patients must learn not to get angry at a nagging wife, or worry about unimportant things like being overcharged or shortchanged. If they learn this essential lesson they not only stay alive, but live longer and more happily than if they had never had a chest pain. "But," he added, "only 25 percent of the people with angina are able to avoid emotional stress and keep calm in the face of aggravation and frustration." It is all too clear that nothing more than emotion, uncontrolled and ill-used, can simply destroy the human body. Yet how can it be otherwise in the face of life as it is?

Indeed this is only one of the ways in which emotions have a profound effect on the body; there are other mechanisms as yet not so clear or so well known as these particular autonomic reactions. Let us look at certain of these effects—some of them the subject of the most recent and fascinating research in medicine —and then consider in detail the emotions involved.

The Body Taking the Brunt

Medical men have known for a long time that illness can be a means of escape from anxiety or other emotional upset. There are

13. At the program of the American College of Cardiology, held at Scripps Clinic and Research Foundation in La Jolla, California, in December 1965.

many reports of cases in which a physical disorder appears to be a psychological necessity to the sick person, and he reacts to physical cure by developing another, more serious ailment. This is known as a conversion reaction or illness, the emotional difficulty being converted into a bodily disorder.

One delightful story is told of a young man who came from South America to study in New York. He found the wild life of the great city far more interesting than his studies, and when examination time rolled around he was unprepared. He became conveniently sick with stomach trouble so severe that he had to be sent back to his own country under medical care. He was not goldbricking; this was genuine illness, but one from which he recovered quickly when he was safe at home. One cannot tell a person with this kind of illness just to snap out of it, however, and expect him to get well. This is just what he cannot do. If one has no way of resolving an emotional conflict except by neurotic illness, treatment may differ, but he is just as sick as if he had measles.

In other cases this kind of illness may show up as a means of controlling other personalities. In the textbook *Psychosomatic Medicine*, one of the authors recounts an instance of this kind to show how he learned early in practice that "treating sick people consists of something more than a knowledge of disease."[14] A young woman, under his care for headaches, grew steadily worse instead of getting well. When she finally had to be hospitalized with intestinal complications, an older physician was called who quickly put his finger on the sore spot. The girl's only brother, for whom she cared deeply and who carried family responsibility, was planning to marry. The patient's illness expressed her opposition, and when she understood its meaning she promptly recovered.

14. Weiss and English, *op. cit.*, 2d ed. (1949), p. vii.

Most of us know at least a little about such illness. Perhaps one
has known some woman who never married because Mama's
heart invariably went bad at the sight of an eligible suitor. Or if
one has had any real neurotic trouble himself—and my experience is that most people fall into this class—he has probably
thought at some time or another, "If only I could be just sick
enough to get off the hook!"—or perhaps the body has in fact
done it for us. Then one wishes that all he had were his neurosis,
once he discovers how difficult it can be to change these ways in
which the body expresses emotion on its own. And these are far
from being the only such effects.

It is now certain, for instance, that diabetes, one of the leading
causes of death today, can be triggered by an emotional crisis. In
one recent study twenty-five new cases of full-blown diabetes
were investigated, none of which had shown any previous sign
of the disease. Twenty of these persons had either lost someone
close to them or suffered a severe personal setback shortly before
their symptoms were discovered. Other patients were also studied who had been doing well on insulin until they had to face a
personal crisis and the disease suddenly went out of control
again.[15] At present, at the University of California at Los Angeles
alone several research teams are working on problems like these,
trying to learn how the mind and nervous system are involved.

They have discovered for one thing that sexual function (and
dysfunction as well) is directly controlled by certain parts of the
brain, which apparently keep a constant check on the body's need
for particular hormones. When a need for ovarian hormone is
determined, the hypothalamus puts out a chemical message telling the pituitary to turn on a supply. But if the experimenters
interrupt the process in the brain,[16] there is no message and no

15. Paul F. Slawson *et al.*, "Psychological Factors Associated with the Onset
of Diabetes Mellitus," *Journal of the American Medical Association* 185 (July 20, 1963):
166 ff.
16. By implanting a solid piece of ovarian hormone in the hypothalamus, an
impression of adequate supply is given to the brain, and the communication

hormone is produced; in a small animal the ovaries simply wither away. In human beings unconscious images, ideas, and emotions clearly affect the hypothalamus and can produce just as damaging interruptions in bodily processes. In this way emotions may well exert a very direct influence for sickness or for health.

Various questions are being asked today about the body's immunity system and how it is affected by the hypothalamus, sometimes called "the drugstore in the brain." The direct effect of mental distress on the body's defenses is known; an increase in the production of "stress" hormones can slow down the formation of antibodies to fight an invading organism. At Stanford University Dr. George F. Solomon is asking what this may have to do with resistance to cancer. Dr. Robert A. Good of the University of Minnesota, leading authority on the immune mechanism, has supported his theory that this system originally developed to dispose of cells altered by mutation, and suggests that cancer cells develop and are disposed of in this way every day in most human bodies. Yet the system can apparently be interrupted by stress. Other men are studying the inverse relation of certain allergies and of rheumatoid arthritis to this whole question of immunity and emotions.

A great deal of research is being done on the chemicals produced by the hypothalamus during sleep. Scientists at Duke University have discovered that angina attacks frequently occur during dreaming,[17] and the increased flow of body chemicals that

system breaks down. But the same implant made directly in the pituitary gland has no effect; the brain still senses the body's need, decides, and sends a message, and the pituitary does as it is told. The hypothalamus appears to be a unique part of the brain; it not only senses, but also functions like a gland, secreting the chemical messengers that tell the system, through the pituitary gland, what to do next. This has emerged from research done under Dr. Charles H. Sawyer at the University of California at Los Angeles.

17. Dr. J. B. Nowlin and his associates monitored several patients during sleep, by electroencephalograph recordings which show when dreams are occurring. Out of 39 attacks that occurred during the study, 32 coincided with periods of dreaming.

happens during dreaming periods is being studied. Dr. Arnold J. Mandell, at the University of California at Los Angeles, suggests that the emotional content of certain dreams may be responsible for many heart attacks that occur during the night when the heart is supposedly being rested. These dreams cause changes in the body's chemistry that can increase the load on a heart both directly and indirectly. Thus dreams—which at the very least are an expression in images of unconscious emotion—can have an effect on one's health.

The growth process of children can also apparently be interrupted by chemical changes initiated by the hypothalamus. This process is governed by hormones secreted by the pituitary, and it can be essentially halted by conflict in the home. The child who seems dwarfed will often grow from five to ten inches in a single year if he is removed from the contradictory environment. If he is returned to the same unhappy home, the growth stops again.

This is only one of the ways that children, by picking up the conflicts of their parents, can start life with emotionally inherited difficulties and so with problems of physical illness. Physicians' files are full of stories like one told me by a psychiatrist of a five-year-old who began a long bout with ulcerative colitis suddenly when her goldfish bowl was upset and one of the fish died.[18] Often only a psychiatrist can pinpoint what atmospehre in a "normal" home has brought about a result like this. But there is one dramatic parallel in the work of experimental psychologists on animals.

This involves Liddell's neurotic sheep at Cornell University. These animals were given as fine a barn as the laboratory could arrange, and were disturbed only for short sessions in which they

18. After intensive medical care and then months of psychiatric help, the youngster is now essentially free of symptoms. But the physician who told me about the case commented on the mother's inability to adjust to the daily demands of life without guilt and apprehension; he remarked that she had had only superficial support for her own problems and had not changed very much.

learned to stand quietly when a metronome began ticking, only flexing one leg that was given a mild electric shock. They adjusted quickly and went on with the placid life of normal sheep. But then, if they were brought in and either given more frequent shocks, or if the metronome was started repeatedly *without* giving a shock, at this point the sheep suffered nervous breakdown with many of the human symptoms—sleeplessness, rapid heart beat, and irritability. If they were removed to pasture and left for a year or so, the heart rate quieted down and other symptoms improved; but when they were brought back the first sound of the metronome, even the smell of the laboratory barn, produced trembling, palpitation, and all the other functional disturbances.[19]

"Do you think that children are any less sensitive than sheep?" Rebecca Beard has commented. When parents tick with unpredictable pressures, so that children are emotionally unsure of their environment and cannot depend on it, then the children may suffer just as the sheep, but with worse consequences. Put either an adult or a child in a situation where expectations and the required response keep shifting, and both his emotional life and his physical health can be permanently damaged. While medicine has taken almost incredible steps toward understanding the processes involved, they are so complex and so interrelated with the personal factors that often a person cannot be helped to recover until his confusing environment has been changed.

19. Howard S. Liddell, *Emotional Hazards in Animals and Man* (1956), pp. 61 ff.; also, "Conditioning and Emotions," reprinted from *Scientific American* for January 1954 by W. H. Freeman & Co. of San Francisco. None of the studies was designed to produce neurosis. In the first instance the animal was learning a more difficult task, to flex its leg for a shock on the sixth click of the metronome, and the schedule was doubled to get the results in time for a scientific meeting. The second result occurred when the signal (in this case a buzzer) was given without the expected shock in order to extinguish the animal's conditioned reflex; instead the flexing was intensified, along with varied signs of neurosis.

Deep-seated emotional disturbances can bring a person to meaninglessness and so to death. While this is sometimes put into words, I wonder if its truth is ever clear until one has experienced the physical effects of meaning restored to a life. In my work I recall a particular occasion when this became reality. A young man whom I had known for a long time was suddenly taken to the hospital so ill with ulcerative colitis that his doctor was afraid he would not live. I was called, and went with great concern, for I knew that the boy had very deep and real fears about himself. He had married on the spur of the moment, and his attractive wife had left him not long before.

I went back again and again, and as we talked the realization emerged for us both that he did not want to live because he saw no future in life. It finally came out that his fear of homosexuality had kept him from real relationship in marriage. As soon as he had faced his fear and how unfounded it was, his physical condition began to improve. I was able to find his wife and talk with her; when he saw possibilities open up ahead instead of hopelessness and felt a need to try to fulfill them, he made a steady recovery. Until his attitude changed, the best of modern medicine had only been able to hold the line. I know of no more rewarding experience than to feel oneself a part of such a change in another person's life and to see the effects materialize. The results, both emotional and physical, of intelligent caring for others can hardly be overestimated.

Freud was one of the first to show the physical ramifications of our emotional states and to demonstrate that physical illness can disappear when the neuroses from which it often springs are resolved. One delightful story from Freudian annals has been used by Flanders Dunbar. As Dr. Dunbar told it to a group, a woman with an exophthalmic goiter had been seen by a surgeon and an operation decided on. But when the surgeon saw how tense she was, he was not at all happy with the risk this presented and so sent her to a psychiatrist first to help with her anxieties. Six months later she came back—minus the anxieties *and* the goiter.

Harold Wolff at Cornell has shown migraine patients their need for emotional insight by demonstrating to them the contrast between the physiological effect of their fears and that of faith. They saw the sharp pulsation waves of the distended temporal artery recorded in tracing as grievances were talked over and a headache came on abruptly. With an injection of simple salt solution, which the patient believed to be a powerful constricting drug, the pulsation waves subsided as suddenly as they had magnified, and the headache was entirely gone. Faith in the power of the physician and his medication had constricted the arteries in the brain.

Many such startling changes in physical condition have been observed by psychologists and physicians as the tensions, anxieties, fears, and guilts of patients have been converted to new purpose and the individual has come to a more mature adjustment to reality. If these can be the results of the psychologist's work, is it too much to believe that God can do as much? Certainly the sense of well-being and wholeness that comes from a mature relationship to God might work the same way. Is it absurd to believe that God cannot have at least the same influence on the human body as the analyst, if we believe in God at all?

John Sutherland Bonnell, noted pastor and former president of New York Theological Seminary, has written about the effects of just such faith in God, presenting an impressive array of examples in his recent book *Do You Want to be Healed?* In it he shows how frequently physicians today are turning to the clergy as allies in helping people come to health of body, as well as of emotion. The modern doctor knows the effect emotion can have on our physical structure.

What Parts of the Body Can Be Affected?

In reality no part of the body is immune to the possible ill effects
of emotion. As we have seen, beginning with Dr. Dunbar's original study there is an enormous amount of material, which for our
purposes may be outlined quite briefly. Why certain organs seem
to become a target for emotional disturbances is not clear. Physical medicine has generally found the reason in the inherited
structure. Some illness seems to be symbolic of specific fears and
concerns, and psychiatry and psychosomatic medicine have
looked for the causes in personality structure, and today in the
emotional environment as well. New developments in psychology, and also in genetics,[20] point to the importance of the inherited psyche. Most likely all have a part in determining why a
person often has trouble in one part of his body and not in
another.

At any rate, it is interesting to realize how much easier it is to
admit that we have a poorly functioning heart or glands than to
admit that our emotions may be poorly directed and controlled.
If it is the body, we see ourselves as victims of fate. If it is our
emotions, we feel a responsibility. As I write these words, I think
of my own physical troubles and how easy it is to blame them on
physical weakness rather than to seek the cause in emotional
difficulties.

But a "weight on the chest" can mean that in reality one has
a "load on his mind." Emphysema, asthma, and hay fever are
unmistakably connected with emotional troubles, and it is
becoming increasingly recognized that respiratory infections,

20. Work with plants at the controlled environment laboratory at California
Institute of Technology has produced a pea that "remembers" the environment
in which the seed developed and under new conditions reproduces the growth
patterns evoked by the old environment.

the common cold, and tuberculosis in particular are related to emotional stress.

Both the skin and the eye have been thoroughly studied as organs of emotional expression. We know that the skin often expresses emotional conflict in blushing, pallor, and perspiration, while many allergies and skin eruptions have been traced to like causes, although the emotional basis is often difficult to identify. The eye is especially sensitive to individual feelings; it has been called the window of the soul, and for medicine it is a diagnostic window. Glaucoma, among other eye conditions, is often tied to emotional shock or tension. In addition, a person's eyes may be partly responsible for his individual immunity to airborne infection when he is able to release feelings through tears; the lysozyme contained in tears is a powerful germ-killer —also present in the nose—which can inactivate even the polio virus on a few moments' contact.

There is no question about the response of the gastrointestinal system to conflict and fear. Digestive ailments all the way from the difficulty in swallowing known as cardiospasm to simple constipation can represent the body's adjustment to tension, overwork, or anxiety. The many studies of this relationship are well known. We have shown some of the more critical ways in which the cardiovascular system responds directly to the deeper emotions and how, especially in hypertensive conditions, other parts of the body are seriously affected. Arthritis, particularly the rheumatoid condition, is now being studied as a possible reaction of the body to its own antibodies, as well as in relation to the effect of stress on the skeletal muscles.

Bedwetting in older children is one indication of the way the genito-urinary tract is affected by emotions. Feelings so naturally underlie all sexual disturbances that their psychic beginnings have been widely understood but seldom put into words. The studies of sexual infertility and impotence, difficulties in pregnancy and childbirth,[21] and menstrual and menopausal disorders show clearly not only emotional causes but a relation to the cause of other diseases.

Both the central nervous system and the entire glandular system are even more the middlemen of the body. Insomnia, headaches, neurotic and psychotic disorders, and even certain tumors are warnings of nervous reaction to stress; they can also be symptoms of the distress of another part of the body. It is well established that the endocrine system, in the same way, often takes the brunt of emotional strain and distributes the effects like lesser shock waves. Dr. Jung notes that he has seen the temperature of a patient rise two degrees from only emotional causes; this is simply one indication that can be easily recorded of how the glands take mental, psychic, and instinctive activity and turn them into physical metabolism. In turn, this system is also extremely sensitive to a playback of conflict from other disrupted functions. Contrary states like fatigue and hyperactivity, obesity and emaciation, are acknowledged as physical conditions that result, at least in part, from the effect of emotional stress on glandular function. Diabetes is more and more seen as related to psychic disturbance, probably through the hypothalamus.

Whatever else is influenced by one's emotions, it would seem that his teeth should certainly stand as a sure rock of physicality. Yet dentists are busy developing their own theories of psychosomatic dentistry. I have before me the outline of a University of California extension course held not long ago for our local practitioners, with a prominent neuropsychiatrist as lecturer. It puts

21. Consider simply the fact of natural childbirth under hypnotic suggestion; or the effect of adopting a child on a couple who have thought one or the other of them to be sterile, and how often pregnancy comes as a surprise after they have become parents by adoption. It is also interesting that "the pill" acts in the brain, working through the hypothalamus, or higher up, to give orders to the glandular system.

together facts that dentists see every day. The diseases of the mouth show a clear emotional correlation, and even tooth decay and erosion and difficulties in occlusion can be affected by anxiety and other psychic influences.

What next? The hospital accident ward has revealed a persistent behavior pattern that seems to allow rebellious people to let off steam without going through the complexity of a neurosis or physical disease. When Flanders Dunbar and her associates were looking about for a group of normal, healthy people with whom to compare diabetic and heart patients, they chose as a control group those who had submitted to hospitalization "accidentally."[22] Instead they were disconcerted to find that the fracture patients selected were not particularly normal at all. Their emotions were just as disturbed as those of other patients, but they took it out in being accident-prone. What easier way could be found to avoid meaninglessness than to let one's unconscious psyche direct an interesting or even fatal injury? As Dr. Jung also observed, frequent physical injury can reflect inner conflict just as much as frequently hurt feelings, and a broken leg may well be a distress signal as to one's psychic "standpoint."

Is the fight for control never done? Tremendous physical energy can, half known to the mind, go into bypassing a clogged blood vessel or rebuilding damaged nerves; or the body can unconsciously choose another route for the same energy that misdirects cell reproduction to the growth of cancer. It can turn creative force to recovery from tuberculosis or to resisting an invasion of polio or the common cold; on another level the same force may direct harmful bacteria to fight back by breeding new and stronger strains. The body can secrete innumerable chemical

22. At about the same time, industry was beginning to take a serious look at the employee who is involved in more than one accident, and a number of psychiatrists were making a careful study of the emotional states that lead to particular accidents.

compounds—to digest food or fight poison, to stimulate its own reproduction or get the highest brain cells into action; or it can secretly turn these secretions on itself, to digest or poison or overstimulate itself.

In some ways this seems to be a realm apart, a field where the material and the immaterial join, where good or evil are determined by an unknown force. But research in this field is really just beginning to reveal the complex interactions, the chemical and electrical changes that take place between the cells and through the brain in their fluid environment. Today one can watch on slow-motion film the vastly magnified lymphocytes attack a foreign cancer cell, and consider why they succeed in one human being and fail in another. There is ample room here for both scientific knowledge and religious wonder. For very possibly answers to a number of questions about disease may lie in the latter area—in religious consideration of problems of the emotions and resistance, of the mind and its proneness to production of creative or malignant energies.

When an elder statesman of physical science like Dr. W. F. G. Swann has had the courage to suggest that science investigate the truth of the soul, it may be time for the church to start working with these problems in people, developing a world view in which such human experiences have a place.

The scientists who wrestle with these mysteries are now convinced that there is no fundamental difference between mental and physical illness, and that "all illnesses have both psychological and somatic components."[23] Some of the recent psychiatric treatment of psychosomatic illness also sounds strangely more religious than medical. The article on concepts of psychosomatic medicine in the *American Handbook of Psychiatry* states:

23. C. P. Kimball, "Conceptual Developments in Psychosomatic Medicine: 1939–1969," *Annals of Internal Medicine* 73 (August 1970): 307. Dr. Kimball, who teaches at Yale, was writing for the American College of Physicians.

Fortunately, effective therapeutic work with patients does not depend upon knowledge of how emotional conflicts are translated into physiologic malfunctioning or upon resolution of problems concerning specificity. *The physician who orients treatment to the patient rather than simply to the disease* and who can utilize the doctor-patient relationship therapeutically can often alleviate emotional problems and ameliorate the physical illness.[24]

To the physician today man's inner, often unconscious feelings are of the utmost importance. Let us look at those that have the greatest negative influence on the body.

Emotions That Play a Part

A psychiatrist from one of the leading hospitals in the United States, when asked what emotions create the most havoc, once listed these four: anger-resentment-hostility, fear-anxiety, guilt–self-punishment, and egotism–self-centeredness. There is no question that these are destructive reactions and complexes, but in the relationship of religious care for human beings one finds others more subtle but no less destructive of mental or physical health if long indulged. In despair, sorrow, and depression there is loss of value, whether from actual deprivation or bereavement or from some inner loss of the value of persons or things that still exist. Inward conflict may arise simply from ambivalence, with the feeling of being pulled apart over every necessary decision and relationship. Finally, there is an emotion that is indefinable except as psychic pain and oppression, an element in all pathological depression. These emotional reactions are the concern of vital religion; they can be changed by a vital religious life and sacramental acts that touch the depth of the psyche.

The negative emotions can sometimes be dealt with by comparatively simple means. One psychologist has remarked that

24. *American Handbook of Psychiatry* (1959), 1: 654. Italics mine.

many people practice excellent psychotherapy without knowing it simply by friendly warmth, along with the positive suggestion of heartfelt encouragement. Bruno Klopfer, the authority on the Rorschach test, once expressed to me the opinion that 50 percent of all psychic therapy consists of warm, positive concern.

How very important it is to avoid negative suggestion in the course of a disease or, for that matter, in any crisis in a person's life. One cannot estimate the amount of misery caused by unthinking negative suggestion. Probably each of us has had the experience of feeling quite well until several people casually remark that he is not looking at all well; it takes a very strong personality not to be influenced by such statements. When the suggestion comes from an authority, the effects may be tragic indeed. I once worked for many months with a young man who had had just this experience. He had been getting along remarkably well until he went to a physician for a routine checkup. In the ordinary exercise test his blood pressure rose a good bit more than the normal. The physician's voice registered shock that a sensible man would get himself into so much trouble by not having proper medical care for such a dangerous condition. My parishioner reacted by going to pieces, and it was not until he was completely reasssured of the hidden healing ways God has given the mind and body that he was able to get on with his normal work and life. It turned out medically that he simply had a blood pressure mechanism that fluctuated easily; he is healthy and busy at the work of two men today.

Most patients are quite capable of complicating their own illnesses without such medical suggestion; their need is for the powerful healing effect of positive but sensible confidence. The effectiveness of "sugar pills" or placebos, when given by a doctor who inspires faith, has long proved this. The double blind test, that impish research tool, has made it even more clear. In a series of studies several years ago tranquilizers were given to one group of psychoneurotic patients and placebos to a control group. Neither the patients *nor* their physicians knew which of them got pills out of the numbered bottle and which were given sugar pills. When the results were checked, it was found that as many as 35 percent had improved on placebos.[25] A number of tranquilizers have been advertised in the journals on a claim of 17 percent or similar effectiveness. How strange—when a placebo can do twice as well!

Sometimes a straightforward discussion of the problems themselves can resolve the trouble they are causing. One of our psychologists not long ago talked over with me a case I had referred to him. A young woman had come to me, obviously glossing over feelings of resentment toward her husband and making much of her own illness. She did have stomach trouble, with constant fear of an ulcer, but her physician had not found any cause. The psychologist wanted me to know that a few talks had revealed the basic sexual problem, and her pain and nausea had immediately disappeared.

However, all emotional problems are not so easily solved. It is the unconscious, the unrecognized hostilities, fears, sorrows, guilts, and psychic pains that cause the most devastating physical reactions. Conscious knowledge itself gives one at least a handle to counteract the effect of known feelings. But when these emotions are difficult to pin down, let alone resolve, then the person often needs help in understanding his own inner reactions if he is ever to be whole either emotionally or physically. Such hidden emotions are far more common than we generally realize.

I know of no method of healing the illnesses that result except to dig into these repressed fears, hatreds, and guilts. This is a dangerous process, but the damage to the body that can come from them is equally dangerous, not to mention the psychologi-

25. Henry K. Beecher, "The Powerful Placebo," *Journal of the American Medical Association* 159 (December 24, 1955): 1602 ff.

cal misery often induced by these repressed feelings. It is always best of course to use the simplest and most direct method available to resolve the difficulty, and not go deeper than necessary. If physical remedies will work, then one should be grateful and let well enough alone. On the other hand, how much more healing and permanent it is when the emotional life can be brought into harmony, so that drugs are no longer needed to counterbalance the depressed physical system. Many persons are able to abandon medication when the tensions causing their physical imbalance have been resolved.

These harmful emotions can be caused by a conflict within the individual, by a conflict between one individual and another, or by a conflict between the individual and his total world. Within the individual the conflict may be between two opposing attitudes, perhaps a sense of duty toward a parent and the desire to go out into the world, or—what many young people today are so set on avoiding—a duty toward parental values that have never been examined and are unconsciously stumbled over with each step in the world. Again, for an individual who has not made good relationships with others and finds them difficult, uncreative, a source of irritation and pain, all sorts of conflicts can arise. The most persistent depression and misery may be caused by a lack of feeling loved and cared for. Harry Stack Sullivan has based a whole theory of psychological illness upon such effects of interpersonal relationships.

Finally, the conflict of the individual with his world, his whole *Weltanschauung* or world view, can cause unending difficulty. If the universe is viewed as basically meaningless or hostile, the whole emotional life of the individual may be greatly affected. How can one be free from fear, emptiness, and rebellion if one's life is seen as no more than a holding action against meaningless forces that will ultimately crush or snuff it out? Indeed, all the negative emotions are likely to be aroused when one sees himself as a mere atom, moved about either mechanically or by blind chance. With no relationship to any continuing meaning, there can be no forgiveness, no real way to cope with the deep sense of guilt that most men bear, nor is there any way to stand against the condemnation of man and society. How can one help but be egotistical if man is the only purposeful entity in the universe— if all is transitory, without inherent value in either people or things?

If one looks into the heart of being, to find only mechanism or blind indeterminacy, there is likely to be a response of utter despair, abiding sorrow, and deep psychic pain, or at best an existential courage, anxious and stoic. Here the part of religion in providing for the individual an adequate world view and a way of relating to transcendental reality cannot be denied. Real religion in action can touch the psyche of the individual directly, and his body through the psyche, when nothing else can. An emotion of confidence, of outgoing love and caring, when released by real religious faith can work miracles. Dr. Jung has investigated especially this area of conflict, with depth and insight and almost single-handed.

Certainly one must conclude that mental attitudes and emotional responses, both conscious and unconscious, have a profound effect upon the body. One of the earliest works on psychosomatic medicine, already cited, quoted the German clinician F. Mohr, who wrote: "There is no such thing as a purely psychic illness or a purely physical one, but only a living event taking place in a living organism which is itself alive only by virtue of the fact that in it psychic and somatic are united in a unity."[26] Since then careful research has shown the truth of this understanding. Recent issues of the journal *Psychosomatic Medicine* have suggested that we are simply using different language when we

26. Flanders Dunbar, *Emotions and Bodily Changes* (1954), p. 428.

describe illness as physical or emotional—that grief, for instance, causes so many physical changes that it might well be treated as a disease. They also include an excellent summary of the whole subject by Dr. Ludwig von Bertalanffy in his report on a recent conference.[27]

There is a great deal of profound literary support for the contention that the individual's moral and religious life influences his body directly. One modern author has risked his life and reputation to propound this thesis from behind the Iron Curtain. Pasternak's witness is all the more impressive because he has known the experiences that go on underneath the rigid structure of materialism and mechanical determinism that rule his country. In the conclusion to *Doctor Zhivago* he wrote:

> Microscopic forms of cardiac hemorrhages have become very frequent in recent years. They are not always fatal. Some people get over them. It's a typical modern disease. I think its causes are of a moral order. The great majority of us are required to live a life of constant, systematic duplicity. Your health is bound to be affected if, day after day, you say the opposite of what you feel, if you grovel before what you dislike and rejoice at what brings you nothing but misfortune. Our nervous system isn't just a fiction, it's a part of our physical body, and our soul exists in space and is inside us, like the teeth in our mouth. It can't be forever violated with impunity. I found it painful to listen to you, Innokentii, when you told us how you were re-educated and became mature in jail. It was like listening to a horse describing how it broke itself in.[28]

There is no sharp line of demarcation between the religious, spiritual, emotional, and physical; between the body and the psyche. If it can be shown that religious life has a vital effect upon that vehicle of man's subtler and more central experience which

27. *Psychosomatic Medicine: Journal of the American Psychosomatic Society* 31 (November-December 1969): 510–21; 29 (January-February 1967): 52–71; also 26 (January-February 1964): 29–45.
28. 1958, p. 483.

Christians are apt to call the soul, then it may be assumed that it will have a like effect upon the body of the believer. However, it must be clearly noted that just because psychic causes predominate in some illnesses, it is not admissible to jump to the conclusion that every illness is predominantly psychic in origin. It must also be realized that the psychosomatic relation is a two-way street: profound and lasting sickness of the body can have a profound effect on the psyche, on the mental and emotional attitudes of the sick person, and also on his religious life.

Let us turn to the possibility that religious experience and faith are significant factors in the health of the psyche, in counteracting and integrating negative, destructive emotional states, and in releasing positive and creative emotions and so health in our bodies.

11

Healing the Emotions

Clinical psychology and psychiatry together form the youngest of the healing professions, one that did not even begin until long after religious healing had ceased to be an accepted part of Western culture. In fact, there was little interest in what was hidden in the troubled souls and minds of sick people almost until the century in which Freud made his original far-reaching discovery.[1] It is hard to realize that scarcely a hundred years before this discovery, Westerners witnessed the last beheading of a witch on the continent of Europe.

It is also difficult to believe how the mentally ill were treated up until that time. Until almost into the nineteenth century, most "mad" people were kept in chains, often in dungeons. They were beaten, dosed with purgatives and emetics, and left to brutal keepers on the theory: "the more painful the restraint, the better the results."[2] Humane treatment was first tried in Italy, at the Hospital of St. Boniface in Florence, beginning in 1789. Three years later in England, where the recurring insanity of George III aroused feeling and questions, the Quaker William Tuke began the reform that finally changed hospitals in that country.

1. Jointly with Joseph Breuer and first published in 1893, followed in 1895 by their book, *Studies in Hysteria* (1961).
2. Franz G. Alexander and Sheldon T. Selesnick, *The History of Psychiatry* (1966), p. 116. This book gives the best picture available of the development of the present understanding of mental illness.

But ironically, it was in Paris during the reign of terror that medical psychiatry was born. In 1793 Philippe Pinel undertook his duties at the Bicêtre, the institution for insane men, and he was thought mad himself when he removed the chains from his patients and gave them real medical care. But Pinel was a quiet thinker who intended to change the treatment. The results were so good that two years later he was asked to do the same thing for the women at the Salpêtrière. There in 1817 Esquirol, who succeeded Pinel, established the first psychiatric clinic, giving physicians a chance to look at the psychotic patient as a medical problem.

Twenty years after the death of Esquirol, Jean Martin Charcot came to the Salpêtrière as professor and physician-in-charge. It was in a lecture hall of that hospital, under a painting of Pinel striking off the chains of inmates, that Charcot had among his students the young man from Vienna, Sigmund Freud. Here Freud found a neurologist—the leading neurologist of the time —who looked with lively but objective eyes at his difficult patients.

Hysteria was one of the main problems, and it is no wonder that the first successes of psychotherapy were with these patients. Charcot saw this ailment, not with fear of being fooled by a malingering woman, but as an illness to be studied and treated. He also followed an intuitive as well as objective approach to medical problems; he did not consider that, once the cause of a disease appeared to be known, this ruled out all other factors. He was not afraid to investigate hypnotism, or to recognize the psychic influences that affected so many people physically. Like Freud at that time, however, Charcot was interested in the physical causes of nervous diseases; he did not actually comprehend the psychological problems he was raising. Instead it was Freud who, later in Vienna, began to discover that his patients did not fit the ideas of personality he saw expressed around him.

Nineteenth-century Vienna, like the rest of the world at the time, considered human personality as relatively simple. Children were expected to listen to their elders, and obviously they would be fed the right mixture of experience and learn the right ideas to produce acceptable adults—correct, law-abiding citizens. There was no worry about any other kind of influences; so far as this period was concerned, a person came into the world like a lump of clay, and it was society's duty to mold him into a reasonable individual. In other words, he took on the conscious rationality of the molder, assisted by a system of rewards and punishments.

Of course there were those who did not turn out that way, and imperial Vienna had its closets for family skeletons as did Victorian England. But for the most part it was expected that the shaping could be corrected. Even if people had a perverse will and resisted, they could be remolded by punishment, or shown where they had to shape up and accept right ideas and habits of action. It was society's responsibility to provide the punishments and institutions of correction for those whose wills needed altering, such as criminals and the mentally ill. But if this failed to bring a person in line, then the poor devil simply had to be removed from society so that his evil behavior would not become contagious.

These ideas were based, of course, on a very old theory of personality, a psychology which assumes that man's psychic structure is built solely out of conscious rationality. Up to the time of Pinel there were almost no voices raised against it. It not only provided the rationale for a penal system from debtors' prisons to the guillotine, but also the only real basis for treating mental illness until almost the nineteenth century.[3] This psychology has bequeathed to us a punishment system which still

3. For instance, irritants were even applied to the skin of insane persons to be sure they would feel the chains and carry the scars.

does more to promote antisocial behavior than it does to keep people out of jail. Mental institutions have been changed only because a handful of men were willing to risk reputation and livelihood to try something different.

This theory of personality which we have discussed at some length, in contrast to the attitude and psychology of Jesus of Nazareth,[4] was essentially implicit in the ideas of Aristotle. Because it was adopted by medieval Scholasticism in the name of all Christians, this view of man entered the modern world without being questioned. It was the basis of practically all legal codes everywhere, including ecclesiastical censure, and once the Christian church accepted it there were few who cared to question. Most men simply took for granted this idea of personality as fact.

Today a similar personality theory is still held by many people who would be quite indignant if it were suggested that they had any psychological viewpoint at all. It exerts such a tremendous hold on persons who are unreflective that they meet any challenge of this assumption with determined resistance. In addition, it has recently been revived as a theory of personality and restated with sophistication by certain modern psychologists who rely largely on rewards rather than on punishments.[5]

Freud on the other hand was trying to see what lay behind the illness and pain, the psychic distress, of his patients. His great contribution was to offer a theory of personality that takes these

4. See chap. 4, pp. 59 ff.

5. A closely related point of view is presented by the behaviorist B. F. Skinner in *Science and Human Behavior* (1953) and *Walden II* (1960). Behaviorism denies the reality of both consciousness and the unconscious, and sees treatment as a process of conditioning the individual through positive stimuli. Man's behavior is only a matter of physical conditioned responses which can be varied by appropriate stimuli to produce the desired results. As one student remarked to me, he certainly did not discuss his real problems with the behavioristic psychology professors, since he did not want to be manipulated and treated as a thing. See reactions against Freudian theory in William Glasser's *Reality Therapy* (1965); also O. Hobart Mowrer's *The Crisis in Psychiatry and Religion* (1961) and *Learning Theory and Behavior* (1960).

experiences into account and thus allows room for other things that happen to human beings which do not originate in rational consciousness. From the very first of his discoveries, Freud had to make room for healings that were anything but rational experiences.

The Discoveries of Freud

In Vienna Freud began to work with Joseph Breuer in an effort to understand hysteria, still one of the hardest maladies to comprehend. It can produce the effects of almost any disease, and patients came to them disabled by pains and seizures without apparent cause—by anything from nausea or coughing to paralysis or even loss of some brain function. In one unusually intelligent and disturbed patient Breuer had seen the results of stirring up (in hypnotic trance) the memory of earlier seizures.

This was the famous case of "Anna O.," who gave a history of her experiences when she was hypnotized and told that she would recall something about a symptom. Without fail, she recounted each occurrence in order, working back from the latest to a time when her father had been ill. The task went on week after week, uncovering each occasion when a symptom had appeared, and the emotional experiences that had come with it. As she came to the starting point of each aspect of her illness, the girl became increasingly disturbed under hypnosis. She seemed to be facing things she had preferred not to notice. But when the recital was over, the story was finished and the symptom itself disappeared. In this way she had "talked out" or "related away" each facet of her disorder until she was well.

The fact of hypnosis left little question about the importance of psychic processes, since other patients came who responded in quite similar ways. It was clear that the suggestion of one person could initiate changes in the behavior and physical reactions of another who was unable to accomplish this for himself. From these findings Freud went on to a very radical "new" idea, that of psychic determination. He proposed the hypothesis that psychic, mental events could not only influence other such events without going through any physical or material medium, but could have causal relation to physical events in the same way. He also suggested that psychic life consists of more than consciousness and has an autonomy quite apart from physical, material reality.

The things Freud first came upon through hypnosis were later verified in various ways. He found that in many cases a patient was aware of the experiences that had contributed to his illness, while the *ideas* he associated with such experiences were often quite unconscious. Since they did not come into question, no conscious reflection was given to them, and so they resulted in actions which conflicted with what the person "thought" he wanted to do or to be. Freud called many of these ideas phantasies, because he found them also in conflict with outer reality— sometimes pure fiction, sometimes interpretations of what had actually happened. Yet the same ideas were held by so many different persons that he came to consider them *primal phantasies*, and suggested that they originated in the actual experience of man in past ages.

Although Freud was by no means the first modern student to question whether there might be unconscious parts of man's mind, this was still a relative innovation in men's thinking. As L. L. Whyte has pointed out, Western languages did not even speak of "the unconscious" or "an unconscious mind" until after Descartes had arbitrarily defined mind and thought as solely a clear, conscious, rational process. Interestingly enough, Descartes did not seem to notice that he had left out something of importance for comprehending the human mind and personality, even though his own understanding had come through a process that was hardly clear, conscious, or rational. His inspiration came to him in dreams on the night of November 10, 1619, in one of those experiences of the unconscious which he eliminated so well that the modern world, after all Freud's careful evidence, still has trouble grasping them.[6]

Freud was the first to give careful, verifiable proof of the reality of the unconscious. Knowing that he had means to deal with the illnesses that came to him, that "symptoms vanish with the acquisition of knowledge of their meaning,"[7] he began to look at the ways people express an underlying conflict. When a patient's basic problem was revealed to him by his words and actions, he suddenly became aware of reactions in himself which had been kept under cover until then. With the right help to focus on them, one could understand and learn to handle these things. Freud therefore studied the mistakes of his patients, their slips of the tongue, free associations, and dreams.

He continued to build up evidence showing how the conflict between unconscious, autonomous contents and the conscious attitudes of a person could keep him constantly upset without

6. In my book *Dreams*, p. 194, there is a brief account of the development of interest in the unconscious. Lancelot Law Whyte's book *The Unconscious Before Freud* (1960), offers the best general study of early thought on the subject and also some idea of the beginnings of modern psychological understanding.

Charcot, however, probably had more influence on Freud in the beginning than any of the philosophers or other physicians. Charcot was still getting his training in the wards when he discovered in the Salpêtrière hospital "the wilderness of paralyses, tremors, and spasms" for which there was no name or understanding. He remained enthusiastic, and much the same desire to understand and heal these patients inspired Freud. Charcot's contribution is discussed by Alexander and Selesnick, *op. cit.*, pp. 190 f.; by Freud in the *Collected Papers* (1955), 1: 9 ff. and 294 ff.; as well as by various biographers of Freud.

In *Studies in Hysteria* (Breuer and Freud, p. 200), Freud has shown how his own ideas began to develop as he found that hypnosis was only one approach that could remove symptoms, but often failed to cure the disease or stop the formation of new symptoms. Freud's *Interpretation of Dreams* and his lectures published as *A General Introduction to Psychoanalysis* contain the basis of his understanding and method.

7. *General Introduction to Psychoanalysis* (1960), p. 292.

knowing the reason. Simply because he was unconscious of these contents, he was powerless against the conflict, and this, Freud concluded, was responsible for neurosis and even the more serious psychological disorders.

His descriptions of the results of inner tension have stood the test of medical practice. This conflict causes both compulsive actions and phobias, subjecting one person to foolish fetishes or extremes such as stealing, fighting, or emotional rage, and keeping another from things he does want to do because he is afraid, say, of studying, or crowds, or high places, or closed-in ones. The tension may manifest itself in floating anxiety, depression, and despair, the very emotions that have the most devastating physiological responses. Finally, if it becomes intolerable, the individual ego is fragmented or dissolved and the result is schizophrenia, the most tragic of mental illnesses.

As Freud realized that patients were driven by ideas, feelings, and emotions that had been repressed and buried since childhood, and that much of this conflict related to sexuality, it became clear why the resulting disturbances could so often be "talked away." When a patient became aware of these drives and learned to deal with them consciously, his psyche no longer automatically compensated for his ignorance and innocence by destructive tension or neurotic and physical illness. As is even better understood today, once a conflict becomes conscious, there are other channels of discharge than through the autonomic or other central systems of the body.

As we have seen, Freud realized not only the importance of very early experience, but also the fact that, whether originating in phantasy or in actuality, these experiences had a common ground somewhere in human history.[8] But Freud was essentially

8. The American theologian, Horace Bushnell, anticipated many of Freud's ideas about the importance of childhood experience in his *Christian Nurture*, published in 1847. Bushnell, in general a dissenter from Calvinistic orthodoxy, sought our release from the strict Puritan image of children as monstrous little

alone in being able to approach the sexual problems that were so disturbing to people. Vienna was the last bastion of puritanical Catholic morality, and he found that the popular religious attitude only reinforced the repression of these ideas and feelings, rather than helping to make them conscious. And so Freud went ahead to formulate a theory of personality that would account for the facts he had found.

Sexuality, broadly understood as the pleasure principle, he saw as the primary life force which was seeking to find expression. Opposing the sexual or pleasure drive, which he called the *id,* was another aspect of the unconscious, the *superego* which embodied the restraining and moralistic attitudes of society, making civilization possible by holding down the wild impulsivity of the id. These two, id and superego, came to warfare on the battleground of the ego, or conscious personality. As long as the ego kept the conflict conscious, handling the situation with will power and rationality, a cold-war truce could be maintained and the individual was more or less healthy. But when the conflict was not consciously undergone, the price was paid in compensatory neurotic behavior or the personality went to pieces in psychosis, and either outcome was likely to take its toll on the body.

One can hardly overemphasize the importance of this theory for all later thinking about the nature of personality, although not many people hold to it totally today. In later years Freud himself came to see another drive operating besides the id. In *Beyond the Pleasure Principle* and *Civilization and Its Discontents* he described the death wish, or *thanatos,* a regressive desire to return to the nonbeing of inorganic matter. But he found little reason to change his view that against these conflicting powers the conscious ego stands alone. In the beginning he wrote:

adults, entitled to no life of their own, who must be disciplined and curbed if they were not to become monstrous mature adults.

One receives a delusive impression of a superior intelligence outside of the patient's consciousness, which systematically holds a large psychic material for definite purposes, and has provided an ingenious arrangement for its return into consciousness. I presume, however, that this unconscious second intelligence is really only apparent.[9]

Through the years he found in religion an even more delusive attempt to return to the womb. Only the God of *Logos* was available, whom he invoked in the closing words of *The Future of an Illusion*. And for Freud this God was weak against the power of these unconscious and hostile psychic forces which man faces, alone and almost helpless, with no hope of final resolution or ultimate peace.

Most of his followers continued his basic schema; even Alfred Adler merely substituted the principle of the will to power for the id–pleasure principle. The one man who was originally closest to Freud, however, and who continued to build on the same empirical foundation, came to a radically different conclusion. This was Dr. Carl Jung, who was forced, in spite of his friendship and admiration for Freud, somehow to make clear that Freud's system did not take all the data into account. He tried at first to convince Freud that there were personal factors and also some very strange experiences which he was not considering. On one occasion Freud replied, "That is sheer bosh," and in another discussion, "But I cannot risk my authority!"[10]

It was just these facts, with important implications for religion, that made it necessary for Jung to propose an entirely new hypothesis. His work offered telling support for religious healing. Besides giving evidence of the reality of healing, he saw that man's consciousness cannot stand alone against the destructive aspects of the unconscious. Only, in fact, as man finds through

9. Breuer and Freud, *op. cit.*, pp. 203 f.
10. C. G. Jung, *Memories, Dreams, Reflections* (1963), pp. 155 and 158. For the full meaning of these remarks the entire chapter, pp. 146 ff., should probably be read.

the unconscious a creative power which can offer protection and integration, does he come to a resolution of inner tensions and conflicts. Such a power for healing, Jung insisted, can be sought only by religious means.

Jung, Religion, and Healing

Jung started his medical practice with the ordinary belief that man inherits a psychic structure, much as he does a physical one, and that everything that fills this structure must come from personal experience. But as he studied the experience of patients who came to him from all over the world, and also took careful note of his own psychic experiences, he found that contents and images were sometimes expressed which could not be explained on the basis of personal background. He began adding to his voluminous knowledge of how such images were expressed in myth and folklore. On the basis of these comparative studies, he came to the conclusion that there is a reservoir of common psychic contents lying beyond and beneath the store of individual memories, and that particularly in dreams and phantasies the individual is in touch with unconscious contents that go beyond his own personal experience of the physical world.

While at first he considered only the possibility that these contents must come from an archaic and primitive level in the mind, Jung's later findings suggested quite conclusively that human beings are in touch through the unconscious with a vast body of objective psychic reality which can have a direct effect on the individual life and consciousness.[11] Even more startling

11. Jung almost never announced that he had changed his outlook, nor did he go back to correct his earlier views. He appeared to assume that anyone interested enough to read his works would follow the growth and development of his ideas. In his earliest writings there are contradictory statements; his later works, as his experience and synthesis became more adequate, are the key for understanding his mature point of view.

was his discovery that in this kind of experience a power was sometimes found affecting a person in ways that were superior to ordinary consciousness. In connection with one series of such dreams, Jung wrote:

> The assumption that the human psyche possesses layers that lie *below* consciousness is not likely to arouse serious opposition. But that there could just as well be layers lying *above* consciousness seems to be a surmise which borders on a *crimen laesae majestatis humanae*. In my experience the conscious mind can only claim a relatively central position and must put up with the fact that the unconscious psyche transcends and as it were surrounds it on all sides. Unconscious contents connect it *backwards* with physiological states on the one hand and archetypal data on the other. But it is extended *forward* by intuitions which are conditioned partly by archetypes and partly by subliminal perceptions depending on the relativity of time and space in the unconscious.[12]

Thus Jung opened the door to the possibility of contact through the unconscious with an objective reality superior to human consciousness, which is able to order and vitalize human life when ego-consciousness is unable to do so. If the human psyche can thus act as a bridge between the physical body and the power of a transcendental reality, then religion and religious experience, particularly healing experiences, become a real and most significant possibility.

How did Jung come to this conclusion? The first time I visited him I asked where his belief in the collective unconscious and its religious implications first arose. He told me that it had come gradually and quite against his will. He had been raised in the materialism and rationalism of the early twentieth century, but had come to see that this outlook could not account for the data that were forcing themselves on him from the unconscious depths of his patients. He then told me how he was first "bitten"

12. C. G. Jung, *Collected Works*, 12: 132. See Bibliography for volume titles and edition.

by this realization, a story which is discussed in *The Structure and Dynamics of the Psyche.*

In a mental hospital in Zurich Jung had a patient who had been an ordinary clerk until he became schizophrenic in his early twenties. He had not been outside the hospital for years. One day he stopped Jung beside a window and, in an awed voice, instructed him how to look at the sun so as to see the phallus hanging down; it would move from side to side, he said, and this was the origin of the wind. This was an unusual experience and Jung took careful note of it. Some time later he was reading a recent translation of a magic papyrus, probably from the ancient cult of Mithras, when he stopped short. Among the incantations and visions recorded in Greek centuries before, and by no means available to the sick man, were almost his patient's exact words. It told how one would see hanging down from the disc of the sun a so-called tube that moved back and forth, and this was the origin of the ministering wind.

It is no wonder that this incident opened Jung's eyes to such material. A psychotic patient was trying to tell him the importance of consciousness. Gradually he became convinced of the autonomous nature of these psychic contents that intrude themselves into human awareness at various times and places. He reminded me of the meaning of the word convince, which comes from the Latin root "to conquer." The trouble with so many people in the modern world, he said, is that they try to convince themselves, whereas real conviction is possible only as one is conquered by something beyond ego-consciousness. Conviction is given, not self-induced.

Like Freud, Jung began to write about healing almost from the first. But this first work to reach the general public—in English *The Psychology of the Unconscious*—was one of his most difficult. He later reedited it completely, referring to it as one of the follies of his youth. Published as *Symbols of Transformation*, it tells a fascinating story of the visionary experiences of a young woman on the verge of schizophrenia, and the healing that could have come had she understood the mythological content of the images that came spontaneously to her. In her visions Dr. Jung traced one after another most of the mythological motifs of mankind, showing what a fundamental and healing correction they offer to our present ideas about life.

In various contexts he speaks of the healing effect of an adequate relation to the unconscious and its symbolic and mythological meaning. Discussing the effects of the unconscious upon the physical world and particularly upon man's body, he wrote,

> The same relationship of complementarity can be observed just as easily in all those extremely common medical cases in which certain clinical symptoms disappear when the corresponding unconscious contents are made conscious. We also know that a number of psychosomatic phenomena which are otherwise outside the control of the will can be induced by hypnosis, that is, by this same restriction of consciousness.[13]

To show the reality of the psyche, in the first part of *Psychology and Religion* he gave examples of these physical effects that he had seen in his own practice:

> Since my readers may not be familiar with these medical facts I may instance a case of hysterical fever, with a temperature of 102°, which was cured in a few minutes through confession of the psychological cause. A patient with psoriasis extending over practically the whole body was told that I did not feel competent to treat his skin trouble, but that I should concentrate on his psychological conflicts, which were numerous. After six weeks of intense analysis and discussion of his purely psychological difficulties, there came about as an unexpected by-product the almost complete disappearance of the skin disease. In another case, the patient had recently undergone an operation for distention of the colon. Forty centimetres of it had been removed, but this was followed

13. *Ibid.*, 8: 232.

by another extraordinary distention. The patient was desperate and refused to permit a second operation, though the surgeon thought it vital. As soon as certain intimate psychological facts were discovered, the colon began to function normally again.[14]

In discussing dreams he wrote that they often show "a remarkable inner symbolical connection between an undoubted physical illness and a definite psychic problem," so that in many cases it looks as if the physical disorder were directly mimicking the psychic condition. Although Jung did not stress this problem— for, as he pointed out elsewhere in relation to glandular disorders, it is hard to know which is cause and which effect—he went on to say:

> It seems to me, however, that a definite connection does exist between physical and psychic disturbances and that its significance is generally underrated, though on the other hand it is boundlessly exaggerated owing to certain tendencies to regard physical disturbances merely as an expression of psychic disturbances, as is particularly the case with Christian Science.[15]

Thus Jung found that when a man tries to live as if he could simply break all connection with the unconscious and avoid its symbolic and mythological meaning by forgetting about it and consciously directing his life to things outside, he generally gets sick. And very often, as psychologists everywhere have found, the symptoms he develops look like a mock-up of what is going on in his unconscious.

The unconscious, as Jung saw, contains both negative elements and creative and healing ones. Its numerous archetypal contents are by nature ambivalent—destructive or creative depending on how the individual deals with them.[16] There is one aspect or

14. *Ibid.*, 11: 11 f. From the Terry Lectures, given at Yale University in 1937.
15. *Ibid.*, 8: 261.
16. These contents, or archetypes, are highly complex realities that produce the most involved reactions in the individual. But for our purpose they may be

element, however, which seems to be ultimately destructive. This kind of content, which drives men to physical and mental illness, is not only represented in the New Testament; it is depicted, for instance, by the witches in *Macbeth* and Mephistopheles in *Faust*, and also by the Evil One so accurately portrayed in the film *Rosemary's Baby*. Jung has described his own personal encounter with this destructive element with terrifying reality in the sixth chapter of his autobiography, *Memories, Dreams, Reflections*.

He has also made important contributions to the problem of dealing with evil, and one of the most significant of these is found in his poetic outburst, *The Answer to Job*. As he was recovering from what had been an excruciatingly painful and nearly fatal illness, he tackled this problem through identifying in feeling with Job. Toward the end of this book he wrote,

> Everything now depends on man: immense power of destruction is given into his hand, and the question is whether he can resist the will to use it, and can temper his will with the spirit of love and wisdom. He will hardly be capable of doing so on his own unaided resources. He needs the help of an "advocate" in heaven, that is, of the child who was caught up to God and who brings the "healing" and making whole of the hitherto fragmentary man.[17]

described fairly simply as elements of the psychic environment which produce attitudes or generalized feelings about the experiences that come one's way, and which thus determine how one reacts or responds to his life experiences. One may react like the "eternal youth," or a Victorian father, or (a woman) like the mother of everyone she deals with, or another person as the savior destined to bring order into other people's lives or even society as a whole. The various reactions are numerous, and—again—they are far from simple. But in general it may be said that the less conscious a person is, the more likely he is to react according to some pattern accepted by his culture and allow the inevitable conflicts with his own desires and those of others to be reflected in automatic ways —by saying or doing things offhand and letting the body develop tensions and other direct reactions.

17. *Collected Works* 11: 459.

Jung remonstrated with those who see evil only as the absence or deprivation of good (the *privatio boni*). He was convinced that evil is a reality of experience with which men are required to deal. They cannot philosophize it out of existence. Indeed he saw this tendency as a dangerous one because it made men unconscious of the evil within them, so that instead of dealing with it they projected it out onto others. In the midst of a long discussion of the *privatio boni* in *Aion*, Jung remarked with some exasperation; "One could hardly call the things that have happened, and still do happen, in the concentration camps of the dictator states an 'accidental lack of perfection'—it would sound like mockery."[18]

The person who ventures into the depth of the unconscious will confront the source of such evil, and he is helpless against this destructive archetypal content unless he is guided and guarded by a power greater than his own. But at the same time, in the real experience of these depths the very meaning of religion is revealed in its essence, as a binding force which guides and protects one through the dark waters. Jung devoted most of the last part of his life to understanding and describing the creative, restoring aspect of the unconscious, and this integrative complex, which he called the *self*, is detailed in works like *Psychology and Alchemy*, *Aion*, and others. So important were these religious and numinous contents that unless a patient began to find relationship to them, he did not come to a full use of his capacities or recover fully from his neurosis and its complications.

Once a patient began to come into vital relationship with these contents and to find some understanding of them, a remarkable change often took place in his life. Though this took courage, dedication, even suffering, he found greater creativity and wider consciousness, as well as a healing influence upon himself and

18. *Ibid.*, 9, pt. 2: 53.

others. It was from facts such as these that Jung originally made the statement of his conviction about religion, which has been so widely quoted:

During the past thirty years, people from all the civilized countries of the earth have consulted me. I have treated many hundreds of patients, the larger number being Protestants, a smaller number Jews, and not more than five or six believing Catholics. Among all my patients in the second half of life—that is to say, over thirty-five—there has not been one whose problem in the last resort was not that of finding a religious outlook on life. It is safe to say that every one of them fell ill because he had lost that which the living religions of every age have given to their followers, and none of them has been really healed who did not regain his religious outlook.[19]

He also remarked:

It is after all only a tiny fraction of humanity, living mainly on that thickly populated peninsula of Asia which juts out into the Atlantic Ocean, and calling themselves "cultured," who, because they lack all contact with nature, have hit upon the idea that religion is a peculiar kind of mental disturbance of undiscoverable purport. Viewed from a safe distance, say from central Africa or Tibet, it would certainly look as if this fraction had projected its own unconscious mental derangements upon nations still possessed of healthy instincts.[20]

Jung was not speaking here of intellectual or rational religion, but of religion which uses images, symbols, dreams, ritual, and myth to keep man in touch with spiritual reality, just as sense experience puts him in contact with physical reality. Man cannot remain well psychologically or physically—let alone socially—if he loses contact with the unconscious and its symbolic and mythological life. Thus the real business of religion, Jung maintained, is to mediate men's contact with this level of reality and to guide

19. *Modern Man in Search of a Soul* (1933), p. 229.
20. *Two Essays on Analytical Psychology* (1956), pp. 215 f.

the individual to the source of healing with which he can be in touch through his own psyche.

To clarify these ideas let us try putting them in a diagram, which may help to reveal some of the relationships whose philosophical and theological implications will be discussed in the next chapter.

Here the triangle in the center represents the human *psyche;* and the whole area of the diagram, the experiences that converge upon it, divided by a line down the center. To the right of the line is the world of *consciousness* and sense experience—experiences of the space-time world. Much of the data accepted by psychology today is limited to this world, since most academic psychology automatically excludes any facts which do not appear to be objectively verifiable by the senses.

The psyche, however, extends into the world of *unconscious experience* on the left, with a small section representing things once known which have become unconscious by being forgotten, while in a larger section are all those experiences which have yet to become conscious. This part of the psyche, as we have already noted, has profound effects on man's physical and mental health. Impinging upon it are various archetypes, the complexes that determine so much of the individual's reactions and behavior,[21] shown with arrows to indicate how often they work at cross-purposes, causing conflict and tension. *Destructive tendencies* impinge upon this part of the psyche, indicated by the dark area below. This reality appears to come from beyond the personality and, invading man's psyche, seems to leave him powerless against it.

The upper angle of dotted lines stands for the "advocate" or *self,* to use but two of the words Jung applied to the powerful experience of integration which fends off the disintegrating as-

21. Discussed briefly in note 16 on page 292.

PSYCHOLOGICAL WORLD VIEW

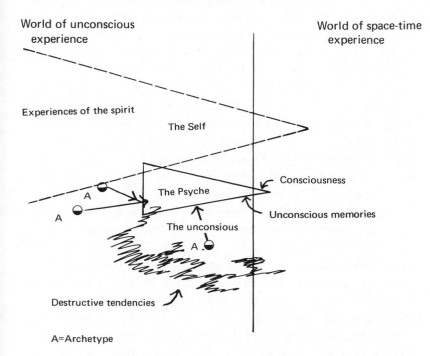

World of unconscious
  experience

World of space-time
  experience

Experiences of the spirit

The Self

The Psyche

A

A

Consciousness

Unconscious memories

The unconsious

A

Destructive tendencies

A=Archetype

pects of experience and brings healing and wholeness. It touches man as with a magic wand. This is an experienced reality which can touch man through the inner, less known part of the psyche and give direction to the conflicting forces that enter into it. Thus it can direct a man's life and protect him from both inner and outer disaster. It is the one reality that seems able to give men the power to reach wholeness— that enables the Holy Spirit to become incarnate in men's lives. The observable action of such a reality paves the way for genuine faith in the actuality of the Holy Spirit and its power.

Dr. Jung recognized what an important and profound insight had been given him, and also how closely his understanding held to the view expressed in the New Testament. As he came to see the immediate urgency of men's spiritual need, he turned to the clergy, asking them to "join forces" with psychotherapy "to meet this great spiritual task" of helping men discover the reality of the Self.[22] But the church, particularly in Europe, was not ready to break out of the rationalistic and materialistic shell that still keeps most of us from finding answers for our pressing spiritual problems.

In this paper Jung had spoken of healing as a religious problem, and he and his followers went on studying experiences of the unconscious psyche as realities nudging man's spirit. Almost alone, they supported the thesis that man can find help from beyond himself, enlisting forces that will bring wholeness, healing, and restoration of mind and body, and that only as he does reach out for such help can the opposing forces—those that lead to sickness, disintegration, destruction—be effectively countered. In case after case this understanding brought new life, physically and emotionally.

In my own life I have had the same results from working with Jung's basic ideas—at first with the aid of another person—in getting solutions for some of my own problems. Jung's thinking also gave me an hypothesis about human personality useful in finding many of these answers. I have seen others reach similar solutions as they were assisted, by mutual discussion, in approaching their problems with the same understanding. In the process I have seen the hypothesis verified again and again, pro-

22. *Modern Man in Search of a Soul, loc. cit.* This section was originally given as an address before the Alsatian Pastoral Conference in Strasbourg in 1932. The paper "Psychoanalysis and the Cure of Souls" was also written for this purpose (*Collected Works* 11: 348 ff.).

ducing both results and other associated data which cannot be adequately explained on the basis of any other theory that I know of.

Thus this point of view—which Jung developed in order to understand the experiences his patients encountered as they began to recover from psychological illness—has significance for religious healing, particularly Christian healing, that no other way of thinking offers. Before sketching the historical background of this outlook, let us examine briefly Jung's understanding of the way in which these healings occur.

The Process of Healing

As Jung stressed again and again, it was not he as psychiatrist who achieved the healing of a sick person. His task was rather to bring the individual to a source of healing found within the psyche, yet which seemed to come from outside it, like a spring bubbling up into a little pond. Primarily his task was to remove the debris that cut off or choked the source. How, then is this accomplished? From this point of view, psychological therapy involves four basic developments.

1. The first is to help the individual become aware of his own unique psychic structure and his relation to the storehouse of unconscious contents, both personal and collective. Thus he can be released from bondage to the negative elements and find his own relation to the creative and integrative contents in the unconscious. But this process begins with a task of self-discovery, which can hardly be undertaken alone. One has to face his mistakes and the guilts and fears with which an imperfect society burdens the individual. In the presence of the therapist, who is not shaken by what he finds, a person has the courage to look within himself.

Most individuals come to therapy because they have stood so

rigidly against the unconscious that one symptom or another has erupted. A person may have known neurotic flight, or depression, perhaps a manic state. But even if he has only experienced a vague guilt for being alienated—from himself and others, as T. S. Eliot shows so well in the figure of Celia in *The Cocktail Party* —his need is to express those aspects of his unconscious which personal distaste has kept him from facing. The therapist's job is to be someone with whom he can be comfortable, so that he can reveal his worst secrets as easily as possible. The therapist then, instead of being a creator in his own image, is a midwife.

Yet this is anything but a mean task. In order to allow this person, this individual, to contract for his own unique, creative meaning from the objective unconscious, someone must walk with him through the darkness who has withstood it himself. It is up to the therapist to know the structure of the unconscious, to be able to recognize intimations of the Self, and to have *faith* that they will become manifest in the life of this patient. He must also know experientially his own personal and collective darkness, so that he is not overwhelmed by the inner agony which has created the patient's neurotic problems. Indeed, anyone who deals with the depth of the unconscious will be touched by some of this agony. The way of wholeness is costing, as Baron von Hügel used to say of the genuine religious path. Even to a casual observer it is evident how similar this first stage of the healing process is to the practice of confession in profound spiritual direction. One can neither direct nor be directed until the data are on the table.

2. The second element, the developing of real relationships, is equally important in this process of growth toward healing. The way of individuation or integration is *not* a process characterized by detachment or lack of personal involvement. To the contrary, it is seldom possible outside of a deep concern for the other person, the individual involved in the encounter. Jung saw the

transference phenomenon not merely as a neurotic one, but as a major experience leading into a deeper encounter with unconscious reality. He discussed this technically in one of his more difficult essays, "Psychology of the Transference."

In addition, at the close of his long and fruitful life, Jung concluded his autobiography by observing that the realm of Eros, or love, is an area "in which rational understanding and rational modes of representation find scarcely anything they are able to grasp." Love, he suggests, may be the first condition of all cognition, "for we are in the deepest sense the victims and the instruments of cosmogonic 'love.' " Man is at the mercy of "love."

He may assent to it, or rebel against it; but he is always caught up by it and enclosed within it. He is dependent upon it and is sustained by it. . . . "Love ceases not"—whether he speaks with the "tongues of angels," or with scientific exactitude traces the life of the cell down to its uttermost source. Man can try to name love, showering upon it all the names at his command, and still he will involve himself in endless self-deceptions. If he possesses a grain of wisdom, he will lay down his arms and name the unknown by the more unknown, *ignotum per ignotius* —that is, by the name of God. That is a confession of his subjection, his imperfection, and his dependence; but at the same time a testimony to his freedom to choose between truth and error.[23]

The person who is unable to let love work consciously in his life, or shuts it out because of the dangers, loses the only way man has been given to come to wholeness, integration, or healing. This is essentially the same attitude as that of the Christian tradition at its deepest and best. The similarity to the Christian emphasis on community, relationship, and charity is obvious enough without further elaboration. Many recent writers about spiritual and sacramental healing, including Agnes Sanford, Starr Daily, and Evelyn Frost, have also stressed the importance

23. *Memories, Dreams, Reflections,* pp. 353 f.

of love in an effective healing ministry.

3. The next stage of education follows with the realization "that no confession and no amount of explaining will make the ill-formed tree grow straight, but that it must be trained with the gardener's art upon the trellis before normal adaptation can be attained."[24] The healing of personality from which emotional and physical healing flow is not an automatic process. It requires training and discipline to bring the conscious will into harmonious teamwork with unconscious contents.

One must learn, on one hand, that there are other ways of relating to the world besides only thinking or sensing, for instance, and then develop his inferior or less developed functions. It is also essential to learn how to keep a relation going with the unconscious so that the widening of one's consciousness will not come to a halt. One of the main methods for such confrontation of the unconscious, described by Jung in *Two Essays on Analytical Psychology*, is the process of active imagination. Many of the classics of the devotional life are records of just such active dealing with the unconscious by men who realized the importance of these images for their lives. John Bunyan's *Pilgrim's Progress* and T. S. Eliot's *Four Quartets* are two of the best known examples of this.[25] Indeed, many people have called my attention to the fact that this process corresponds almost exactly to the practice of religious meditation.

24. *Modern Man in Search of a Soul,* p. 46.
25. M. Esther Harding's *Journey into Self* (1956), is an excellent study of *Pilgrim's Progress,* showing that this Christian classic is a fine piece of active imagination. This is certainly true of Jakob Böhme, William Law, Scupoli, and John Woolman, as well as such ancient works as *The Shepherd of Hermas* and modern ones like *The Midnight Hour* by "Nicodemus" and Auden's *The Age of Anxiety* and *For the Time Being.* One of the best modern books of devotion, *A Testament of Devotion* by Thomas Kelly, is another excellent example. One analyst has pointed out that this process is represented in an Egyptian text telling about a man's conversation with his soul, and also in the remarkable dialogue with his soul recorded by Hugo of St. Victor.

4. Important as this effort is, however, it does not actually resolve the basic inner conflict. The patient's situation at this point is paradoxical. All he can do to develop understanding and will and consciousness does not constellate the Self, and yet without his conscious hard work usually nothing happens. It reminds one of the dilemma of orthodox Christianity. Salvation is not achieved by our own efforts; the church had to consider this idea very carefully in order to quash it in the heresy of Pelagianism. Yet neither are we saved entirely by the action of God unrelated to our own efforts, as the predestinarian holds. We must try as hard as we can, knowing that it is not enough and that God gives salvation as his own free gift. What Jung has described as a psychological process has essentially the same quality as the religious way.

In fact, in this final development, religious virtues of the highest nature are needed if one is to continue seeking growth and integration in the face of his own inability to pull together the fragmentↄ of his personality. When he is doing the best he knows how, and still nothing happens, he must have patience, persistence, courage, and faith. He must be able to bear the tension of conflict and unresolved opposites within himself, and also within those around him, until the solution is *given*. A patient generally finds the analyst of great help and strength at this time.

It is such times that the saints have described as the dark night of the soul. These are the men who give others the courage to bear on through the darkness until light appears, even though it seems that they will never pass through themselves. Without courage one cannot hope for success; after doing all he can, he often finds it is not enough. His stalemate is like that of Job and his friends. They had argued through three rounds of discourse with no solution; instead the conflict only became more violent and bitter. But Job persisted.

The individual who persists on, neither backing down nor

giving up, then often finds the conflict solved for him on a higher level. As with Job, God appears in a whirlwind to set things right and resolve the stalemate. In fact, several cases have been reported of a solution coming to a patient as he dreamed of a whirlwind. What he could not do for himself was done for him. Then opposites are reconciled and conflict solved by being raised to a new level, where it loses its bitter poignancy. This is the experience of the constellation of the Self, in which an unknown arises in the life of the individual to bring order out of chaos— to integrate the conflicting tendencies and parts of his personality. Theologically this is known as the religious experience. Jung speaks of a transforming symbol by which the difficulties are resolved irrationally. In the religious experience the fragmented parts are united by common meaning and values; a satisfying sense of wholeness and value is given by God, who still remains the unknown. There is a real similarity to the experience of a Christian in former times who stood before a martyr's shrine in need of healing, and found himself healed and his life changed as well.

Jung observed an instinctual drive toward wholeness within the psyche. In his words, "To strive after Τελείωσις—completion—in this sense is not only legitimate but is inborn in man as a peculiarity which provides civilization with one of its strongest roots. This striving is so powerful, even, that it can turn into a passion that draws everything into its service."[26]

Very much as nature abhors a vacuum, the psyche abhors separation and division. One manifestation of this instinctual drive is transference, in which the unity is obtained symbolically as one comes close to another person who carries an essential part of the psyche for him. And if this instinctual drive is followed through to its own conclusion, it leads to a genuine wholeness

26. *Collected Works* 9, pt. 2: 69.

such as is experienced in real religion. Thus it may be said that man is instinctively religious and that he cannot be truly whole in soul, mind, and body until he has come to this experience, or —to use religious terms—until he has been touched by the reality of God. In this experience he is welded into a whole and given meaning. In the last analysis, real health of body and mind depends upon one's religious life.

Man continues to grow in this world, however, and this is not a once-and-for-all experience. One has an intimation of it, and finds his life whole. Then, while living as fully and consciously as possible, new conflicts and problems arise, and so there must be a new experience of the Self, a new integration and transformation. In other words, the task of achieving consciousness goes on and on. On the one hand, contact with the unconscious, which gives power, can almost imperceptibly swallow us. On the other hand, we cannot abide our own egos when they stand out of relation with the unconscious depth. So we remain always between the danger of being swallowed and inflated or of being spiritually dehydrated. Hence the religious quest must always go on in this positive and creative tension.

Indeed, this process has no limit or end; man is given far greater capacity for growth than he ordinarily realizes. In Christian thinking the religious experience was not understood as a final encounter which ended the need for further growth. It was seen rather as an initiation into the religious way, which leads one ever further and deeper into the mysteries of reality. Real integration and religious life are both growth *processes*, equally seeking the goal of fruition of life without bounds. While ultimate goals, of course, are not for this life, one does obtain many intimations of this.

It would seem that if we are to stay well, emotionally as well as in body, we must keep on a path of growth both psychologically and religiously, not so much in order to reach a destination as to remain on a religious journey.[27] Indeed, Jung saw the analytical process as no longer bound only to the consulting room of the doctor. He said very specifically of analytical psychology: "We might say that it transcends itself, and now advances to fill that void which hitherto has marked the psychic insufficiency of Western culture as compared with that of the East."[28] Western man, he went on to suggest, was about ready to forgo compulsion and start building a bridge, stone by stone, toward the development of the psyche and to serve those who have a right to health.

If Dr. Jung and his followers are right about the nature of the psyche and its relation to a nonphysical world, they have something very important to say about our physical and mental health. They have something to say to us very close to the original message of Christianity. But this is only an isolated, interesting fact unless people do something about it. Can a point of view like Jung's be currently accepted? Supposing it is worth acting upon, what unconscious assumptions will it meet among modern thinking men? In particular, how does it fit with our present scientific knowledge of the world? Let us consider these questions rather carefully before drawing certain conclusions about healing for ourselves and others today.

27. One of the most interesting studies of the correspondences between the Christian way and depth psychology at its most comprehensive may be found in an anthology, *The Choice Is Always Ours* (1960), compiled by Dorothy Phillips and other editors. Here great passages of Christian devotion are placed side by side with passages from depth psychology and deep human experience. It often becomes clear that each discipline is expressing, simply in different words, practically the same experiences and insights as the other.

28. *Modern Man in Search of a Soul*, p. 53.

12

A Place for Religious Healing in the Modern World

Either there is a place for Christian healing in today's world or there is not, and this can only be decided on facts. But Christian theology does not seem to be looking at the facts—although, as we have seen, these are certainly not lacking. Instead, one has the distinct impression of a foregone conclusion. The most comprehensive survey of recent theology, John Macquarrie's *Twentieth Century Religious Thought,* makes this quite clear. Healing is simply overlooked today. Of the hundred and fifty theologians discussed in that book, *not one* emphasizes the effect of man's religious life on his mental and physical health, as do the more perceptive psychiatrists and students of psychosomatic medicine. Few of these religious thinkers, in fact, even bother with the arguments against healing.

Of course there are some who, on the side, poke fun at the theological vagaries of Mary Baker Eddy and others, or decry the extravagances of "faith" healers. But the real reasons for ignoring the possibility of healing are much deeper than this. Our culture has no place for such experiences. Men feel helpless when confronting them, and theology has no answer. Indeed, Christian thinkers cannot consider experiences of healing today because of the tacit acceptance, philosophically and theologically, of a world view which allows no place for a breakthrough of "divine" power into the space-time world. Such a breakthrough as healing is simply considered an impossibility.

Both theology and philosophy attempt to be consistent. They attempt to put experience into a rational framework. Since they see the world as a closed mechanical system, with man limited to it, consistency requires that he be understood within the system and human experiences be explained logically. But it is difficult to explain incidents of religious healing within a system which contains everything that can possibly touch man and admits no intervention from beyond this space-time realm. The only choice is to ignore a supposed healing—or rationalize it, say, as coincidence or the result of some natural force not yet understood. One cannot, with logical consistency, withhold judgment and see whether the experience implies other, perhaps more desirable alternatives.

This, as current studies show, is the framework within which all influential modern theologians operate, whether they realize it or not. If religious healing is to have a hearing, it will be necessary for Christians to take off these philosophical blinders and consider facts which our modern world view shuts out entirely. To do this, we must first understand the present outlook quite clearly. While it is not possible to go into this fascinating story in detail, we shall look briefly at how it started and was later adopted into Christianity in preference to the alternative, and in fact original, point of view. This will give some idea of how important one's outlook is in determining the facts we are able to accept.

We shall then look at the facts that make necessary a different point of view—one that takes healing into account. As we shall see, one cannot isolate the spaciotemporal world from a non-physical or psychic realm as the modern philosopher does. Perhaps the separation is obvious to him, but the "obvious" is usually what one has not fully understood.

The task of providing a new point of view, of taking a new

theological stance, is a difficult one. We must consider where we have been and where we are going. Let us look together at this ancient and modern history, trying to open up a new conscious understanding for tomorrow. The following sketch is brief and technical, but necessary to understand the rejection of religious healing among most modern theologians. I have provided a more detailed account of this development in my book, *Encounter With God: A Theology of Christian Experience.*

A Closed System

The idea that man lives within a closed rational and physical system, receiving information only by his sense experience and his reason, was first worked out in detail by Aristotle in the fourth century B.C. Other philosophers had suggested that man might be only a material being, but Aristotle was the first to develop the implications of this idea. In opposition to both the philosophy of Plato and the popular view of his time, he maintained that there is no reality apart from the known world of sense experience and reason. Forms or ideas, he held, have no separate existence and become real only as they are expressed in material substance.

It was incongruous to Aristotle to believe that man might be influenced by a reality independent of the physical world. For one thing, it offended his one-way concept of human freedom and morality that something should be able to break in upon man and change his life; so he ignored or denied the significance of dreams, prophecy, and other emotional and nonrational aspects of man's experience as having anything to do with reality emanating from God. In not looking very carefully at the basis of his own belief, he failed to see the logical absurdity to which this understanding would lead.

Although Aristotle was not very popular in the ancient world, his thinking was later seized by Islam and became the basis for the brilliant Arab civilization of the Middle Ages. And at length his influence was felt in western Europe, and against his crisp and logical ideas the thinking of the church, based on a misconceived and otherworldly Platonism, did not stand a chance. A new world view emerged, which represented an attempt to synthesize the Christian and Aristotelian points of view.

The most careful and sophisticated representative of this school was Thomas Aquinas, whose Scholasticism was head and shoulders above most of the thought of his time. On the basis of his work, the church erected a system in which the certainties of Aristotle's logic and metaphysics were applied to teachings and ideas of Christianity considered essential to a theology or knowledge of God. Whatever was not logically essential, including most intrusions from the spiritual world, was left out. Man was saved, not through contact with God, but by accepting the system *in toto*. In the thinking of Aquinas little room was left for the gifts of the Spirit Paul enumerates in his first letter to the Corinthians.

Aquinas, as we have seen, quite naturally had difficulty with healing. Unless one believes in a very actual spiritual reality, which not only exists apart from the material world but interpenetrates it, sacramental healing *is* a logical absurdity. In other books I have shown also the trouble he had with dreams and tongue speaking. Angels and demons got into the act as rational creatures by a feat of logic—as Father White has shown in his *God and the Unconscious*. This Scholastic and Aristotelian thought has had a far more pervasive and lasting influence upon both Catholic and Protestant ideas than most people realize. It was not seriously quesioned—largely because until quite recently secular thinking followed the same track.

So pervasive is this influence that it seldom occurs to us that there is another traditional outlook which gives an entirely plausible view of religious healing. This is the more popular tradition, stated with clarity and profundity by Plato. It was also the basic point of view of Jesus, the fathers of the church, and the whole of eastern Christianity. This viewpoint finds man interacting not only with a real physical world, but with a real nonphysical one as well. From this stance, healing is one of the direct ways in which the Spirit makes its impact on men. It is one of five such ways described at length and thoroughly discussed in the New Testament;[1] indeed nearly half the verses of the New Testament deal in one way or another with these direct experiences of nonphysical reality.

Yet modern Christians very rarely wonder about these things, even though an understanding and acceptance of them would make it possible to comprehend the facts about religious healing which are accumulating more and more rapidly today. Instead of trying out this line of understanding, most of us allow a certain other view of life and reality to determine unconsciously which facts we will seriously entertain and which we do not see at all. A *world view* has this power, actually screening the data that get into our consciousness; and it would be wise for us to know how our present outlook came to prevail so universally, and who have been its most influential supporters. As briefly as possible, hitting only the high spots, let us glance at the main developments of modern philosophy.

Modern thinking takes off from the Aristotelian-Scholastic base in a quest for certainty about external reality, as well as about logical ideas. It was inaugurated by Descartes when he tried to find solid ground for what we know by fitting all experience into the model of analytical geometry, which he had discovered. In the Cartesian system all unclear or shadowy ideas and beliefs were eliminated, and all else was to be doubted until

1. They are 1. dreams and visions, 2. special divine knowledge and wisdom, 3. prophecy, 4. experiences of angels and demons, and 5. healing.

proved true. Qualities became stripped objects, seen only quantitatively, while the subject was seen as separate from the object, with no mathematical way to prove the existence of the object from thought alone.

In addition—quite a refinement of Aristotle—the subject (or thinking person) was viewed as pure consciousness—although, as we have seen, Descartes did not operate on this basis even in developing his method. But before the Cartesian web collapsed, finally poked full of holes by later thinkers, it had caught enough flies to leave the imprint of its ideas at work in the philosophic mind.

In England this was followed by the great deductive system of Thomas Hobbes, who anticipated many of the rationalistic conclusions of modern thinking, including disbelief in the healing miracles of the New Testament, which did not fit into his system. In turn Hobbes was succeeded by the empiricists, led by John Locke, who held that the only sure knowledge is mathematical, all else being derived from sense experience.

The dangers of this view were sensed by the brilliant and graceful Bishop Berkeley. Proposing the first Western idealism, Berkeley made a competent rescue of the material world—as ideas held in the mind of God—thus bridging the gulf in Cartesian dualism that extended to skepticism about matter itself. He remained an influence until Western philosophy ruled out metaphysics in the 1930s. But meanwhile David Hume carried the ideas of the empiricists to their logical conclusion in a total skepticism in which the individual knows only the stream of impressions that come before him, nothing more—not even his own identity.

Kant, however, soon reestablished the dualism, maintaining that man can never know either the object in itself or the subject in itself. For him, experience was the product of the interaction of these two unknown realities, with only the conscious aspects of the subject considered. He left man with real phenomenal knowledge, but with final doubt as to whether he will ever know reality in itself. Kant defined the limits of human knowing, and many thinkers believe that his critical conclusions have yet to be overridden. He also cast doubt on all the customary Scholastic arguments for God and tried to base his belief in God on entirely different grounds, on man's moral sense. It never occured to him, in the closed system of sense experience, that the divine had any other way to break through and touch man.

At the same time practical philosophers were gradually coming to have great confidence in man's reason and his knowledge of the world around him. The confidence of Descartes in his skepticism was backed up by the Enlightenment, and then given further support by the work of Newton and Darwin. By the late nineteenth century this view was solidifying into dogma: the material alone was real, and evolved according to rational and mechanical laws which would eventually be understood *in toto*. Man himself was a prisoner in this closed and unalterable system, since his psyche was merely an epiphenomenal by-product, "nothing but" the result of this material process.

Since then most philosophy has been occupied in trying to support or deny the results of this dogma. Popular thinkers from Comte and Spencer to Mach and Skinner have developed its implications. The behaviorist utopia is even provided in Skinner's novel *Walden II*. Hegel, on the other hand, tried to escape the uncertainty of Kant and support the autonomy of "mind" and "idea" by proving dialectically, with logical certainty, that the entire experienced world is a manifestation of "mind." But with no place for the individual, Hegel's "ideal" system left man as much a prisoner of an unvarying order as he had been in the materialistic system. It was on the basis of Hegel's dialectic, of course, combined with the materialism of the current science, that Karl Marx gave the modern communist movement its philosophic base, thus providing a materialistic dogma for large sections of the modern world.

Kierkegaard and the existentialists who followed him reacted violently to Hegel's magnificent dialectic. Realizing that man's unique individuality was lost in it, they turned their attention to the individual, yet did not question the idea that he is utterly caught in a closed physical system. It was as impossible for Kierkegaard as for the naturalists to believe that God or Spirit could break through into the here and now, into history.[2] Since they saw no way for extraneous meaning to come in, or for man to reach out to it, all they could offer was a blind jump of faith into an unknown through the tension of anxiety and dread.

The lead of Hegel was picked up again in phenomenology by Edmund Husserl. In an attempt to arrive at the same certainty as the natural sciences had apparently achieved, he based an entire philosophy on the logical presuppositions of man's conscious, intentional act. He saw no way by which man could reach meaning except through intellectual analysis. He dismissed the unconscious as a meaningless concept, accepting also as axiomatic that nothing breaks through into the closed system of man's consciously understood space-time world.

Strangely enough, the strongest influence on theology today has come from a synthesis of the thinking of these two men. Working from the ideas of Kierkegaard and Husserl, a group of Europeans, notably Heidegger, Jaspers, Sartre, Marcel, and Merleau-Ponty, have produced the significant movement of existentialism. Although there are many differences between these men, philosophically they are all existentialists. They all hold that man can know only his own conscious existence—perhaps best known through contemplation of death and dread, and understood through ontological analysis. None of them suggests any

2. See particularly his *Training in Christianity* (1944).

experience of a transpersonal realm or of any reality other than the personal, and thus the idea of religious healing for these men is simply absurd.[3]

The influence of this philosophy on modern theology—through Barth, Bultmann, Bonhoeffer, Tillich, and their popularizer John A. T. Robinson—has been enormous. While Barth actively denies any influence, he still goes along with their assumption that God does not break into the space-time world, finding various reasons for seeing the biblical period as the one exception. Bultmann and Bonhoeffer frankly acknowledge their dependence on these philosophers, and the Tillich of the *Systematic Theology* is clearly related to them. None of these theologians can conceive of any possibility but a closed system in which man lives and dies, and they do not consider evidence that might indicate any other possibility. The idea of a transpersonal reality breaking into man's psyche or influencing his body for sickness or health is not worth discussing seriously. No wonder we found their ideas on the subject so negative in chapter 2. Their rejection of a healing ministry is on philosophical grounds rather than upon evidence, which would at least make sense to today's science-oriented world. As I have said before it is not my purpose to provide this evidence, but in various places I have referred the reader to the works of others where it can be found.

There is one other approach in current philosophy, that of the British school of empiricism. Building on the genius of Wittgenstein, Russell, and Whitehead, this group has taken a different tack. They see logic as tautological and not productive of any new knowledge; rather, all knowledge is derived from empirical observation, from experience. Since one cannot know with logical

3. For a more detailed treatment of this school, see my article, "Is the World View of Jesus Outmoded?" *Christian Century* 86 (January 22, 1969): 112 ff. In some of Heidegger's most recent thought, however, there are new insights into the importance of intuition, suggesting a somewhat broader view.

certainty what new experiences will bring, all knowledge is then only probable and hypothetical. As A. J. Ayer shows in his brilliant exposition of these ideas in *Language, Truth and Logic*, this school has not denied that men could have other levels of experience than that of the senses, or that another realm of reality might break in and affect man's life. But by pushing aside other possibilities, they have gone along with the assumption that man is contained in a closed physical system, and so they write off metaphysics, theology, and moral theory with a stroke of the pen.

One need not look far to find the connection between the religious ideas of our time and these concepts of philosophy. In modern studies of how man knows God, the present understanding of philosophy is accepted as almost axiomatic, with the conclusion that men must infer their knowledge of God from events of this world and not from any direct or immediate experience of the divine.[4] It is clear in these studies how closely philosophy and theology are linked. The fact is that when man's understanding of the world places him unquestioningly in a setting in which the entire meaning of his life derives only from his personal actions and relationships, theology can whistle in the dark for all anyone cares. It may concoct all kinds of intellectual notions about meaning and healing, but practically no one will be taken in.

Only as men begin to understand human life and other reality (and this is *philosophy*) in terms of a viable meaning beyond the purely personal, can they then explore and elaborate the possibility that there are experiences—for instance, like those of healing —in which men find relationship to this meaning (which, over-

4. For instance, see F. R. Tennant, *Philosophical Theology* (1956); Douglas Clyde MacIntosh, *The Problem of Religious Knowledge* (1940); John Baillie, *The Idea of Revelation in Recent Thought* (1956), also *The Sense of the Presence of God* (1962); John H. Hick, *Faith and Knowledge* (1966); and Bernard J. F. Lonergan, S.J., *Insight: A Study of Human Understanding* (1957).

all, is *theology*). It would seem obvious that the two go hand in hand. If one's understanding of life excludes belief in any possible relationship to a meaning that could be called God except through his organizational principles from organic chemistry on up, then one can learn very little from theology. He would do better then to study evolution, or law, or politics, and compare notes with scientists in other fields, if he would learn how God works.

There are indications, however, that a new understanding of the world is growing, involving quite a different view of man's place in it and the meaning he finds through it. This is occurring in two different but related areas: one is in the scientific world as a whole and the other in psychology.

New Facts

Early in the twentieth century awareness was growing that the nineteenth-century outlook—the rational materialism which saw man within a closed naturalistic system—was too narrow to take in the data now becoming known about our world. Through the work of Becquerel and the Curies, of Planck, Heisenberg, and others, the substantial atom exploded into an increasing number of particles which could not be understood on a basis of Newtonian mechanics. Einstein, in one of the greatest intuitions of this age, came to the conclusion that space might not be Euclidean in nature, and his studies of the speed of light brought a new concept of time.

Man's whole conception of time and matter and scientific truth were undergoing a traumatic change. The scientific method had not produced final and certain truths after all, but only hypotheses which could be overturned by new research and replaced with new understanding. Scientific "laws" could no longer be seen as ultimate truths; they were like maps, increasingly accurate but still only maps of a territory that could never be fully known.

In biology and paleontology it was found that the idea of survival of the fittest does not always fit the facts, that the relation between genetic factors and what Darwin observed appears to be directed in far too complex a way to be expressed without some idea of purpose. Thus, through thinking about evolution, the idea of teleology was reintroduced into the study of man. Pierre Teilhard de Chardin has stated these facts with brilliance and clarity in his several books. We have already shown some of the evidence adduced by psychosomatic medicine in this area.

But this thinking has not taken hold generally. Although it is making a deep impression on the philosophy of science, the idea has not occurred to many philosophers that these new conceptions may have a relation to man's own life, to his search for meaning in this universe. Instead the basis for a new philosophical understanding was produced almost single-handed by one man in the field of psychology, because, as we have seen, he had to find ways to help people recover from psychological illness.

This of course was C. G. Jung, who was grounded as few other scientists in the history of philosophy, but came to use this interest for very practical rather than theoretical reasons. He found that the difficulties of his patients, usually including a variety of symptoms, could arise simply from loss of meaning. Being a committed physician, he did whatever he could to help them recover, even turning to philosophy and theology to fill the gap left in their lives by the loss of a traditional approach to religion.

Jung was also trained in the most rigorous scientific method, as well as having a wealth of empirical data available to him about man and his ways of finding meaning. Through the experience of hundreds of patients, he was able to describe from direct inner experience the processes which Teilhard de Chardin and others described from the outside. Building on this evidence,[5] he carefully sketched out an empirical framework in which man's psychic, unconscious experiences were given the same value as experiences of the physical world. At the same time Jung was participating in the growth of a new attitude within the scientific community itself.

He realized that theories of the unconscious were as difficult to understand or accept from the nineteenth-century point of view as theories of quantum mechanics. In fact Jung often drew attention to the analogy between quantum mechanics and depth psychology. He saw that in taking the unconscious seriously as an operative part of man's personality, he was breaking with philosophic tradition from Kant on, and also with the popular psychological ideas of Wundt on which today's experimental psychology is based. He was prepared to support his position; while he did not write a great deal about his methodology and philosophical presuppositions, he was well aware of them, and they were clearly formulated in passages scattered throughout his writings.[6]

Jung and Modern Thought

Jung frankly accepted the philosophic realism of modern science and its organic and empirical emphasis. But he did not limit his empiricism only to facts that can be verified in a physical sense. He applied the method of the physical sciences to personal encounters with the unconscious, testing them with basically the same questions: How does it work? Is it repeated? What is the

5. I have suggested the nature of the evidence in the discussion on pp. 288 ff.
6. Jung was quite close to the physicists Wolfgang Pauli and Max Knoll. He collaborated with the Nobel prizewinner in one publication, while Knoll (one of the inventors of the electron microscope) supplemented and amplified some of Jung's ideas, particularly in "Transformations of Science in Our Age," *Papers from the Eranos Yearbooks 3, Man and Time* (1957): 264 ff.

result in the individual? As Raymond Hostie put it in describing Jung's work at some length in *Religion and the Psychology of Jung*, his method was actually a "non-experimental empiricism."[7] Jung was fond of remarking that in experimental research the scientist asks the questions, while in clinical practice the patient and nature ask it, and that it is not hard to see which asks the more difficult questions. Scientific experiment gives carefully defined data about a small area of nature. Jung's method gives less defined data about the nature of man himself, data which can direct the next step and even be roughly verified.

Philosophically Jung started from the base of Kant's critical study of man's reason, but considered the subjective component of the experiencing act to include unconscious contents and processes. This part of the subjective component—perhaps the major part—was made up of contents not always as personally subjective as they might appear. They were experienced subjectively, but this is also the way we experience the physical world, and there were many contents that seemed to come into the individual psyche from outside itself, and to have the same givenness as sense experience.

Thus Jung maintained that man has contact with an objectively real physical world, which of necessity is experienced subjectively; plus an equally real world of collective or autonomous psychic contents, also experienced only subjectively by necessity; plus—finally—an equally real world of personal psychic contents which are experienced directly, inwardly, and of course also subjectively. All these experiences give only phenomenal knowledge. None gives final or certain knowledge of "the thing-in-itself," but only what can become known through its reaction with the subject. The experience of the subject tells us all we can know about either the physical object or the psychic content,

7. 1957, pp. 9 ff.

although this knowledge can be made more certain as more attention is directed to the phenomena themselves.

What Jung wrote to me in 1958 summarizes his understanding especially well; in this letter he wrote:

> The real nature of the objects of human experience is still shrouded in darkness. The scientist cannot concede a higher intelligence to Theology than to any other branch of human cognition. We know as little of a Supreme Being as of Matter. But there is as little doubt of the existence of a Supreme Being as of Matter. The world beyond is a reality, an experiential fact. We only don't understand it.

Or again, he stressed that "natural science is not a science of words and ideas, but of facts,"[8] found through or within man, where two different kinds of reality meet and interact in a special way.

Let us look for a moment at how the physical scientist handles the facts of experience. He does not ask them to be something more than his own experiences with matter. Instead he asks what these empirical observations mean. Then by induction or analogy, nearly always based on intuitive insight, he makes an educated guess—an hypothesis which he proceeds to test. In this way he reaches a theory that tries to put all the facts into relationship. Each new experience that does not fit his hypothesis requires an expanded or often entirely new hypothesis. One inconsistent fact, small enough to be overlooked by most observers, may even require a whole new world view. It is at this point that logical thought, right down to mathematical relationships, is most needed to work out the implications and details of new hypotheses and a new theory.

For instance, one such fact, which literally started a chain reaction in science, was Becquerel's experience in 1896 of finding his sealed photographic plates mysteriously exposed by a sup-

8. *Collected Works* 16: 317. See Bibliography for volume titles, here and below.

posedly inert metallic salt. Once Marie Curie became interested in this experience, it was no longer an isolated phenomenon. The properties of uranium, thorium, and radium were discovered, followed by work with neutrons, protons, "heavy" atoms, and finally—the blast. And it struck home, even to unsophisticated people, that matter is not very dead or inert. A new understanding was needed, which, as we have seen, began to develop in various parts of the scientific world.

Jung, who began his work a few years after Becquerel and the Curies, came upon his evidence just as unexpectedly. Listening to the people who came to him for healing, he found they were experiencing strange images and other contents thrusting into consciousness. Many of these patients were practical scientists, schooled in scientific certainty, who had neglected the whole area of feeling and unconscious experience since it had no conceivable place in that framework. As they encountered and dealt consciously with these unconscious contents, these people not only found healing but often experienced strange elements of mythology and extrasensory perception. In many instances it was through an experience of just this nature that a patient began to find meaning and new energy. To help understand this, Jung began an intensive study of mythology and dream symbols, and also of experiences synchronized with similar or identical events in the outer world.

Thus he came to new and detailed knowledge of the unconscious, which—coming from the most complex aggregations of matter, human beings—showed that a new hypothesis was needed to understand both consciousness and the unconscious and their relation to the material world. The older theories were no longer adequate, and Jung suggested a new hypothesis which stepped beyond the deterministic naturalism of the nineteenth century and therefore offered meaning for wide areas of man's life. The implications of his theory are both philosophical and theological.

This direction was supported by a strong pragmatic bent. Jung believed that electing a course of action that results in permanent healing—in human wholeness—comes closest to living with reality as it is. He was much influenced by the pragmatism of William James, whose writings he knew well and often quoted. Much as James did, he expressed the assumption that runs unexpressed through much of modern science: that what works in practical life is closely correlated with what is real.

In pragmatism there is a further hypothesis which Jung accepted: that life is more than just a chance and meaningless epiphenomenon. If there is ultimate meaning in the universe, and if man's life expresses a high level or stage of that meaning, then what furthers and develops human life is likely to correspond to that same meaning in the universe. And alternatively, what blocks or destroys human life—including neurotic and physical illness—is alien to that meaning, while living life fully and completely is likely to express it. Jung offered the theory that nature is meaningful in itself, and then adduced volumes of evidence from man's inner life to corroborate this thesis.

This approach was reinforced by Jung's realization, discussed above, that there are experiences of unconscious contents which are not merely primitive and atavistic. The unconscious can produce understanding which is often *superior* to the reasoning of consciousness, although it usually presents these understandings in images rather than as abstract concepts. But, as Jung carefully demonstrated in his introduction to *Symbols of Transformation*, man is quite capable of thinking in this way, as well as by using the directed, conceptual reasoning of practical science and Aristotelian philosophies. Man uses the intuitive, symbolic "thinking" that comes in images from the unconscious to convey his deepest insights and his emotional meaning. Art, drama, liturgy, folktales, mythology, and scientific intuition all make use of archetypal images, and each night the dream also presents its significance in similar symbols and pictures.

It is important that our logic be broad enough to deal with these aspects of experience. When man loses touch with his capacity to think symbolically, as most of us have today, he is no longer able to understand either his own myth and dreams and sickness or his relationship with the world around him. This is one fact which scientific men are beginning to appreciate today.[9]

Mapping a New Understanding

If Jung's evidence from the unconscious is taken seriously, then man clearly has need for a new understanding of the total world of experience and of his place within that world. The hypothesis that Jung offers is very different from the materialistic rationalism that has swept the house bare for most of us. Instead, it finds man faced with an *experiential* dualism. From this point of view, man is confronted not only with the objective reality of a physical world, but also with experience relating to the objective, autonomous reality of the psychic world. These worlds interact; Jung's studies of synchronicity describe these outer interactions. Aniela Jaffé has discussed these in her little book, *From the Life and Work of C. G. Jung*. It is, however, within man that they come to the most profound and meaningful interplay. Man is a very significant bridge between these two worlds.

The vast psychic world with which man is presented through unconscious contents and meanings, Jung found, is as objectively real, and as meaningful and possible to experience, as the physi-

9. Evidence of the transformation in scientific thinking is found in Max Knoll's article mentioned in the footnote on p. 319, and also in Friedrich Dessauer's "Galileo and Newton: The Turning Point in Western Thought," in *Papers from the Eranos Yearbooks* 1, *Spirit and Nature* (1954): 288 ff. Two other leading scientific thinkers who profess the same Platonic point of view are Werner Heisenberg, who speaks for himself in *Physics and Philosophy: The Revolution in Modern Science* (1962), and Kurt Gödel, whose complex presentation is discussed by Ernest Nagel and James R. Newman in *Gödel's Proof* (1964). See also Stephen Toulmin's excellent summary of recent thought, *The Philosophy of Science: An Introduction* (1960), and Mary Hesse, *Models and Analogies in Science* (1966).

cal world of space and time. In our present state of knowledge we cannot, for the sake of logical tidiness, reduce either one of these worlds to the other. In his comprehension of this Jung came very close to Plato's understanding of "Ideas," which he (Jung) saw as the philosophical version of his "psychically concrete" archetypes, rather than as eternal concepts.[10] He also agreed in principle with Plato that man does not come to experience and know the realm of the "Ideas" through the exercise of reason, but only through just the kind of irrational means Plato described as prophecy, dreams and healing, art, and love. As we have already seen, Jung stresses each of these areas and shows particularly his appreciation of love and its cognitive value.

Let us look again at the model or schema of this point of view, considering it philosophically rather than only psychologically.

The psyche, again represented by the completed triangle, exists in two worlds, like a bridge between two countries. In other words, two kinds of phenomenal experience impinge upon man through the psyche. Both are realms of experience of great complexity. Both are equally real from an ontological point of view, although each is conditioned by the experiencing subject. But both worlds can be known more and more fully as the individual opens himself to more and more significant experiences and then lets his rational and analytical capacities play upon them. Man in relation to the psyche is somewhat like a sightseer in Glacier International Park, who can cross the Canadian-U.S. border freely with only the bother of going through customs when he leaves the park.

The "Self" (the open triangle) represents those creative and suprapersonal experiences which are so meaningful for human development both scientifically and psychologically. From ex-

10. *Collected Works* 8: 191.

PHILOSOPHICAL AND RELIGIOUS WORLD VIEW

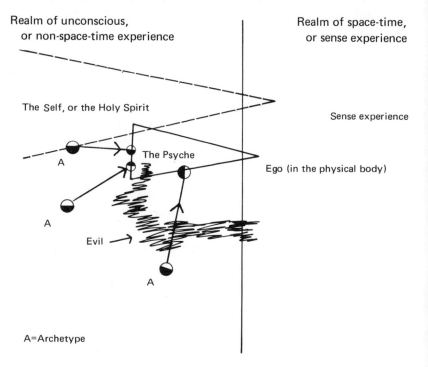

Realm of unconscious,
    or non-space-time experience

Realm of space-time,
    or sense experience

The Self, or the Holy Spirit

Sense experience

The Psyche

A

A

Ego (in the physical body)

A

Evil →

A

A=Archetype

periences of the "Self" come intuitions of the total world and also of man's own meaning. The experiences of evil (shaded) are those described, for instance, in Jung's account of his encounter with the unconscious in chapter 6 of his *Memories, Dreams, Reflections.* A few of the possible archetypes are suggested, showing both their creative and destructive effects on one's orientation toward life (half-shading). All these realities impinge upon the human psyche in addition to the constant bombardment of physical experience through the five senses. Because consciousness in the Western world is usually turned toward this sense experience, the realm of psychic affect is only occasionally considered and is rightly termed "unconscious."

If Jung has correctly mapped the territory of man's experience (and our schema of his word map, of course, has its limitations), then man is indeed in touch with complex realities of two kinds. There are those that he can handle physically and others that he cannot deal with in this way—realities which can be known only as men have the courage to encounter this other realm and try to understand and relate to it. In fact, Jung's thinking can provide a philosophical base for a modern experiential theology with an approach to healing—just as Plato's world view provided such a framework for the church fathers to express their experiences of Christ and Christian healing in the first vital centuries of the church's life.

Religious people in all ages and among all peoples have spoken of a "spiritual world" apart from the physical world. As one of the great modern physicists, Werner Heisenberg, has reminded us, words like these which come from the natural language express a more direct connection with reality than even the most precise abstractions of science.[11] Since Jung's evidence shows that there is a realm in which men have come into contact with a healing function superior to human consciousness, the idea of a healing God appears not to be mere metaphysical speculation after all, but rather the name which religious people have applied to their experience of such a healing reality. In Jung's world view the religious undertaking and the religious object are not only potentially meaningful; they are necessary if men are to survive as whole, healthy individuals. Jung has laid the foundation, and empirical theology can build upon that base.

Two of Jung's own statements, late in his work, clearly point out what we have sketched. In the first he wrote:

11. *Op cit.*, pp. 200 f.

I have, therefore, even hazarded the postulate that the phenomenon of archetypal configurations—which are psychic events *par excellence*—may be founded upon a *psychoid* base, that is, upon an only partially psychic and possibly altogether different form of being. For lack of empirical data I have neither knowledge nor understanding of such forms of being, which are commonly called spiritual. From the point of view of science, it is immaterial what I may *believe* on that score, and I must accept my ignorance. . . . Nevertheless, we have good reason to suppose that behind this veil there exists the uncomprehended absolute object which affects and influences us—and to suppose it even, or particularly, in the case of psychic phenomena about which no verifiable statements can be made.[12]

The other remark, which Jung made in his British Broadcasting Company interview, is almost too well known to be repeated, but it crystallizes all the other ways he tried to put this over: "Suddenly I understood that God was, for me at least, one of the most certain and immediate experiences. . . . I do not believe; I know. I *know.* "

In addition, Jung's understanding of the problem of evil has almost equally important implications for healing. He suggested that empirical theologians take this problem more seriously. His experience made him balk at the Aristotelian position that evil is only the absence or deprivation of good, with evil naturally belonging to man's nature—the *privatio boni*—and so he had to deal with the problem. He did so as creatively as anyone in our time, thus opening a real place for theological encounter.

He would have agreed with the author of Ephesians that "our fight is not against human foes, but . . . against the superhuman forces of evil in the heavens." (6:12, NEB) Man has to wrestle with darkness to find out its nature, and then either integrate or reject it. Jung believed that the doctrine of the *privatio boni*, first laid down for the church by Augustine and later developed by

12. *Memories, Dreams, Reflections* (1963), pp. 351 f.

Aquinas, crippled him in this struggle. It deceives him about the seriousness of his struggle. "The growing awareness of the inferior part of the personality," Jung wrote, "should not be twisted into an intellectual activity, for it has far more the meaning of a suffering and a passion that implicate the whole man."[13] Dealing with unconscious contents or with God can be a painful process, a *via crucis* which most men will avoid at any cost. This emphasis on creative suffering has much in common with the teaching of the New Testament and the church fathers.

The destructiveness—the very reality that we call evil—results in separation and disintegration within the psyche, which leads in turn to emotional ill health and ultimately to physical illness. Healing of either mind, emotions, soul, or body involves throwing back the forces of evil. But when evil is seen as merely an accidental lack of perfection, man is left with no approach to the psychic forces of destructiveness in which all sickness is rooted at least partially. To see evil as nothing but the absence of good leaves man with no ground to stand on for a fair fight against these forces. Instead they are able to operate in the unconscious autonomously and without interference. Unrecognized, evil is then given free rein to take control of the psyche.[14]

Thus when no one worries about it, evil either causes destruction within the psyche and the body or uses the individual psyche to promote destruction in the outer world. In one case we have emotional and physical ills, in the other social ills. Religiously the results are no better. If evil has no reality, then either man's ills must come from the direct action of God or one must end in denying that God has power to act. Either God becomes a mon-

13. *Collected Works* 8: 208.
14. This is an obviously complex problem which cannot be completely discussed here. A fuller treatment is offered in my paper on "The Mythology of Evil," to be published in the *Journal of Religion and Health*. One of the most recent works offering real insight into this problem for the individual is Adolf Guggenbühl-Craig's *Power in the Helping Professions* (1971).

strous being—somewhat less moral than man, as Jung pointed out in *The Answer to Job*—or else man finds himself in a meaningless world, with no real answer for his sickness, physical or spiritual, as Sartre and Camus have found. In the long run there seems to be no alternative when people are unable to see the reality of evil.

To admit the reality of evil, however, puts a different kind of responsibility on man. It is then up to him to deal with the unconscious or spiritual forces of evil, and this involves the whole person. This is a process of finding creative relationship with the unconscious so as to turn back the dark, destructive side of it. For most individuals this process involves one's whole being in relation to another person. Jung saw this very clearly. For him love was as much the powerful, revealing, restoring daemon as it was for Plato. Evil, he found, is seldom overcome or forced to withdraw until, through human love, man has opened himself to the power of divine love, which then forces the destructive powers into retreat. Indeed the process of healing requires and results in deepened human relationships.

We shall touch in the concluding chapter on ways of helping the individual to open himself to new life through the "Self" or the Holy Spirit. This, however, is a separate subject which must wait for more detailed treatment in another work.

Christian Theology and Healing

The world view we have sketched opens up a way for new appreciation of the vital experiences of Christianity and the concepts that formerly kept them alive and meaningful. One of the most central and living of these was the idea that the Christian became a source of healing, essentially and simply as a continuation of Christ's life through his church. As Irenaeus and Justin Martyr both held, it was understood that Jesus became what we are in order that we might become what He is. Healing was as basic a part of early Christian thought and experience as it had been in the life of Jesus. Thus the continuation of healing in the church's ministry can best be understood in its integral relation to the other fundamental ideas of Christianity. Let us look at these ideas of the incarnation, the atonement, the sacraments, and the church as they relate to healing.*

Once the *natural* interpenetration of the spiritual and physical worlds is understood, one is no longer startled or offended by the idea of the incarnation. In a very real sense every man *is* spirit incarnate. Difficult as this is to describe in terms of Aristotelian categories, the data accumulating today show that man is just such a hybrid of flesh commingled with what can only be called spirit. Ordinary people today, when they encounter this realm, have uncanny experiences far outside the mode of physical being. Is it then difficult to imagine that the Spirit of God himself could become incarnate in one human being, first received in the womb of a woman and then born as a human infant, or to see that at such a time there might have been the star, the visions of angels, the dreams of Joseph and the Wise Men, the forewarning and flight into Egypt? These things are scarcely incredible; rather they show the incarnation actually to be the ultimate extension of the action of Spirit in human life.

But for the early Christians there was something even more behind this doctrine. The apostles who had lived and suffered with this man were awed by what they met in him. They knew that something beyond the ordinary had occurred before their eyes. There was an unearthly wholeness and power in this man. Through Jesus they were touched by the numinous, the transcendent—the same experience they had in the most profound of their religious encounters which they experienced as good Jews.

*The material of this section is found in similar form in my *Encounter With God: A Theology of Christian Experience*, chapter 7.

In the healing of the sick and demon-possessed, a degree of love and harmony and wholeness was manifested that left them thunderstruck.

Then in the resurrection came the confirmation of all their deepest intuitions about Jesus. The man they had followed was not conquered by the actions of men under the influence of the Evil One. They hung him to a cross, and then God wrote, in actual fact, into history—into the fabric of the physical world—the mythical dream which had beaten in upon the intuition of man from the dawn of time. What had touched man in dream and vision and myth they now saw actualized. With this experience they realized that the realm of the Spirit ruled over all reality and that in the end there was nothing to fear. Through the master who had led them until his death, and then returned, they could still find the same new quality of life which he had imparted as a living man.

Unquestionably this experience is difficult to describe. But experiences of a person returning to someone he cared for are reported so often that this evidence is denied only by those who are unable to consider such facts. In ancient times Ambrose told of consoling encounters with his deceased brother Satyrus. Sulpitius Severus carefully described his vision of Martin of Tours almost at the time Martin, unknown to him, was dying. I have at least one modern letter describing a similar experience, and in May 1970 an incident in the United States near Gary, Indiana, was in the news all over the country: of a father who was guided by the voice of his murdered son, step by step, to the killer. Particularly at the time of a death, living men seem to have the capacity to experience the psyches of the departed directly and not through ordinary sense experience. If this can happen when ordinary men and women die, how much more likely it was for this man if he actually did bear the very Spirit of God in his human body.

There is also evidence that several people sometimes experience the same vision at the same time, and the resurrection appearances are easily understood as *at least* a numinous breakthrough of such a collective vision. Jung has described this phenomenon, and sees the flying saucer as a more mundane example of it.[15] Various instances have been reported of different men having the same dream. This does not, however, in any way hinder the possible factualness of an objective physical appearance. If the man Jesus was the incarnation of the very force that created the world, then what could prevent this objective spiritual reality from taking to itself the dead and torn body of Jesus, giving it new form and new splendor. Those who know anything of the "emptiness" and energic quality of matter will certainly not dismiss it as implausible. Such experiences of a resurrected body, of sudden appearance and disappearance and passing through doors, are only incomprehensible in terms of nineteenth-century physics.

In the ascension this particular manifestation of matter returned in a blaze of glory to the Creator. This experience should not overwhelm men who understand the moment-by-moment destruction and creation of atoms in a star, and have seen men create new atoms and turn carefully selected ones into a blaze of power in the atomic bomb. If man himself can collect just the right particles to do these things, I do not find it hard to believe that God was able to do a somewhat similar thing in the resurrection and ascension of Jesus, rounding out his creativity by the salvation of men whom he loves.

After the ascension the followers of Jesus were given a new awareness of the Spirit along with the almost tangible manifestation of an ecstatic speech. These men had lost everything but the hope of new life. As I have written elsewhere:

15. *Collected Works* 10: 307 ff.

The Jews indeed carried a burden, a crushing burden. Their task was to make God's righteousness manifest in their external lives. They carried it through suffering and exile; political subjection only intensified it. They yearned for some direct manifestation of God. While Jesus was with the group, he appeared to meet and satisfy their Jewish thirsting. But after the crucifixion and the ascension they were alone again. The only stability these men had was to sit still and wait as they had been told, both by Jesus and in a vision; being men who had known suffering and hope, they did just that. They stayed together and prayed, not knowing what might come. It was then that the experience of glossolalia first occurred. This experience was evidence to them that God's spirit was with them. It helped give them the conviction which sent them courageously into a hostile world.[16]

The encounter with the Self, described by Jung, is just such a central and vital experience. Again and again he observed that an objective, nonphysical reality like this could bring wholeness—indeed, health and harmony—to an individual's life, once he could allow it to operate. If ordinary men, then, have experiences of a power like this, one would expect it even more for the followers of Jesus after all they had experienced and suffered. When the Spirit did break through, it came not only with the evidence of tongues, but with the power to heal, which continued and was passed on to other converts.

These common experiences made the church, the fellowship, necessary. Men found that they were more open to the transforming power of the Spirit as they met together with one spirit. Their worship experiences even had the flavor of Pentecost itself and were anything but sedate experiences. Out of this common worship grew a fellowship of love and caring which was the most remarkable characteristic of the early church. Ecstatic worship, individual experience, a fellowhip of concern reaching out to those in need, and the healing ministry—all were parts of one complex whole.

16. *Tongue Speaking: An Experiment in Spiritual Experience* (1964), pp. 18 f.

The experience of being filled with the Holy Spirit is a kind of mysticism usually found only in Western thought, specifically in Christianity. In it the ultimate religious experience is seen as one which does not annihilate the ego. In Plato's thinking there was a foretaste of this; he saw the ultimate experience as a love relationship between the psyche and the divine which ceases to be meaningful if the ego is dissolved. Christian thinking, in terms of the schema we have presented, sees the Holy Spirit infilling the psyche (covering it), bringing harmony out of the tension of discordant contents (and spirits), integrating as much of man's unconsciousness (which often appears as evil darkness) as possible, and forming a shield against irreconcilable evil. The psyche is brought to an entirely new level of reality. Far from entering the void of nirvana, or losing itself by seeking to be transcended as in the later Platonism,[17] the ego is transformed. It is made a harmonious part of a total human psyche, which now has a new center and focus. The old center and the new remain in relation, a new relationship of wholeness.

This experience is one of the most moving a man can sustain, but our human condition does not allow it to remain fixed. Wholeness is tasted for a moment and then becomes a goal, the end to be sought in life and finally found, hopefully, in the next life. One can even turn his back completely after such an experience and reject it at any time, because there is no static end to this process. It is a *way*, not a safe harbor at the end of a journey.

Whoever enters this way is faced with ever greater consciousness and the task of integrating more and more of his own unconsciousness which so often appears as destructive darkness. Each such experience brings new harmony of purpose, often with a

17. In the Neoplatonism of Plotinus, for instance, the final aim was to allow the divine content to take over entirely, reducing the ego to next to nothing. This was very similar to the nirvana of Oriental religious thought, and it became the ideal of such Christian mysticism as Hesychasm in the eastern church. Plato's understanding was quite different; for a further discussion of his thought on this subject, see Paul Friedländer's *Plato: An Introduction* (1964), chaps. 1–3.

sense of creative peace, and also physical healing because the tension that produces so much disease is relieved. Each experience opens one further to intrusions of the Spirit in dreams and visions. It also brings greater understanding and compassion for others, changing the destructive critical nature in each of us; one is more kind, or more firm when necessary. In fact the surest way to tell whether the Spirit has had a hand in such an experience is to see whether the person has become more forgiving and charitable. If not, he may be possessed by some archetypal power, partial and ambivalent, rather than filled with the Spirit of God, of wholeness.

The Spirit that broke through in such a dramatic way on Pentecost resulted almost immediately in the healing of a crippled beggar. As the Spirit continued to show in the lives of Christians by such actions, it also brought understanding of these experiences. A sophisticated doctrine developed of the soul as mediator of the spiritual world. In discussing these beliefs about how the Spirit speaks to man, the Rev. John Sanford has shown how close a parallel there is between the thinking of Dr. Jung and the ideas of the fathers of the church.[18] These early Christians saw clearly that God and the world of spirit made a direct impression on man's soul. A new imprint, they saw, sprang first from the fact that God had been revealed in Jesus, and the same power and revelation continued in healings, visions, dreams, intuitions, and prophecies.

There was nothing far out about revelation. God had been reaching out to touch men through all the ages. Once he had broken through into historical time and space, and meaning had been unveiled, the way was open, and men were in a better position to appreciate the experiences he could give them. Thus the experiences of individuals, shared and tested by the fellow-

18. In an unpublished manuscript on the epistemology of the church.

ship, gave personal guidance and understanding as well as direction to the struggling church. Knowing as they did that God loved man enough to become embodied in the physical world, it was not hard to believe that he would continue to break through to them in visions and dreams, in prophecies and healing. It would have been surprising if he had not.

The early church apparently held little of the idea that men's brokenness and sin are so repellent to God that he will have nothing to do with them. The apostles told of God touching their lives, not only in clear messages, but also in images on which they had to meditate as Peter did after his dream-ecstasy in Joppa. The same tradition continued, for instance, in the *Shepherd of Hermas* and the account of St. Perpetua's martyrdom, among the ante-Nicene fathers, and then in all the doctors of the church.[19] We have sketched the experiences of healing the church has set down from the earliest days to the present. With their understanding that the soul participates in the spiritual world, these men did not question the need to listen to these experiences. If God or the Holy Spirit might break through at any time, it was up to the individual to be open to the spiritual world and whatever it brought in dream and vision—in intuition or spiritual and mental transformation. It was also their job to pass on to other human beings whatever a person was able to receive in understanding and healing experiences.

There was one danger in this. Being so open to the spiritual world, the Christian was open to evil as well as to the Holy Spirit. Indeed, it was expected that the more one was committed to the Christian community and its life, the greater his influence in the world, the more he would be selected as a target by the Evil One. Christians would be tested again and again. As Tertullian re-

19. In chaps. 4, 5, and 6 of my book *Dreams*, most of these materials from the New Testament and the important fathers of the church up through the fifth century are discussed in some detail.

marked with characteristic exaggeration, the devil was fully known only to Christians. But they also had the experience of being able to withstand these attacks through keeping alive and vivid the experience of the cross and resurrection.

Through the fellowship of the church, its sacraments and symbols, through experiences of healing—particularly in laying on of hands and exorcism—Christians were able to meet evil, much of it incredibly destructive, and not go to pieces in one way or another. From such experience the doctrine of the atonement developed. Somehow through the cross and resurrection, it was found, the forces of evil had been turned back. In his crucifixion and resurrection Jesus seems to have wrought a change in the objective nature of the spiritual world, and those who were close to him were given protection and saved from evil. At present this was partial, but in the last days his kingdom would come fully and evil would be cast out.

The atonement in terms of the world view we have presented is the spiritual result of a victory worked out by Christ, as Spirit, in the physical world through Jesus, as man. If, as it appears, the outer actions of ordinary men can influence events in the psychic, nonphysical world, through active imagination even changing both psychic and physical circumstances, then the atonement is the supreme example of such action. What happened in Judea when Pontius Pilate was procurator there was a spiritual drama made concrete in that time and place, with eternal consequences in a world that is not subject to time and space like that of our five senses. Christ's struggle with evil was fought out in both outer and inner worlds, and thus his victory was fixed in the eternal spiritual world.

But this doctrine of the atonement was not conceived just intellectually. In the early church it was the hypothesis developed to account for the experience of freedom and power men knew as they came into the Christian fellowship, often finding themselves no longer subject to mental and physical illness, to demons, or simply to giving up in the face of persecution. Indeed as Christians took part in the Mass, joining in the celebration of the Last Supper, they found themselves transformed by the Spirit. The living presence of the risen Christ, it was seen, broke through, infusing the bread and wine and the worshipers who gathered to make the sacrifice. This sacrament became the experience, par excellence, in which men could be touched and transformed, and sometimes physically healed, by the Spirit.

This and the other sacraments of the church, in the framework of our model, are events in the space-time world through which men can come into contact, touching and participating, with realities at work in the spiritual world that seek healing and other such effects. As Jung has written in regard to one sacrament,

> Baptism endows the individual with a living soul. I do not mean that the baptismal rite in itself does this, by a unique and magical act. I mean that the idea of baptism lifts man out of his archaic identification with the world and transforms him into a being who stands above it. The fact that mankind has risen to the level of this idea is baptism in the deepest sense, for it means the birth of the spiritual man who transcends nature.[20]

It was just this experience, this sense of transformation, that led to the doctrines surrounding this sacrament and helped to perpetuate it.

The Communion service is just such a rite, through which the individual participates in the death and resurrection of the Lord. Just as it was believed that the spirit is carried by men's material bodies, and that Christ was incarnated in a human body, so this rite is, basically, a structured situation in which it is possible for the individual to find contact with realities in the spiritual world that have moved Christians since the first century. Of this Jung

20. *Collected Works* 10:67.

has written in "Transformation Symbolism in the Mass," "If the inner transformation enters more or less completely into consciousness, it becomes one of the vividest and most decisive experiences a man can have of his individual fate."[21] Through the centuries this experience has kept the living mystery of the Mass alive, and from this the church developed its teaching and dogma of the Lord's Supper.

Once the possibility is considered seriously that a spiritual world does exist alongside of the physical world, independently and in relationship with it, then the idea of life after death becomes quite natural. There are not only numbers of occurrences which men have described as coming from beyond the borders of this life, as Jung did in *Memories, Dreams, Reflections*,[22] but the resurrection itself stands for the permanence of the human soul as no other event in history.

When man is conceived of as a physical structure housing a psyche that is integrated into matter but still able to relate to the independent nonphysical world, then it is not reasonable to insist that the whole psyche—which has already reached out beyond the body—must dissolve with the dissolution of the body. The idea of a destiny beyond this puts man's life in quite a different perspective, giving him a very different picture of how he wants to live it. It also has decided effects upon the individual's mental and physical health.

The early church was specifically a healing community. Men and women came to the church as they had to the temples of Aesculapius, and often they were healed. As early as Plato, the ancient world recognized that psychic disorder would cause sickness and infirmity in the body. It was only natural that a fellowship whose experiences brought wholeness and salvation to the individual psyche would bring healing to sick bodies and minds

21. *Papers from the Eranos Yearbooks* 2, *The Mysteries* (1955), p. 336.
22. See pp. 100, 104 ff., and 190 ff. of that work.

as well, and this was the experience of the followers of Jesus and the early church.

These people saw sickness, not as the result of God's disfavor, but as caused by the actions of the Evil One and his minions. Since the church had been given power over evil through the conquest of Jesus on Golgotha, on this same basis it also received healing power over mental and physical illness. The experiences of healing, which are found everywhere in the church's history, thus were interpreted within a framework essentially in agreement with the world view we have presented. Christian healing was one of the natural results of God's particular breaking into the space-time world in this special way. But this view, quite obviously, leaves some fairly difficult questions hanging fire.

Some Unanswered Questions

Strangely enough, the question that seems the hardest on the surface is actually the easiest to approach. How can a miracle happen? As we have seen, the most intelligent minds today find that man so far does not achieve any final knowledge of the world around him. Since most "laws" are actually only statistical averages—road maps as it were—there is not much meaning, scientifically or theologically, in the idea that a miracle is some event which is clearly an impossibility. The world is more fluid than nineteenth-century science could comprehend, and miracles seem to be those unusual occurrences which tell us something about its movement and direction. They help us to understand the teleological, "spiritual" aspect of reality which seems to be moving in and through physical reality. This irregular movement in man's evolutionary history has been charted with remarkable success by Teilhard de Chardin in his many works. In the case of religious healing, the unusual or miraculous quality most often has to do with the time factor, and this becomes little problem when one views time in the relative manner of modern thought. Instantaneous healing is no more a breach of natural law than air-lifting a fifty-ton cargo.

Indeed there is no reason to limit God to one final and inflexible plan. Investigating the miraculous is a way of learning something about God. These events confront one with the evidence that this is God's world, after all—a dangerous and vital world of unlimited, living possibilities, in which no open-minded man can become bored. It is the kind of world for which man longs, but for which he had not dared to hope. People whose minds have no place for these strange happenings deny the reality of such a God and his world, and are not dealing with life as it is.

A second question is a good deal more difficult. Why are some persons healed when others are not? This is a problem for which there are some partial explanations, but no satisfactory answer. It can really be considered only in connection with the problem of evil. But the fact that we cannot answer the question is no reason to doubt the actuality of religious healing. It does not upset the evidence of healing any more than the inability of nuclear physicists to pinpoint the movement of particular electrons disproves the fact of atomic radiation. That we do not understand why one person is healed and another not, is a reflection on our imperfect human knowledge, not on the power of the Spirit to heal. Because we cannot encompass the Spirit does not mean it does not work.

Why then is there evil, and what is its source? Again, there is no final answer. As Jakob Böhme and others have defined it, evil is a partial good that takes over the whole by pretending to be the total good. Or, as Whitehead so beautifully says, "Evil is the brute motive force of fragmentary purpose, disregarding the eternal vision."[23] This is true of a psychic complex that rises up and runs

23. *Science and the Modern World* (1948), p. 192.

the whole personality. In a way it applies to an invading organism or cancer cell which takes over and makes the human body
a factory for its own uses. But this does not tell us very much
about the forces that cause such things to happen. We cannot
even foresee how a particular evil will affect us, and there is
certainly no easy way to deal with it. Even Jesus was able to deal
with evil only by the drastic action of being born among men to
be crucified and resurrected. Christians, it seems clear, cannot
expect final answers to these questions.

One of the evils associated with healing is the inflation of the
healer who comes to believe he is a special agent of God or better
than his fellows. This attitude is common for many gifts. Even
singers have been known to display it, and all church choirs are
not noted for their humility and perspective. This does not mean,
however, that singing is not a gift and cannot be used to touch
men religiously. With all its profound significance, the same
surely applies to healing.

Christians are faced with man's illness and misery as it is.
Obviously men who are tied up in knots, whether by physical
illness or neurosis or psychosis, are not as free to find real relationship with God. If Christians are to help, they must of course
have all the knowledge they can to deal with man's collective or
social problems, his unconsciousness, even his sometimes willful
estrangement. But man's reconciliation with God does not, in the
end, depend upon final answers, scientific or metaphysical. It
depends upon his experience, and perhaps in the last analysis on
that particular experience of love which Paul described in his
letter to the Ephesians, when he spoke of what had been revealed
to him, and asked for the churches:

That he would grant you, according to the riches of his glory, to be
strengthened with might by his Spirit in the inner man; that Christ may
dwell in your hearts by faith; that ye, being rooted and grounded in love,

may be able to comprehend with all saints what is the breadth, and length, and depth, and height; and to know the love of Christ, which passeth knowledge, that ye might be filled with all the fulness of God. (3:16 KJV)

Healing, however sporadic in effect and incompletely understood, is an important evidence of that love. To offer healing is one way in which Christians can express it—that love which is so much needed by people today.

13

Healing in the Church Today

The case for spiritual healing rests. We have set forth facts supporting its reality, from earliest times down to the most recent findings of medical science. We have examined the theological arguments that reject such healing for people today, seeing how little force such theology has when put up against the understanding originally expressed by Christians. We have also considered evidence which suggests that today's unilateral understanding of reality is inadequate, and that a less partial view of the world is needed if man is to know the truth about healing, as well as about a good many other things that happen to him.

To sum up, we have found in most religions, including Judaism, an appreciation of nonphysical or spiritual realities that influence man's life and contribute to healing. But only in the New Testament tradition have we found a consistent practice of healing based on a fully developed understanding of God's love and a divine will for men. On this basis Western culture was founded, with the same unique interest in healing generally expressed. Not until the time of Gregory the Great was there a definite change.

Then, as civilization went to pieces before the barbarian invaders, the church for the first time began to forget the love of God and emphasize his retribution instead. Men like Gregory feared so much the loss of all they knew to be good that they saw only *one way* to cope with that changing world—to hold onto God by using their moral faculties almost exclusively. Even healing had to be tested for the possibility of ulterior motive and effect. Little by little the church began to overlook man's ability to turn to God for direct help in such matters.

In the thirteenth century Scholasticism completed this framework. Its exclusive emphasis on reason and morality in man's immediate life made it difficult for intellectually sophisticated people to believe that healing, or any direct action of God, was available to human beings in this world. At the same time, men were beginning to gain on the outer world through knowledge. As their capacities in the physical world were progressively extended, it became harder and harder to see a need for help from beyond themselves, in whatever sphere. Even so, where religious life has been alive and vital, healings have continued to occur, right down to the present.

But today it has become apparent to many people that something is lacking in human life. As more and more persons have sought psychiatric help, with others turning to drugs or violence, the awareness has grown that the modern limited view of life cuts man off from something he does need. This has been expressed in various ways, and meanwhile scientific thinkers have added a new understanding of the material world. As science has discovered in this century, man's universe is far from rigid or limited, as had been thought, but is influenced along lines difficult to define physically.

In no realm has this been truer than in the field of medicine, particularly in the psychiatric and psychosomatic areas. Man's health, it is now clear, depends to a great extent on emotional factors and thus in the end on "psychic" elements, which are certainly not simply the creation of either his own psyche or the physical world. Thus health and illness are, in great measure, controlled by nonphysical forces that affect man and the world in which he is immersed.

Dr. Jung and his followers have offered the evidence that relates these facts to an understanding of God. They find, as religion has maintained, that there is a purposeful center of reality with which man needs conscious contact. They also find that men seldom stay well mentally and physically without finding some way to relate their lives to this center of being whom they call God. This relating may be unconscious as in the dedicated lives of many atheists. What a man believes is better shown by what he does than what he says he believes. But aware or not, man's health and very life require a standpoint—made conscious by someone—that takes God and his direct influence on the world into account. In such a point of view, religious healing is a most significant fact. It is one of the experiences that can give men a knowledge of God and needed relation to him. The fact that healings do occur is also one of the best evidences that a relation to God is possible and needed, and that this view of the world is reasonable.

If so much is true, then we come to a very practical question. How, specifically, can the church mediate the kind of spiritual influence that will lead to healing? We have five suggestions to offer for the clergy and the church. First of all, an understanding of the issues is essential. Offering an opportunity to discuss them runs a close second. Then, it is up to the group to create an atmosphere of healing concern. A fourth task is to provide an actual healing ministry of both clergy and lay people, and— finally—a ministry of counseling and spiritual direction.

Providing Understanding

It is almost impossible for anyone, clergy or lay person, to share wisely in a ministry of healing without an adequate intellectual and theological framework from which to understand what is happening. When the healing movement lacks such a framework it tends to let emotionalism or gimmickry take the driver's seat, or humility is simply lost. Much of the damage done by religious healers is caused by their inadequate background, which allows the individual to forget that he is only the agent of a greater power. Unfortunate cults of personality are the result, and this is dangerous both to the individual healer and to those who follow him.

To avoid this, the person interested in healing needs a firm belief that there is some other-than-material reality which can make a creative change in the souls and minds and bodies of men. In Christian terminology, the first requirement is for a theology in which the Spirit with the gift of healing has an essential place. If this is accomplished before anything else, then the healing ministry becomes a natural part of our religious activity and function. It can hardly become an end in itself, an isolated, over-weighted goal, since with such a theology one is only amazed—filled with wonder—that the Spirit can use him. Faced with the possibility of a healing, he has an attitude of humility—his reaction is something like this: if something of value happens, then I am grateful that the Spirit has used me; if nothing happens, then I am sorry that something within keeps me from being a good instrument of the Spirit.

There is then no conflict between the practice of medical healing and the legitimate healing ministry of the church. The church's job, for both clergy and laity, is to provide one essential condition, one part of the spiritual and emotional soil in which healing can occur. To do this, cooperation with the physician is essential. Once the person representing the church believes that he has something to offer in the healing process, and values himself and his contribution, cooperation is possible instead of the either/or isolation in which both professions have worked so long. It is then up to the ministry to provide some reasonable formulations for the doctor, whose training is not in this field, and to help offer a basis for dialogue between medical men and those in the church interested in healing.

As part of this undertaking, it is necessary to reexamine the Gospels and later documents, studying the healings and other nonrational experiences that occur in the New Testament and in church history. One has to come to terms with these stories in relation to the present. It is very helpful for the clergy to preach on these events so as to introduce the people of the church to this essential Christian tradition. The minister who has not done so may be in for some surprises as his congregation sees correlations with their own experience and needs.

One purpose of this book is to gather together this evidence for clergy and lay people so that such a task may be more easily undertaken.

A Place for Discussion

A second task of the church is to provide a place where there can be frank and honest discussion of the issues involved and the questions that come up. There is great need for groups where the basic ideas and experiences of Christianity can be examined and understood. Since this is a matter of education, undoubtedly the best method for it is in small group discussions. People seldom get much education from simply being told; instead they learn by becoming involved in questioning and discovery. Nearly all modern educational research emphasizes the superiority of this kind of learning—compared, for instance, with the methods so often used in churches.

There is no real reason to fear being hung up on questions or doubts, once one knows the reality of Christian experience. Healing is one aspect of the latter, and simply talking about such experiences opens up deeper levels of people's awareness. They begin to break through the resistance petrified from unexpressed questions and doubts. Then, as they discuss what happens in healing and experiment with it, most often a new depth of faith and commitment is found.

At the church of which I was rector for many years, such discussion groups became the focus for a growing nucleus of newly vitalized and dedicated Christians. Up to two hundred adults met each week to discuss basic religious questions on a college seminar level. This program has continued, and the planning and direction of these groups still takes about half the time of a professional educator, who also teaches in one of the local universities.

Of course this takes money—the church has no right to ask for services and pay less than the secular world—but I know of no other way for Christianity and its basic message to touch people who are enmeshed in the secular world and its point of view. This is not only for lay members of the church; most of us who are professional clergy also need this kind of experience. The question is simply: How important is the healing message of the Christian church for our community? And of course healing is only one of the subjects that can be brought into this focus.

In addition, it is helpful to meet with members of the medical and psychological professions, particularly for those who are most deeply involved in the healing ministry and life of the church. I have discovered that church people who want this communication will find medical men who are truly interested and quite willing to share understanding. One of the really stimulating experiences for me has been a semimonthly luncheon with a psychiatrist who, besides being a thoroughly enjoyable friend, has kept me abreast of medical developments and given me a place to refer people with serious problems. We have also shared something of our respective understanding of meaning, and he has been a sounding board for many of my ideas on philosophy and religion.

Anyone seriously active in the church's healing ministry needs this kind of fellowship with his opposite number in the healing profession. It not only keeps one's ideas within sensible limits, but to share the real need for the healing power of the Holy Spirit puts a different light on the religious calling. If one can talk over actual experiences in this way, he is likely to find himself less defensive about his religious life and more effective in action.

The Religious Community

Probably the most important condition the church can provide for healing is the sense of a loving community. By this the early Christians were known. This sense of belonging, this amazing love, gave the early church so much vitality and made it so much a healing instrument of the Spirit that it became a mark by which Christians could be told from other people. As one French scholar has commented, "If Christians had not had this quality, the world would still be pagan. And the day when this quality is no longer there, the world will be pagan once again."[1] It is in such fellowship that the relation to God which brings about healing is most often found; and as we have suggested, such love also has a cognitive quality.

But the average traditional church is not the easiest place to find this kind of fellowship and relation to God. In fact, such a relationship involves a transformation of the whole person, an entirely new sense of being and vital purpose—which seems to be the last thing most churches today are looking for. Instead the

1. A. J. Festugière in the *Revue de Théologie et de Philosophie* (1961), quoted by E. R. Dodds, *Pagan and Christian in an Age of Anxiety* (1965), p. 138.

average church has become a conventional institution concerned with keeping things as they are, almost protecting men from real relation to God. Far from offering a renewing, healing encounter, in many churches people look upon those who have had a soul-shattering reconstituting experience as odd and even dangerous. Yet an experience like that of Pentecost is one way in which people's lives are touched by the Spirit today, and fellowships formed. It is tragic when people with such events in their lives find it necessary to leave their traditional churches to find fellowship.

Admittedly it is difficult for modern men to believe that God can change their lives. It was probably easier to change the morals of ancient pagans than it is to break through the point of view of people today who find nothing real or valuable except the material and the rational, with man as he is the only center of meaning. The experience of friends of mine, however, who have taken the experiential Christian message to both rural Indonesia and sophisticated Taipei and Hong Kong, suggests that we have something to learn from the early Christians about imparting that message of fellowship and love. It was done, they found, much as the book of Acts describes.

In the first place, the early Christians healed pagans whether they were interested in the church or not. Some, of course, were irresistibly drawn to the Spirit who had healed them, and those who did come into the church were expected to become vital centers of Christian life. They were expected to preach, teach, and heal as other Christians did. *There was no such thing as a purely passive or receiving Christian in the early days of the church's life.* Paul, for instance, wherever he could, worked for several months or more to develop a group of vitally changed, growing people who wanted to share the new life they had found.

In the centuries that followed, converts were generally given three years' training as catechumens. Before they were baptized and admitted to full fellowship, they learned a totally new way of life. Gradually they came to share their lives with the group; they confessed and received penance, and learned how the direction of the Spirit was given through the sacraments. Then with baptism and confirmation, the new Christian became a center of the Spirit of God, a source and transmitter of this power himself. Healings often occurred at this time; as the church knew, spiritual transformation like this resulted in the regeneration of body, mind, and soul together.

This new life was sustained and strengthened in the fellowship of the church, particularly in that of the Eucharist, which was the central, revitalizing contact with Christ. It healed not only lapses and weakness of mind and soul, but also sickness of the body. In addition, when members of the church were sick, holy unction with laying on of hands was frequently used for the express purpose of conveying an extra measure of the same spiritual power as in the other sacraments. And while certain people were found to be especially gifted by the Spirit to do this, any person acting for the caring and committed fellowship could accomplish the same thing through the agency of this sacrament.

Obviously the early church took a great deal of trouble to insure a creative, caring fellowship of men and women growing in love and experience of God. Some of the same effort will be required today if we are to have a church that is more than nominally Christian, a church that once again expresses the reality for which so many people are searching today. Once the Christian group seeks a vital and growing relation to the reality of the Spirit through a fellowship of love and concern, healing will come naturally. Men and women, once set upon this *way*, will heal as an expression of God's creative wholeness, because this is the nature of such a fellowship, as it was Christ's nature.

Besides effort, probably the prime requirement is for individuals who are seeking, who know that they need something beyond themselves. To find these persons, inside the church or out of it, calls for the first step of this kind of fellowship. That is: simply to listen, to hear and perceive what another's need is, in quiet assurance that the Spirit is at work. As such a group grows, members will want to join in informal prayer groups, as well as gathering for the larger, more formal services of the church. In such smaller groups imagination can be most effectively used as suggested by Agnes Sanford in her books on healing. These groups usually become the vital center of a church's religious life and its healing activity.

As a church finds itself centrally guided in this way, healing will come not only through the sacrament of unction and laying on of hands. It will come at conversion and baptism, and through absolution and spiritual direction as the psyche is unburdened and relieved of its distress, and given new ways of meeting life's perplexities. It will come through the Eucharistic fellowship; also through the actions of individuals endowed with special gifts of healing. It will come through teaching and preaching, as well as from the direct activity of the Spirit through prayer, and also in the experience described by modern Pentecostals as the "baptism of the Spirit." These all convey grace when they come from a living Christian fellowship, a community moved and directed by the Spirit of God.

As both the early Christians and modern medical men have seen, when spiritual grace is given, it is usually given to the total man. Since the human being is a totality of which soul, mind, and body are parts, it is impossible to separate the grace directed toward the soul from that directed toward the mind and body. Thus in a fellowship which expresses the love of Christ in action faith is also given, which Dr. Jerome Frank has described as a specific for many diseases of our time. In such a church the grace of faith and that of healing go hand in hand.

The Healing Sacrament

Obviously those who are interested in healing will not wait until such a Christian fellowship is fully established to begin a practice of sacramental healing, for then there would be almost no healing ministry at all. Once a minister, or lay person for that matter, is convinced of the biblical and theological basis for a healing ministry, he can move quite naturally into its practice wherever a need appears. He does not have to start with a formal declaration of intention if he simply follows obediently the suggestions of Jesus about a threefold ministry of teaching, preaching, and healing. This particular sacramental ministry, of course, is not the totality of one's Christian life and commitment; but although subordinate, it is an essential part as one clear expression of caring empowered by the Spirit.

In this sense, as we have suggested, healing offers no usurpation of the medical function, but instead supplies the base for effective medical care. The fact that some groups who undertake nonmedical healing insist that such healing can take place only when the individual turns away from medical care does not mean that sacramental healing is tied to such assumptions. Indeed, it is because of the rather questionable philosophical and theological framework of these groups that such ideas are maintained. They simply fail to see that healing is the natural effect of the creative Spirit moving in a man. As Agnes Sanford has so aptly remarked to many groups, "One should have the best doctor and nurse possible when someone is sick, and then pray with depth, wisdom and sincerity."[2]

When nonmedical healing occurs, it is usually the result of the

2. Specific suggestions about how to get on with the healing ministry are found in Agnes Sanford's *The Healing Light, Behold Your God, The Healing Gifts of the Spirit,* and also in her novels, *Oh, Watchman! Lost Shepherd,* and *Dreams Are for Tomorrow.*

loving concern of a Christian fellowship and of the one who acts
as bearer of that Spirit. As the minister of healing, he needs to
be backed up by real caring, by agape. The quickest way to
discourage a healing ministry is by lack of charity for other
religious representatives whose understanding may differ in
some way or other. Lay people who are either derisive or hostile
toward a minister, for instance, for his apathy about healing only
make genuine interest in healing more difficult to bring about. It
is also wise not to rush in to offer healing; tact and sensitivity are
requirements for an effective healing ministry.

Where results are concerned, obedience is far more important
than belief. In making pastoral calls at the hospital, for instance,
the minister can lay his hand upon a sick person quite naturally
while he prays. He does not have to feel any burning faith in his
ability to heal, nor does he have to announce what he is doing.
Some of the most surprising results in my own ministry occurred
on three or four of the occasions when I have been called out in
the night and, very humanly, did not want to get up at all except
for my commitment to Jesus Christ. This obedience works in the
same way for the lay ministry of healing. When it is expressed
in this way, with no promises as to what is going to happen and
with as little human pride as possible, the Spirit seems to act with
increasing effect, and few if any persons are hurt.

Once a church has become interested enough in the healing
movement to institute healing services, it is valuable to begin an
educational program at the same time to help the general membership understand the biblical nature of the ministry and the
reasons for it in terms of theology and modern thought. It may
seem wise to have a healing mission led by some well-known
leader in the field. It is probably also well to hold the service at
a time when those who do not care to participate need not be
involved. In most churches where a program has been instituted
in this way, there is a wide acceptance of this aspect of the

Christian ministry, with little misunderstanding. In the parish of which I was rector for twenty years, we tried all these various methods, and for several years at least three regular services have been offered during the week at which those who wished could participate and receive the healing sacrament.

The institution of such services calls attention to the healing function of the church and to the power of God to touch every aspect of our lives. It tends to encourage an increasingly vital participation in the church, as those who receive healing strength turn their new conviction and vigor to activity in support of the Spirit they have found. In the years of my own active ministry, there were quite a few problems in my church, but none because of the healing ministry.

The Counseling Ministry and Healing

Through a counseling ministry the minister can, in still another way, help to bring healing to individuals in spiritual, psychological, or physical need. Here one brings the impact of his own Christian and individual personality into contact with another person so that in the end the Spirit may move freely within the other. Such counseling is at least as old as St. Antony; it was described as one of his great gifts by his biographer, St. Athanasius, and since then has been used by many of the saints.

Interestingly enough, when I asked Dr. Jung what the nearest method to his counseling practice was, expecting him to name one psychological school or another, I was told, "The classical direction of conscience of the nineteenth-century church in France." This was precisely the direction of which I had read in the works of the great theologian Baron von Hügel, of which he speaks so highly from personal experience. The same kind of Christian direction is desperately needed in these days of myriad emotional and physical problems—not to mention our spiritual and moral problems. Through this approach a minister (or any church-related trained person) can help many people, particularly because of the archetype which is projected upon him. My medical friends often refer people to the church for this very reason. Of course special training in this area is sorely needed.

Since the need for this ministry is so great, the clergyman will probably find that he cannot meet the needs of all those who seek to counsel with him, and he can then call upon others in the counseling profession to help carry the load. One soon discovers how many people are seeking to find the roots of their own meaning, and how often they are confused by meaninglessness and by doubts and problems which lead to physical as well as emotional illnesses. In the church of which I was rector, we had four persons trained in counseling who assisted the two clergymen, with most of them busy all the time they had to give.

In addition, the program of classes made available in that church help to supplement the counseling in two ways. They offer a great many people an understanding in depth of vital religion, and they also train lay people who in turn train others to continue the growth of this understanding. The work of Dr. Ollie Backus in organizing this program at St. Luke's is still unique.

The need of people for meaning is, if anything, growing today. When it can be met in ways like this, there are spiritual and psychological effects, besides physical ones, which awaken new life in the Christian church. Given a chance to embody the spiritual reality of which a Christian fellowship is capable, the church becomes a center of caring concern, as well as of worship in which the holy is sensed; then the healing of neurosis can take place here as well as in the psychiatrist's office. Perhaps this is one of the church's most proper tasks.

In these ways healing comes to be seen in a new light. As we have seen, this understanding or context is both old and new. In brief: physical healing is a living process, and as such it is an inner mystery, in the end known only to the cells themselves which are involved and to the One who created them. Thus it is a process about which we must keep learning as much as we can, both physically and spiritually. In the end healing is given by the creative center of things, who is not only living, but needs all the help he can get from us. With knowledge and preparation, we can give such help physically through medicine, emotionally through psychotherapy, and spiritually through sacramental action and spiritual direction.

In particular, healing occurs when the conditions are right. There are physical conditions which only the physician is qualified to know and prepare. There are also emotional conditions which can be made ready by those trained in psychotherapy. And finally, healing requires conditions of a spiritual nature which can best be seen and helped along by those trained and practiced in the unique traditions of the vital Christian church. Together they make a team of which God has need.

APPENDIX A

The Healing Christ*

Christianity has traditionally considered physical healing as somehow related to its primary concerns. This is no mere accident. Always there has been before it the figure of the Master who, as portrayed by those who knew Him best, was more often engaged in acts of healing than in almost anything else. Despite the major inroads of a Hellenistic soul-body dichotomy, and the Gnostic and Manichean down-grading of matter which so profoundly influenced early Christian thought, despite a later monastic tendency to confuse sickness with saintliness, over the centuries the healing Jesus remained a figure to be reckoned with. Although the true meaning of His Ministry may often have been obscured by attempts to reconcile it with the Church's overt hostility toward undue concern for the "body," it was impossible to deny that the "body" had been an important object of His concern.

The actual life of Jesus was spent in a cultural milieu which knew little of sharp Hellenistic soul-body distinctions. Surprisingly, only in recent years have Christian theologians begun to note this fundamental difference between the Hebrew (and consequently primitive Christian) conception of man, and that of the Greeks with which Christianity eventually came to terms.

The Hebrew conception of man, as the late Dr. Wheeler Rob-

*Quoted in full from the *Current Medical Digest*, for December 1959.

inson reminded us in a now famous sentence, "is an animated body, not an incarnated soul." Or, as John A. T. Robinson has phrased it in his monograph on the body in Biblical thought: "Man does not have a body, he *is* a body. He is flesh-animated-by-soul, the whole conceived as a psychophysical unity." On the other hand, in the dominant Greek view the soul was regarded as the essential personality, imprisoned in a body that was non-essential. Indeed, as expressed later in Gnosticism and Manicheanism, the body was positively evil and ultimately to be eliminated. This view was basically incompatible with the Hebrew conception of the resurrection of the body, an idea that dominated the New Testament. (It will be recalled that it was while discussing the resurrection that St. Paul met his rebuff at the hands of the Athenian philosophers.)

The healing ministry of Christ can be accurately understood only against this backdrop. Jesus thought not simply of "saving souls," to use a familiar Christian cliché. His redemptive concern necessarily encompassed the whole of man, including his body. For example, in His mind there was no sharp cleavage between sickness and sin—the former belonging to the body and the latter to the soul—in the classical sense. Concerning the man "sick of the palsy," He could ask, "Which is easier, to say, Thy sins be forgiven thee; or to say, Arise, and walk?" (Matt. 9:5) His ministry was directed to a total need.

How strangely congenial this aspect of Jesus sounds to our modern ears. Once again we are beginning to consider man not in terms of a division of soul and body or a trichotomy of soul and body and world, but as a psychosomatic or psychosoma-world unity in which whatever affects him in one area has implications for the whole of him. We have come to think of disease not only in isolated terms of organ pathology or disturbed physiological processes, but also in terms of disrupted interpersonal relations—of guilt and the need for love.

Although greatly influenced by non-Christian interpretations of man's nature, the Post-Apostolic Church often saw the healing ministry of Jesus, and that committed to the Church, as radically opposed to the methodology of "pagan" physicians of the period. It was miracle against scientific method—Christ's healings were miraculous, not scientific! But the early Church often failed to distinguish between "miracle" and "magic." Healing is always miracle—and never more so than when at its center is the greatest of all miracles—love.

Tragically, the Church generally tended to make magic the normative element of healing; thus the later scientific investigator with his dissecting tables, his microscopes, and his pharmaceuticals was left to feel that the Great Healer, as healer, did not truly belong to him. This was to miss the central significance of Jesus. Not method but redemptive concern lay at the heart of His ministry—concern that encompassed the whole man—the making of the whole man, whole. The physician, if informed and alert to the modern implications of his vocation, cannot miss this real point of identity with Christianity's real figure. Insofar as he is aware of the total need of his patients, insofar as his ultimate concern transcends mere objective method, and insofar as he as a physician is characterized by agape, to use the New Testament word for Godly love, he walks today in the steps of the Master.

It has become traditional to identify modern doctors in spirit with a long line of historic greats reaching back to the impressive Hippocrates. This notable Greek, a veritable pinnacle in ancient medicine, often called the "Father of Medicine," largely set the pattern for current professional attitudes and relationships. But sometimes it is forgotten that medicine owes its greatest debt not to Hippocrates, but to Jesus. It was the humble Galilean who more than any other figure in history bequeathed to the healing arts their essential meaning and spirit. During this Christmas season physicians would do well to remind themselves that without His spirit, medicine degenerates into depersonalized methodology, and its ethical code becomes a mere legal system. Jesus brings to methods and codes the corrective of love without which true healing is rarely actually possible. The spiritual "Father of Medicine" was not Hippocrates of the island of Cos, but Jesus of the town of Nazareth!

JACK W. PROVONSHA, M.D.,*
Contributing Editor

*Dr. Provonsha is Professor of the Philosophy of Religion and Christian Ethics, Loma Linda University, Loma Linda, California.

APPENDIX B

Biblical Criticism and Healing

Some of the most careful and critical recent studies of Jesus' life and teachings affirm the necessity of recognizing the reality of his healing ministry.

Günther Bornkamm in *Jesus of Nazareth* (1960) points to the relation between faith and miracle. "At the same time," he writes, "there can be no doubt that the faith which Jesus demands, and which alone he recognizes as such, has to do with power and with miracle. And this not in the general sense, that God is all-powerful and can work miracles, but in a very concrete sense: faith as very definitely counting on and trusting in God's power, that it is not at an end at the point where human possibilities are exhausted." (p. 131)

Norman Perrin, in *Rediscovering the Teaching of Jesus* (1967), discusses the history of Biblical criticism and points out that modern prejudice should not blind us to the reality of the healing aspect of Jesus' ministry. He then goes on to compare this ministry of Jesus to pagan parallels, suggesting that

A further problem is that many of the most characteristic sayings about faith in the gospels are associated with miracles, especially healing miracles, and critical scholarship has found this aspect of the tradition very difficult. Liberal scholars tended either to rationalize the stories, or to speak movingly of "the supreme meaning of Jesus' wonders: God's will of mercy and salvation was expressing itself through him," and then

365

move quickly to a more congenial subject! Form criticism, building on the foundations of the immense comparative studies of the *religionsges-chichtliche Schule*, dismissed the stories as typical products of the legend-making propensities of ancient religious movements, to be paralleled in both Jewish and Hellenistic religious literature. In either case, there was no desire to discuss the concept of faith involved in these stories as an aspect of the teaching of Jesus. . . .

Today, however, it is being increasingly recognized that the tradition of miracle stories in the gospels deserves much more serious attention than either the older liberal or the earlier form-critical scholarship gave it. . . .

The view of the miracles held by critical scholarship has, then, changed, and for this there are a number of reasons. One is that parallels quoted from Jewish and Hellenistic literature have been more carefully examined, and they turn out to be not completely convincing as sources for all that we find in the synoptic accounts. (pp. 15 ff. and 131 ff.)

BIBLIOGRAPHY

Alexander, Franz G., and Selesnick, Sheldon T. *The History of Psychiatry*. New York: Harper & Row, 1966.

Ambrose, Saint. *Theological and Dogmatic Works*. Translated by Roy J. Deferrari. Washington, D.C.: Catholic University of America Press, 1963.

American Handbook of Psychiatry. Edited by Silvano Arieti. Vol. 1. New York: Basic Books, 1959.

Anderson, Odin W., and Lerner, Monroe. *Measuring Health Levels in the United States, 1900–1958*. Research Series no. 11. New York: Health Information Foundation, 1960. (Pamphlet)

Anderson, Sir Robert. *The Silence of God*. Grand Rapids, Mich.: Kregel Publications, 1952.

Andrieu, Michel. *Les Ordines Romani du Haut Moyen Âge*. Louvain: Spicilegium Sacrum Lovaniense, 1931–1948.

Anglo-Saxon Missionaries in Germany, The. Translated and edited by C. H. Talbot. London: Sheed & Ward, 1954.

Anointing and Healing: Statement. Adopted by the adjourned meeting of the 1960 convention of the United Lutheran Church in America, June 25–27, 1962, Detroit, Mich. (Pamphlet)

367

Anson, Harold. *Spiritual Healing: A Discussion of the Religious Element in Physical Health.* London: University of London Press, 1924.

Ante-Nicene Fathers, The. Grand Rapids, Mich.: Wm. B. Eerdmans Publishing Co., various dates.

Apostolic Fathers, The. Translated by Archbishop William Wake. Vol. 1. Edinburgh: John Grant, 1909.

Aquinas, Saint Thomas. *The "Summa Theologica."* Literally translated by the Fathers of the English Dominican Province. London: Burns, Oates & Washbourne, various dates.

Auden, W. H. *The Age of Anxiety: A Baroque Eclogue.* New York: Random House, 1946.

————. *For the Time Being.* London: Faber & Faber, 1946.

Augustine, Saint. *The City of God.* Translated by Gerald G. Walsh, S.J., and Daniel J. Honan. New York: Fathers of the Church, 1954. Books 17–22.

————. *Letters (204–270).* Translated by Sister Wilfrid Parsons, S.N.D. New York: Fathers of the Church, 1956.

Aulén, Gustav. *Christus Victor: An Historical Study of the Three Main Types of the Idea of the Atonement.* New York: The Macmillan Co., 1951.

Authorized Daily Prayer Book of the United Hebrew Congregations of the British Empire, The. With a new translation by the Rev. S. Singer. London, 1912.

Ayer, Alfred Jules. *Language, Truth and Logic.* 2d ed. New York: Dover Publications, 1946.

Babylonian Talmud, The. Edited by Rabbi Dr. I. Epstein. London:

Soncino Press, Vols. 23 and 24, *Sanhedrin*, I and II, 1953; vol. 32, *Seder, Kodashim, Bekoroth, 'Arakin,* 1948.

Baillie, John. *The Idea of Revelation in Recent Thought.* New York: Columbia University Press, 1956.

_____. *The Sense of the Presence of God.* London: Oxford University Press, 1962.

Banks, Ethel Tulloch. *The Great Physician Calling.* San Diego, Calif.: St. Luke's Press, n.d. (Pamphlet)

Banks, John Gayner. *Healing Everywhere: A Book of Healing Mission Talks,* San Diego, Calif.: St. Luke's Press, 1953.

Baragar, C. A. "John Wesley and Medicine," *Annals of Medical History* 10, no. 1 (March 1928): 59 ff.

Barth, Karl. *Church Dogmatics.* Edited and translated by G. W. Bromiley, T. F. Torrance, and Others. Edinburgh: T. & T. Clark, 1936–1969.

_____. *Epistle to the Romans.* Translated by E. C. Hoskyns. London: Oxford University Press, 1963.

Basil, Saint. *Ascetical Works.* Translated by Sister M. Monica Wagner, C.S.C. New York: Fathers of the Church, 1950.

Batten, Loring W. *The Relief of Pain by Mental Suggestion: A Study of the Moral and Religious Forces in Healing.* New York: Moffat, Yard & Co., 1917.

Beard, Rebecca. *Everyman's Goal: The Expanded Consciousness.* Wells, Vt.: Merrybrook Press, 1951.

_____. *Everyman's Mission: The Development of the Christ-Self.* Evesham, Eng.: Arthur James, 1952.

_____. *Everyman's Search.* New York: Harper & Brothers, 1950.

Bede's Ecclesiastical History of the English People. Edited by Bertram Colgrave and R. A. B. Mynors. Oxford: Clarendon Press, 1969.

Beecher, Henry K. "The Powerful Placebo." *Journal of the American Medical Association,* 159, no. 17 (December 24, 1955), 1602–1606.

Berry, George Ricker, ed. *The Interlinear Literal Translation of the Greek New Testament.* Chicago: Follett Publishing Co., 1960.

Bishop Sarapion's Prayer-Book. Edited by John Wordsworth, Bishop of Salisbury. London: Society for Promoting Christian Knowledge (hereafter S.P.C.K.), 1923.

Blatty, William P. *The Exorcist.* New York: Bantam Books, Harper and Row, 1971.

Blum, Richard and Eva. *Health and Healing in Rural Greece.* Stanford, Calif.: Stanford University Press, 1965.

Boggs, Wade H., Jr. *Faith Healing and the Christian Faith.* Richmond, Va.: John Knox Press, 1956.

Bonhoeffer, Dietrich. *Letters and Papers from Prison.* New York: The Macmillan Co., 1953.

Bonnell, John Sutherland. *Do You Want to be Healed?* New York: Harper & Row, 1968.

Book of Common Prayer, The. According to the Use of the Anglican Church of Canada. Toronto: Anglican Book Centre, General Synod of the Anglican Church of Canada, 1962.

Book of Common Prayer, The. According to the Use of the Church of England. Oxford: The University Press, 1970.

Book of Common Prayer, The. According to the Use of the Protestant Episcopal Church in the United States of America. New York: Church Pension Fund, 1945.

Bornkamm, Günther. *Jesus of Nazareth.* New York: Harper & Row, 1960.

Botte, Bernard, O.S.B., ed. *La Tradition Apostolique* [Hippolytus of Rome]: *D'Après Les Anciennes Versions.* 2d ed. Paris: Éditions du Cerf, 1968.

Breuer, Joseph, and Freud, Sigmund. *Studies in Hysteria.* Boston: Beacon Press, 1961.

Bultmann, Rudolf. *Existence and Faith: Shorter Writings of Rudolf Bultmann.* Translated by Schubert M. Ogden. New York: Meridian Books, 1960.

————. *Jesus Christ and Mythology.* New York: Charles Scribner's Sons, 1958.

————. "The New Testament and Mythology." In *Kerygma and Myth: A Theological Debate.* Edited by Hans-Werner Bartsch. New York: Harper & Row, 1961.

Butler, Cuthbert. *The Lausiac History of Palladius.* Hildesheim: Georg Olms, 1967.

Butler, Josephine. *Catharine of Siena: A Biography.* London: Dyer Bros., 1878.

Cadbury, Henry J. ed. *George Fox's 'Book of Miracles.'* Cambridge, Eng.: The University Press, 1948.

Calvin, John. *Institutes of the Christian Religion.* Translated by Henry Beveridge. Grand Rapids, Mich.: Wm. B. Eerdmans Publishing Co., 1953.

Castaneda, Carlos. *The Teachings of Don Juan: A Yaqui Way of Knowledge.* Berkeley, Calif.: University of California Press, 1968.

Charisma in Hong Kong. Hong Kong: Society of Stephen, n.d. (Pamphlet)

Chertok, L. "Psychosomatic Medicine in the West and in Eastern European Countries." *Psychosomatic Medicine* 31, no. 6 (November-December 1969): 510–21.

Christian Faith and the Ministry of Healing. Approved by the Church Council of the American Lutheran Church, Minneapolis, July 1965. (Pamphlet)

Christiani, Leon. *Evidences of Satan in the Modern World.* New York: The Macmillan Co., 1962.

Christmann, Harold L. *A Pattern for Healing in the Church.* San Diego, Calif.: St. Luke's Press, 1959. (Pamphlet)

Chrysostom, Saint John. *Baptismal Instructions.* Translated by Paul W. Harkins. Westminster, Md.: Newman Press, 1963.

Church's Ministry of Healing, The. Report of the Archbishop's Commission. Westminster, Eng.: Church Information Board, 1958. (Pamphlet)

Clark, Glenn. *How to Find Health Through Prayer.* New York: Harper & Brothers, 1940.

Clarke, W. K. Lowther, ed. *Liturgy and Worship.* London: S.P.C.K., 1954.

Coleridge, Henry James. *The Life and Letters of St. Francis Xavier.* London: Burns & Oates, 1881.

Cullman, Oscar. *Immortality of the Soul or Resurrection of the Dead?*

The Witness of the New Testament. New York: The Macmillan Co., 1959.

Daily, Starr. *Recovery.* St. Paul, Minn.: Macalester Park Publishing Co., 1948.

———. *Release,* New York: Harper & Brothers, 1942.

Dalmais, Irenée Henri. O.P. *Eastern Liturgies.* New York: Hawthorn Books, 1960.

Daniélou, Jean. *The Bible and Liturgy.* Notre Dame, Ind.: University of Notre Dame Press, 1956.

Dearmer, Percy. *Body and Soul.* London: Sir Isaac Pitman & Sons, 1909.

Desert Fathers, The. Translated by Helen Waddell. London: Constable & Co., 1936.

Dessauer, Friedrich. See *Papers from the Eranos Yearbooks.*

Dix, Gregory, ed. *The Treatise on the Apostolic Tradition of St. Hippolytus of Rome.* Rev. by H. Chadwick. London: S.P.C.K., 1968.

Documents of Vatican II, The. New York: America Press, 1966.

Dodds, E. R. *The Greeks and the Irrational.* Boston: Beacon Press, 1957.

———. *Pagan and Christian in an Age of Anxiety.* Cambridge, Eng.: The University Press, 1965.

Dorothea Trüdel, or the Prayer of Faith: With some particulars of the remarkable manner in which large numbers of sick persons were healed in answer to special prayer. London: Morgan & Chase, 1865.

Duchesne, Mgr. Louis. *Christian Worship: Its Origin and Evolution.* 5th ed. London: S.P.C.K., 1919.

Dunbar, Flanders. *Emotions and Bodily Changes.* 4th ed. New York: Columbia University Press, 1954.

Dwyer, Walter W. *The Churches' Handbook for Spiritual Healing.* New York: Ascension Press, 1960. (Pamphlet)

Early Christian Biographies. Edited by Roy J. Deferrari. Various translators. New York: Fathers of the Church, 1952.

Easton, Burton Scott. *The Apostolic Tradition of Hippolytus.* Ann Arbor, Mich.: Archon Books, 1962.

Eliade, Mircea. *Shamanism: Archaic Techniques of Ecstasy.* Princeton, N.J.: Princeton University Press, 1970.

Eliot, T. S. *The Cocktail Party.* New York: Harcourt, Brace & World, 1950.

_____. *Four Quartets.* New York: Harcourt, Brace & World, 1968.

Evans, Lester J. *The Crisis in Medical Education.* Ann Arbor, Mich.: University of Michigan Press, 1965.

Feifel, Herman, ed. *The Meaning of Death.* New York: McGraw-Hill Book Co., 1959.

Ford, Peter S. *The Healing Trinity.* New York: Harper & Row, 1971.

Fox, George. *The Journal of George Fox.* Edited by Norman Penney. Cambridge, Eng.: The University Press, 1911.

Frank, Jerome D. *Persuasion and Healing.* New York: Schocken Books, 1969.

Freud, Sigmund. *Beyond the Pleasure Principle.* Translated by James Strachey. New York: Liveright Publishing Co., 1961.

_____. *Civilization and Its Discontents.* Translated by Joan Riviere. Garden City, N.Y.: Doubleday & Co., n.d.

———. *Collected Papers*. New York: Basic Books, 1955.

———. *The Future of an Illusion*. Translated by W. D. Robson-Scott. London: Hogarth Press, 1949.

———. *A General Introduction to Psychoanalysis*. New York: Washington Square Press, 1960.

———. *The Interpretation of Dreams*. New York: Basic Books, 1955.

———. See Breuer, Joseph, and Freud, Sigmund.

Friedländer, Paul. *Plato: An Introduction*. Translated by Hans Meyerhoff. New York: Harper & Row for the Bollingen Foundation, 1964.

Friedman, D. B., and Selesnick, S. T. "Clinical Notes on the Management of Asthma and Eczema: When to Call the Psychiatrist." *Clinical Pediatrics* 4, no. 12 (December 1965): 735–38.

Frost, Evelyn. *Christian Healing. A Consideration of the Place of Spiritual Healing in the Church of To-day in the Light of the Doctrine and Practice of the Ante-Nicene Church*. London: A. R. Mowbray & Co., 1940.

Garrison, Fielding H. *An Introduction to the History of Medicine*. 4th ed. Philadelphia: W. B. Saunders Co., 1929.

Glasser, William. *Reality Therapy*. New York: Harper & Row, 1965.

Good Angel of Stamford, The: Or an Extraordinary Cure of An Extraordinary Consumption, In a true and Faithful Narrative of Samuel Wallas *Recovered By the Power of God, and Prescription of an Angel*. Reprints of English Books 1475–1700, edited by Joseph Arnold Foster, no. 17. London: Ingram, 1939. Originally printed in London, 1659.

Goodspeed, Edgar J. *The Story of Eugenia and Philip.* Chicago: University of Chicago Press, 1931.

Gordon, A. J. *The Ministry of Healing.* 2d ed. Harrisburg, Pa.: Christian Publications, 1961.

Graham, David T. "Health, Disease, and the Mind-Body Problem: Linguistic Parallelism." *Psychosomatic Medicine* 29, no. 1 (January-February 1967): 52–71.

Grégoire, Georges Florent [Gregory of Tours]. *Les Livres des Miracles et Autres Opuscules.* Translated by H. L. Bordier. 2 vols. Paris: Jules Renouard et Cie., 1860.

_____. *Selections from the Minor Works.* Translated by William C. McDermott. Philadelphia: University of Pennsylvania Press, 1949.

Gregory the Great, Saint. *Dialogues.* Translated by Odo John Zimmerman, O.S.B. New York: Fathers of the Church, 1959.

Gregory of Nyssa, Saint. *Ascetical Works.* Translated by Virginia Woods Callahan. Washington, D.C.: Catholic University of America Press, 1967.

Gross, Don H. *The Case for Spiritual Healing.* New York: Thomas Nelson & Sons, 1958.

Guggenbühl-Craig, Adolf. *Power in the Helping Professions.* New York, Spring Publications, 1971.

Gusmer, Charles W. "Anointing of the Sick in the Church of England." *Worship* 45, no. 5 (May 1971): 262–72.

Guze, Samuel B. "Hysteria and the GP's Role." *Psychiatry 1970,* edited by Eli Robins, New York: *Medical World News* publication, 1970, p. 11.

Hamilton, Mary. *Incubation (or the Cure of Disease in Pagan Temples and Christian Churches)*. London: Simpkin, Marshall, Hamilton, Kent & Co., 1906.

Handbook on the Healing Ministry of the Church. Toronto: The Bishop's Committee, n.d. (Pamphlet)

Harding, Esther. *Journey into Self*. New York: David McKay Co., 1956.

Hastings, James, ed. *Encyclopedia of Religion and Ethics*. New York: Charles Scribner's Sons, n.d.

Hatch, Alden. *Le Miracle de la Montagne: L'Histoire de Frère André et de L'Oratoire Saint-Joseph à Montreal*. Paris: Librairie Arthème Fayard, 1959.

Healing Church, The: The Tübingen Consultation 1964. World Council Series no. 3. Geneva: World Council of Churches, 1965. (Pamphlet)

Heisenberg, Werner. *Physics and Philosophy: The Revolution in Modern Science*. New York: Harper & Brothers, 1962.

Herolt, Johannes [Discipulus, ca. 1440]. *Miracles of the Blessed Virgin Mary*. Translated by C. C. Swinton Bland. London: George Routledge & Sons, 1928.

Hesse, Mary. *Models and Analogies in Science*. Notre Dame, Ind.: University of Notre Dame Press, 1966.

Hick, John H. *Faith and Knowledge: A Modern Introduction to the Problem of Religious Knowledge*. Ithaca, N.Y.: Cornell University Press, 1966.

————, ed. *Faith and the Philosophers*. New York: St. Martin's Press, 1964.

Hillman, James. *Emotion: A Comprehensive Phenomenology of Theories and Their Meanings for Therapy.* 2d ed. Evanston, Ill.: Northwestern University Press, 1964.

Hippocrates. *Works.* Vol. 4, *Regimen.* Translated by W. H. S. Jones. Cambridge, Mass.: Harvard University Press, 1957.

Hostie, Raymond. *Religion and the Psychology of Jung.* New York: Sheed & Ward, 1957.

Husserl, Edmund. *Phenomenology and the Crisis of Philosophy.* Translated by Quentin Lauer. New York: Harper & Row, 1965.

Ikin, A. Graham. *New Concepts of Healing: Medical, Psychological, and Religious.* New York: Association Press, 1956.

Interpreter's Bible, The. New York: Abingdon-Cokesbury Press, 1952–1965.

Ionas, *Vitae Sanctorum Columbani* (Scriptores Rerum Germanicarum). Edited by Bruno Krusch. Hanover: Impensis Bibliopolii Hahniani, 1905.

Jaffé, Aniela, *From the Life and Work of C. G. Jung.* New York: Harper and Row, 1971.

James, William. *The Varieties of Religious Experience.* New York: Longmans, Green & Co., 1925.

Jaspers, Karl, and Bultmann, Rudolf. *Myth and Christianity: An Inquiry into the Possibility of Religion Without Myth.* New York: Noonday Press, 1958.

Johnson, Thomas W. "Japan's New Religions: A Search for Uniformities." *Kroeber Anthropological Society Papers,* (University of California), no. 42 (Spring 1970): 112 ff.

Jouhandeau, Marcel. *St. Philip Neri.* New York: Harper & Brothers, 1960.

Juliani Imperatoris, *Quae Supersunt Praeter Reliquias apud Cyrillum: Omnia.* Edited by Friedericus Carolus Hertlein. Vol. 1. Lipsiae: B. G. Teubneri, 1875.

Jung, C. G. *Collected Works.* New York: Pantheon Books for the Bollingen Foundation,

Vol. 5, *Symbols of Transformation,* 1956.
Vol. 7, *Two Essays on Analytical Psychology,* 1953.
Vol. 8, *The Structure and Dynamics of the Psyche,* 1960.
Vol. 9, pt. 2, *Aion: Researches into the Phenomenology of the Self,* 1959.
Vol. 10, *Civilization in Transition,* 1964.
Vol. 11, *Psychology and Religion: West and East,* 1958.
Vol. 12, *Psychology and Alchemy,* 1953.
Vol. 16, *The Practice of Psychotherapy,* 1954.

————. *Memories, Dreams, Reflections.* Recorded and edited by Aniela Jaffé. New York: Random House, 1963.

————. *Modern Man in Search of a Soul.* New York: Harcourt, Brace & Co., 1933.

Kaplan, Melvin H., and Frengley, J. Dermot. "Autoimmunity to the Heart in Cardiac Disease: Current Concepts of the Relation of Autoimmunity to Rheumatic Fever, Postcardiotomy and Postinfarction Syndromes and Cardiomyopathies." *American Journal of Cardiology* 24, no. 4 (October 1969): 459–73.

Karagulla, Shafica. *Breakthrough to Creativity,* Los Angeles: De Vorss & Co., 1968.

Kasturi, N. *The Life of Bhagavan Sri Sathya Sai Baba.* Prasanthi Nilayam, South India: Sanathana Sarathi, 1969.

Keenan, Sister Mary Emily. "Augustine and the Medical Profession." *Transactions and Proceedings of the American Philosophical Association* 67. Haverford, Pa. (1936): 168–90.

_____. "St. Gregory of Nazianzus and Early Byzantine Medicine." *Bulletin of the History of Medicine* 9, no. 1 (January 1941): 8–30.

Kelly, Thomas R. *A Testament of Devotion.* New York: Harper & Brothers, 1941.

Kelsey, Morton T. *Dreams: The Dark Speech of the Spirit.* Garden City, N.Y.: Doubleday & Co., 1968.

_____. *Encounter with God: A Theology of Christian Experience.* Minneapolis, Minn.: Bethany Fellowship, 1972.

_____. "Is the World View of Jesus Outmoded?" *Christian Century* 86, no. 4 (January 22, 1969): 112–15.

_____. *Tongue Speaking: An Experiment in Spiritual Experience.* Garden City, N.Y.: Doubleday & Co., 1964.

Kemp, P. *Healing Ritual: Studies in the Technique and Tradition of the Southern Slavs.* London: Faber & Faber, 1953.

Kepler, Milton O., M.D. "The Importance of Religion in Medical Education," *Journal of Religion and Health* 7, no. 4 (October 1968): 358 ff.

Kerényi, C. *Asklepios: Archetypal Image of the Physician's Existence.* New York: Pantheon Books for the Bollingen Foundation, 1959.

Kerin, Dorothy. *The Living Touch.* London: Hodder & Stoughton, 1965.

Kierkegaard, Søren. *Training in Christianity.* Translated by Walter Lowrie. Princeton, N.J.: Princeton University Press, 1944.

Kimball, C. P. "Conceptual Developments in Psychosomatic Medicine: 1939–1969," *Annals of Internal Medicine* 73, no. 2 (August 1970): 307 ff.

Klausner, Joseph. *Jesus of Nazareth: His Life, Times and Teaching.* Translated by Herbert Danby. New York: The Macmillan Co., 1929.

Kluger, Rivkah Schärf. *Satan in the Old Testament,* Evanston, Ill.: Northwestern University Press, 1967.

Knoll, Max. See *Papers from the Eranos Yearbooks.*

Kooiman, W. J. *By Faith Alone: The Life of Martin Luther.* Translated by Bertram Lee Woolf. London: Lutterworth Press, 1954.

Krause, Allen K. *Environment and Resistance in Tuberculosis.* Baltimore: Williams & Wilkins Co., 1923.

Kuhlman, Kathryn. *I Believe in Miracles.* Englewood Cliffs, N. J.: Prentice-Hall, 1962.

Kyle, William H., ed. *Healing Through Counselling: A Christian Counselling Centre.* London: Epworth Press, 1964.

Laing, R. D. *The Politics of Experience.* New York: Ballantine Books, 1968.

Lambeth Conference 1930, The: Encyclical Letter from the Bishops, with Resolutions and Reports. London: S.P.C.K., n.d.

Large, John Ellis. *God Is Able: How to Gain Wholeness of Life.* Englewood Cliffs, N.J.: Prentice-Hall, 1963.

———. *The Ministry of Healing.* New York: Morehouse-Gorham Co., 1959.

Lesser, Graham. *Why? Divine Healing in Medicine and Theology.* New York: Pageant Press, 1960.

Leuret, François, and Bon, Henri. *Modern Miraculous Cures: A Documented Account of Miracles and Medicine in the Twentieth Century.* Translated by A. T. Macqueen and John C. Barry. New York: Farrar Straus & Cudahy, 1957.

Lewis, C. S. *Christian Reflections.* Edited by Walter Hooper. Grand Rapids, Mich.: Wm. B. Eerdmans Publishing Co., 1968.

Liddell, Howard S. "Conditioning and Emotions: An account of a long-range study in which neuroses are induced to clarify how irrational emotional behavior originates and ultimately to indicate how it may be prevented." Reprinted from *Scientific American* for January 1954. San Francisco, Calif.: W. H. Freeman & Co.

_____. *Emotional Hazards in Animals and Man.* Springfield, Ill.: Charles C. Thomas, 1956.

Lietzmann, Hans. *A History of the Early Church.* Cleveland: World Publishing Co., 1961.

Limitation of Activity and Mobility Due to Chronic Conditions: United States–July 1965–June 1966. Public Health Service Series 10, no. 45. Washington, D.C.: U.S. Department of Health, Education, and Welfare, May, 1968.

Lipowski, Z. J. "Psychosocial Aspects of Disease," *Annals of Internal Medicine* 71, no. 6 (December 1969): 1197–1206.

Lonergan, Bernard J. F., S.J. *Insight: A Study of Human Understanding.* New York: Philosophical Library, 1957.

Luther: Letters of Spiritual Counsel. Edited and translated by Theodore J. Tappert. London: S. C. M. Press, 1955.

Luther's Works. Edited by Jaroslav Pelikan. St. Louis: Concordia Publishing House, 1955–

McCluskey, Neil G., S.J., "Darkness and Light over Konnersreuth." *The Priest* 10, no. 9 (September 1954): 765–74.

MacIntosh, Douglas Clyde. *The Problem of Religious Knowledge.* New York: Harper & Brothers, 1940.

MacMillan, William J. *The Reluctant Healer: A Remarkable Autobiography.* New York: Thomas Y. Crowell Co., 1952.

Macquarrie, John. *Twentieth Century Religious Thought: The Frontiers of Philosophy and Theology, 1900–1960.* New York: Harper & Row, 1963.

Maguire, John Francis. *Father Mathew.* London: n.p., 1864.

Manual of Christian Healing: A Handbook for the International Order of Saint Luke the Physician, and for Other Clergy and Laity Engaged in the Work of Spiritual Therapy. Edited by John Gayner Banks. 11th ed. San Diego, Calif.: St. Luke's Press, 1960. (Pamphlet)

Martimort, Aimé Georges. *L'Église en Prière: Introduction à la Liturgie.* Paris: Desclée & Cie., 1961.

Martin, Bernard. *The Healing Ministry in the Church.* Richmond, Va., John Knox Press, 1960.

"Mass Hysteria." *Time* magazine 95, no. 4 (January 26, 1970): 59 ff.

Meer, F. van der. *Augustine the Bishop: The Life and Work of a Father of the Church.* Translated by Brian Battershaw and G. R. Lamb. London: Sheed & Ward, 1961.

Mehta, Ved. *The New Theologian.* New York: Harper & Row, 1966.

Meier, C. A. *Ancient Incubation and Modern Psychotherapy*. Translated by Monica Curtis. Evanston, Ill.: Northwestern University Press, 1967.

Menninger, Karl A. *Man Against Himself*. New York: Harcourt, Brace & Co., 1938.

————, with the collaboration of Jeanetta Lyle Menninger. *Love Against Hate*. New York: Harcourt, Brace & Co., 1942.

Meyer, Adolf. "The Psychiatric Aspects of Gastroenterology," *American Journal of Surgery* 15, no. 3 (March 1932): 504–509.

Ministry of Healing, The: Report of the Committee Appointed in Accordance with Resolution 63 of the Lambeth Conference, 1920. London: S.P.C.K., 1924.

Miracles de Saint Benoit, Les, écrits par Adrevald, Aimoin, André, Raoul Tortaire et Hugues de Sainte Mariê (Moines de Fleury). Libraire de la Société de L'Histoire de France. Paris: Mme. Ve. Jules Renouard, 1858.

Miraculous Powers of the Church of Christ, The, asserted through each Successive Century from the Apostles down to the Present Time. England: n.p., 1756.

Monden, Louis, S.J. *Signs and Wonders: A Study of the Miraculous Element in Religion*. New York: Desclée Co., 1966.

Morison, James Cotter. *The Life and Times of Saint Bernard, Abbot of Clairvaux*, London: Macmillan & Co., 1901.

Mowrer, O. Hobart. *The Crisis in Psychiatry and Religion*. Princeton, N.J.: D. Van Nostrand Co., 1961.

Nagel, Ernest, and Newman, James R. *Gödel's Proof*. New York: New York University Press, 1964.

Neihardt, John G. *Black Elk Speaks: Being the Life Story of a Holy Man of the Oglala Sioux.* Lincoln, Neb.: University of Nebraska Press, 1961.

Nicodemus [Melville Salter Channing-Pearce]. *The Midnight Hour: A Journal from 1st May to 30th September 1941.* London: Faber & Faber, 1942.

Oursler, Will. *The Healing Power of Faith.* New York: Hawthorn Books, 1957.

Papers from the Eranos Yearbooks. Edited by Joseph Campbell. New York: Pantheon Books, 1954–. Vols. 1–3.

> Dessauer, Friedrich. "Galileo and Newton: The Turning Point in Western Thought." Vol. 1, *Spirit and Nature* (1954), pp. 288–321.
> Knoll, Max. "Transformations of Science in Our Age." Vol. 3, *Man and Time*, (1957), pp. 264–307.
> Wili, Walter. "The Orphic Mysteries and the Greek Spirit." Vol. 2, *The Mysteries* (1955), pp. 64–92.

Pasternak, Boris. *Doctor Zhivago.* New York: Pantheon Books, 1958.

Patrologiae: Cursus Completus (Latinae et Graecae). Paris: Garnier Frères and J.P. Migne, successors, various dates.

Pedalion ["Rudder"], *The.* Translated by D. Cummings. Chicago: Orthodox Christian Educational Society, 1957.

Perrin, Norman. *Rediscovering the Teaching of Jesus.* New York: Harper & Row, 1967.

Phillips, Dorothy, *et al.*, eds. *The Choice Is Always Ours.* Rev. ed. New York: Harper & Row, 1960.

Pieper, Josef. *Love and Inspiration: A Study of Plato's Phaedrus.* London: Faber & Faber, 1965.

Pioneer of Divine Healing: Jon. Chr. Blumhardt. London: Order of Saint Luke the Physician, n.d. (Pamphlet)

Plato. *Dialogues.* Translated by B. Jowett. New York, Random House, 1937.

Powys, John Cowper. *The Meaning of Culture.* New York: W. W. Norton & Co., 1929.

Prayer Book Studies III: The Order for the Ministration to the Sick. The Standing Liturgical Commission of the Protestant Episcopal Church in the United States of America. New York: Church Pension Fund, 1951. (Pamphlet)

Provonsha, J. W., M.D. "The Healing Christ." *Current Medical Digest,* December 1959.

Puner, Helen Walker. *Freud: His Life and His Mind,* New York: Dell Publishing Co., 1959.

Quasten, Johannes. *Patrology.* Vol. 3, *The Golden Age of Greek Patristic Literature after Irenaeus, from the Council of Nicaea to the Council of Chalcedon.* Utrecht: Spectrum Publishers, 1960.

Quimby Manuscripts, The. Edited by Horatio W. Dresser. New York: University Books, 1961.

Ranaghan, Kevin and Dorothy. *Catholic Pentecostals.* New York: Paulist Press, 1969.

Reinhart, John B., and Drash, Allan L. "Psychosocial Dwarfism: Environmentally Induced Recovery," *Psychosomatic Medicine* 31, no. 2 (March-April 1969): 165–72.

Relation of Christian Faith to Health, The. Adopted by the 172nd

General Assembly of the United Presbyterian Church in the United States of America. Philadelphia, May 1960. (Pamphlet)

Report of the Bishop of Toronto's Commission on the Church's Ministry of Healing, The. Toronto, May 1968. (Pamphlet)

Roberts, Margaret. *Saint Catherine of Siena and Her Times.* London: Methuen & Co., 1906.

Roman Ritual, The. Translated and edited by Rev. Philip Weller. Milwaukee: Bruce Publishing Co., 1952.

Ross, James Davidson. *Dorothy: A Portrait.* London: Hodder & Stoughton, 1958.

Ryrie, Charles Caldwell. *Dispensationalism Today.* Chicago: Moody Press, 1965.

Sabatier, Paul. *Life of St. Francis of Assisi.* Translated by Louise Seymour Houghton, New York: Charles Scribner's Sons, 1938.

Sanford, Agnes. *Behold Your God.* St. Paul, Minn.: Macalester Park Publishing Co., 1958.

_____. *Dreams Are for Tomorrow.* Philadelphia: J. B. Lippincott Co., 1963.

_____. *The Healing Gifts of the Spirit.* Philadelphia: J. B. Lippincott Co., 1966.

_____. *The Healing Light.* St. Paul, Minn.: Macalester Park Publishing Co., 1947.

_____. *The Healing Power of the Bible.* Philadelphia: J. B. Lippincott Co., 1969.

_____. *Lost Shepherd.* Plainfield, N.J.: Logos International, 1971.

_____. *Oh, Watchman!* Philadelphia: J. B. Lippincott Co., 1951.

Sanford, Edgar L. *God's Healing Power*. Evesham, Eng.: Arthur James, 1962. Reprinted in 1971.

Sanford, John A. *The Kingdom Within: A Study of the Inner Meaning of Jesus' Sayings*. Philadelphia: J. B. Lippincott Co., 1970.

Sawyer, Charles H.; Kawakami, M.; and Kanematsu, S. "Neuroendocrine Aspects of Reproduction." Chap. 4 in *Endocrines and the Central Nervous System*, edited by Rachmiel Levine. Association for Research in Nervous and Mental Disease, vol. 43. Baltimore: Williams & Wilkins Co., 1966.

Scherzer, Carl J. *The Church and Healing*. Philadelphia: Westminster Press, 1950.

Schlier, Heinrich. *Principalities and Powers in the New Testament*. New York: Herder & Herder, 1961.

Schroeder, Rev. H. J., O.P., *Disciplinary Decrees of the General Councils*. St. Louis: B. Herder Book Co., 1937.

A Select Library of the Nicene and Post-Nicene Fathers of the Christian Church. 1st and 2d Series. Grand Rapids, Mich.: Wm. B. Eerdmans Publishing Co., various dates.

Selesnick, Sheldon T., and Sperber, Zanwil. "The Problem of the Eczema-Asthma Complex: A Developmental Approach." In *Psychoanalysis and Current Biological Thought*, edited by Norman S. Greenfield and William C. Lewis. Madison, Wis.: University of Wisconsin Press, 1965.

Selye, Hans. "The General Adaptation Syndrome and Diseases of Adaptation." *Journal of Clinical Endocrinology* 6, no. 2 (February 1946): 217 ff.

Service Book of the Holy Orthodox-Catholic Apostolic Church [the Euchologion]: Compiled, translated, and arranged from the Old

Church-Slavonic Service Books of the Russian Church and collated with the Service Books of the Greek Church by Isabel Florence Hapgood. Rev. ed., with endorsement by Patriarch Tikhon. New York: Association Press, 1922.

Services for Trial Use: Authorized Alternatives to Prayer Book Services. Protestant Episcopal Church in the U.S.A. New York: Church Pension Fund, 1971.

Sharing, journal of the International Order of Saint Luke.

Silverman, Samuel. *Psychobiological Aspects of Physical Symptoms.* New York: Appleton-Century-Crofts, 1968.

Skinner, B. F. *Science and Human Behavior.* New York: The Macmillan Co., 1953.

———, *Walden II.* New York: The Macmillan Co., 1960.

Slawson, Paul F., *et al.* "Psychological Factors Associated with the Onset of Diabetes Mellitus." *Journal of the American Medical Association* 185, no. 3 (July 20, 1963): 166 ff.

Swann, W. F. G. "The Living and the Dead." *Saturday Review* 43, no. 23 (June 4, 1960): 43 f.

Teilhard de Chardin, Pierre. *The Phenomenon of Man.* New York, Harper & Brothers, 1959.

Tennant, F. R. *Philosophical Theology.* Cambridge, Eng.: The University Press, 1956.

Thomas of Celano. *Tractatus de Miraculis S. Francisci Assisiensis.* Edited by the Fathers of the College of Saint Bonaventura, Rome, 1928.

Thompson, Francis. *Health and Holiness.* St. Louis: B. Herder Book Co., 1905.

Toulmin, Stephen. *The Philosophy of Science: An Introduction.* New York: Harper & Brothers, 1960.

Unesco Courier, The, editorial feature, no. 3 (March 1960): p. 22.

Van Buskirk, James Dale. *Religion, Healing & Health.* New York: The Macmillan Co., 1952.

Villasenor, David V. *Tapestries in Sand: The Spirit of Indian Sand Painting.* Healdsburg, Calif.: Naturegraph Co., 1966.

Visitatio Infirmorum: Or, Offices for the Clergy in Praying with, Directing, and Comforting the Sick, Infirm, and Afflicted. 3d ed. London: Joseph Masters, 1854.

Von Bertalanffy, Ludwig. "The Mind-Body Problem: A New View." *Psychosomatic Medicine* 26, no. 1 (January-February 1964): 29–45.

Weatherhead, Leslie D. *Psychology, Religion and Healing.* New York: Abingdon-Cokesbury Press, 1951.

Weiss, Edward, and English, O. Spurgeon. *Psychosomatic Medicine: The Clinical Application of Psychopathology to General Medical Problems.* Philadelphia: W. B. Saunders Co., 1943. (2d ed., 1949; 3d ed., 1957)

Wesley, John. *The Journal of the Rev. John Wesley.* Edited by Ernest Rhys. London: J. M. Dent & Co., n.d.

Western Fathers, The. Translated and edited by F. R. Hoare. London: Sheed & Ward, 1954.

White, Hugh W. *Demonism Verified and Analyzed.* Ann Arbor, Mich.: University Microfilms, 1963.

White, Victor, O.P. *God and the Unconscious.* Cleveland: World Publishing Co., 1961.

Whitehead, Alfred N., *Science and the Modern World*. New York: Mentor Books, 1948.

Whyte, Lancelot Law. *The Unconscious Before Freud*. New York: Basic Books, 1960.

Wili, Walter. See *Papers from the Eranos Yearbooks*.

Wittkower, E. D.; Cleghorn, J. M.; Lipowski, Z. J.; Peterfy, G.; and Solyom, L. "A Global Survey of Psychosomatic Medicine." *International Journal of Psychiatry*. 7, no. 1 (January 1969): 499–516. Critical evaluations, pp. 516–24.

Wolf, Stewart, and Wolff, Harold G. *Headaches: Their Nature and Treatment*. Boston: Little, Brown & Co., 1953.

Worrall, Ambrose A. and Olga N. *The Gift of Healing*. New York: Harper & Row, 1965.

Year Book of Neurology, Psychiatry and Neurosurgery, The. 1966–1967 Year Book Series. Edited by Roland P. MacKay, Sam Bernard Wortis, and Oscar Sugar. Chicago: Year Book Medical Publishers, 1967.

Young, Richard K., and Meiburg, Albert L. *Spiritual Therapy: Modern Medicine's Newest Ally*. New York: Harper & Brothers, 1960.

Zündel, Friedrich. *Johann Christoph Blumhardt*. A summarized translation by Art Rosenblum. Chicago: privately printed, 1967.

INDEX

Adelbert (bishop), 230
Adler, Alfred, 287
Aesculapius, other healing gods, 45 f.,
47 ff., 59; shrines of, 50, 147, 151, 340
Alcuin (of York), 230
Alexander, Franz G., M.D., 278n, 284n
Alfred (the Great), 196
Altizer, Thomas J. J., 30
Ambrose, St., 160, 188 f., 194, 332
American Lutheran Church, 223n
Anderson, Odin W., 10 (quote)
Anderson, Sir Robert, 24
Andrieu, Michel, 182n, 208n
Anselm, St., 231
Antony, St., 163, 166 f., 184, 192 f., 357
Antony, St. (of Padua), 232
apostles, New Testament authors,
others of the period, 25, 53 ff., 58 f.,
101 ff., 104 ff., 113 f., 117–28, 140, 185,
187, 219, 331 ff.; see also James, Let-
ter of; Jesus of Nazareth; Paul; Peter
Aquinas, St. Thomas, 23, 30n, 198, 204,
205, 209, 213–20, 222, 233, 310, 329
Arians, Arianism, 157, 159, 170, 201,
204
Aristophanes, 50
Aristotle, Aristotelian thought, 23, 47,
62, 201, 204 f., 213 f., 216, 218 ("the
Philosopher"), 220, 222, 281, 309 f.,
311 f., 323, 328, 331
Arnobius, 152
Athanasius, St. (the Great), 159, 163,
166 f., 184, 357
Athenagoras, 143n, 146n

Auden, Wynstan Hugh, 302n
Augustine, St. (of Canterbury), 196,
228
Augustine, St. (of Hippo), 134, 160,
184–88, 191, 193, 198 f., 216 f., 222,
233, 328
Aulén, Gustav, 144 f.
Ayer, Alfred Jules, 316

Babylonian religion, 38 f.
Backus, Ollie, 358
Baillie, John, 316n
Banks, Ethel Tulloch, ix, 55, 57
Banks, John Gayner, ix, 240
Barnabas, Epistle of, 142n, 145n, 146n,
154n
Barth, Karl, 23 f., 67n, 224, 236 f., 315
Basil, St. (the Great), 159 f., 167 f., 170 f.,
172, 174, 198
Basilides, 134
Batten, Loring W., 240
Beard, Rebecca, 257, 263
Becquerel, Henri, 317, 321 f.
Bede, the Venerable, 181, 228 ff.
Beecher, Henry K., M.D., 273n
Bell, Robert, ix
Benedict, St., 195, 231n
Berkeley, George (bishop), 312
Bernard, St. (of Clairvaux), 231 f.
Blatty, Wm. Peter, 66, 153n
Blum, Richard and Eva, 184n
Blumhardt, Johann Christian, 23, 236 f.
Boethius, 204
Boggs, Wade H., 25 f., 41, 85

393